the makerspace librarian's sourcebook

#the makerspace_librarian's sourcebook {

// edited by **ellyssa kroski**

An imprint of the American Library Association
Chicago | 2017

Ellyssa Kroski is Director of Information Technology at the New York Law Institute, as well as an award-winning editor and author of thirty-five books including *Law Librarianship in the Digital Age*, for which she won the AALL's 2014 Joseph L. Andrews Legal Literature Award. Her ten-book technology series The Tech Set won ALA's Best Book in Library Literature Award in 2011. She is a librarian, an adjunct faculty member at Drexel and San Jose State Universities, and an international conference speaker. Her professional portfolio is located at www.ellyssakroski.com.

© 2017 by the American Library Association

Extensive effort has gone into ensuring the reliability of the information in this book; however, the publisher makes no warranty, express or implied, with respect to the material contained herein.

ISBN: 978-0-8389-1504-2 (paper)

Library of Congress Cataloging-in-Publication Data
Names: Kroski, Ellyssa, editor.
Title: The makerspace librarian's sourcebook / edited by Ellyssa Kroski.
Description: Chicago : ALA Editions, an imprint of the American Library Association, 2017. | Includes bibliographical references and index.
Identifiers: LCCN 2016037887 | ISBN 9780838915042 (pbk. : alk. paper)
Subjects: LCSH: Makerspaces in libraries. | Makerspaces—Equipment and supplies. | Maker movement.
Classification: LCC Z716.37 .M35 2017 | DDC 025.5—dc23 LC record available at https://lccn.loc.gov/2016037887

Cover design by Kim Thornton. LilyPad Arduino: photo by Leah Buechley. All others: © Shutterstock, Inc. Text composition by Alejandra Diaz in the Adobe Caslon Pro and Helvetica typefaces.

♾ This paper meets the requirements of ANSI/NISO Z39.48–1992 (Permanence of Paper).

Printed in the United States of America
21 20 19 18 17   5 4 3 2 1

contents

Part One // Creating the Library Makerspace

Part Two // Makerspace Materials, Tools, and Technologies

Part Three // Looking Ahead

figures and tables

Figures

Tables

preface

The *Makerspace Librarian's Sourcebook* is an essential all-in-one guidebook to the maker realm written specifically for librarians. This practical volume is an invaluable resource for librarians seeking to learn about the major topics, tools, and technologies relevant to makerspaces today. Jam-packed with instruction and advice from the field's most tech-savvy innovators, this one-stop handbook will inspire readers through practical projects that they can implement in their libraries right now.

Part I leads librarians through how to start their own makerspaces from the ground up, reviewing strategic planning, funding sources, starter equipment lists, space design, and safety guidelines. It also discusses the transformative teaching and learning opportunities that makerspaces offer, as well as how to empower and encourage a diverse maker culture within the library.

Part II provides hands-on, practical discussions of the eleven essential technologies and tools that are most commonly found in makerspaces of all types. This section serves as a primer on all the major maker tools and technologies ranging from 3D printers, Raspberry Pi, Arduino, wearable electronics, to CNC, Legos, drones, and circuitry kits. It covers what they are, how to use them, how different libraries are using them, and offers project suggestions that are specifically geared toward libraries.

Part III looks ahead to topics such as making your makerspace mobile, sustaining your makerspace once initial grants and funding sources are gone, and the future of makerspaces in libraries.

Authored by knowledgeable maker librarians, this comprehensive resource will guide librarians through all they need to know to make the most of their library makerspace.

—**ELLYSSA KROSKI**
The New York Law Institute

acknowledgments

I would like to express my thanks and admiration to all the insightful authors who dedicated their time and expertise to create this outstanding resource.

Part I

Creating the Library Makerspace

How to Start a Library Makerspace

CHERIE BRONKAR

What Is a Makerspace?

You may have heard the term "makerspace" and wondered what it meant. Makerspaces are, simply put, places where people gather to make things. Although that may sound like a simplistic definition, the things that can be created in a makerspace vary a great deal. Makerspaces can be high tech, low tech, and everything in between. A makerspace's offerings revolve around the needs of the community it serves, but the one thing all have in common is that they bring people together to share ideas.

Typically, the first thing that comes to mind when thinking about makerspaces is 3D printing, but when it comes to what's going on in makerspaces around the world, that's just the tip of the iceberg. Makers create things, ideas, and concepts. Makers work in metal, wood, plastic, fabric, paper, and digital forms. From robotics to crocheting, there are no limits to your makerspace. Let your imagination run wild.

Cherie Bronkar is Director-Regional Library at Kent State University Tuscarawas.

In this chapter, we'll provide the information and ideas to get your makerspaces up and running based on your unique populations and budgets. You'll find a myriad of ways to create your makerspace. You'll also discover ways to ensure your makerspace is fun and functional.

Know Your Makerspace Culture

Makerspace culture developed from hackathons, which were rooted in software and brought together groups with an interest in creating new apps and software. Such ventures nourished the makerspace culture.

The makerspace culture brings together multiple groups with multiple interests, sometimes putting together unlikely pairings to encourage new ways to think and create. What the members of these groups have in common is a love of tinkering, building, and sharing ideas. The makerspace provides space, resources, training, and technology that all enhance the culture.

Because it isn't limited by age or experience, makerspace culture is unique. Often, groups are comprised of those who just have an interest in creating new products and information. The focus is on sharing and learning in a synergetic environment. The key is that whether these groups are solving a problem or simply creating a fun piece of 3D art, they are doing it in a collaborative environment where makers can bounce their ideas off others with similar interests.

How does the maker culture fit a library? Makers create information as well as physical objects. In the past, the librarian's traditional role was to house information. Libraries now take an active part in the production process as well as in developing new information, all the while passing along valuable STEM skills to library patrons through instruction and by providing the tools of production such as 3D printers, 3D modeling software, and more. The maker culture has found a new home in our libraries. We need makers and they need us.

Discover the Major Types of Makerspaces

Makerspaces come in many forms, from low tech to high tech. Each library approaches its vision of a makerspace in its own unique way, often relying on the interests of the local community and potential users. Any library, including specialty libraries, can operate a successful makerspace, but they are more commonly seen in public, academic, and K–12 libraries. Makerspaces offer opportunities for collaboration in our communities and institutions. Offerings and key players vary greatly depending on the type and the size of the library.

Public Libraries

Public libraries offer amazing opportunities to create makerspaces of all kinds. Where else do you get the chance to use fun activities to bring together so many diverse groups? Public libraries come in many shapes and sizes that allow for an array of creative makerspaces. Public libraries are on the forefront of the makerspace movement. They have a broader spectrum of users and an ability to create spaces that meet the needs of their communities. These spaces range from large to small, from high tech to low tech and all provide training to the public. This includes both one-on-one training and public workshops.

The Charlotte Mecklenburg Public Library's Idea Box is a great example of what a larger public library can achieve. The Idea Box (www.cmlibrary.org/idea-box) features 3D printers, laser engravers, vinyl cutters, sewing machines, Raspberry Pi, and more. It offers programs on everything from circuitry to sewing to meditation. The facility is a fully staffed space that's open at specific hours during the week, and it offers programs based not only on technology and available equipment, but also includes an array of creative and crafty pursuits.

Public libraries large and small throughout the United States are eager to embrace the maker explosion. Smaller libraries can easily incorporate fun and exciting programming. Crafting with recycled materials to make jewelry, duct tape crafts, Legos and erector set competitions, and small electronics projects with littleBits, Makey Makey, and Raspberry Pi are filling our libraries with eager learners.

Academic Libraries

Academic libraries operate a bit differently than public libraries. In an academic library makerspace, much of the equipment will be aligned so that it can be applied to the curriculum. Although academic libraries are typically available to enrolled students, some are also open to the public. Training is provided in much the same way as in a public library, but academic libraries also work closely with faculty to develop project-based training.

A typical academic makerspace would include 3D printers, programmable electronics, digital microscopes, video equipment, large format printers, and other items that add to the institution's curriculum.

Case Western Reserve University's Think Box (http://thinkbox.case.edu/home) is an amazing space with many resources. Its equipment is extensive and includes items such as a vacuum chamber, miter saws, digital multimeters, band saws, and milling machines. Its projects range from brain scans turned into 3D puzzles to a human-powered cell phone charger. A space like this gives students endless possibilities to put their education into practice.

Kent State University at Tuscarawas (http://libguides.tusc.kent.edu/maker space) is a regional campus that's turned a section of its Academic Learning Commons into a makerspace featuring 3D printers, an Oculus Rift station, a digital microscope, and LEGO MINDSTORMS to excite and inspire students. Its focus is on problem-solving projects, and it's used its makerspace to solve a problem in its science labs by creating a clip that allows students to attach any type of cell phone to a microscope and take photos and video of their findings. It's also used 3D printers to create prosthetics for animals in conjunction with the Veterinary Technology program.

K–12 Libraries

Much like the academic library, the K–12 library is geared towards curriculum and exploration. The K–12 makerspace provides an environment for students to experience technology and its applications. Training in these libraries is provided to specific classes, often as project-based learning. These spaces are generally not open to the public and are closely monitored.

Equipment in these spaces is often tied to STEM initiatives and includes items like 3D printers (notice a theme here?), littleBits, Makey Makeys, and electronics-based learning materials. (See the chapters in part II on specific tools for more ideas.) K–12 makerspaces also make good use of apps and software to keep their students in touch with technology. 3D-compatible software such as Tinkercad, Google SketchUp, FreeCAD, and MeshLAB are just some of the options. Apps can be downloaded to school computers and made available to students for use. Some popular apps are Motion Café, Garage Band, iMovie, Kodable, ScratchJr, Stop Motion, and Easy Studio, to name just a few. There's literally an app for everything, so look around for one that will amaze students.

The staff of school library makerspace may find they have limited amounts of time to work with students. As a response to little time during the school day, Theodore Robinson Intermediate School established an after-school Maker Club, which takes on projects that experiment with stop-motion animation software and art bots.[1]

Mobile Makerspaces

Your makerspace need not be stationary. Some innovative libraries are creating mobile makerspaces which, much like bookmobiles, deliver materials to remote locations. Mobile makerspaces take the maker movement wherever it is needed. These spaces offer opportunities for collaboration between schools, public, and academic libraries.

Featuring the ever-popular 3D printer, the mobile makerspace offers many pieces of equipment that can travel, such as laser cutters, craft supplies, and even hammers and nails. Much like our bookmobiles, traveling makerspaces like the STEAM Truck (http://community-guilds.org/) bring makerspace innovations to communities that might not otherwise have access to them. What an amazing way to reduce the technology gap for those areas that do not have makerspaces in their libraries or their schools!

Membership Based

Increasingly, makerspaces receive support from membership fees. These makerspaces can be for-profit or nonprofit. For a fee, members are offered access to equipment, training, and the space. This model has also been adopted by a few academic libraries to allow their spaces to be shared by the public.

The focus of membership-based makerspaces varies greatly. From the arts-inspired Artisan's Asylum's (http://artisansasylum.com/), with its huge creative spaces where artists can collaborate, to the TechShop's (www.techshop.ws/) multiple locations and tech focus, there's a wave of membership-based centers sweeping the country. The membership-based makerspace is supported by membership fees, and often funded by grants that support specific programs for youth.

Determine Your Makerspace Focus

As librarians, we all know the importance of narrowing your focus to make information manageable. The same is true with makerspaces. As you research makerspaces, focus on those with populations that best match your demographics and budget. Ask what works for them and consider mirroring an approach that has already proven successful.

Budget, staffing, and community will be major influences on the focus of your makerspace. Costs can run high if your focus is technology-driven. If you have a low budget for starting your space, consider a mixture of a few higher-dollar items augmented with other low-cost but creative ideas.

The maker movement is not solely based in technology. Yes, it's a great way to bring technology to those who might not consider using it, but being a maker is about creativity, collaboration, and producing new ideas. Makers exist regardless of budget, so keep that in mind and develop spaces that your library can support and staff.

Your space doesn't even need to be a space. It can be a series of programs, if that's what fits your library. When funds are unavailable, the focus can be on creative workshops featuring low-cost materials and big ideas. Once you decide what resources you can commit, look for ways to develop programming that fits the demographics of your users.

There are so many directions you can take with your makerspace. A technology-based space is a big draw. Spaces with 3D printing, laser engravers, robotics, and electronics are very popular. These are the typical spaces libraries envision when planning a makerspace.

Crafting and art makerspaces can be created with a little less funding. These spaces can include sewing, quilting, knitting, painting, writing groups, and anything you think will be appealing to your users. Another plus with this type of makerspace is that it can be set up for users of all ages.

Media spaces include video and audio recording studios and go very well with libraries that lend musical instruments. These spaces are becoming more popular, but much like the technology spaces, they require a great deal of staffing, training, and funding.

The focus for your makerspace should reflect your users' interests and your library's ability to staff and fund the space. As with any large project, starting with a focus allows you to ensure you've covered all the bases. It is very easy for your makerspace vision to branch in multiple directions. Keeping a focus will prevent that from happening and allow you to design the best possible space.

Once your space is up and running and you know what you've gotten yourself into, you'll have a better idea of what you might need to add. Makerspaces are spaces of continuous change. Additions will be constant, but starting with a single focus will allow you to face changes and additions without becoming overwhelmed.

Establish Funding

A major component to any new endeavor is funding, and a makerspace is no different. In fact, because of the potentially huge costs, funding them can be even more of a concern. Whether you are funding the space with your current budget or applying for grants, it's important to factor in everything you will need to make your space a success.

A makerspace requires a great deal of planning. Using the information from this book will help you lay out a solid plan, but, as with any large project, there will be things that you never saw coming. To start with, plan for the costs of equipment, repairs, maintenance contracts, supplies, staffing, training, and construction, and then add a contingency to be safe.

Once you've done that, you can determine if you'll need outside help to fund your space. Luckily, makerspaces are appealing to grantors, so the time to apply for grants is now.

How to Win a Grant

Larger libraries and institutions will often have a person on staff to guide you through the grant process. Your grant officer knows what grants are available, and their requirements. This is often the case with schools and universities as well. Institutions that already receive federal funding may have restrictions on what grants they can pursue. Be sure to check with your administration before you seek funding.

Grants come in many sizes from many places. Some are highly competitive, some are not. Use your networking skills and talk to people. Talk to people in public office and your state library, and seek out information from others who've been successful in obtaining grants. Talk to other makerspace librarians, and ask them if they applied for grants and which ones they received.

Federal grants can be very competitive, but this is not always the case. Federal grants offer big rewards, but require detailed paperwork, stipulations, and reporting. When you're seeking grants, research past recipients. This will give you a better idea of what grantors want to fund. Federal grants require a great deal of paperwork, so be ready to have your ducks in a row if applying for a federal grant. The Institute of Museum and Library Services (IMLS) is the largest source of federal funding. IMLS grants serve initiatives outlined in the Library Science and Technology Act (LSTA) and are offered throughout all fifty states, with over 2,500 grants available.[2]

Local grants can be found at the state, county, and community level. These grants can be less competitive than federal grants. They also tend to be more specific and offer less funding. Local grants come from an array of sources, from trust fund distributions to local businesses.

Edutopia.org lists multiple funding sources, including company funding from PG&E Bright Ideas, Botball Robotics, ING Unsung Heroes, and Lowes' Toolbox for Education.[3] Another source for finding grants for libraries and schools is Scholastic's Activities and Programs web page (www.scholastic.com/librarians/programs/grants.htm), which features information on grants and their requirements from an array of sources, including the Paul G. Allen Family Foundation, the MBNA Foundation, RGK Foundation, the National Endowment for the Humanities, and the W. K. Kellogg Foundation.[4]

Crowdfunding is being used to raise money for everything under the sun, so why not for your makerspace? There are many options for setting up crowdfunding; some are open to anything you want to fund and others are specific to education. Give crowdfunding a try. GoFundMe, Kickstarter, Indiegogo, Patreon, and Crowdrise are just a few examples. Educators have found success using DonorsChoose.org, a crowdfunding source that is set up to allow donors to choose educational projects to fund. Some libraries simply share their makerspace-focused Amazon Wish List with patrons and businesses in their local communities.[5] There are many options available today that weren't available just a few years ago. Try them all out and see what sticks.

Grantors love to see collaborations. Makerspaces are perfect for collaborative ventures among schools, universities, businesses, and small-business development agencies. Seek out local agencies to build partnerships that benefit the community, schools, or local businesses.

Your makerspace is in a prime position to promote technology, small-business creation, and job growth. These are all selling points.

Get Started without Funding

We'd love to think every makerspace will receive unlimited funding, but sad to say that will not always be the case. So, what do you do when you desperately want to start a makerspace but don't have the funds? You do what makers are meant to do: get creative.

You can have an inviting and appealing makerspace on a shoestring. There are many ideas out there for items that don't cost an arm and a leg (many of which are discussed in this book). Paper crafts are extremely cost-efficient. From origami to book art (using withdrawn books) to creating apps, you can make it happen on the smallest budget.

The makerspace movement does not rely solely on high-priced technology. Making through shared interests has always been a part of our libraries. We've done this through much of the programming we've always offered. With some adjustment, this same technique can be applied to your budget makerspace.

Making can be as simple as featuring a building contest with Legos or hosting something more technical like a hackathon. Your makerspace does not always have to provide equipment and materials; you can bring together groups to share what they've done and learn from each other.

If you work at a school library, consider hosting a space where students can make and display dioramas, science projects, crafts, and jewelry (something along the line of friendship bracelets). After all, what you want is for students to come to your library and collaborate in fun ways with fellow students. These kinds of activities in your makerspace would also be a great way to get faculty and librarians working together.

Most of us have computers in our libraries. There are many free design websites. Host some training to help your students create videos on their phones and upload them to free video editing apps, run a contest for the best Vine, create a school YouTube site, encourage the English faculty to have students supplement their literature studies with things like funny video spoofs of a book their class has read.

A public library can offer many of the same activities, and with its larger demographic there are even more low-cost options. Public libraries can host local artists in their spaces. Offer a "bring your own supplies" art project that introduces your users to other budding artists who can continue to meet at your library. Crocheting, knitting, graphic design using free software downloads—there is no end to what you can offer on a no-cost or low budget.

Ask for the things you need. Donated items are a great way to build your makerspace. Let your users know what you need; they may have that item to donate. Conduct a tool drive in your community.[6] Local companies are a good place to look for donations of small machinery and used technology.

If you have a small budget, all the better. You can still build a great space. The most important part of your space is simply that it encourages collaboration. If you can include a few tools and inexpensive equipment and suggest project ideas, you have a makerspace. The tools and equipment do not need to be expensive. Equipment for jewelry-making and scrapbooking are inexpensive, yet are fun and creative ways to interest your users.

You can still add an electronics component to your space without incurring huge costs. Edutopia has featured many ideas for what it refers to as "unmaking."[7] Who hasn't wanted to take apart a piece of electronic equipment to discover what's inside? Unmaking uses recycled electronics to allow users to learn about electronics by taking them apart and putting them back together.[8]

Evaluate Your Space Design

There are many aspects to take into consideration when designing your makerspace. The equipment you install in your makerspace will be very different from what's found in a traditional library. The way this space is used will be different than any other library space. The library of the past was based around quiet study.

Although we still need quiet spaces, the makerspace will be noisy. Even if you don't have noisy equipment, a successful space is a collaborative space, and collaboration means people must talk to each other. Excited users are not quiet; nor should they be. Locate your space in an area where talking won't be disruptive to quiet study areas.

Some libraries will be repurposing a current space to house a makerspace. Be prepared to call the electrician. The maxim "you can't have too many outlets" has never been more true than it will be in your makerspace. Because many pieces of equipment will be required to support technology and computers, data ports have become the new electrical outlets. Add more than you need, and then add a couple more.

Some equipment will need proper ventilation, which is a bit easier to address in a new space. If you are repurposing an older space, you'll need to check with an architect to see if ventilation is possible. Heat and moisture can wreak havoc on technology and even some of your supplies. 3D printer filament is temperamental once opened, so a moisture-proof container is a must. Equipment can easily overheat in any environment. Electronics fans are usually inexpensive and can save costly repairs due to overheating.

Supplies can take up much more space than anticipated. If your tools break, you'll need more tools to fix them. These things quickly collect; and having a space already planned for all the extras will ensure you have a clean area and your supplies are organized for easy access.

Dealing with makerspace waste material is sometimes an afterthought. Much of your makerspace waste is recyclable. Having a place to store recyclable materials is a must. In addition to scraps from filament, paper projects, and metal, you may have waste from batteries or that requires specific disposal and recycling precautions. Research your local outlets to learn where you can safely recycle or dispose of these materials.

If it's possible to add plumbing to your space, this can be a real plus. Although not essential, a sink in your space can be quite helpful. Makers make messes too, and a convenient way to clean up is quite handy.

Whether your space is large or small, creating a diagram of the way you will lay out your equipment, work areas, electrical outlets, and data ports is essential. Take measurements of equipment before you order it and allow enough space for the equipment to be used properly. For instance, a large-format poster printer takes up more space than a regular printer. Posters need to be laid flat, and professional large-poster cutters need to be mounted to a table, which can take up a huge amount of space. Although you can easily determine how big the printer will be and plan for its footprint, the space needed to create with printing posters and banners may be a surprise. Legos, Erector Sets, and electronics kits can easily be stored in small areas, but do you have a space designated for users to spread out and use them? If not just improvise, as Diana Rendina did for her Lego Wall at Stewart Middle Magnet School in Tampa, Florida. Diana created space on a wall for building with Legos to optimize her small space.[9]

Computers will take up a lot of space if you are using equipment that needs specific software to operate. 3D printers, vinyl cutters, and data-driven equipment will need space for the computers that support them.

When planning your space, there are many considerations that won't come to mind. Besides planning for electrical, bandwidth, and the size and layout of your equipment, you will need to envision and design a plan that includes space for all the extras. Keep in mind that workspace and supplies storage will be just as essential to your space as the equipment.

Although there are many considerations when creating your makerspace, the main thing is to create a space that fits the needs of your community. Once you determine what kind of makerspace you want to establish, look at the budget you have available and make a plan. Don't be deterred by the cost—there are always ways to create an effective makerspace on any budget.

Getting Started—Equipment Lists

Here are some sample starter equipment lists for you to consider, depending on the type of makerspace you'll be building as well as your library's budget.

Technology-Focused Makerspace Starter Kit
(Estimated Cost $3,300)[10]

- Makey Makey ($50)
- Squishy Circuits ($25)
- Minecraft EDU ($25)
- LEDs ($30)
- LED batteries ($14)
- copper tape ($20)
- Scratch (free)
- Tackk (Free documentation website)

- paper/vinyl cutter ($350)
- 3D printer ($2,500)
- Arduino Adventures parts kit ($60)
- Raspberry Pi kit ($90)
- Legos ($50)
- Snap Circuits kit ($60)

Bigger Budget Technology-Focused Makerspace Starter Kit
(Estimated Cost $21,000)[11]

- OWI Robotic Arm Edge robot arm ($50)
- LEGO MINDSTORMS Education NXT Base Set ($500)
- GCC Expert 24 Vinyl Cutting Plotter with stand and heat transfer vinyl pack ($820)
- 3Doodler pen ($99)
- Anthrotab 20SSPW multi-charging unit ($614)
- Zotac ZBOX-ID90-P Intel Core i7 3770T, 4GB RAM, 500G HDD, Intel HD4000 Graphics integrated by CPU, Mini PC, and 55-inch GVision large format touch screen display (for presentation room) ($595)
- Logitech MK550 Black USB RF Wireless Ergonomic Wave Combo ($80)
- Erector Set ($81)
- Architect Lego set ($160)
- FlipBooKit Moto ($99)
- EL-Wire starter kit, 25 feet ($40)
- Starter Pack for Arduino (includes Arduino Uno R3) ($65)
- Flip video camera—White, 30 minutes ($80)
- Parallax BOEBot Robot for Arduino Kit ($124)
- Ultimaker PLA filament spools (assorted colors) ($65 per spool)
- Microsoft Surface 2, 64 GB ($449)
- Microsoft Surface Power Cover ($199)
- Wakom Intuos Pro Pen & Touch Special Edition ($379)
- Accucut Original Mark IV Super Starter Set—Early Childhood ($1,999)
- Xyron 2500 Machine ($1,480)
- Ultimaker 2 3D printer ($2,500)
- LulzBot TAZ ($2,200)
- Canon imagePROGRAF iPF750 36-inch large format printer ($3,495)
- digital cameras ($259 each)
- green screen and lighting kit ($179)
- Cricut Scrapbooking vinyl/leather/paper cutting machine ($250)
- Sprout 3D scanner/printer ($3,000)
- Adobe Photoshop ($179)

Media—Video-Focused Makerspace Starter Kit
(Estimated Cost $7,200)[12]

Hardware
- Canon PowerShot A2300 digital camera ($211)
- Canon Eos Rebel T3i digital camera ($250)
- Sonny Bloggie camcorder ($175)
- Panasonic camcorder ($500)
- Kodak Play Touch video camera ($200)
- flash drives, SD cards, and readers ($5 each)
- HP Photosmart 5510 color scanner/printer ($385)
- Digital Concepts tripod ($20)
- 85-watt photo light ($15)
- 10 x 9-foot green screen wall ($75)
- two Shure SM28 microphones with stands ($99 each)
- HP Compaq 6200 Pro SFF computer ($215)
- HP Compaq 4000 Pro SFF computer ($109)
- 27-inch iMac computer ($2,000)

Software
- Adobe CS 6 Production Premium—Photoshop, Illustrator, Premiere Pro, and more ($2,600)
- iLife Suite—Garage Band, iMovie, and iPhoto ($45)
- Audacity—for audio recording (free)
- Cyberlink Power Director 8—movie-making software ($25)
- Microsoft Office ($90)

Media—Sound-Focused Makerspace Starter Kit
(Estimated Cost $7,500)[13]

- ProTools ($299)
- Sibelius ($280)
- Audacity (free)
- Garage Band ($45)

Video
- Final Cut Pro ($300)
- Adobe Creative Suite ($1,500)
- iMovie. ($15)

Audio

- iMac with software and 27-inch monitor ($1,763)
- Eleven Rack guitar rack ($699)
- Scarlett 2i4 USB audio interface ($169)
- Novation LaunchKey 49 MIDI board with drum pads ($150)
- Shure SM57 dynamic microphone ($99)
- Blue Yeti Pro USB condenser microphone ($150)
- condenser shotgun microphone ($80)
- Sennheiser headphones ($90)
- handheld boom poles ($125)

Video/Film

- Canon XA10 HD camcorder ($800)
- camera tripod with revolving head ($25)
- three stand-up lights with softbox/diffuser kits ($175)
- green room (green walls/floor) ($100)
- portable green screen ($75)
- Canon Rebel T5i ($600)

Low Budget, Elementary School-Focused Makerspace Starter Kit (Estimated Cost $500–$1,000)[14]

- sewing supplies (needles, thread, scissors, fabric) ($100)
- ribbon, yarn, string ($30)
- Legos, K'NEX, building blocks ($50)
- all types of paper (wrapping paper, card stock, construction paper, printer paper, scrapbook) ($200)
- Post-it Notes ($50)
- markers, pens, crayons, etc. ($50)
- cardboard of any kind, from food packaging to large appliances (free; flattened please)
- cardboard tubes from wrapping paper, toilet paper, paper towel, etc. (free)
- Play-Doh ($20)
- circuitry kits (can be purchased online) ($20–100)
- craft supplies (cotton balls, popsicle sticks, paint, tape, low temperature hot glue gun, glue gun sticks, glue and glue sticks, toothpicks) ($100)
- canvas, art supplies ($100 and up)
- cameras, photography equipment ($50 and up)

- things to take apart, such as old or broken electronics and small devices (donations)
- hammers, screwdrivers, pliers ($100)
- nails, screws, bolts ($50)
- storage containers—tubs, baskets ($50)
- dominos, marbles ($50)
- playing cards (used for building items) ($20)
- batteries (various sizes) ($50)

Dream Budget—Milling/Power Equipment Focused Makerspace
Equipment List (Estimated Cost $30,000—$50,000)[15]

- large Matsuura RA-1F Vertical CNC milling station (Red Dragon) ($2,000)
- tabletop gear lathe (Central Machinery) ($4,000)
- drill press (Speedway) ($100)
- metal lathe (South Bend Lathe Works) ($4,000)
- bandsaw, vertical (Do-All) ($2,000)
- drill presses and table (Rockwell) ($600)
- hydraulic press ($300)
- disc sander ($200)
- bench grinder (Farm & Fleet) ($40)
- cut-off/chop saw (Milwaukee) ($200)
- 7 x 12-inch bandsaw, vertical/horizontal with coolant tank (Wilton) ($2,000)
- bench top lathe (Delta) ($500)
- hand grinder (Skil) ($50)
- drill bits, taps, etc. ($50)
- nuts, bolts, etc. ($50)
- large vise ($30)
- forge ($1,265)
- casting furnace ($55)
- centrifugal spin caster ($500)
- anvil ($100)
- post vise ($1.600)
- forging hammers ($200)
- electric arc welder (Lincoln) ($450)
- ESAB PCM-1125 plasma cutter ($679)
- compound miter saw (Dewalt) ($399)
- CNC router ($2,000)

- router table (Craftsman) ($200)
- scroll saw (Delta) ($45)
- lathe tools ($75)
- combination disc/belt sander (Craftsman) ($89)
- laser cutter ($3,499)
- MakerBot Replicator ($2,500)

Identify Your New Roles

Librarians are no strangers to adapting to new technology and new environments. However, the pace at which we need to adapt is increasing. Librarians who embrace this world of constant change have easily moved into new roles, including the makerspace. Managers of makerspaces and technology-driven spaces must set clear expectations and provide professional development to adequately prepare staff for their new roles. We do a huge disservice to our users and our staff when we roll out new equipment without first providing the training needed to operate and troubleshoot the equipment.

Determine Expectations

We all have lofty expectations for librarians who operate makerspaces. Realistically, we won't necessarily find a librarian who knows everything there is to know about each piece of equipment. In this case, as with any position in the library, we're looking for more than one specific skill set. Ideally, we'd love to fill these positions with librarians who've been trained in engineering and information technology, but that's not very realistic. As with any library position, we look for approachability, creativity, and the drive to be a lifelong learner. These qualities are essential for the makerspace librarian. There will always be users who need friendly, knowledgeable assistance to help them find opportunities to use makerspaces creatively. I've found that users relate well to librarians who've started as novices and learned through trial and error. It seems to introduce a certain comfort level, especially for curious new users who might be intimidated by the equipment.

Construct a Training Plan

Having well-trained staff is essential. That said, we all know there are a lot of mitigating factors in the mix when it comes to a makerspace. If you have unlimited funds, it's possible to hire trainers from various vendors to come to your library and train staff on individual pieces of equipment. If, like most libraries, you don't have unlimited funds, then training can be a bit more frustrating. Luckily, librarians are the sharing sort, so one option is to visit other libraries with makerspaces and learn from those already doing the tasks you're setting out to do. Why re-create the wheel, when you can find one spinning smoothly?

Set a time line for training. Things can get hectic as you set up your space. Multiple pieces of equipment are exciting and overwhelming at the same time. Setting a time line for how and when training will take place will help you stay on track. It's very easy to be caught up in the excitement of opening boxes and setting up equipment. Jumping from discovering one piece to another can be confusing and can result in missed details.

Creating manuals for equipment can be a simple process. Manuals can be in traditional paper format or made available online. If using company manuals in an online environment, link to the company's site if possible. Most companies offer text manuals and video tutorials on their sites. Most of your equipment will come with user manuals; housing those in binders in the makerspace is a handy resource for new users and staff.

Staff

Whether selecting from current staff or hiring new staff for the makerspace, it's important to find people who are excited about the possibilities of a makerspace. Staff who are eager to jump in and learn everything they can about makerspaces will make the training process run much smoother. If you can afford it, hire trainers. If you can't, improvise. Travel to other makerspaces if possible and create connections with other maker librarians. If travel is not possible, well, what do librarians do best? Research! Research your equipment, watch YouTube videos, and sign up for makerspace groups. There are many great groups on social media and listservs.

I've found that having a group, or at least two people who can work together, learn how to operate new equipment allows for a better learning experience and prevents the problem of having only one person who knows how to operate a piece of equipment. As you grow your makerspace you may find that your staff will be able to train volunteers to help new users. Makerspaces tend to draw groups that want to bounce ideas around and collaborate on projects. Use this to your advantage; not only do you get new perspectives, but you'll also find that you're creating your own network of people who all have specialties to share with your users.

An effective way to learn is to create training materials for users while you're learning. This also ensures that step-by-step instructions are available for new staff. Depending on the size, budget, and scope of your makerspace you may want to have print-based training materials, online materials, or even a mixture of both.

Online training materials are more conducive to the nature of a makerspace for several reasons. Creating training materials and housing them online allow easy access and quick additions. Makerspace training will be an ongoing process. Equipment is added and updated often. New tips and troubleshooting methods will need to be recorded on a regular basis. Having the ability to quickly update this information online will save a great deal of time in printing and redistributing information.

Librarians now function as teachers in so many ways. Taking advantage of the training they've received and creating workshops for users should be second nature. I've always believed that to learn a new process, you need to teach it. A great way to start this process is to have makerspace staff create mini-workshops and present them to other members of the library's staff. This gives them opportunities to hone their skills and provides basic knowledge about makerspace operations to the entire library staff. Not everyone in the library needs to know how to operate the makerspace, but everyone does need to have enough basic information to answer questions and help sell the space.

The makerspace will draw many curious patrons. Make sure that your makerspace staff is well trained, that your library staff knows how to point people in the right direction, and that you have materials listing the equipment and the contact information for your makerspace staff.

Makerspaces require a great deal of staff training to operate efficiently. Take the time to do this step right. Before you order your first piece of equipment, make a solid plan that addresses who will staff your space, how they will be trained, time lines for training staff, and how training will be funded. Additionally, make sure your staff know what's expected of them and for which areas they're responsible.

A makerspace is a different kind of service than we might be accustomed to. Staff will need to know how to operate the equipment, how to troubleshoot and repair equipment (unless your budget allows for service contracts—in which case, lucky you!), how to create and establish policies for use, how to generate equipment and material lists for users, and how to devise workshops, handouts, and online materials to assist users.

Just when you think you have it all put together, there will be more pieces to the makerspace puzzle. Once again, based on the size of your library and its funding, you need to factor in ongoing and maintenance costs. Machines break, and materials run out. Someone on your staff will need to organize this information so that you don't discover that equipment is in disrepair or supplies are depleted and you have no funds for repairs and supplies. As with every part of the makerspace, your first year will be a series of trials and errors. Assign a staff person to make notes of the repairs and parts needed and supplies used over the first year so that this can be factored into your operational costs. Keep clipboards by each piece of equipment so that staff and users can jot down issues and fixes.

The final piece will be to set policies for use. These should be included in training. You don't need to start from scratch; makerspace policies can be found with a simple Google search. Piece together what fits your library and create what you don't find. Librarians are sharers of information, but do ask for permission when using someone else's material. Then return the favor and share your policies so that others can benefit.

Users

Your users will come from all walks of life and all age groups. Some will be novices and some will be experts. We need to be prepared for the various levels of user expertise. Ensure that curious onlookers have a friendly staffer to welcome them to your space. Show off the projects that have been created and highlight simple projects.

As mentioned above in the section on staff training, training materials in an online format are easily shared not only with staff, but also with the public. If your information is online, users can learn all about the operation of the equipment, the materials they can use, and find helpful hints to avoid mistakes.

Makerspace users may want to create their own online community to share their ideas. An area for this can easily be added to your online training. Creating a community of users creates bonds to your space. The community, including staff, can benefit from the ideas shared. Consider creating your own Facebook, Twitter, or blog page for your users. Both you and your users can take advantage of existing Facebook pages dedicated to makerspaces. The Makerspace and Participatory Library (www.facebook.com/groups/librarymaker/) and Makerspace (www.facebook.com/groups/255985941160728/) public Facebook groups are just two of the many great places to share and obtain ideas.

Workshops should be held often. Create a schedule of workshops that covers specific pieces of equipment. We instituted "Makerspace Mondays," which featured a new piece of equipment each week. By doing this, we gauged the level of interest through attendance and held the most popular workshops more often.

Because most of your users are newbies, take it slow and start simple. Although we may want to tell new users everything that's possible with 3D printing, showing them everything in one sitting can be overwhelming to both the user and to the staff. Create workshops that are basic introductions and allow some very simple design and hands-on activities. Users can then schedule individual time with makerspace staff to learn more.

Scheduling tours will attract new users. Offer tours to every group you can reach out to. When offering tours, go outside the norm. The first go-to is always schools, but you can add 4-H groups, senior groups, businesses, local clubs and organizations—any group that gathers for meetings is a target group for a tour. You'll be surprised how many new users will come to your makerspace.

Consider partnering with agencies that can provide small business startup workshops or create them yourself. Makerspaces are the perfect place to create entrepreneurs. To ensure that your new entrepreneurs have the skills to go further with their products and ideas, provide them with the information they need to develop those ideas into productive plans. Providing this kind of support will also help you obtain funding. Most states are very interested in supporting initiatives that develop entrepreneurs and small businesses.

Identify and Arrange Professional Development

In times of dwindling budgets, librarians get very creative with professional development. There are professional development opportunities out there that will fit everyone's budget. When it comes to professional development for makerspaces, once again, we're moving beyond traditional venues. Although we are seeing more offerings at national and local library conferences, libraries may also want to look beyond traditional professional development "go-to's" to find ideas and experiences.

Because makerspaces serve such a varied population, the maker movement is taking shape in the industry, education, library, and technology information fields. Each field brings a new perspective on makerspace usage. Unlike many of our services, which are tied closely to libraries, makerspaces aren't necessarily library-centric. This opens the door to many more opportunities for professional development.

Encourage staff to seek out professional development in as many ways as possible. Whether it be library conferences, technology conferences, educational conferences, on-site vendor training, or webinars, it's essential that you offer your staff the opportunity to develop their skills continuously.

Maker Faires are popping up everywhere. Don't overlook these events when looking for professional development. Maker Faires are the perfect places to build your network and learn what is working for others. Although much of your time in a makerspace will be spent learning the intricacies of the machines as well as their uses, Maker Faires have an unlimited supply of people who can offer ideas and troubleshooting tips. I've attended several Maker Faires, and each time I find new connections, useful tips, ideas, and even get to try out new equipment. Seek out these Maker Faires—attend them, participate in them, or even go one step better and host a Maker Faire. You can find local, national, and even international Maker Faires simply by visiting http://makerfaire.com/.

Establish Policy

Policy development is probably not anyone's favorite aspect of planning. Nonetheless, it is a requisite for creating your makerspace. Consider that we are dealing with machinery, some of it potentially dangerous. We are also looking at a user group that differs in age and ability. No one wants problems or conflicts to arise because policy was not clearly defined.

One of the first concerns I heard expressed was: "What will you do if someone wants to print a gun?" Truthfully, at the time I was skeptical, thinking that this person was being overly cautious. Surely this was not a concern we'd ever have! But within the first year, someone did, in fact, approach me and asked to 3D print a gun. Luckily, I had planned for what I thought would be an unlikely scenario, and could point out that our policy prohibits the use of our equipment to create weapons of any kind, or parts associated with weaponry, including guns, bombs, knives, ninja stars, and so on. The lesson here is that if there is a way to find an inappropriate use for your equipment, you must deal with it.

Moving parts, cutting apparatus, and temperatures hot enough to burn are probably new problems for most libraries. Items you never considered could cause injuries, and will, at some point. Set policies that address these issues with users and with staff. Establish policies and procedures to deal with injuries and make certain that staff members know how to handle emergency situations.

Although we want the makerspace equipment to be available to all, we do have to ensure that we are protecting users, especially younger ones. You may find it necessary to set age limitations and require that users attend a training session on safety before working with specific equipment. In some cases, you may want to stipulate parental supervision for users below a certain age.

No matter how well you plan, situations will arise that require you to reconsider your policies. The safety of our users is our first concern, and we also want to protect the library from potential liability.

Consider Costs

Policies for makerspaces cover a broad spectrum, and of course safety should be addressed first, but there are many other considerations including costs. There's no getting around it: makerspaces can be costly. Repairs are expensive and materials costs can quickly add up. Don't forget to consider the hours your staff will spend fixing equipment, loading materials, and helping users create designs.

Grants are often garnered to obtain equipment and a set of supplies to start our makerspaces. That's great—for about the first year. After that you're on your own. Technology is a splendid thing—so long as it's working. The hard facts about technology are that it breaks down, parts need to be replaced and repaired, and equipment becomes obsolete.

It is up to you to decide how you will maintain your equipment and supplies. In many cases, setting a policy based on the cost charged to your patrons for using equipment and materials can offset what could be a sizeable drain on your budget. If you are lucky enough to have funded your space with a grant, the good news is you have some leeway in determining what type of cost recovery you may need. To encourage people to use our space, we allowed users to utilize the space and the materials for free until the grant-funded materials ran out. After that we had to devise a plan for recouping some of the costs.

Libraries are not in the business to make money, so often we are scrambling to provide our services for free. That's not always possible with the expenses associated with makerspaces, so it's important to begin with a policy that outlines the cost for materials and whether there will be any other costs associated with using the space.

Some makerspaces are fee-based. Some allow users to pay a fee for unlimited access to the equipment. Others allow users to use any piece of equipment for free, but charge for the materials used. It is up to you to set a policy that works best for your library.

Most makerspaces are set up so that the equipment use is free. Factor the costs of repair, upgrades, and new equipment into your budget. Materials can be offered at cost, and libraries can offer the option for users to bring their own materials.

Provide your users with clear information detailing the materials costs so that there are no surprises. Most materials are not cost-prohibitive to our users. 3D filament, for instance, is very inexpensive. There are a few areas where costs can get higher, for example, large runs on a vinyl cutter. Just be sure to let your users know the costs associated with their projects in advance.

If you decide to offer the option for users to bring in their own materials, you'll want to set a policy on the types of materials that can be used. Outlining the specifications for materials will be necessary so that users know the correct types and brands of materials that work best with your equipment.

A simple way to let your users know what materials are acceptable for use is to house this information in your user-training materials or equipment listings. If using an online system, simply include a link to a list of acceptable materials. That said, most new users will opt to purchase your materials at cost.

Develop Usage Policies

If you have been around libraries as long as I have, you might remember when we first added computers. It wasn't long until we had people waiting to use them and needed to develop ways to limit usage time so that everyone had a turn. You'll encounter the same thing with makerspace equipment.

Some items will be in high demand and you'll soon find there will be a select few users who will monopolize these items. 3D printers will likely be the main focus of your efforts. 3D prints take up a lot of time. The bigger the print, the longer it takes. Determining the amount of time to allow for an individual to use equipment can be tricky. You don't want to discourage or turn away users, but creating a policy that outlines time limits will help your users work within these parameters.

Children

Depending on the type of library, you may need to set up policies that are specific to children. This could include age limits and parental supervision. Some makerspace equipment is just not suited for use by young children.

Planning Your Makerspace

The planning process for your makerspace can seem like a daunting process. Creating policies, choosing equipment, training, and predicting future costs are all aspects that will need to be addressed. Before you take on those tasks, you'll want to figure out what population you will target with your makerspace.

Determining the focus for your space is a good starting point. As mentioned previously, makerspaces vary by type of library. Understanding the population your makerspace will serve helps determine your focus.

K–12 libraries will obviously focus on users that range from the very young to high school students. A makerspace in a high school has very different equipment and training needs than one located in an elementary school. Academic libraries focus on students and sometimes the community. To increase faculty interest, academic makerspaces are often centered on curriculum. Public libraries have an even wider demographic, because they serve users of all ages and skill levels.

Where to Market Your Makerspace

Marketing your makerspace is essential to its success. Promote your new makerspace as much as possible. Build up excitement for your makerspace and consider holding off on revealing everything until you can hold a grand opening for the space. Plan ahead so that you can roll out information to the public in phases. Begin with hints of what's to come and lead into the grand opening of the space. Be ready to hit the ground running after your grand opening!

Local newspapers and media outlets are great places to spread the word. Makerspaces are exciting news, and you'll find it easy to get coverage. Be prepared with good-quality, publication-ready photos of your makerspace. It's also helpful to have some examples of items that have been created in the makerspace.

Set up speaking engagements. Kiwanis, Rotary, and community groups and agencies are always looking for speakers. They will be thrilled that you have something new and exciting to share at their meetings. Show them ways to leverage the equipment in your space. These groups are also great places to elicit support in the form of local grants.

Public and academic libraries should also consider planning school visits for the makerspace along with regular school visits. The more people you reach, the more traffic you will see in your makerspace.

Traveling with your makerspace is something you should consider. We've talked a little about mobile makerspaces. There are a few ways you can set up a traveling version of your makerspace. A mobile unit would be ideal, but that's not feasible for everyone. For most of us, putting together a system to mobilize a few key pieces of equipment is a good start.

Visits to schools, Maker Faires, and community events will expose your makerspace to new audiences. To ensure you aren't caught off guard when asked to show off your makerspace outside the library, make arrangements for how you will transport your makerspace equipment. When traveling with your equipment, ensure you have containers that can safely house your equipment, flyers, and displays. It's worth it to purchase good professional quality displays and containment systems.

A big piece of marketing will be what you want to say about your makerspace. Consider how you will promote your space and the outcomes you expect. A general brochure outlining your makerspace, including why you created it, what it contains, its hours, and contact information is a must. These brochures are a first glimpse of your space for those who are new to the concept.

Marketing doesn't stop after your initial roll out. You don't want your makerspace to be a fad, so continuing marketing and programming highlighting your makerspace is necessary. The dark side to new initiatives is that sometimes your space takes off like a rocket, but in a year, it's empty. Don't let that happen—ensure that you continue to market your space to new users.

NOTES

1. Kathy Ceceri, "How to Build an Art Bot," *Wired,* May 16, 2012, www.wired.com/2012/05/ff_artbot.
2. "Grants to States," Institute of Museum and Library Services, www.imls.gov/grants/grants-states.
3. Paloma Garcia-Lopez, "Six Strategies for Funding a Makerspace," Edutopia, September 5, 2013, www.edutopia.org/blog/6-strategies-funding-makerspace-paloma-garcia-lopez.
4. "Library Grants," Scholastic Inc., www.scholastic.com/librarians/programs/grants.htm.
5. Phil Goerner, "Creating a School Library Makerspace: The Beginning of a Journey," *School Library Journal: Tech Tidbits,* January 19, 2015, www.slj.com/2015/01/technology/creating-a-school-library-maker-space-the-beginning-of-a-journey-tech-tidbits/#_.

6. "Spring Tool Drive," *Gorge MakerSpace,* April 15, 2014, www.gorgemakerspace.com/2014/04/15/spring-tool-drive/.

7. "Dissecting the Un-Makerspace: Recycled Learning," Edutopia, November 24, 2014, www.edutopia.org/blog/dissecting-un-makerspace-recycled-learning.

8. Ibid.

9. "How to Build an Epic LEGO Wall," *Renovated Learning,* September 12, 2014, http://renovatedlearning.com/2014/09/12/the-epic-library-lego-wall-how-to-build-one/.

10. "Classroom Makerspace Resources," *Digital Harbor,* www.digitalharbor.org/resources/classroom-makerspace/.

11. "Makerspace," Kent State University at Tuscarawas, http://libguides.tusc.kent.edu/makerspace.

12. "Creation Lab Inventory," Fayetteville Free Library, https://fflib.org/creation-lab/inventory.

13. "MakerSpace Audio/Visual," Johnson County Library, www.jocolibrary.org/makerspace/audiovisual.

14. "Farnhamville Elementary Maker Space Supplies List. Southeast Valley Schools," www.southeastvalley.org/vnews/display.v/ART/5481fe3850974.

15. "Equipment List," *Milwaukee Makerspace Wiki,* http://wiki.milwaukeemakerspace.org/equipment.

Pedagogy and Prototyping in Library Makerspaces

LAURA COSTELLO, MEREDITH POWERS, AND DANA HAUGH

T he print-to-digital shift has transformed the way library spaces are used. As print resources migrate online, libraries have mirrored this migration. Across all types of libraries, spaces once dedicated to stacks of physical books and individual study have transformed into informal, collaborative learning areas. In addition to repurposing old configurations into open working areas with whiteboard walls, librarians are also experimenting with makerspaces and innovation labs— spaces that can host meaningful, tangible experiences that foster creativity. Many libraries are already adding hardware development kits (e.g., electronics, physical computing, digital design and fabrication) to their circulating collections, and so providing spaces where communities can gather to tinker, experiment, and create with technology seems like a natural progression. Implementing a makerspace not only enhances traditional library offerings, but also revitalizes the library as a center of learning.

Although we typically think of the classroom as the place where learning happens, other environments are vitally important for reflection, study, collaboration,

Laura Costello is Head of Research and Emerging Technologies at Stony Brook University. Meredith Powers is Reference Librarian at Brooklyn Public Library. Dana Haugh is Senior Reference Librarian at Queens Public Library.

and active engagement with both content and other people. Libraries—whether connected to formal education institutions or not—often serve as such informal learning spaces, but fruitful interactions do not occur by chance. The importance of intentionally designing physical environments like makerspaces to support collaboration, experimentation, and other goals should not be underestimated, but it is equally critical to consider a variety of pedagogical approaches and plan how you will use any technologies within the space. When makerspaces and emerging technologies are aligned with traditional library resources, there is potential for technology, pedagogy, and space to converge in a blaze of innovation and creativity. Whether you approach your library makerspace with a specific pedagogical framework in mind or need to be open to a number of approaches, this chapter will help you develop a laser-sharp focus on your community's needs via prototyping activities and programs within your makerspace.

Pedagogy

As librarians have identified and responded to the transforming needs of their patrons, the way we approach teaching and learning has also transformed. Educators and librarians have options beyond traditional lecture-style teaching methods and new types of learning spaces to help support collaborative and interactive pedagogical approaches. Makerspaces have the capacity to support a variety of collaborative, active, and interactive learning activities. Employing a variety of educational techniques will not only make your programs more successful but will help engage an assortment of learning styles so you can reach a larger audience. We'll start by familiarizing ourselves with some of the most effective pedagogical approaches and then work our way through to how we can employ these techniques in our makerspaces to support our institution's pedagogical objectives. Let's get started!

Pedagogical Approaches

Active Learning

Learning is an active process. We learn by doing. Only knowledge that is used sticks in your mind.

—DALE CARNEGIE

Active learning is the process in which students participate in activities to facilitate understanding and retention. Active learning is a term we can apply to any form of learning that goes beyond traditional lectures to engage students in contributing to their own comprehension of a topic. This can include reading, writing, discussion, group-work, investigative research, and questioning. The pedagogical approaches outlined below are all examples of active learning.

Collaborative Learning

Teamwork is the ability to work together toward a common vision. The ability to direct individual accomplishments toward organizational objectives. It is the fuel that allows common people to attain uncommon results.

—ANDREW CARNEGIE

Perhaps the most well-known and frequently used active learning style, collaborative learning involves two or more people working together to understand a concept. The term "collaborative learning" has its origins in health sciences education and has been practiced across all levels and disciplines of education in the United States since at least the 1980s (Bruffee, 1984). The philosophy of collaborative, discussion-based problem-solving that informs this strategy has much in common with the student-centered approaches that John Dewey advocated in the early twentieth century and the practice of learning through collaboration almost certainly goes much farther back in human history.

Collaboration is one of the most powerful forms of learning because it gives students the opportunity to discuss ideas and flesh out concepts through an iterative and evaluative process. Collaborative learning generally takes the form of group work, but can be categorized as any exploration of an idea with two or more minds involved. Individuals working in groups generally retain more information and understand a concept more fully than those working alone. Utilizing a collaborative learning method is one of the best tools in your teaching arsenal when attempting to explore a particularly complex or esoteric topic.

Inquiry-Based Learning

Sometimes questions are more important than answers.

—NANCY WILLARD

Inquiry-based learning is the process of learning by posing questions, problems, or scenarios. The advantage of this method is that it provides a scaffold for student learning but allows students to explore and develop a better understanding of concepts instead of simply presenting the facts or providing a linear path to established ideas (Hmelo-Silver, Duncan, & Chinn, 2007). Inquiry-based learning is an intuitive form of pedagogy, because learners are naturally inclined to question unfamiliar ideas. With inquiry-based learning, students are at the center of the learning process and are responsible for questioning ideas to foster their own comprehension. Using inquiry-based learning to teach an idea often means that no two learning sessions will be the same. Students pose questions based on their personal perspectives, which makes the process of understanding a topic more engaging and effective than linear lecturing.

Project-Based Learning

It's not that I'm so smart, it's just that I stay with problems longer.

—ALBERT EINSTEIN

Project-based learning uses a project goal as context for student exploration of relevant questions as they arise over time. Projects are complex, multilayered learning experiences that require students to develop critical thinking and problem-solving skills. The Buck Institute of Education has developed seven main elements for effectively using project-based learning as a pedagogical approach, which we will outline below. These suggestions are offered to educators to ensure the best possible learning results.

To start, present a compelling and challenging problem for your students to consider. Once a problem is proposed, students are *encouraged* to explore this topic through extensive inquiry, research, and information application. One of the most important aspects of project-based learning is ensuring that the topic at hand is timely and authentic. Students will benefit most from exploring real-world issues and topics they can relate to personally, which will make their research and findings more interesting. Additionally, students should have a say in how they work and what they want to ultimately produce. Be sure to foster an atmosphere of reflection by encouraging students to share their challenges, triumphs, and progress. As the project draws to a close, organize a time for critiques and revisions, and allow students to collaborate with their peers for feedback and support. Finally, have students share their results with peers and other audiences. When deployed successfully, project-based learning can increase student engagement, foster self-confidence, and build skills for lifelong success.

Constructionism

For the things we have to learn before we can do, we learn by doing.

—ARISTOTLE

Constructionism is inspired by constructivist theory, which focuses on student-centered learning and discovery as the means to acquire knowledge. The theory posits that people learn better when they are actively making things. In this pedagogical approach, students are encouraged to build or create tangible objects to understand the world around them. This learning method is perhaps the most closely linked with makerspaces and the idea of that tinkering stimulates personal and intellectual growth. Instead of teaching *at* a person, constructionism supports the idea of assisting learning through trial and error. Educators become facilitators instead of lecturers, and act as resources in a student's personal learning journey.

When using constructionism as a teaching approach, it's important to encourage students to test their ideas without the fear of failure. Approaching problems and challenges in a creative or nonlinear way may not always end in success, but it does allow students to develop a more comprehensive understanding of an issue.

How Makerspaces Support Learning: Connecting Theory to Practice

Now that we have spent some time exploring various teaching techniques, we can begin to understand why makerspaces are gaining traction as an important tool in education. Not only do they support and enhance students' opportunities for learning, they also provide a physical space outside of the classroom where students can explore ideas at their own pace. Makerspaces are safe spaces where learners are *encouraged* to fail to test boundaries and explore creative limits in pursuit of intellectual growth and understanding. Libraries have long been responsible for bringing new technologies and resources to the public, by offering a place to experience and assess software and equipment that is still too expensive or complex for home use. The equipment in makerspaces often addresses this usage gap and can help users experiment with new technologies as they become more accessible. Because makerspaces are free of the rules governing noise and mess in classrooms, students are free to explore and test ideas without limitations. These spaces encourage collaboration and shared excitement, reinforcing project-based and collaborative learning in a space that is entirely directed and inspired by whatever a curious mind can concoct.

Makerspaces also reinforce a variety of literacies important for cognitive and character development. These spaces promote technology literacy—the ability to use technology effectively—because students are regularly asked to investigate and experiment with existing technology to produce a desired effect. Through work in makerspaces, students can hone their computer and digital literacies and experiment with visual, media, and information literacies. In addition, learners are given the opportunity to interact with a variety of people at skill levels, increasing their ability to collaborate effectively while developing crucial communication and problem-solving skills that are important for success.

Though work in makerspaces helps build important skills and literacies, the most engaging and rewarding benefit of makerspaces is the opportunity to play with educational technologies. Where else would you have the opportunity to build a computer from scratch, construct simple robots, experiment with 3D printers, or program your own wearable? Failure in a makerspace is an opportunity, not a roadblock. There are no tests, no assessments, no limits. Makerspaces offer a place for like-minded individuals to explore technology together to create amazing things.

How Library Makerspaces Support Institutional and Pedagogical Objectives

Access

One function of the librarian, as he saw it, was to blunt the edge of these differences and to provide a means whereby the rich and poor could live happily side by side. The public library was a great leveler, supplying a literature by which the ordinary man could experience some of the pleasures of the rich, and providing a common ground where employer and employee could meet on equal terms.

—REMARKS BY LEWIS H. STEINER ON LIBRARY BRANCHES, NEWARK PUBLIC LIBRARY
OPENING EXERCISES. OCT. 16, 1889 (CITED IN DITZION, 1947)

The library is an engine for the democratization of knowledge and information, and an access point for new technologies. Before computers, printers, and even the Internet were commonplace in most homes, libraries offered people a chance to try these newly affordable technologies out for themselves—and get help using them. Most public and private institutions consider it their mission to provide and increase access to information and technology; however, access alone is not enough. Although many of the technologies common in makerspaces are becoming increasingly affordable for the home consumer, acquiring the skills to use them effectively is not always as straightforward as acquiring the products themselves. The value and role of librarians are not only to provide access to new technologies, but also to educate and help improve users' technology skills, engagement, and understanding.

Library as an Agent of Change

Good novels, if we are ready for them, transform us. Good curricula should have the same effect.

—N. V. OVERLY & E. SPALDING, 1993

Libraries have the ability to transform communities. At the same time, modern libraries must continuously define and redefine, establishing best practices and inhabiting new roles at the same time. The transformation of maker librarians from technology supporters to teachers using technology tools is both a reimagining of the role of librarians and a continuation of the capacities and functions of instructional librarians. A comparison of the top competencies and skills for information professionals in learning labs and makerspaces (Koh & Abbas, 2015) with ACRL's 2008 report on the proficiency standards for instruction librarians shows many skills common to both roles. Librarians have traditionally occupied many posts: they've served as teachers, facilitators, collaborators, researchers, and technologists in a variety of settings and organizational contexts. Managing makerspaces, then, is a natural extension of most traditional librarian roles, and the ability to run an educational makerspace is a valuable addition to any instructional or service-oriented librarian's toolkit.

More importantly, libraries can spark and support innovation in education. Teachers and schools are reimagining classroom lessons to meet new standards for digital literacy and technology skills; in higher education, colleges, departments, and individual faculty are developing new assignments that encourage students to explore new media technologies and engage more deeply with course content. Libraries can do more than offer collaborative workspaces for students to work on their assignments. Librarians can help teachers and faculty develop new curricula, extend support for the technical aspects of these new assignments, offer technology training workshops to students and staff, and provide new materials, tools, and technologies as part of the library collection—all of which supports the development of new and exciting curricula by taking some of the pressure off individual departments or teachers. Crucially, this support team includes not just maker librarians, but a wide variety of library staff including but not limited to information literacy librarians, reference librarians, instructional designers, technologists, subject specialists, and data specialists.

Maker Education

Though librarians may share similar missions across a variety of libraries, different institutions will still have different pedagogical objectives and educational goals. Makerspaces for tinkering and exploration can exist outside of an educational framework; learning is apt to happen naturally in any makerspace, but it is not the primary objective of every makerspace. Libraries have an established role in promoting new technologies to patrons and supporting the use of those technologies, but makerspaces go beyond this mission to support learning beyond the use of new technology.

Maker education is a learner-driven process. In an ideal educational makerspace, the line between "student" and "teacher" starts to blur through collaboration and mutual participation in projects. As learners encounter obstacles and challenges, their peers and collaborators can offer solutions, ideas, and advice—effectively taking on the teaching role—in a fluid, constantly shifting process. Though the learner-driven environment of an educational makerspace may look anarchic, it is probably more accurate to think of it as a controlled chaos. There is always a teaching strategy undergirding successful educational makerspaces, and a plan to gently guide students to discover, question, experience, and understand the concepts they are intended to absorb. Whether the students in an educational makerspace are aware of the learning goals or not, it is vitally important that the person managing the space (and guiding the learning outcomes) models the makerspace ethos for all the participants. Resist the impulse to answer questions too quickly or too frequently—one of the chief advantages of active learning within a makerspace environment is that there are no single experts, only fellow experimenters with expanding areas of expertise.

Prototyping as Pedagogy

Earlier in the chapter we looked at different types of pedagogical approaches often used in teaching. All of them centered on the idea of active learning, the process of engaging students in the act of learning through collaboration, investigation, and inquiry. These approaches to pedagogy have been shown to resonate strongly with students, leading to better understanding and retention than traditional lecture-style learning. The last idea we looked at was constructionism, the act of learning by building. Perhaps the most "active" of the different approaches we explored, constructionism involves the physical manipulation of the space around learners to help them grasp concepts or ideas more completely. Constructionism can be said to be a kind of controlled prototyping, where the student is given a task and asked to make sense of it or solve it using the information and tools she has at her disposal. A constructionist learning approach gives the student control over her own understanding of an idea, which often leads to better comprehension and retention.

In a makerspace, prototyping as a pedagogical approach seems like a natural choice for fostering an educational atmosphere because students are given complete control. Through this approach, students learn from their successes and failures to advance their knowledge of the ideas they decide to explore. Prototyping in a makerspace environment is a low-stress, high-reward process that empowers students of all abilities. Whether you are creating something as simple as an electrical circuit or as complex as a robot, students will walk away feeling accomplished because the reward is in the process of making. The ability to tinker, build, break, and create something you envisioned is an incredibly powerful lesson, and to work alongside makers of all skill levels reinforces the idea that we are all learners and we all need help to succeed.

Making the Most of Your Makerspace

How the makerspace environment feels to potential users is probably the first consideration when it comes to creating the space itself, because a makerspace can thrive or die depending on how well it attracts and inspires library users. But once you have established a space that invites curiosity, playfulness, and a sense of wonder, what do you actually do with it? How do you create not just an environment conducive to learning and exploration, but a set of activities or guidelines that support, direct, and assess learning?

The Basics of Instructional Design

What is basic [in education] is not a certain set of texts, or principles or algorithms, but conversation that makes sense of these things. Curriculum is that conversation. It is the process of making sense with a group of people of the systems that shape and organize the world that we can think about together.

—M. GRUMET, 1995

Although you might want students to pose their own inquiries, develop their own projects, and learn at their own pace, you still need to have a plan or guiding strategy. Instructional design models can draw from a variety of pedagogical frameworks; you can approach instructional design from the perspective of cognitive and behavioral psychology, constructivism, or a hybrid view. Although it is important to find a good fit for both instructor and learner, most of the models focus on the same basic elements and may be interchangeable and adaptable. Whatever your approach when planning and implementing curriculum, you will need to address the learners, the learning objectives or goals, the method of instruction, and assessment or evaluation. How you structure your learning activities is up to you, but considering each of these elements enables you to set appropriate goals, tailor your lessons for specific situations, assess learning outcomes, and develop strategies for improvement. This holds true whether you are drawing from existing curricula, developing a single lesson plan, or creating a suite of learning experiences and environments. Furthermore, thinking about your learners, whether they are your current users or a new audience you hope to reach, and considering potential learning goals ahead of time can also guide you as you consider what types of technologies to include in your library's makerspace.

Instructional Design Models

Ideally, the process of creating instructional experiences is informed by educational research and pedagogically tested theories of learning. Many instructional design models are based on the five-phase ADDIE (analyze, design, develop, implement, evaluate) model, which was originally developed at Florida State University (Branson et al., 1975) and has been revised and updated continually over the years. The ADDIE model is versatile enough to be adapted for a variety of contexts, including student-only settings, which is characteristic of many maker activities and experiences. The ADDIE framework addresses five components of instructional design:

- *analysis,* which defines instructional problems and goals, and identifies learners, the learning environment, pedagogical considerations, and any constraints;
- *design,* which focuses on specific learning objectives, assessment measures, lesson planning, and other details;
- *development,* which refers to creation and assembly of content and other assets (e.g., storyboards, software, textual materials);
- *implementation,* which covers curriculum delivery, procedures, training, and carrying out the instruction with students; and

- *evaluation,* which includes both the final assessment of the overall instruction as well as the kind of internal evaluation present throughout each stage of instructional design.

Though the framework is easily described in a linear fashion, it is a much more dynamic and responsive process in practice. Internal assessment can be performed at any stage and used to revisit and revise previously completed stages.

Rapid Prototyping

In the context of instructional design, rapid prototyping is related to the ADDIE model, and places particular emphasis on the implementation and evaluation stages. Rapid prototyping is not just an instructional practice; it has applications in software development, architecture, user experience, and other design fields, where it is used to catch design problems in the early stages when they are easiest to fix. Paper prototyping for user-experience design is a good example of rapid prototyping. Instead of spending time creating elaborate digital mockups, paper versions of software interfaces can be used to test design assumptions and user expectations cheaply and quickly. Rapid prototyping lends itself especially well to maker curriculum design, as both instructors and students may need to create and evaluate prototypes to truly understand the problems, obstacles, and solutions that arise during active learning sessions.

Backward Design

A discussion of instructional design would be incomplete without mentioning backward design, a term first used by Grant Wiggins and Jay McTighe in *Understanding by Design*—although its conceptual roots stretch much further back in the history of curriculum design. Essentially, backward design starts with the endpoint of a lesson—the desired learning outcome—and works backwards to develop the learning activity itself. Like rapid prototyping, backward design shares commonalities with the ADDIE model. It covers the same components within a condensed, simpler framework, although it offers less flexibility as a much more linear design process. The three main steps cover the entirety of what instructors need to plan a lesson: identify the desired outcomes (what knowledge, skill, behavior, or attitude should change in your target audience); determine what evidence you will need to show that students achieved the outcomes; and design learning activities (including teaching methods and resources) that will lead to your desired results.

Perhaps the main advantage of backward design is that it is strongly oriented toward assessment. Not only are all activities designed to reach a specific goal or outcome, but backward design builds into its existence the evidence for the value and worthiness of the learning activities and learning environments. This can be a useful technique to advocate for your library's makerspace, and this process can provide ample justification for maintaining and updating the space long after its novelty wears off. On the other hand, backward design can focus a little too heavily on standards and formulated assessment—a real disadvantage for settings like libraries that do not necessarily need (or want) to use the government-mandated learning standards that schools are often required to follow. Over-adherence to a set of structured learning activities can even run counter to the maker ethos of experimentation and exploration. Still, the emphasis on evaluation and assessment makes backward design a useful tool for librarians and instructional designers if it is employed thoughtfully and there is a little flexibility built into the activities and environments that will ultimately guide learners to an intended goal.

The Eight Learning Events

Colloquially, a learning event can be anything: a workshop, a lecture, a research project, a series of classes, and more. In the field of education, "learning event" can also take on a much more specific meaning. Dieudonné Leclercq and Marianne Poumay's (2005) Eight Learning Events model is an instructional design model that describes content- and context-independent, observable, specific learner activities: imitate, receive information, exercise, explore, experiment, create, self-reflect, and debate. Each learner activity is paired with a teacher activity rooted in at least one learning theory and suitable for specific domains of knowledge and learning. Leclercq and Poumay's eight learning events can be used in any combination to form a learning strategy, lesson plan, or learning scenario. At first glance, the learning activities imitate, exercise, explore, experiment, and create will immediately jump out as particularly well-suited to maker education. These activities will probably form the basis of most of your learning strategies. Yet any of the eight learning events can work in the context of a makerspace. For example, building in opportunities for learners to engage in self-reflection can help them apply their maker experiences to other aspects of their lives. Moreover, incorporating a variety of learning events can assure that you are connecting with a diverse range of learners.

Designing a Learning Event

Curriculum . . . is a design of events that brings about conversion. Curriculum . . . is not worth the journey if it does not convert those who participate in it into something better.

—W. H. SCHUBERT, 1991

When it comes to designing pedagogy and programs for your makerspace, you may want to combine several lesson-planning strategies. The ADDIE framework can help you plan specific goals and activities for specific learners and learning environments. While backward design may prove too rigid for every kind of makerspace activity, it is still a good idea to determine your overall goals for an activity including any pedagogical objectives or desired outcomes to create and configure objects, activities, and spaces in an environment that is likely to lead you and your students to meet your goals. When developing actual programs or classes for your learners in a makerspace, it may be helpful to think in terms of Leclercq and Poumay's Learning Event model, and valuable to include a few different types of activities to support a broad range of domains—and a broad range of learners.

Creating Lesson Plans and Activities

Planning ahead is one of the most important steps in developing effective instruction, and maker education is no exception. Good lesson plans identify learners, learning goals, methods of instruction, and assessment strategies. In a practical sense, lesson plans help organize materials, time, and other resources. Because maker education relies heavily on a well-designed environment for learning to occur, lesson plans are a valuable tool. However, although lesson plans are often used to communicate goals and assessment methods directly to learners in a classroom setting, maker educators need not explicitly tell learners what it is that they're intended to learn; part of the value in maker education is allowing learners to direct the experience. Yet even learner-driven activities require planning and guidance, and creating a lesson plan can be a helpful means of organizing the tools needed to guide the learning experience.

The following worksheet is a somewhat generic outline for writing a lesson plan, but it can be useful to have a basic guide when developing them for the first time. Although it's possible to approach a lesson plan using any framework, this template guides you to determine goals and outcomes before creating an action plan.

LESSON PLANNING WORKSHEET

1 **Background and rationale**

Define what you are doing—whether it's a workshop, program, series, or other event—and its value proposition. Who are the learners, or the target audience? This can be a short summary, or it can include detailed background information, but it may help to think of this as a pitch: why would anyone want to be part of this event?

2 **Goal**

What is the main point of this lesson, activity, or program? Thinking in broad strokes is acceptable here. (In the ADDIE model, this is part of the analysis phase.) There can be more than one goal, but think of it as the main idea—don't try to do too many things in one shot.

3 **Learning outcomes**

This should be more specific that the overall goal. What changes in knowledge, skill, behavior, or attitude should learners undergo? In other words, what will they be able to do, or what will they know and understand after the lesson? There will likely be more than one learning outcome. Most instructional models require outcomes to be measurable in some way, so you can assess whether the outcomes are achieved. A common structure in many instructional models is to use active verbs (create, explore, consider, describe, use, etc.) to articulate outcomes. For example:

– Learners will be able to create a three-dimensional model using CAD software.

4 **Action plan**

An important part of planning a learning activity is documenting your process so that you or someone else can replicate it. Although you may not be able to plan the actions of the learners ahead of time, it's useful to have some idea of what might happen—and you should be able to detail all the resources and strategies you have at your disposal, even if you can't predict exactly what will happen in learner-driven contexts. At the very least, it's helpful to be as detailed as possible so that you can replicate successful events, and have a good starting point for reviewing and revising less-successful events. It might be valuable to consider the Eight Learning Events model when determining the types of activities to include. Some questions and considerations to address:

– What materials are needed to teach your lesson?

– What is the general plan? Even in a learner-directed setting, it might be helpful

to introduce it to learners. This might be your elevator pitch, but it's also an opportunity to find out about their prior knowledge and skills that can shape the activities.
- Are there any mini-lessons embedded in the overall learning event? For example, do you need to explain any new skills or tools? If so, will you teach any or all of this, or will learners teach each other as collaborators? Do you need to prepare or gather any materials such as step-by-step instructions, videos, or sample projects? How can the event be tailored for learners at different skill and knowledge levels working in the same space?
- What is the main project or process in which learners will engage?
- Will you include any time for reflection on the process or project? This could be an ongoing discussion throughout the activities, a sharing-out session at the end of the event, or even reflective writing which will provide learners with some documentation of the activity.
- How will you engage in assessment or evaluation? Will the learners be aware or unaware of the assessment?

It is worth noting that some makerspace activities may not require as much detail in each step as more traditional classroom lessons; however, planning what learners are intended to accomplish or master and how to assess the outcome is a good practice in any learning context. Even though learners may be encouraged to experiment, explore, and create without fear of failure or assessment, the makerspace itself and the related learning activities should be evaluated for effectiveness.

Finding Curricular Materials

Of course, you do not have to build every event or program from scratch; there are numerous freely available resources already in existence to support maker education. The George Lucas Educational Foundation maintains Edutopia, a comprehensive website and online community that emphasizes project-based learning, comprehensive assessment, integrated studies, social and emotional learning, and technology integration. In addition to the online community, Edutopia also aggregates case studies, teaching strategies, projects, and practices from K–12 schools, and offers its own downloadable lesson plans and assessment rubrics that support or are easily adaptable for maker education. Maker Ed is another nonprofit organization with an extensive resource library of projects and learning approaches for maker education, as well as research and data on making in education. The Digital Harbor Foundation also provides ideas, tips, and projects for library programming; aggregates a library of free resources related to makerspaces, digital app-making, and 3D printing; and offers workshops on making, 3D printing, and electronics for educators. Though there is not much in the way of national and state standards for maker curriculum, Stanford University pioneered a fellowship program to bring together researchers and educators with an interest in maker education. Funded by the National Science Foundation, the FabLearn Fellows program offers an open-source library of curriculum, resources, information, and research about the maker movement in education.

There are many other online resources for maker education, but perhaps the most significant asset for the twenty-first century librarian is the Open Educational Resources (OER) Commons. Here you will find teaching and learning materials including lesson plans, worksheets, activities, ebooks, and full university courses. The content is downloadable and reusable in many cases. Most OER materials are licensed through Creative Commons or GNU, in which case you can freely use, adapt, and share them. The OER Commons has a somewhat limited, but growing, library of resources specifically related to maker education, but the OER mission of openness, collaboration, cocreation, and participation are true to the ethos of the maker movement.

Implementing and Evaluating Programs in a Library Makerspace

Even after setting achievable goals, developing lesson plans, and browsing other curricular materials, it can still be challenging to come up with good programs to implement in your makerspace. Whether you are new to makerspaces or to implementing library programs in general, it can be helpful to come up with a few starter projects that can be completed relatively quickly with a low level of expertise. Sites like Instructables can offer a wealth of starter project instructions, but they can also be intimidating because of the sheer enormity of ideas available. However, there are some tried-and-true projects that can easily be adapted for different age groups and skill levels, such as:

- learning how to solder
- deconstructing anything, including appliances and electronics
- building simple circuits with LEDs
- making musical instruments

- creating things with duct tape
- designing a maze with Scratch coding
- constructing (and launching) basic rockets
- fixing broken appliances

No matter what projects you decide to try, the most important thing to do when you are starting out is to document everything. Documentation is key when it comes to evaluating your maker programs. In addition to the kinds of standard program-evaluation questions librarians often pose to users (e.g., what was the most important thing you learned from the program, how well did the program meet expectations, was there anything about the program that you would change), a record of projects that worked and did not work can help inform your next steps and enable you to adapt and tweak your programs in the future. Furthermore, by documenting your work, you will be poised to share it with others both within and beyond your library. Depending on your goals, you may wish to keep a private log of your maker activities or maintain a public blog; project binders, photos, videos, online tutorials, and digital narratives are also good ways to document your work.

Building a Community of Practice

Once you have established a consistent program series, a community of regular participants, or even a maker club, it may be time to start thinking beyond your own makerspace and start connecting with the larger maker community. Coordinating a visit to a Maker Faire, whether with your users or other members of your organization, is one way to get involved. Participating in or even hosting a "make-a-thon" is another strategy for engaging with makers outside your institution's walls. Competitions and existing design events like the Digital Harbor Foundation's FabSLAM—a multi-session, team-based, digital fabrication competition where kids and young adults learn and practice design, iteration, and rapid prototyping skills—can be another fun way to introduce your users to other makers, and encourage them to tap into a larger community of software engineers, digital designers, architects, industrial designers, and problem-solvers from a multitude of disciplines.

Ultimately, for an educational makerspace to flourish, it helps to develop community partners to ensure a healthy flow of new technologies, ideas, and people. Just as librarians and teachers often share the same goals for student learning, a library makerspace can benefit from tapping into a network of individuals and organizations beyond the library. Although outreach is often thought of as a method to attract users by advertising services and resources, it can also be a powerful mechanism for making connections with like-minded organizations. A makerspace operating on its own, without new inputs, can easily slip into obsolescence by becoming stale and rote. Building genuine partnerships between different libraries, museums, schools, universities, nonprofits, organizations, and even individuals can help bring in diverse pedagogical perspectives and keep people engaged in learning, making, and growing.

REFERENCES

Association of College and Research Libraries (ACRL). (2008). *Standards for proficiencies for instruction librarians and coordinators: A practical guide.* Chicago, IL: American Library Association.

Branson, R. K., Rayner, G. T., Cox, J. L., Furman, J. P., & King, F. J. (1975). *Interservice procedures for instructional systems development. executive summary and model.* Florida State University Tallahassee Center for Educational Technology.

Bruffee, K. A. (1984). Collaborative learning and the "conversation of mankind." *College English,* 46(7), 635–652. http://doi.org/10.2307/376924.

Ditzion, S. H. (1947). *Arsenals of a democratic culture: A social history of the American public library movement in New England and the middle states from 1850 to 1900.* Chicago, IL: American Library Association.

Grumet, M. (1995). The curriculum: What are the basics and are we teaching them? In J. L. Kinchloe & S. R. Steinberg (eds.), *Thirteen questions: Reframing education's conversation.* 2nd Edition. New York, NY: Peter Lang.

Hmelo-Silver, C. E., Duncan, R. G., & Chinn, C. A. (2007). Scaffolding and achievement in problem-based and inquiry learning: A response to Kirschner, Sweller, and Clark (2006). *Educational Psychologist,* 42(2), 99–107. doi:10.1080/00461520701263368.

Koh, K., & Abbas, J. (2015). Competencies for information professionals in learning labs and makerspaces. *Journal of Education for Library and Information Science,* 56(2), 114–129.

Leclercq, D., & Poumay, M. (2005). *The 8 Learning Events Model and its Principles.* Release 2005.1 LabSET. University of Liège.

Overly, N. V., & Spalding, E. (1993). The novel as a metaphor for curriculum and tool for curriculum development. *Journal of Curriculum and Supervision,* 8, 140–156.

Schubert, W. H. (1991). Curriculum inspired by Scrooge or "A Curriculum Carol." In G. Willis & W. H. Schubert (Eds.), *Reflections from the heart of educational inquiry: Understanding curriculum and teaching through the arts* (pp. 284–292). Albany, NY: State University of New York Press.

RECOMMENDED READING

Brown, T. (2009). *Change by design: How design thinking transforms organizations and inspires innovation.* New York, NY: Harper Business.

Durrance, J. C., Fisher, K. E., & Hinton, M. B. (2005). *How libraries and librarians help: A guide to identifying user-centered outcomes.* Chicago, IL: American Library Association.

Fleming, L. (2015). *Worlds of making: Best practices for establishing a makerspace for your school.* Thousand Oaks, CA: Corwin Press.

Honey, M., & Kanter, D. E. (Eds.). (2013). *Design, make, play: Growing the next generation of STEM innovators.* New York, NY: Routledge.

Huang, R. (Ed.). (2015). *Ubiquitous learning environments and technologies.* Springer Berlin.

Ito, M., et al. (2009). *Hanging out, messing around, and geeking out: Kids living and learning with new media.* Cambridge, MA: MIT Press.

Jenkins, H., Purushotma, R., Weigel, M., Clinton, K., & Robison, A. J. (2009). *Confronting the challenges of participatory culture: Media education for the 21st century.* Cambridge, MA: MIT Press.

Martinez, S. L., & Stager, G. (2013). *Invent to learn: Making, tinkering, and engineering in the classroom.* Torrance, CA: Constructing Modern Knowledge Press.

Rowe, P. G. (1991). *Design thinking.* Cambridge, MA: MIT Press.

Thomas, D., & Brown, J. S. (2011). *A new culture of learning: Cultivating the imagination for a world of constant change.* Lexington, KY: CreateSpace.

Wiggins, G. P., & McTighe, J. (2005). *Understanding by design.* Alexandria, VA: Association for Supervision and Curriculum Development (ASCD).

Wilkinson, K., & Petrich, M. (2013). *The art of tinkering: Meet 150+ makers working at the intersection of art, science & technology.* San Francisco, CA: Weldon Owen.

Wyatt-Smith, C., Klenowski, V., & Colbert, P. (Eds.). (2014). *Designing assessment for quality learning.* Dordrecht, Netherlands: Springer.

ADDITIONAL CONTENT

Design Thinking on a Dime: Using Cheap Materials for Experimentation and Prototyping

Cardboard

The Cardboard Book, Naralle Yabuka

The Art of Cardboard: Big Ideas for Creativity, Collaboration, Storytelling, and Reuse, Lori Zimmer

Duct Tape

Awesome Duct Tape Projects, Choly Knight

Dazzling Duct Tape Designs, Tamara Boykins

Clay

Creating with Polymer Clay: Designs, Techniques, Projects, Stephen Ford and Leslie Dierks

Polymer Clay Surface Design Recipes: 100 Mixed-Media Techniques Plus Project Ideas, Ellen Marshall

Foam

Foam Patterning and Construction Techniques: Turning 2D Designs into 3D Shapes, Mary McClung

Foam Crafts on the Go, Lorine Mason

Wax

Miriam Joy's Wax Design Techniques, Miriam Joy

Beeswax Alchemy: How to Make Your Own Soap, Candles, Balms, Creams, and Salves from the Hive, Petra Ahnert

Metal

Wire + Metal: 30 Easy Metalsmithing Designs, Denise Peck

Stamped Metal Jewelry: Creative Techniques and Designs for Making Custom Jewelry, Lisa Niven Kelly

Discarded Electronics

62 Projects to Make with a Dead Computer (and Other Discarded Electronics), Randy Sarafan

Unscrewed: Salvage and Reuse Motors, Gears, Switches, and More from Your Old Electronics, Edwin J. C. Sobey

Design Thinking on a Dime: Favorite Inexpensive Tech Tools

Arduino: An open-source electronic prototyping platform that allows users to create interactive electronic objects.

Google Apps: A collaborative tool that allows multiple users to share and edit in real-time, which gives students and learners a free resource for brainstorming.

Google Cardboard: A viewer that transforms phones into a virtual reality or augmented reality headsets.

Kano: A simple computer kit that allows anyone to assemble a working computer.

LightUp: An electronics construction kit that enables users to learn about electrical currents through trial and error.

Lollybot: The design specs for Thomas Tilley's prize-winning entry for the 2012 African Robotics Network (AFRON) $10 Robot Design Challenge enables anyone to build truly affordable robots, which is available free online at www.tomtilley.net/projects/lollybot/.

Makey Makey: An "invention" kit that allows users to turn anything that's capable of conducting a small amount of electricity into a touchpad that can be connected to a computer.

Osmo: A gaming accessory that transforms the way an iPad is used, bringing the digital world into the physical world.

Ozobot: A tiny robot that expands STEM and computer science learning through a collection of game-based activities and digital apps.

PocketLab: A wireless sensing and analytics platform for science experiments.

Soda Can Robug: A kit to build a recycled robot out of an old soda can.

WriteIt: An educational storytelling application for users of all ages.

Low Assembly Required: Ready-Made Maker Kits for Time-Limited Librarians

Cubelets: A set of blocks that produce different functions when connected to each other, encouraging robot-building exploration and experimentation.

Dash and Dot: Toy robots that teach users how to code on Apple and Android tablets and phones.

LEGO MINDSTORMS: A robotics construction kit includes sensors, motors, and a programmable brick that lets users build and direct their own robots.

littleBits: Easy-to-use electronic building blocks for all ages.

Zombonitron: A robot construction system designed to help kids invent and build their own robotic creations.

Encouraging a Diverse Maker Culture

AMY VECCHIONE, DEANA BROWN, GREGORY BRASIER, AND ANN DELANEY

What Does It Mean to Have a Diverse Maker Culture?

Libraries have a long tradition of making accessible that which is not accessible. We are now shifting from a single focus on content consumption to a model that includes content creation. Makerspaces are known for providing access to current and emerging technology. Indeed, many of us believe that equipment is the hallmark of makerspaces, which "typically provide access to materials, tools, and technologies to allow for hands-on exploration and participatory learning" http://acrl.ala.org/techconnect/post/makerspaces-move-into-academic-libraries (Fisher, 2012). But to succeed, makerspaces must balance equipment and culture.

How do you define a makerspace? Is it defined by the equipment or the making? A makerspace is defined less by *what* is being made and more by *how* its community uses it. A critical aspect of makerspace design involves developing an empowering community. To create a makerspace that is truly innovative, a library must use a set of best practices to help empower the community it serves.

Amy Vecchione is Head of Web and Emerging Technologies at Albertsons Library, and Associate Professor at Boise State University. Deana Brown is Librarian at Albertsons Library, and Assistant Professor at Boise State University. Gregory Brasier is a student at Boise State University. Ann Delaney is a graduate student at Boise State University.

A makerspace focused on inclusion will help users to feel empowered, rather than intimidated, when they enter the space. They should feel that they belong there.

A makerspace is a design thinking workspace where the actual space itself is a design thinking problem. A room can have all the technology in the world, but its success also depends on the way individuals and groups are empowered, how the community interacts, and users' radical trust in the makerspace.

Often, makerspace organizers begin by focusing on technology, facilities, and staffing models. These are important considerations, but are secondary to user engagement. Healthy user engagement and empowerment are necessary to develop a successful makerspace that focuses on people and purpose rather than on things. Space and budgets can be addressed after user engagement has been realized, when the library better understands what users need. Harnessing user demand, and engaging deeply with makerspace users to iterate the space, will help to procure the best equipment.

This chapter's goal is to help libraries define what a makerspace is in the context of their home institutions. (We may use a few terms that may be new to the library literature.) When designing a makerspace, first consider user needs. No two makerspaces are alike, and no two makerspaces will have the same equipment. *Diversity* is the level of differences between the individuals using the makerspaces. A successful makerspace should be an informal learning space where many users can come together as teams to solve problems. *Levels of engagement* are the ways that users interact with a space and its services. By starting at an introductory level and progressing to a high level of expertise, makerspace users will increase their activity, knowledge, expertise, and responsibility. As a best practice, *radical trust* is a concept embraced in a great makerspace wherein users are trusted to act as experts who can manage the equipment, service, or product. Levels of engagement can be used to advance users' levels of knowledge. Makerspaces do not require the available types of maker technology, but can create a glide path to other institutions or organizations that do provide access. Connecting users to these other organizations will help advance their skills. *Radical inclusion* embodies the idea that anyone can be a part of the makerspace.

Makerspaces are ultimately a creative balance between a carefully designed culture and emerging technologies. This balance sets the stage for the interactions and types of innovations that will occur. For true innovation to take place, a willingness to expand or change services or design structures is necessary. Ideas can only grow if given enough space; much like a plant in a pot whose root structure is bound, users in a makerspace may need larger, or different, pots, or sometimes they won't want to be in a pot at all. To drive engagement, makerspace equipment must excite the user base. (3D printers are generally the easiest piece of technology that will accomplish this.) This combination of equipment, excitement, change, and culture will direct users to develop innovative ideas.

Makerspaces should draw users from a diverse group of backgrounds and experiences. They will come from different disciplines, and have different skills and areas of expertise. *Transdisciplinarity* is the concept that problem-solving tools exist in every discipline. Makerspace users, as teams or individually, can learn from other experts in a variety of fields and adopt problem-solving techniques to solve their unique issues. If a makerspace is on a college or university campus, users' majors and demographic makeup should reflect the entire institution. If not, focus on transdisciplinary team-building by practicing specific outreach and inclusion strategies. Projects will be more successful because of the diversity of opinions informing the design strategies.

Transdisciplinary thinking is a skill valued by hiring committees. Companies are looking for robust problem-solvers who can think on their feet, take risks, and troubleshoot issues. Makerspaces are places where library staff encourage their users to troubleshoot, try new things, adopt new ways to problem-solve, and take calculated risks.

Library staff who manage makerspaces should ask questions about maker activities. What is the mission of the space? What is the purpose behind the activities? What would a successful makerspace look like at your institution? What are the passions and strengths of the organizers? As Erin Fisher points out, "makerspaces are defined not by specific equipment but by a guiding purpose to provide people with a place to experiment, create, and learn" (Fisher, 2012). Whether you start your mobile or static makerspace from scratch, or are presented with a piece of equipment and given a mandate, determining the purpose of your makerspace and services will be crucial to inform future decisions. Will your space serve as a spot to create, ideate, or showcase—or all these? Who will your space serve? What level of service will you provide? What resources will be available?

Planning is critical, because a makerspace won't be perfect from the outset. Using the design thinking methodology, makerspaces will become places where library staff will model ideation for the space. If staff ideate and prototype different kinds of spaces, soliciting user input and ideas to revise and improve them, the makerspaces will become better the more they are used. Starting small and then scaling to become inclusive, are critical. Developing deep empathy for those who use the space is crucial to help expand the space and better engage more individuals.

Radical Inclusion

As mentioned above, a successful makerspace has at its heart an organizational culture that focuses on design thinking. The staff working in the space will learn from the community, create a safe and equitable environment, and develop a culture focused on the empowering users. Radical inclusion is the idea that anyone can be a maker, and everyone can be included. Practicing radical inclusion and providing access to a clear pipeline of resources will help a makerspace community thrive.

It is important to acknowledge that not everyone identifies as a maker. By casting a broad net of inclusion for all types of individuals, a makerspace can radically embrace and help them find their place in the makerspace, and begin to identify as makers. Some individuals may not think of themselves as makers due to preconceived notions about what happens in a makerspace, but they may have some incredible ideas. Suzette Duncan explains that makerspaces need to use a broad definition of making to be completely inclusive:

> Use the most inclusive definition of making. Many times people assume that making only includes coding, physical computing, 3D printing, soldering, and the like. People who are involved in textile or culinary arts, for example, may not identify as makers, or can feel excluded from the Maker movement with its emphasis on STEM. (Duncan, 2016)

Giving users the chance to explore will allow those ideas to develop. Asking them about their motivations and interests will help the library makerspace staff to provide programs about the types of making that interest them. Users will feel included in the space because their interests and ideas are honored.

Inclusion can mean providing outreach to nondominant groups to give them a chance to be perceived as makers. Furthermore, by creating a space that is safe for experimentation, makerspace organizers allow users to acquire technical skills in an informal and nearly risk-free environment. Because there is no assessment in a makerspace, there is no blame if a project doesn't work quite right. In a makerspace, every iteration is a learning opportunity worth celebrating. Inclusion also means allowing individuals to envision themselves in the space, and see it as a place for people like themselves. Suzette Duncan, a teacher at the AltSchool, cites research that found "girls need to see young women who look like them involved in making and STEM activities to believe that they can get involved themselves. In other words, mirrors that reflect these girls' experiences are essential" (Duncan, 2016). This can be as simple as sharing stories about how leaders or makers from every background succeeded, describing how they ran into challenges along the way, and how they triumphed. This can also be accomplished via peer makers from different groups. Generally, peers are best at bringing in new makerspace users, and library staff can cultivate and support these micro-communities in a variety of ways.

The Boise Public Library is a great example. Although the Boise Public Library does not have a makerspace, it does offer many programs, books, databases, and resources about coding, programming, and app development. Ryan Zehm used the Wi-Fi when he was homeless (Reynolds, 2016) to build a game app that made enough money for him to rent an apartment. Providing access and supporting super users in this way help our most vulnerable populations.

User Visions

The concept that a makerspace can define its own direction will work better in some environments than in others. On a college campus, an academic library will attract a segment of the population who value learning, and therefore have self-selected to participate in higher education. Public colleges, and universities also serve the community, and may engage businesses, alumni, or other individuals who elect to utilize their local college libraries. Thus, success may be easier to achieve in an academic library than in a public library. A public library serves the entire populations of the area, some of whom may be less focused on learning. This may prove to be a barrier; however, being inclusive is more important to engage users and provide the same status to people at all socioeconomic levels. By engaging relevant users from all demographics, a public library can also help empower some of the most vulnerable populations.

The Digital Divide and Participatory Maker Culture

Libraries running makerspaces will benefit from developing tiered levels of engagement. Users can situate themselves on a ladder of expertise. For example, newcomers to a makerspace shouldn't start off independently on equipment that might cause injury. After a training session on safety, these users can advance up the levels of engagement to develop responsibility and gain greater access to tools. By setting up levels in an informal learning environment, users can scale up their own skills as much or as little as they prefer, depending on the nature of their projects. The higher students progress up the tiered structure, the greater their expertise will become. Levels can be developed based on a core user group, and then iterated as the population grows. Because the users are also the creators of the space, their presence and needs will modify the space.

People at the introductory level might be interested in the technologies and have small projects in mind. Commonly, they will have found something on Thingiverse and want to 3D print the object. These are individuals who are interested in a specific technology and want to complete one small project with the technology. Their needs are met through instructional sessions that provide training on the equipment. Sometimes casual users don't advance beyond this point, which is fine, because not everyone will want to move up the ladder.

A user who indicates a certain level of curiosity and displays the capacity to learn more has progressed to the second level. An example would be someone who attends a workshop and learns how to modify a Thingiverse model in Tinkercad or to design his or her own model in Tinkercad. Such users will return to the space after an instructional session, or learn how to use the software on their own and work toward becoming members of the space and developing ownership of the tools and services.

Third-level users in a makerspace begin to identify as makers and start to recognize their skillsets. They demonstrate the capacity to complete projects. They communicate about their ideas with the community in the makerspace. These users will also meet with a librarian to determine the best steps to take next, or to determine which technologies will be best to complete their projects. This level is critical because it will engage users in self-evaluation of technical skills. This is a place of true empowerment where users will express what they desire to accomplish. With the makerspace librarian's help, they will begin to identify the gaps in their skills.

Once users have developed a significant skillset they tend to join the core community of the makerspace. They reach the fourth step when they identify themselves as makers, and feel as though they belong in the makerspace. They return regularly either because they enjoy the safe space and culture of inclusion, or because they like learning about emerging technologies. They troubleshoot the technologies with the community regularly and become known as experts in specific technologies, such as printing with flexible filament or editing green screen videos. Individuals in this category identify themselves as makers who add value to the makerspace community.

The fifth level of maker progresses from the core community to become a leader within the space, generally by becoming a volunteer, employee, peer trainer, or ambassador for the space. These users tend to request service changes on behalf of others in the makerspace, and even meet with the library administration to determine how to make those changes. They regularly engage in prototyping and troubleshooting, and reflect critically on their projects. This level of community would best function in an official capacity, for example, as a maker-led executive committee or executive board, because they would be best suited to run and manage the space in future iterations.

The sixth level of makerspace user takes on responsibilities, either as an official employee of the makerspace or as a regular volunteer. These users may meet with the librarians regularly, discuss the future of the space, and train other makers in the various market segments. At the sixth level, users may, for example, constantly iterate better ways of organizing the 3D printer filament. Generally, they take responsibility for training and mentoring a large group of users with whom they most closely identify. These users offer workshops about what they have learned, and may turn their ideas into businesses. Users at the most advanced level will have significant expertise in one or more areas and offer workshops to others about the details of their projects. They troubleshoot efficiently.

When users enter the makerspace, the makerspace staff should focus on moving them up this informal chain of engagement to help them feel successful and develop confidence in their abilities. When staff allow the space to be managed by the individuals who use it, the community grows. Get to know the people who use the makerspace, and give them a sense of ownership by empowering them to work through the levels at their own pace and as far as they wish.

Staff members in a makerspace should inquire about what the various teams are working on, and assist when appropriate. Makerspace users may also request time to meet with staff for informal discussions about ideas and equipment. As with all services, there are limits and boundaries to the types of support provided in a makerspace. When something is outside of the scope of the maker team, refer people to other resources that can better support their needs. Many businesses need prototypes developed, and come to a makerspace to find someone to create a prototype for them. Although some users might be able to perform this role, be prepared to refer the businesses to other resources.

Developing Partnerships

As library staff engage with groups across the community, seek out and actively partner with both dominant and nondominant user groups. Patricia Gomes (2016) writes that "equity and diversity will not happen by accident" in a makerspace. It is up to the makerspace staff to take ownership of this important issue, and that "educators should be intentional in creating opportunities so that minorities and low-income students feel a sense of belonging in these spaces." A diverse makerspace should strive to exemplify inclusion of all ideas, technology, cultures, and people. Doing so ensures continued support for those already engaged in the space, while reaching out to groups and individuals who are either unaware of the space, or did not think of it as a place for them. To ensure everyone's needs are met, these connections should start with a conversation about the users' needs.

As you seek partnerships, recognize that each partner you work with will have different strengths. Some institutions already have great avenues for engaging and showcasing maker work, but need an influx of ideas to energize their community. Some groups might have funding that can help supply something that your makerspace needs, and they in turn will want to partner because of the culture in the makerspace. Seeking these kinds of partnerships will maximize effectiveness and help transition your makerspace toward success.

As you engage one-on-one with new users, you might find it best to determine their needs by engaging them in conversations about their projects. Makers tend to enjoy talking about what they're working on and, if you have created a safe space, will happily share their struggles and successes. This can help you identify their knowledge gaps, determine needed resources, and connect them to available services and resources that will fill those needs.

An increased awareness of makerspace resources in your community will lead to more opportunities, connections, and resources. When working with a group leader to learn about a group's needs, remember there may be only one chance to connect with the entire group the leader represents. In academic libraries, faculty planning class visits may request opportunities to access different kinds of equipment. These will depend on the instructor's desired learning outcomes, the length of a class, students' technology skills, and available resources. When librarians in academic libraries plan visits with group leaders, it is important to agree on expectations before the session, and make sure they are both attainable and meaningful. Short class visits might be more effective if the session focuses on raising awareness of available resources, whereas longer class visits allow for hands-on time with the technology. This will help to avoid having a group arrive for a session expecting to have hands-on time when you have only prepared a brief tour. Although having a planned curriculum is helpful, it is important to remain flexible, because technological issues might arise and library staff will need to respond accordingly. The important thing to remember is that each interaction has the possibility to grow your network of connections.

Think about the library community's network of innovators. Whom does it include? Whom else could it include? What resources could they offer? Are there barriers to access? Can those barriers be eliminated? Who might be potential partners? This glide path results in users collaborating with larger innovation centers, including business incubators, community makerspaces, community centers, the public library, the state library commission, the municipality, and local business owners. Developing partnerships will connect communities. Consider similar types of makerspaces where access can be expanded or provided depending on library makerspace user needs.

In instruction sessions, new makerspace users become more skilled as their confidence increases. As they move from introductory to higher levels, their confidence grows and they spend more time as part of the community.

Librarians should employ constructivist and team-learning theories to help provide a safe environment where students can engage with the technology to take risks without experiencing stress about becoming experts. Fostering a safe environment during instruction sessions can be accomplished by creating teams that include members of all skill levels. Employ team-based learning participation surveys so individuals can indicate how familiar they are with specific technologies. Users who are at the most advanced levels of proficiency should be the team captains. Teams are stratified by combining all different levels into one team.

Team-based learning gives makers opportunities to have questions asked and answered informally. As teams engage with a technology, library instructors can also provide more anonymous methods for asking questions, such as writing them on a whiteboard, and addressing them at the end of the session. This allows all voices to be heard, and encourages peer-to-peer learning. Often other users will respond to other teams' questions by replying on the whiteboard. These class instruction sessions can enable libraries to reach a broader section of the campus community. Another outcome of these partnerships will be increases in requests for instruction from schools, businesses, associations, and more.

Community Outreach

When a core group of makerspace users is established, it's time to broaden the user base. Makerspaces serve unique needs of specific groups that might not be met elsewhere. This insight should drive library staff to look more critically at who is currently using the space and reach out to those who aren't currently using it. This tactic of having user research serve as inspiration for new services, rather than merely as a justification of current services, is discussed in Kris Cohen's 2005 conference presentation, "Who We Talk About When We Talk About Users."

A makerspace should reflect the demographics of a library's community, but women are often underrepresented. A 2012 study from *Make* and Intel reported that 81 percent of makers are male. In fact, over a nine-year period, 85 percent of the cover images of *Make*'s own publications featured males (Buechley, 2014). To counteract these numbers, and ensure that user demographics reflect the community, identify groups to partner with who represent those constituencies. Choose organizations working to bring more female and underrepresented users into makerspaces. Any organization that encourages engagement with STEM-related technologies is also applicable.

Host events designed to facilitate inclusion. Name them carefully—don't call an event targeted to women "Ladies' Night." Our library uses the title "Breaking Barriers" for events designed to encourage diverse users to participate in making a different type of environment.

Library staff should photograph users at work in the space, and encourage users to share images that show works in progress and completed projects. Showcasing these images in a rotating slideshow display will help makers identify themselves as part of the community. New users will see individuals who resemble them, and whose projects look like something that they find interesting. This allows them to visualize themselves and their peers in the space and quickly fosters a sense of ownership. This feedback loop immediately helps to develop community. A Slack channel offers this same kind of feedback loop, where community users benefit from everyone's positive contributions, ideas, and perspectives. When one user encounters an issue, others can chime in to help provide solutions. Slack can be instrumental in identifying and developing a core group of makerspace users.

Fostering an Inclusive Culture at Albertsons Library's MakerLab

Albertsons Library's MakerLab team focuses on empowering the user to make decisions that will positively impact the process. Rather than providing advice and stating why a certain project turned out poorly, we ask targeting questions to help guide the user into critical reflection. This allows the user to look at and review a product based on how it is both designed and used to identify why something went wrong.

The team focuses on the positive aspects of user-created designs. We refer to this as *micro-empowerment*. Library makerspace staff can implement this by remembering a few basic ideas: state positive attributes about projects and ideas, offer potential solutions to problems, connect users to other user experts, emphasize that a user is the expert on specific issues (e.g., by stating "You are the expert in _____ so I trust you on that.") When users in the makerspace ask if they can do something, tell them you trust them to do so (considering the needs of all relevant stakeholders). This practice helps users to see themselves as having developed skills, which in turn helps build confidence and provides support. Creators and users contribute and create services as well as use them—as they build expertise, their confidence levels grow.

The library staff and faculty at the MakerLab have partnered with many groups, associations, clubs, and companies to advance the resources of the space, deeply engage a core user base, provide opportunities, and expand the number of individuals using the space. These include a range of campus entities: first-generation college students (McNair Scholars); the eight programs that fall under the federal TRiO Student Success Programs at Boise State, whose mission is to help students from disadvantaged backgrounds; the Louis Stokes Alliance for Minority Participation in STEM fields; and Concurrent Enrollment, where students in high school take college-level courses. Many student clubs have partnered with the MakerLab, including the Creative Technologies Association, the Association for Computing Machinery—Women (ACM-W), the Microgravity Team, and Space Broncos. The goal for each of these groups is to help the students feel at home in the MakerLab, and they do. Beyond the campus, the MakerLab has aligned itself with other makerspaces, a startup incubator named Trailhead Boise, a maker network named Open Lab, and a meetup group called Girl Develop It. Any library will find these kinds of affiliated groups in its community.

Culture Leads to Skill Development

A successful makerspace has at its heart an organizational culture that focuses on design thinking, learning from the community, a safe and equitable environment, and a culture focused on the empowerment of the users. A combination of radical inclusion and a clear pipeline to help facilitate user access to resources will help a makerspace community thrive. We define radical inclusion as the idea that although anyone can be a maker, not everyone identifies as one. Inclusion requires providing outreach to nondominant groups to offer them the chance to become makers. Furthermore, by creating a space that is safe for experimentation, makerspace organizers help users to acquire technical skills in an informal and nearly risk-free environment. The acquisition of these skills can help resolve the technical skills gap that exists in today's workforce. Per a survey by Deloitte Consulting, 52 percent of managers and respondents indicated that their employees have inadequate problem-solving skills, and 36 percent of respondents have deficient computer skills (Morrison et al., 2011). A makerspace helps students and users develop their computer skills and problem-solve when, for example, 3D printing doesn't go as planned. Problem-solving in a maker environment leads to this type of skill acquisition. Students find that "maker experiences help [them] learn to pursue their own passions and become self-directed learners, proactively seeking out knowledge and resources on their own . . . [and] learn how to problem-solve, to iterate, to take risks, to see failure as opportunity, and to make the most out of unexpected outcomes" (Agency by Design, p. 4). A makerspace environment will embody this philosophy regardless of the technology.

Design and prototyping can be done with paper, scissors, and other common office supplies, because high-tech equipment is not the only key to a makerspace's success. A culture that combines experimentation, empowerment, and learning is critical when working with any form of technology. Makerspaces are design thinking hubs where experimentation and learning take place. Design thinking is defined by Nelson and Stolterman (2003) as, "the action of bringing something new and desired into existence—a proactive stance that resolves or dissolves problematic situations by design. It is a compound of routine, adaptive, and design expertise brought to bear on complex dynamic situations." The focus on design thinking helps users of the makerspace to include their own approaches. This process helps create better services, products, and ideas that meet their needs, and help them to be more successful. Developing empathy is one component of the design thinking toolkit.

Makerspaces should aspire to attract a diverse group of people with different backgrounds, experiences, and expertise. If a makerspace is on a college or university campus, then it should reflect a variety of majors. By focusing on interdisciplinary team building, projects in the makerspace will be more successful because of the diversity of opinions contributing to the design strategies.

Makerspaces work best when they serve a wide variety of skills and expertise. The more varied the background, skills, and abilities of the individuals in the makerspace, the higher the likelihood of great ideas. Diversity of ideas can help enable everyone to make connections that solve all kinds of social problems. Because "tinkering is as much a form of cultural production as a technical one" (Dunbar-Hester, 2014), the focus on the cultural production is significant to develop a makerspace where nondominant voices are heard. Because makerspaces work by creating a nonhierarchical culture where the initiatives are run by the users, it's critical to facilitate inclusion and diversity in all aspects.

Makerspaces are places to demystify technologies that are used by experts. Creating an environment that is open and inclusive to all is critical to "combat the hoarding of technical knowledge and power by experts, and undermine elite forms of technocratic decision making more generally" (Dunbar-Hester,

2014, p. 77). Through this process of openness and encouraging levels of engagement that allow anyone to be trained and learn how to use specialized maker equipment, anyone running a makerspace can expand the number of individuals who identify themselves as makers, and help them grow into entrepreneurs or small business owners.

Typically, places such as makerspaces attract individuals from high socioeconomic groups. According to Farnham et al. (2014), this is because makerspaces require "the specialized skills, education resources, and funds required for works using technology as a creative medium . . . . Furthermore, given the gender discrepancy of those in the technology industry, it also trends towards being more male" (Farnham et. al., 2014, p. 18). The MakerLab at Boise State University Albertsons Library attempts to include nondominant groups through a variety of practices: instructional techniques, communication styles, user empowerment, and strategic outreach.

Users in a makerspace need to feel that they can make decisions to improve the space, help to modify and improve services, and take charge of their own learning experiences. The concept of the participatory library is that the library puts users in charge of making decisions about the library. It is critical to empower users, not only because they will feel responsible for the space, but because they will learn a great deal more about the technologies. Users feel a sense of ownership, and this helps them identify as someone who uses the emerging technologies that are present.

Library makerspaces have a mission to increase the skill level of their users. Following practices that help them to feel empowered, reducing barriers to access, and encouraging risk taking (while in a safe environment) eliminate the distinction between expert and novice. Users will quickly begin to see themselves as proficient and creative, and they will begin to think of themselves as makers.

Using the concept "let's let them," listening to ideas from users and letting them make improvements, changes, and decisions about the makerspace is critical. Staff must realize when it is necessary to step out of the way and when they need to help provide direction. Letting users explore, test, ideate, prototype, and push boundaries, individually as well as in teams, is the kind of entrepreneurship that is required to use new inventions to advance the economy.

When users participate by suggesting changes in the space, and then see that the library maker team is considering or implementing their ideas, their confidence grows. Additionally, this helps facilitate more ownership over the space in which they work. For users who might not believe that they belong in a makerspace, or who didn't previously identify as makers, this can be hugely helpful to illustrate that they do belong. The makerspace then serves as a radically inclusive community with a clear pipeline to resources that allow students to design ideas, objects, and dreams.

User engagement is a critical aspect of the rebirth of a new library model. "The cornerstones of participatory library were found, including: connection, sharing, peer support, authority, prosumption, playground, and comfort" (Nguyen, 2015; Nguyen, Partridge, & Edwards, 2012). As well, a "participatory library is one that fosters community among the users, librarians, and broader society. It encourages the empowerment of all library users and provides them with a holistic experience in both physical and virtual library spaces" (Nguyen, 2015).

In a makerspace, staff and teams can follow practices to facilitate user participation. Some best practices that we have implemented include allowing for multiple points of access to the makerspace resources. Library makerspace staff can greet individuals by name when they walk into the space, and if they don't know the users, introduce themselves, and offer a tour of the space. By engaging super users, makerspace staff can ask them to volunteer to conduct peer-to-peer training. Doing this helps members of different market segments and populations to find peers that they trust to help them through the process. Additionally, by promoting members from traditionally nondominant groups and elevating them to the higher-level status of peer trainers helps those groups see themselves as welcome in the space. Make training sessions as brief and as empowering as possible, allow students to lead their own workshops and training sessions, advertise in as many different places as possible, and avoid setting too many parameters about who can use the space and for which purposes.

The Pima County library system in Arizona worked with its teen users to design teen space, choosing different elements that encouraged user participation, such as services design, furniture, and colors. Using the concepts of the participatory library, any team in a makerspace can engage a group of users to help facilitate their ownership over a space. By recognizing the unique talents of those individuals, one can help embolden their confidence and generate more passion, expertise, and interest. Per Harvard's Agency by Design, Project Zero, makerspaces are places where "students come to see themselves as capable of effective positive change in their own lives and in their communities" (Agency by Design, 2015, p. 4). Our hope is to allow students who may not see themselves as makers to grow into the role. Because the makerspace is open to anyone, all students may walk in and become a part of the space, and increase their ability to create positive change.

When a space and service design follow this kind of empowerment and training, students gain many skills that go beyond manufacturing. Through 3D printing a user engages in downloading and uploading files, managing file systems, and running 3D printing configurations. All these tasks require complex digital fluency skills, which users are more likely to acquire in this environment.

The additional skills that are gained include the ability to design human-centered solutions based on real-life problems, confidence building, and even finding pathways into other majors and aptitudes that users previously thought were not for them.

Makerspace Communication

Communication outside of the space is critical to help foster communication. Consider using some type of chat, message board, or real-time messaging tool like Slack (slack.com) to facilitate asynchronous communication about the makerspace. Once established, private channels can be used to help establish safety and teamwork, but keep general chat areas open to all members. This online chat can then be promoted to users as a digital version of the makerspace. As such this space serves as a place where users can present ideas, ask for feedback, and encourage questions.

Some users feel safer in a semi-anonymous environment such as this where users can speak up without fear. And makerspace staff can monitor communications and flag, edit, or address ideas that need to be challenged. Individual community members can directly correspond with makerspace staff through this technology and get rapid-fire answers to their questions. In addition, the community members share pictures, post links, and connect with other users. In the virtual version of the makerspace, users mirror the culture of the physical space, where all voices are acknowledged and valued. Access to the channel may be made private or by invitation, and users can set up their accounts with their real names or pseudonyms. Invitations must be managed by makerspace staff, and extended to any current or potential user of the makerspace. The staff and faculty in the space must take into consideration ideas posted on Slack, and do their best to make those suggestions come to fruition, much as they do in the physical makerspace. They can do this by providing technical expertise and supplies that will help ideas become a reality.

An ideal makerspace establishes a positive culture. Staff can do this by creating a culture of happy accidents and inside jokes, and by showcasing ideas. A makerspace allows people from many backgrounds to share ideas. The projects and the users benefit from the variety of areas of expertise that come together in the space.

Every makerspace needs to showcase successful projects, and it's also important to create a critical-reflection station. This can be as simple as a table of failed prints for users to analyze. Anyone can pick up one of the pieces and evaluate it by asking themselves what went wrong, and how it might be solved. Troubleshooting is a life skill, and by troubleshooting these emerging technologies themselves, makerspace users will gain valuable skills.

Creating Community

Getting to know the maker culture at a library will help develop community. As mentioned above, library staff can develop programming opportunities to allow individuals to interact. Makerspace users with similar goals and different approaches benefit from sharing ideas. Holding events like Maker Mixers allows your makerspace users to interact and connect. Learning the user's needs, providing events for connecting, and introducing users with similar or divergent interests can only encourage creativity.

Before developing a physical makerspace, library staff will benefit from holding open houses or mixers to identify potential partners and gauge the level of interest. Open these events to anyone who's interested, and send invitations to others who are likely to be interested. Through maker programming, library staff can easily identify super users who want more programming like this and want to help support the initiative.

If libraries have not yet begun maker programming, sending targeted invitations will require a defined strategy. Identify local groups who are working with emerging technologies, or otherwise making in some way. Designing an event to be an active learning environment where attendees are encouraged to rotate through a variety of high- and low-tech stations will facilitate engagement. Low-tech making stations will increase the comfort level for attendees who might be less familiar with emerging technology, but are interested in learning about it. Low-tech making is still making! These events create happy collisions between individuals and technology, and strengthen the maker community.

At Albertsons Library's MakerLab, the Creative Technologies Association (CTA) was founded by students. At that time a group of six students was spending a lot of time with the original 3D printer and learning how to establish precision settings. By the end of the semester, they had pitched library administration to establish a network of individuals including students, staff, and faculty at Boise State University to help develop new skills in emerging technologies.

The club aims to create "a campus-wide network of informational, social, and physical resources" (Tuck, 2015) that allows its members to take the lead on new technologies, move up to higher levels of expertise, and showcase their skills to potential employers. Members of the club have considerable expertise in specific technologies that they then share with the other club members. They also hold workshops for the greater Boise State community and provide instruction on these technologies on a regular basis. If someone comes into the MakerLab with a question about projection mapping or virtual reality or 360° video or printing in Ninjaflex, experts on those technologies contribute their expertise at the point of need. The members of the Creative Technologies Association fuel the space, because a good number of members spend their free time in the space working on homework, personal projects, and helping others.

The constitution for the CTA also states that members will "develop and use creative thinking skills that are highly applicable to a multitude of modern careers—ultimately being able to present their work in the CTA as part of a resume to future employers" (Tuck, 2015). Involvement in the CTA allows students to take ownership of a technology they want to learn, connects those students with resources and expertise, and then showcases their final projects.

The communication aspect of users' expertise should not be underestimated. This experience of sharing informally, in workshops, and in personal instruction sessions allows the students to learn how to explain complicated technologies to someone who may be a novice. This experience will help them in their careers because they will likely always be eager to learn new technologies and share their experiments. Because the expertise is diversified throughout the group, the information is open and tacit knowledge is continually exchanged in the lab. Anyone in the MakerLab can learn a great deal. Additionally, as more users utilize the new technologies, they will encounter different problems. As a team, the group gets excited when there is a new problem because it's a chance to learn something new that will help them improve their designs later.

What a Successful Makerspace Looks Like

The exchange of tacit knowledge in a makerspace is critical. Technologies change rapidly, and one single staff member cannot possibly spend enough time learning about all the possible glitches that can occur. When a group solves a problem together, this builds teamwork and skills, and helps to alleviate the burden of needing library staff always on deck to solve every 3D printer ailment.

A successful makerspace will have a robust community whose members express themselves, their ideas, and projects. Teams will shake up and change regularly. If done well, library makerspace staff will hear all kinds of suggestions to make changes about both equipment and culture.

When it comes to correcting cultural problems, a top-down approach is not always the best. Coaching, mentoring, and modeling behavior are critical. When library makerspace staff start to hear that someone isn't following the rules, pay attention—it means the culture is about to shift to accommodate new needs, and you will need to get the attention of users who have been setting the culture.

University Innovation Fellows and Designing Your Own Makerspace

The desire for the MakerLab to grow is enormous. Individual users and faculty members would like deep integration into the space, emerging technologies, and innovative practices. These users are in every college across the university, and reflect a diversity of disciplines. The demand for services exceeds the capacity and resources at the library. We have investigated a number of opportunities to grow access to the makerspace, increase the community, expand the space, acquire more technology, and gain greater technical expertise. Students continue to voice how important it is throughout this process to maintain the culture, community, and focus on inclusion.

Other Models

Many models for makerspaces vary from what is described here, and every culture will be different. Each model depends on its unique constraints. These can include budgets, staffing, space, administrative support, user support, time, engagement levels, and resources. If a library wants to overcome these limitations, it must capitalize on its existing strengths and then find partners which need those strengths. As mentioned above, strategic partnerships will open many doors. Often partners are open to ideas and possibilities, and may have access to venture capital or equipment. Combining these strengths, and collaborating with open minds, can go a long way to providing greater access to resources.

The Invention Studio at Georgia Tech (which is not housed in its library), works students through levels of responsibility and skill. Users design and develop the equipment and also serve as leads by taking on roles like Shop Manager or master of a specific piece of technology. The Georgia Tech initiatives include a community of practice. The students engage in informal learning. They have conducted a small study ($n = 50$) on the outcomes of the makerspace, and consider it a success based on its specific goals. These goals include serving as a cultural hub for discussions, providing a place to access state-of-the-art equipment, encouraging team engagement, using design thinking, and tackling real-world open-ended problems. Based on survey results, "the data indicate that the Studio is achieving its expressed goals at a better than proficient level" (Forest et al., 2014, p. 18). Libraries may want to make plans to conduct these surveys in the future to see how their makerspace goals are being met.

Summary

Makerspaces are hubs for design thinking where users come together to experiment and learn, and where failure as considered a learning opportunity. Through projects and team-based learning, students create successful projects that result in the acquisition of technical and digital fluency skills. Practicing radical inclusion and inclusive excellence keeps a positive balance of nondominant groups in the space, which allows them to envision themselves as makers should they choose to identify as makers. Providing levels of engagement can help makerspace users develop their expertise and work towards becoming entrepreneurs for their amazing ideas. By including everyone, we can acquire a multitude of perspectives that will improve the design of the service, product, or idea that the student is iterating.

Through this process, any library can develop its own unique culture of making, which will create the demand to fuel initiatives to build capacity in its makerspace. First, reach out to all possible groups. Develop partnerships with groups with similar missions and functions. Design hand-crafted makerspace user learning experiences. Stress informal learning opportunities and make clear that the makerspace is a risk-free environment. Remember to help empower everyone to develop ownership and expertise in any area. Move users up the levels of engagement where applicable. Practice the idea of letting them lead the way. Welcome the users, empower them, and bring them back to the makerspace.

Makerspaces may not be about equipment, but they are places that challenge the status quo, safe places to ask questions, places to acknowledge and honor differences, places to talk about solving societal issues, places to embrace design thinking strategies, and places where users feel safe enough to tackle the questions that matter the most.

REFERENCES

Agency by Design (2015). *Maker-centered learning and the development of self: Preliminary findings of the agency by design project.* www.agencybydesign.org/wp-content/uploads/2015/01/Maker-Centered-Learning-and-the-Development-of-Self_AbD_Jan-2015.pdf.

Boise State University Facts and Figures 2015–2016. https://news.boisestate.edu/wp-content/blogs.dir/1/files/2016/03/FF2016_online.pdf.

Buechley, L. (2014, June). Presentation at Eyeo 2014. Vimeo video, 32:11. https://vimeo.com/110616469.

Cohen, K. R. (2005). Who we talk about when we talk about users. *Ethnographic Praxis in Industry Conference Proceedings,* (1): 9–30.

Dunbar-Hester, C. (2014). Radical inclusion? Locating accountability in technical DIY. In M. Boler and M. Ratto (Eds.), *DIY Citizenship: Critical making and social media* (pp.75–88). Cambridge, London: The MIT Press, 2014.

Duncan, S. (2016, May 23). Three ways the maker movement can be more inclusive of women and people of color. *EdSurge News.* www.edsurge.com/news/2016-05-23-three-ways-the-maker-movement-can-be-more-inclusive-to-women-and-people-of-color.

Farnham, S. D., Brice, J., Tremblay, G, Carey, C, & Pinto da Silva, A. (2014). *Fostering a community of innovation at the intersection of art + technology in the Pacific Northwest.* www.ieticornish.org/wp-content/uploads/2014/10/PDF-download-here.pdf.

Fisher, E. (2012, November 28). Makerspaces move into academic libraries. *ACRL Tech Connect.* http://acrl.ala.org/techconnect/post/makerspaces-move-into-academic-libraries.

Forest, C., Moore, R., Jariwala, A. S., Fasse, B. B., Linsey, J., Newstetter, W., Ngo, P., & Quintero, C. (2014). The invention studio: A university maker space and culture. *Advances in Engineering Education,* 4(2), 1–32.

Gomes, P. (2016, May 11). "Diversity does not happen by accident" and other lessons about equity in the maker movement. *EdSurge News.* www.edsurge.com/news/2016-05-11-diversity-does-not-happen-by-accident-and-other-lessons-about-equity-in-the-maker-movement.

Make & Intel. (2012). *Maker market study and media report: An in-depth profile of makers at the forefront of hardware innovation.* http://cdn.makezine.com/make/sales/Maker-Market-Study.pdf.

Morrison, T., Maciejewski, B., Giffi, C., DeRocco, E. S., McNelly, J., & Gardner, C. (2011). *Boiling point? The skills gap in U.S. manufacturing.* www.nist.gov/mep/data/upload/A07730B2A798437D98501E798C2E13AA-2.pdf.

Nelson, H. G., & Stolterman, E. (2003). *The design way: Intentional change in an unpredictable world: Foundations and fundamentals of design competence.* Englewood Cliffs, NJ: Educational Technology Publications.

Nguyen, L. C. (2015). Establishing a participatory library model: A grounded theory study. *The Journal of Academic Librarianship*, 41(4): 475–487.

Nguyen, L. C., Partridge, H., & Edwards, S. L. (2012). Towards an understanding of the participatory library. *Library Hi Tech*, 30(2): 335–346.

Reynolds, J. (Jan. 24, 2016). Once homeless, Boise man creates video game outside library, resets life. *Idaho Statesman*. www.idahostatesman.com/news/business/article56427875.html.

Robison, S, & Cooke, J. (2007). *Engaging YOUTH in community decision making*. www.cssp.org/community/constituents-co-invested-in-change/other-resources/engaging-youth-in-community-decision-making.pdf.

Tuck, K (2015, May 22). Student club encourages creative technology. http://news.boisestate.edu/update/2015/05/22/student-club-encourages-creative-technology/.

Safety and Guidelines in the Library Makerspace

KEVIN DELECKI

Makerspaces can be filled with inherently dangerous items—sharp edges on hand and power tools, extreme heat on 3D printers and soldering irons, lasers, and fumes from laser cutters. There is no way to eliminate this risk entirely, nor should there be. Most maker activities can entail real risk. But they also carry the possibility that a child will discover a love of STEM, a teen will learn a new career skill, a small businessperson will develop a new product or streamline a process, parents will learn something new alongside their children, or a senior will rekindle an old hobby. People must be allowed to take risks and to push themselves outside of their comfort zones. This will increase the chance of minor injury—nicks and cuts or minor burns, but will also increase the possibility of discovery and accomplishment (Lewis, 2013).

It is possible, however, and essential, to minimize the danger of serious injury to students, patrons, volunteers, and staff. As the power and complexity of tools offered by library makerspaces increase, so do the serious dangers that are introduced. By taking steps at the outset to provide basic safety equipment, offering

Kevin Delecki is Head Librarian at Xenia Community Library—Greene County Public Library.

and requiring training for staff and patrons, creating a well-designed workspace, and emphasizing a culture of safety, libraries can develop spaces where patrons and students will enjoy a safe and welcoming place in which to create.

Creating a Culture of Safety

Before beginning to address the individual tasks that will ensure the safe and effective use of the library makerspace, the staff and administration must commit to creating a culture of safety. A culture of safety occurs when the staff of the makerspace is not only encouraged to work toward the well-being of patrons and students, but directly act when needed (Institute for Healthcare Improvement, 2016). This involves proactively identifying safety risks and addressing them, integrating and embedding safety procedures into every task performed by staff, volunteers, patrons, and students, and developing a physical space that encourages the safe use of equipment. Without a culture of safety, none of the individual actions taken to ensure the well-being of makerspace users and equipment will be as effective, and there will be a much greater chance of preventable danger being overlooked.

Creating a culture of safety does not mean that patrons and students using the library's makerspace need to be made afraid of using the available tools. Although accidents are possible when tools are used carelessly, millions of people use potentially dangerous equipment every day without issue. Instead, the goal is to create an environment where everyone who uses the makerspace does so without hesitation, because safety has been built into every aspect of the space, and all users instinctively protect themselves and are prepared to use tools properly every time. (Hlubinka, 2013).

Within a culture of safety, patrons and students partner with staff and volunteers to watch out for the safety of themselves and those around them. They respect the equipment, and address situations that do not seem safe, even if they cannot identify exactly why they are uneasy. This culture should be at the core of everything the staff and volunteers of the makerspace do, and must be taught and consistently reinforced for every person who uses the space. Creating a culture of safety is not a one-time process that is put in place and left alone; it is a living creation that must be constantly addressed and remade to ensure that the safest possible environment for patrons and students is provided.

Supervising the Makerspace

Perhaps the most important contribution to creating a makerspace that embodies a culture of safety comes from the people who supervise the space. All making activities, from the lowest tech to the highest, involve at least some amount of risk, and therefore require at least some amount of supervision. The selection of who staffs a makerspace and how they are trained, in addition to the policies and procedures that help supervise users of the space, are an integral part of creating a safe and welcoming location for patrons and students.

In creating a makerspace, libraries must determine how to staff the physical space, whether by paid staff, volunteers, or a combination of the two, as well as the number of staff that the space will need. Regardless of how the space is supervised, it is imperative that a comprehensive training plan is created and implemented with each new person who will staff the space. This training plan needs to center around the creation of a culture of safety as detailed above, as well as address the specifics of the space, including first aid, personal safety, and safety equipment use; how to safely use and teach users to operate every piece of technology and machinery in the space; how to care for the space and equipment; and what to do in case of emergencies or accidents.

It is also important that the makerspace is always staffed when equipment is in use. It only takes one small error to create a dangerous situation, and without trained staff present, a dangerous situation can turn into a disastrous one quickly. Exceptions can be made to this in limited situations, such as a Maker-in-Residence program, or when current staff of the room are working on projects when the space is not open to the public, but in general, it is safest for everyone involved if a trained staff member is present whenever the space is being used by the public.

For staff of the makerspace to be able to help patrons and students use the space safely, there need to be policies in place to handle the most obvious situations. There are hundreds of examples of makerspace policies available online, and each space will need to adapt these to their own situations, spaces, age ranges, and available equipment. However, there are some major categories that should be addressed in every space.

- *Procedures for working safely:* This includes detailing who is authorized to enter and use the space, and what steps need to be taken to become authorized. In addition, it addresses what to do when unsafe working conditions or behaviors are observed.

- *Personal safety:* This includes detailing what steps users of the space must take to keep themselves safe, including actions, safety equipment, and appropriate dress.
- *Underage/minor policies:* This includes detailing what ages are approved to use the space, and under what conditions (i.e., supervised by a parent or guardian, unsupervised but with a signed parental agreement, etc.).
- *Safety plans:* This includes basic safety steps to take with the equipment—unplugging equipment before repairing, not disabling safety features, etc.

In addition to creating policies for the makerspace, all users need to fill out and sign an agreement stating that they have read and understand the policies, and agrees to abide by them. This helps protect the makerspace, and ensures that there is a common point of reference for all users of the space.

User Safety in the Makerspace

In addition to the policies and procedures that have been set up for the makerspace, there are specific steps that users of the space need to take to help keep themselves safe. These steps need to be clearly defined by the makerspace, and communicated to all users. These steps fall into two categories: personal safety/equipment and patron training. Both are essential to the safety of users in the makerspace, and need to be incorporated into the culture of the space.

There are simple steps that each user of the makerspace can take to increase their personal safety. These steps should be made clear to every user, posted clearly in the space, and upheld for each user with no exceptions.

- Appropriate face and/or eye protection must be worn when powered equipment or hazardous materials are present. Provide a selection of face and eye protection for your users, as well as guidelines about when the protection must be worn. Sample guidelines can be found in the Occupation Safety and Health Administrations' Personal Protective Equipment Booklet (www.osha .gov/Publications/osha3151.pdf).
- Proper hand protection must be worn based upon the hazards present. Provide a selection of gloves, as well as guidelines as to when the protection must be worn.
- Users must not wear open-toed shoes, sandals, scarves, neckties, loose-fitting clothing, or jewelry when entering the makerspace. These items can be caught in even the most innocuous-looking equipment, and cause injury.

- Users must secure long hair when entering the makerspace. Hair is extremely flammable, and can be caught in many different types of equipment.
- Unless a specific exception has been made, no one may work alone in the makerspace. If an exception is made, the person using the space must be able to communicate how the space will be safely used, and how contact with emergency personnel will be handled if necessary.

Although users need to be responsible for their personal safety, the makerspace also has the responsibility of equipping the user for the best possible opportunity to stay safe. Makerspaces must train users on the correct use of the equipment in the space, especially if users are given the freedom to operate the equipment unattended, and must make sure that these procedures are being followed. There are two ways to do this: individual patron training and certification, and group training.

The best way to ensure that users best understand the safe operation of the equipment in the makerspace is to train and certify each person individually on the equipment she is interested in using. Makerspace staff or volunteers sit with each user and go over the safe operation of the equipment the user wishes to use. The user then demonstrates that she can operate the equipment per the guidelines set forth by the makerspace. This certification is then recorded in a place where all staff and volunteers of the space can refer, to ensure that only users who have been trained and certified are utilizing the equipment. While staff-intensive, this approach ensures that users will have the instruction and tools necessary to safely operate the equipment in the space.

Alternatively, the makerspace can require that all users attend a group class on the operation and safe use of one or more pieces of available equipment before using that equipment unsupervised. These classes would cover much of the same material as individual training and certification, and would provide the attendees with the necessary information to utilize the equipment safely. Although this approach cuts down on the amount of time staff and volunteers spend teaching individual users how to operate the equipment, it does not give users a chance to demonstrate their knowledge before being allowed to operate the equipment unsupervised.

If the makerspace is uncomfortable with or unable to train each user on the safe operation of the equipment, then an alternative would be to require that all equipment is set up and operated by the trained staff and volunteers of the makerspace. This approach is time-consuming for staff, and could result in longer wait times by users, but is effective in keeping users safe in situations where it is difficult to ensure that users are properly trained in the use of the equipment.

Workspace Safety

One of the easiest ways to help patrons and students stay safe in the makerspace is to create a physical environment that supports and is designed for safety. Whether a new space is being built or an existing space is being modified or adapted, there are steps that need to be taken to ensure that the space itself encourages and emphasizes safety. However, it is important to remember that before building or modifying a makerspace, it is vital to verify with local government authorities whether building permits are required—often even the most innocuous change in physical space may require a permit. Although there are different safety considerations based upon the physical size of the makerspace, there are many factors that need to be considered for any space.

The design and layout of the makerspace needs to be executed with an eye toward safety. Makerspace design should be done with the goal of having everything a patron or student needs for a project within the same work area. This keeps users from having to walk near others using the equipment as often. In addition, each piece of equipment should be given as much space as possible. This allows patrons and students to be comfortable as they use the equipment and lay out their projects, and in the case of hand and power tools, as well as motorized machines (CNC routers, laser cutters, etc.), it helps ensure the safety of both the person using the equipment and those in the general vicinity. Consider whether there is adequate lighting in each work area. Although different pieces of equipment have different lighting needs, it is important that, in general, the makerspace is well and evenly lit.

The flooring of the makerspace is also important. Although it might not be possible to change the flooring type in a space that is being repurposed, the floor should be level and free of any cracks or variations in height that could cause a tripping hazard for someone carrying a tool or project. Floors should also be nonslip and easy to clean. Carpet creates a nonslip surface, but may be hard to keep clean. Many wood, laminate, and concrete floors are easy to sweep and mop, but may become slippery when dusty or wet. The goal is to create a floor that minimizes both hazards as much as possible, and then create a plan to minimize the rest of the danger through regularly followed procedures. Additionally, the floor should be kept as clear from hazards created by power cables and extension cords. These should be confined to the walls as much as possible, and covered when it is necessary to run them across the floor.

Many pieces of equipment in the makerspace require air filters or ventilation. This is especially important if the makerspace is located in an interior room without easy access to a window or roof. Many machines that require ventilation can be vented out of a window. If this is not an option, then an air filter designed for use by that machine will need to be used. However, even without machines that need specific filtration, it is important that the makerspace is well ventilated, and that there is good airflow. Dust particles and volatile organic compounds (VOCs) can be created by many of common makerspace tools, and steps should be taken to ensure these particles do not linger in the space.

The physical layout of the makerspace also needs to be designed to be easily organized for safety. There are many ways in which to accomplish this, but all of them boil down to ensuring that patrons and students can use the space with the fewest preventable safety hazards. This includes things like ensuring that consumables for each piece of equipment are in the same work area so that users do not need to travel to multiple areas to gather what they need, power and hand tools are in specific places in so that accidents do not occur when reaching for something that is misplaced, and placing sharp and potentially hot or otherwise dangerous items out of the reach of children.

After the physical layout where the makerspace will reside is complete, there are still additional steps that should be taken to encourage safe use of the space, and inform users of potential dangers and how to react if there is an accident.

- Immediately next to the entrance, place coat hooks or a coat rack so that coats, loose clothing, and jewelry can be stored immediately. This space can also be used to store aprons, gloves, eye protection, and other personal safety equipment so that patrons and students can equip themselves as soon as they enter the space.
- Each piece of equipment in the space should have a sign attached that lists the main or ideal use of the equipment as well as some essential safety guidelines.
- First-aid kits and first-aid information should be located at strategic locations around the makerspace, and staff of the space should have at least basic first-aid training. Ideally, an eye-wash station, or at least an eye-wash bottle, should be located within the space.
- Fire extinguishers should be located at strategic locations around the maker-space, in easy-to-see areas between 3 and 5 feet from the ground. Staff should be trained on their use.
- Accidents and injuries should be reported immediately by the patron involved to a staff member or volunteer, no matter how seemingly insignificant. Logs of these accidents and injuries should be kept, and all information should be reported to a selected member of the administrative team for the organization overseeing the makerspace. This will help protect the makerspace, and will give good empirical data on where injuries and accidents are occurring more often than they should, and will allow changing and adapting the space to help prevent future injuries.

Though it is impossible to prevent every dangerous situation, advance thought and planning can mitigate the worst of the issues. Makerspaces also must continually adapt as new hazards are identified and new safety measures are created, and implement these into the space.

Even a safely designed makerspace can become dangerous, however, if it is not cleaned properly. Keeping the space clean is a job that needs to be adopted by all users of the space: staff, volunteers, patrons, and students. Tools and equipment need to be cleaned of dust, debris, and excess material after each use. This will prolong the life of the equipment, and allow for their continued safe use. Workspaces need to be kept clear of mess and debris, and have all equipment returned to its proper place when it is finished being used. The floors need to be kept clear of dust and liquids, as these can lead to slips and falls, which in conjunction with the equipment being used in the makerspace may have potential for greater injury. Users of the space need to be made aware that they are responsible for cleaning the tools and equipment they use, for keeping their work areas organized, and for notifying staff or volunteers if a spill or mess on the floor has occurred. The staff and volunteers of the space need to continually check for the cleanliness of the space, and have a plan in place to ensure that the entire makerspace has been cleaned and reorganized at the end of each day.

Makerspace Equipment Safety

The biggest area for potential danger in a makerspace is the equipment it contains. Even when used appropriately, things that are sharp or hot, that move quickly, or that have moving gears are inherently dangerous. However, with proper training, good maintenance, and careful use of the equipment, most of these dangers can be drastically mitigated.

Tools and equipment in the makerspace need to be carefully maintained. Steps to achieve this will vary greatly based on the equipment in the space, but on the most basic level, it means ensuring that tools and equipment are cleaned properly after each use; that manufacturers' guidelines are followed when it comes to replacing consumable parts, oiling moving parts, and upgrading internal electronics; and confirming that all safety features inherent to the equipment are enabled and working correctly. This is especially important when purchasing and using secondhand tools and equipment, as the safety history of the tool is unknown. When purchasing new equipment, it is also a good idea to look for items that include new or next-generation safety features. Examples include:

- Fully enclosed CNC machines such as the Carvey or Nomad 883, which offer the benefits of a CNC router without the danger of exposed cutting blades, mitigate the amount of dust and debris projected into the work area.
- Laser cutters with integrated air filtration systems such as the BOSS LS-2436 or the Glowforge (which is still in development at the time of writing).
- Power tools with automatic brake features in case of contact with skin, such as the SawStop.

With all tools and equipment in the makerspace, disconnect the power and remove from publicly accessible areas any piece of equipment that is not working correctly, needs to be repaired, or is due for major maintenance. Always ensure the tool is disconnected from its power supply before beginning any repair or maintenance.

One of the most exciting aspects of makerspaces in libraries is the almost unlimited configurations of tools, equipment, and technology that can be located in each individual space. Listed are some of the most common items found in makerspaces, and some basic safety suggestions for each. However, it is imperative that each makerspace identifies, adapts, and creates specific safety instructions for the exact tools and equipment located in their space—this is truly a case in which one size does not fit all!

- *3D Printers:* Often a library's first foray into makerspace technology, 3D printers allow for the additive creation of objects by adding material one thin layer at a time. Currently, the most common types of 3D printers, known as fused filament fabrication (FFF), create the objects by pushing melted plastic filament through an extremely hot nozzle, and laying down the melted plastic one very thin layer at a time. The hotend of a FFF printer reaches temperatures of over 200 degrees Celsius, and can cause severe burns immediately if touched. If the makerspace's 3D printers are manufactured with an enclosed printing chamber, it is imperative that children are supervised when using the printers. As 3D printers gain in popularity, studies have begun to show that the melting of plastic filament at high temperatures can release VOCs into the air. Although the emissions are much higher when using ABS plastic rather than PLA (the two most commonly used types of filament at the time of writing), both filaments released at least some VOCs. (Merlo & Mazzoni, 2015.) It is important to use 3D printers in well-ventilated areas, and to research the various filament materials before using them. Keep in mind there are also varying levels of toxicity in 3D printing filament, with ABS being toxic and nonbiodegradable, and PLA being nontoxic, biodegradable, and produced from sustainable resources such as cornstarch or sugarcane.

- *CNC Machine:* In general, a computer numerical control (CNC) milling machine is safer than its manual counterparts because it is designed to be as safe for the user as possible. Many desktop machines are designed in a way that the spindle will not start cutting until the guard is in place. However, if the makerspace's CNC machine does not have an enclosure with a guard, it is essential that hands are kept at least 6 inches away from the spindle whenever the machine is in use—the router will not stop if it is touched, and could cause serious injury. It is also important to secure the material being cut firmly to the work surface of the machine to ensure it does not come loose during the cutting, and to choose materials that do not contain knots or other objects that will break free when cut, or break the bit of the router—both could lead to flying objects and injuries to the user or other people using the space. There are also safety concerns when choosing the materials that will be cut on the CNC machine. Each machine will have a different tolerance for the types and thicknesses of materials, and it is up to the staff of the makerspace to ensure that users are adhering to those tolerances. Cutting materials that are too thick or dense for the machine or use the wrong mill end can result in damage to the machine and danger to the user. Be sure to check the user guide, as well as online resources, for specific instructions on what materials and end mills to use with each specific machine.

- *Laser Cutter:* Already one of the more useful and popular tools in professional makerspaces, laser cutters are growing in popularity in library makerspaces as they become more compact, easier to use, and safer. However, even with recent safety upgrades, laser cutters still have inherent dangers that must be addressed. Laser cutters use, not surprisingly, high-powered lasers to cut. This means that users must wear proper eye protection, as must anyone else working in the same area who might come into contact with the laser cutter. Most newer laser cutters are enclosed to help mitigate this risk, but it is still important to have eye protection. Laser cutters also have restrictions on the type of materials that can be used in the machines. PVC and vinyl should never be cut, because they will release hydrochloric acid, which is dangerous to humans and will corrode machines. In addition, other materials can release harmful vapors or VOCs. It is essential that laser cutters have equipment-specific air filtration and ventilation systems installed, and that unknown materials are never used in the cutter. As with the CNC machines, each laser cutter has different tolerances for materials, and the staff of the makerspace need to know what materials are safe for use in their specific machine.

- *Sewing Machines/Sergers:* Although not as obviously dangerous as the other high-powered equipment discussed previously, sewing machines and sergers have the potential to cause injury, especially when used inattentively. Though it may be obvious, sewing machines use sharp needles that move at a very rapid pace. Clothing, hair, and fingers must be kept well away from these needles. Additionally, ensure that used or broken needles are disposed of in a way that will not endanger anyone—mint tins are good for this. Like CNC machines and laser cutters, sewing machines have different tolerances for the materials they use. It is important to know the limitations of the makerspace's sewing machines, and ensure that users do not try to force the machine to sew through something thicker than it can handle.

- *Hand and Power Tools:* Depending on the size of the makerspace, there are several options for tools that could be housed in the space. From electronic screwdrivers to massive table saws, tools can be used to create or assist in the creation of nearly every project in the space. However, because hand and power tools are meant to amplify the ability of the human body, they also increase the potential for injury to the user and those around the user. It is essential that patrons and students are trained to use each tool that will be used and understand the potential hazards, and that they only use the tools for their intended purposes.

- *Soldering Irons:* If the makerspace is going to include any electronics projects, then soldering irons are going to be a necessity. Like 3D printers, the ends of soldering irons become extremely hot. Users need to take great care not to touch the heated irons, melted solder, or items that have been touched by a hot soldering iron. In addition, safety glasses need to be worn when working with soldering irons, as the solder can pop and send bits flying. In addition, melted solder releases fumes that need to be ventilated or purified. There are several solder fume extractors available; the makerspace will want one for each soldering station that is going to be available to users.

These lists and safety tips are not intended to be an all-encompassing safety plan for the makerspace. Instead, they are intended to jump-start the necessary conversations about the safety and well-being of the patrons and students using the space. Every space will need to create detailed safety plans for each piece of equipment, and ensure that patrons and students are trained on how to use them safely and that the guidelines are being followed at all times.

REFERENCES

Hlubinka, M. (2013, September 2). Safety in School MakerSpaces. *Make Magazine.* http://makezine.com/2013/09/02/safety-in-school-makerspaces/.

Institute for Healthcare Improvement. (2016). Develop a culture of safety. www.ihi.org/resources/Pages/Changes/DevelopaCultureofSafety.aspx.

Lewis, D. (2013, January 30). Maker dad: Defining safety in makerspaces. *EdSurge.* www.edsurge.com/news/2013-01-30-maker-dad-defining-safety-in-makerspaces.

Merlo, F., & Mazzoni, S. (2015). Gas evolution during FDM 3D printing and health impact. *3D Safety.* www.3dsafety.org/3dsafety/download/mf2015_eng.pdf.

RECOMMENDED READING

Building a makerspace? Safety considerations for 3D printers, drones, and laser cutters (2015, March 6). *The DHMakerBus.* https://dhmakerbus.com/2015/03/05/building-a-makerspace-safety-considerations-for-3d-printers-drones-and-laser-cutters/.

Common rules poster. (2013). *Makerspace playbook: School edition,* San Francisco, CA: Maker Media.

Gurstelle, W. (2011). The safe workshop: Rules to make by. In *Ultimate Workshop and Tool Guide.* San Francisco, CA: Maker Media.

Kemp, A. (2013). *Make: The makerspace workbench.* San Francisco, CA: Maker Media, Inc.

Smith, S. (2016, April 1). Eight safety necessities for your workshop. *Make Magazine.* http://makezine.com/2016/04/01/8-safety-necessities-your-workshop/.

EXAMPLE SAFETY GUIDES, RULES, POLICIES, AND WAIVERS

Fayetteville Free Library. Fab Lab maker agreement. www.fflib.org/images/fflfablabmaker agreement2015.pdf.

Fayetteville Free Library. Fab Lab safety guide. www.fflib.org/images/pdfs/fflfablabsafety sheet.pdf.

SLO MakerSpace rules and general safety. (2013, December). *SLO MakerSpace.* www.slomakerspace.com/wpcontent/uploads/2013/12/SLOMakerSpaceRulesand GeneralSafety.pdf.

University of California at Berkeley. Makerspace safety policy https://supernode.berkeley .edu/training/assets/safety-form-4f9d9cdeb3dff18739d5e45851721efd6ee61de761f 65543b6864cf5460f18f2.pdf.

Part II

Makerspace Materials, Tools, and Technologies

A Librarian's Guide to 3D Printing

BOHYUN KIM

What Is 3D Printing?

3D printing refers to the additive manufacturing process that builds a physical object from a three-dimensional digital model created by computer-aided design (CAD) software. Before the introduction of 3D printing technology, the most common type of manufacturing was subtractive. Also known as "machining," subtractive manufacturing creates an object by taking a block of raw material and cutting pieces from it to give it a certain shape. By contrast, in additive manufacturing, material is added to create an object. 3D printing makes things by adding layers one by one. Although there are many different types of 3D printing technologies, all of them share this characteristic.

Different Types of 3D Printing Technologies

3D printing was invented by Charles Hull and patented in the United States in 1986.[1] The type of 3D printing technology that he invented was stereolithography

Bohyun Kim is Associate Director for Library Applications and Knowledge Systems at Health Sciences and Human Services Library, University of Maryland, Baltimore.

(SLA). SLA uses a UV laser and a curable photopolymer, usually liquid resin, which hardens when exposed to light. A UV laser moves following a specific path, and the liquid resin on that path is exposed to the UV light and becomes solid. This process is repeated layer by layer until a three-dimensional object is built out of those layers.

Digital light processing (DLP) is a similar 3D printing method. DLP also uses liquid photopolymer resin, but its curing mechanism utilizes a light projector instead of a laser beam. The light projector can change the amount of projected light, unlike the UV laser used in SLA. This allows DLP to cure resin at different levels.

Selective laser sintering (SLS) uses powder as its raw material. "Sintering" refers to the process in which powder material is heated to just below the boiling point to fuse particles in it. As a result, the powder solidifies and forms an object. SLS can use multiple types of powder materials such as nylon, ceramic, and even metal.

Jetting is another 3D printing technology. Jetting 3D printers work like inkjet printers. The printer head jets out layers of liquid photopolymer. A UV light attached to the printer head cures those drops instantly, forming a plastic layer that adheres to one another.

Fused deposition modeling (FDM) is the 3D printing technology that is most widely adopted by today's hobbyist desktop 3D printers. FDM 3D printers take in plastic filament, squeeze out the melted plastic through the extruder, which is heated to melt the plastic filament, and then lay down the melted plastic along the paths specified by the 3D model file. Each cross-section of an object is laid down as one layer. Once all layers are printed and fused on top of one another, you get a three-dimensional object.

There are many videos online that show how these different 3D printing technologies work if you would like to see the process. Although most of the popular ones are covered, there are more 3D printing technologies, such as electron beam freeform fabrication (EBFF) and laminated object manufacturing (LOM).[2]

3D Printers and Materials

High-end 3D printers are expensive and often used for industrial and commercial purposes. Those create realistic high-resolution models and can print large objects. On the other hand, desktop 3D printers target hobbyist consumers. Most entry-level desktop 3D printers use the FDM 3D printing technology. The FDM 3D printer uses less costly material but produces less accurate and smaller models in comparison to high-end 3D printers that use different 3D printing technologies such as SLA, DLP, and SLS.

For example, MakerBot Replicator 2X, one of the popular FDM desktop 3D printers, is capable of 3D printing an object as large as 9.7 inches long, 6 inches wide, and 6.1 inches high.[3] Using the FDM technology, it prints outs objects in the resolution of 100 microns (0.1 millimeter). That means each layer is 0.0039 inches high. In comparison, 3D Systems' ProX950 3D printer uses the SLS technology. It can produce much larger objects with greater details and accuracy to the original 3D model. Its maximum build volume is 59 x 29.5 x 21.65 inches, and its resolution is 0.0005 inches.[4] Stratasys' PolyJet 3D printer model J750 is an even more sophisticated 3D printer. It can create an object in more than 360,000 different colors as well as a vast array of materials and material properties in the same part, from rigid to flexible and opaque to transparent.[5]

Today's 3D printers can take a wide range of materials from ceramic, resin, metal, clay, plaster, cement, and even biological matter.[6] But the most commonly used material is plastic. Most desktop 3D printers use either PLA (poly lactic acid) or ABS (acrylonitrile butadiene styrene) plastic. PLA is made of plants such as corn, potato, or sugar cane. ABS is petroleum-based and a widely used material for desktop 3D printers. PLA has a more pliable quality than ABS. ABS is stronger and harder than PLA. PLA can be printed on a cold surface. On the other hand, ABS melts at a much higher temperature (220–235°C) than PLA does (180–220°C) and requires a heated platform. There are also wood, bronze, polyester, flexible, dissolving, and other types of specialty filaments that can be used with FDM desktop 3D printers.

How 3D Printing Works

The first step in 3D printing is to create a digital 3D model using one of the CAD software applications. The digital model file should be in .stl (stereolithography) or other file types supported by one's 3D printer. Second, the 3D model file is loaded on the software that works with the 3D printer. Third, the software will translate the 3D model data into information about individual layers to be laid down and create the G-code instructions. This process is called "slicing." G-code is a text-based protocol that is generated based on a 3D model. It specifies the speed and the X, Y, Z coordinates that the 3D printer's extruder will follow, which is also known as the "toolpath."[7] Most 3D printers come with their own control software, which performs slicing and allows a user to send a machine code file from the computer to the 3D printer and to change 3D printing parameters such as the speed and temperature of the extruder.[8]

3D Printers on the Market

What You Need to Know before Purchasing a 3D Printer

One of the most common misconceptions about a 3D printer is that it will print out a three-dimensional object as quickly as a conventional printer would print out a paper document. However, 3D printing jobs take a much longer time than most people expect. Even a small object that is only several inches in width, length, and height can take a few hours to 3D print. In addition to the size, the complexity and density of the model are also variables that determine the actual 3D printing time of a 3D model.

Another little-known fact about desktop 3D printers is that many 3D print jobs fail due to a variety of reasons, from design defects in the 3D model to mechanical issues with a 3D printer. For example, not all 3D models created on a computer are 3D printable. For a 3D model to be successfully 3D printed, it should meet certain conditions of geometry. A 3D digital model is often created through the mesh modeling process, which is one of the 3D modeling techniques. A mesh is a collection of vertices, edges, and faces that defines the shape of an object. For the illustration of vertices, edges, and faces, see figure 5.1. All faces in the mesh should be properly closed, meaning there must be no open gaps or holes, non-manifold edges, self-intersections, zero-length edges, naked edges, degenerate faces, duplicate faces, or inverted faces.[9] These may sound complicated, but what it means is simply that a digital 3D model should be solid and watertight to be 3D printable. I will discuss how to detect and repair some of these pesky mesh errors in a later section of this chapter.

FIGURE 5.1

Elements of Polygonal Mesh Modeling

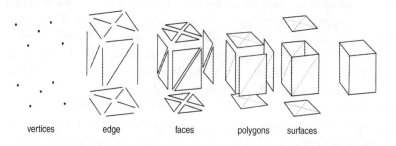

| vertices | edge | faces | polygons | surfaces |

3D print jobs can also fail for technical reasons such as the build platform being not completely level or insufficiently heated, the extruder being clogged, and the lack of raft or support. Desktop 3D printers have gone mainstream in recent years as a consumer product, and people can now buy them at retail stores such as Amazon and Costco. But those 3D printers are still far from being appliances that just work at the press of a button. As a matter of fact, desktop 3D printers require a lot of tweaking and troubleshooting on a regular basis.

Many 3D printers come with their own control software, either proprietary or open source. The 3D printer control software slices a 3D model into layers; creates the G-code, which specifies the toolpath for the 3D printer's extruder; converts the G-code instructions to the binary format; and then sends it to the 3D printer. For example, the proprietary .x3g file type is the binary format of the G-code that 3D printers manufactured by MakerBot 3D printers understand. If you load a 3D model in the MakerBot Desktop application and export the print file, you will get a .x3g file.

The most common 3D model file type is .stl. It is accepted by almost all 3D modeling programs and 3D printer control software. There are other 3D model file types that are also accepted by 3D printers. For example, MakerBot Replicator 2X comes with the MakerBot Desktop application that accepts the files types of .stl, .obj, and .thing.[10] The Afinia H480 3D printer also has its own software, and it accepts files in the .stl format only.[11] The application that works with the LulzBot Taz 5 3D printer is the customized LulzBot edition of Cura, an open-source software.[12] It accepts file types of .stl, .obj, .dae, and .amg.

Popular Brands and Models

Most libraries choose a FDM desktop 3D printer because it is less expensive and easier to handle than other types of 3D printers. You can read a few purchase guides available online to get a good idea about what some of the popular FDM desktop 3D printer brands and models are. The price range for most of those 3D printers is $1,000 to $3,500 although there are also both cheaper and more expensive ones.

3D Hubs (www.3dhubs.com), a website that lets people find a 3D printer available near them, publishes an annual 3D printer guide. Its "2016 Best 3D Printer Guide" recommends twenty 3D printers based upon over 5,350 verified reviews on 441 different 3D printer models.[13] The guide aims at measuring the user experience of a range of 3D printers in terms of print quality, ease of use, build quality, reliability, failure rate, customer service, community, running expenses, software, and value. This guide recommends 3D printers in five different categories: Enthusiast, Plug 'n' Play, Kit/DIY, Budget, and Resin (the category for SLA printers). Each category lists several 3D printers along with their specifications for accepted material, maximum build capacity, resolution, and more, and reviews the pros and cons of each. Also included are detailed reviews by users of each model. This guide is very helpful in narrowing down possible purchase choices because each category prioritizes different performance areas of a 3D printer: print quality, reliability, support, value/cost, and ease of use.

3D Hubs' "2016 Best 3D Printer Guide" recommends the Zotrax M200 ($1,990) as the best 3D printer in the Plug 'n' Play category. CEL Robox, Beeeverycreative Beethefirst, and LulzBot Mini received the next highest ratings. In the Enthusiast category, Makergear M2 ($1,825) scored the most points, followed by LulzBot Taz 5, DeltaWASP, FlashForge Creator Pro, Ultimaker 2, and BQ Witbox.

Make Magazine (makezine.com) also tests FDM desktop 3D printers and publishes its recommendations online. *Make Magazine's* 3D Printer Buyer's Guide provides a list of FDM desktop 3D printers recommended in several categories: Best Overall, Best Value, Best for Schools, Most Portable, Outstanding for Open Source, and Best Large Format. Readers can filter the results by bed style, materials, filament size, hotend, build volume, and operating system. This guide provides a detailed review for each 3D printer and its overall score in addition to its performance in multiple areas such as finish, accuracy, overhang, and support.

The most recent 3D Printer Buyer's Guide by *Make Magazine* recommends eighteen FDM desktop 3D printers.[14] The one that received the highest score is LulzBot Taz 5 in the category of Best Overall priced at $2,200. Zotrax M200 and SeeMeCNC Rostock MAX v2 scored 34 and 33 points each; their respective prices are approximately $2,000 and $1,000.

PC Magazine also provides a list of the ten best 3D printers of 2016.[15] It evaluates both FDM and SLA 3D printers. This guide provides a great overview of recommended 3D printers in several categories: editor rating, dimension, weight, maximum build area, frame, LED/LCD screen, 3D printing technology used, number of extruders (if FDM), number of colors, highest resolution, ports, SD card slots, wireless connectivity, and supported materials. The ten 3D printers recommended in 2016 are Formlabs Form 2, LulzBot Mini, MakerBot Replicator, Ultimaker 2, Formlabs Form 1+, XYZprinting Nobel 1.0, Flashforge Finder, MakerBot Replicator Mini, Ultimaker 2+, and XYZprinting da Vinci Jr. 1.0.

The desktop 3D printers recommended in these three guides provide a good starting point for determining which 3D printer to purchase. Make sure to read about the pros and cons of each model and check if the specifications, such as the maximum build volume, resolution, and supported materials, meet your library users' needs. It is also a good idea to find out what 3D printers other libraries and local makerspaces use and how they perform. "Makerspaces and the Participatory Libraries," a public Facebook group (www.facebook.com/groups/librarymaker/), and the American Library Association/Library and Information Technology Association's Maker Technology Interest Group (formerly the 3D Printing Interest Group) (www.ala.org/lita/lita-maker-technology) are both good places to make such inquiries.

Because FDM desktop 3D printers tend to require a good deal of trouble-shooting in everyday operation, it is highly recommended to purchase an extended warranty and a service plan for two to three years. Since new models continue to come on the market and prices are going down, it is reasonable to expect to replace the 3D printer within three to five years if there is sufficient use and demand by patrons to continue the 3D printing service. In choosing a 3D printer model to purchase, also make sure that there is an active user community that is supported by the 3D printer manufacturing company itself.

3D Printing Step-by-Step Using MakerBot Replicator 2X as an Example

This section reviews how to 3D print an object using a MakerBot Replicator 2X as an example. Some aspects of the instructions below may apply only to this specific 3D printer model, but no matter which FDM desktop 3D printer you buy, the tasks you will perform with your 3D printer will include the steps mentioned below, such as loading and unloading filament through the printer head and leveling the build plate.

A desktop 3D printer requires a little bit of assembly although most of them come largely preassembled. The package will also include an instruction sheet. If you follow those steps in the instruction sheet, you shouldn't encounter any serious problems. There are also many online videos that show how other 3D printer users unpacked and assembled various models of 3D printers. If you think such a video will help you with the process, watch one before you unpack and assemble your own. In the case of MakerBot Replicator 2X, the MakerBot company provides a detailed video of unboxing and assembling the Replicator 2X, which is posted on YouTube at www.youtube.com/watch?v=02sRfXSuQGo.

The two most important parts in any FDM desktop printer are the extruder and the build platform. The extruder heats and melts the plastic filament, and the build platform is a plate where the 3D model is built. MakerBot Replicator 2X accepts ABS filament of 1.75 mm diameter only and comes with two extruders. Its maximum build size is 24.6 L x 15.2 W x 15.5 H cm, and its highest resolution is 100 microns (0.1 millimeter).

Once you complete the assembly of your 3D printer, you will want to test a few things. First, you will need to become familiar with the menu options presented on the screen. When you turn on the Replicator 2X, the small screen at the lower bottom corner will light up. This is where you will find the following categories of the menu options: *Build from SD, Preheat, Utilities,* and *Info and Settings.*

Build from SD is used to print a 3D model directly from a file on a SD card plugged into the MakerBot Replicator 2X. Most FDM 3D printers connect to the computer so that you can send the 3D print job directly from a computer. Some 3D printers also allow 3D printing directly from a file on a USB drive or a SD card plugged into the 3D printer. MakerBot Replicator 2X accepts an SD card, but not a USB drive.

Preheat allows preheating the right and the left extruder and the platform. *Utilities* includes *Monitor Mode, Change Filament, Level Build Plate, Home Axes, Jog Mode, Run Startup Script, Enable Steppers, Blink LEDs,* and *Calibrate Nozzles.* The *Info* and *Settings* includes *Bot Statistics, General Settings, Preheat Settings, Version Number,* and *Restore Defaults.* Some of these options will be rarely used. But it is always good to know what information you can get directly from the screen on your 3D printer.

Load and Unload Filament

Loading and unloading the filament is the first thing you want to become comfortable doing with your 3D printer. In the menu screen, select *Utilities> Change Filament.* You will see four options: *Load Right, Unload Right, Load Left,* and *Unload Left.* Select *Load Right.* Replicator 2X will start preparing the right extruder by heating it. The changing temperature will be displayed on the small screen of the 3D printer. To load the filament to the extruder, the extruder should be sufficiently heated to melt the filament that passes through it.

Once the extruder reaches the desired temperature, bring the filament into the top of the extruder. Apply slight pressure to gently push the filament into the extruder until you feel the sensation of the filament being sucked into the extruder. The thin thread of melted plastic will start coming down from the bottom end of the extruder towards the build plate. The plastic should come down in a straight line until it reaches the build platform.[16] Once you are satisfied, stop the action using the menu option in the screen.

To unload the filament, select *Utilities> Change Filament> Unload Right.* Replicator 2X will start preparing the right extruder by heating it up again. Once the extruder is ready, grab the filament and gently pull it away from the top of the extruder. The filament will slowly come out of the extruder. Repeat this with the left extruder. Practice multiple times until you feel comfortable doing this.

Level the Build Platform

The next task is to level the build platform. Although some 3D printers can level the platform automatically, Replicator 2X requires manual adjustment. Correct leveling is crucial for a 3D print job to succeed. If the platform is not level, the extruder will end up laying down plastic at wrong points. Even slight unevenness in the build platform can cause distortions in the details of the 3D model or the failure of the 3D print job itself.

Select *Utilities> Level Build Plate* on the screen. Replicator 2X will bring up the build plate close to the two extruders. The step-by-step instruction will be displayed on the screen. Follow it and proceed to the next step by pressing the blinking "M" button next to the screen. The leveling process consists of adjusting three knobs under the build plate, one back in the middle, one at the front right, and the last one at the front left. By adjusting these three knobs, you make the build plate even. Start by tightening each of the three knobs under the build platform about four turns. After that, the Replicator 2X will move the extruder around to different positions. Adjust each knob, just enough that the nozzle almost touches the build plate. Then take a piece of paper and test the space between the extruder and the platform at each corner. The space should be just enough for the paper to pass through with a little bit of friction.

Every time you adjust one knob, it affects the space between the nozzle and the platform above all other knobs. So, it is important to repeat the leveling process more than once. You will adjust the knobs three rounds to make it sure that the platform is completely level. If you move the printer around, the platform can easily become uneven, and you must level the build plate again to ensure the 3D printer functions properly. It is recommended that you regularly level the build platform.

Prepare the Build Plate

Once the build platform is leveled, clean it with rubbing alcohol to remove any dust. Apply blue painter's tape on the surface. This will make it easy to remove the 3D model object from the platform once it is completely printed.

Download a 3D Model File

Unless you already have a 3D model file that you would like to print out, head out to one of many 3D model repositories online such as Thingiverse, Instructables, 3D Warehouse, GrabCAD, Ponoko, Nervous System, Yeggi, NIH 3D Print Exchange, and Smithsonian X 3D.

You will find 3D model files in many different file types. The Replicator 2X accepts .stl, .obj, and .thing file types. All 3D printers and 3D modeling applications accept .stl files as a de facto standard file type. So, it is best to download the .stl version of the 3D model that you would like to 3D print.

When choosing a model, bear in mind that some of the 3D models, particularly those created by a 3D scanner, will require a great deal of repair and modification to be successfully 3D printed. This requires picking a model to test our new 3D printer. So, pick a 3D model that is relatively simple and well-tested by others. One of the common choices for testing a new 3D printer is the Stanford Bunny, a 3D model developed at Stanford University in 1994. The .stl file for the Stanford Bunny can be downloaded at Thingiverse at www.thingiverse.com/thing:11622.

Open and Modify Your 3D Model File in the MakerBot Desktop Application

Download and open the MakerBot Desktop application at www.makerbot.com/desktop. This is a proprietary software that works with 3D printers manufactured by MakerBot. If you have a different 3D printer, you will be using the application that is compatible with your 3D printer. Those applications will let you perform tasks such as loading a 3D model file; scaling; rotating; positioning the model on the platform; setting various parameters such as the infill ratio, the temperature of the extruder, and the build platform, raft, and support; and most importantly, preparing the G-code based upon the 3D model and sending the 3D print job to the 3D printer along with other settings information for the 3D printer.

Launch the Maker Desktop program and open the 3D model file that you have downloaded by selecting *Add File* on the menu bar. The model may be bigger than the maximum build size of your 3D printer or simply too big or small for your purpose. In that case, you will need to scale the model. You may also need to move and rotate your model using the control options on the left side of the screen. Make sure to place the model directly on top of the build plate with no gap in between. If there is a wide and flat side in the model, that side should be on the platform. This will make the 3D printed object be more stable while it is being printed.

The home icon on the left-hand side will take you to the default view. You can also use the + and the − icon to change the zoom level. In the *View* control shown as the eye icon, you can also select *Top, Side,* and *Front* to change the viewing angle. If the model needs to be rotated, select the *Rotate* control box represented by the icon of two circling arrows. Make sure to select the model first by clicking it to activate the *Rotate* control option. After rotation, part of the model may go below the platform as shown in figure 5.2. Click the *Lay Flat* button inside the *Rotate* control option menu to place the model on the platform.

You can see the *Dimension* control option by selecting the rectangle icon on the left. The *Dimension* control allows you to easily find out the size of your 3D model in millimeters. You can also scale the model here. If you want to scale your model proportionately in all three dimensions, make sure to mark the checkbox for *Uniform Scaling.* If you want to change the model size in width only, change the number in the x-axis. To change the model size in height only, change the number in the y-axis. You can also use the *Maximum Size* or the *Reset Scale* option to set the model to be the maximum size for Replicator 2X or to set the model to its original size.

FIGURE 5.2

3D Model of the Left Shark Loaded in the MakerBot Desktop Application with the *Rotate* Control Option Selected *(Note That Part of the Model Is below the Build Platform)*

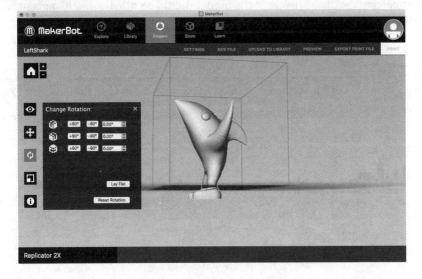

Now let's have a look at the *Settings* section in the MakerBot Desktop application. Click *Settings* in the menu bar. When Replicator 2X is connected to the PC, the MakerBot Desktop program will set the default values automatically here. But you can change them in this section later. You have two options—*Quick* or *Custom*. If you are unfamiliar with the detailed mechanics of the 3D printer, you can use the *Quick* setting, which is shown in figure 5.3. You can select *High, Standard,* or *Low* for *Quality.* The better the quality is, the longer it takes for the 3D printer to build an object. You can also select the checkbox for *Raft* or *Support* to add them to the object here.

If you select *Raft,* the 3D printer will build the raft first to use it as a heated surface on which it will start building the 3D model. *Raft* is useful to prevent a small model from warping. It can be also useful in removing the first few layers that are distorted on the heated platform.[17] If you do not select the *Raft* option, the 3D printer will directly start building the 3D model on the build plate. The *Support* option means the 3D printer will add support to the model if it has an overhang or an arch. For example, if you want to 3D print a tree with a long branch whose angle is less than 45° from the ground, then you will probably need to add support. Both raft and support must be removed after the model is printed. They also increase the amount of material required and the printing time. Select these options only if your model needs them.

You can also view and change *Layer Height, Infill, Material, Extruder Temperature,* and *Platform Temperature* in the *Quick* tab of the *Settings* menu option. *Layer Height* determines how detailed or less detailed a model will be. *Infill* refers to the material that will be filled inside a 3D printed object. Here, you can specify what percentage of the inside of the model should be filled out. 100 percent will make a model 100 percent solid.

FIGURE 5.3

Settings Section of the MakerBot Desktop Application Connected to Replicator 2X with the *Quick* Tab Displayed

---

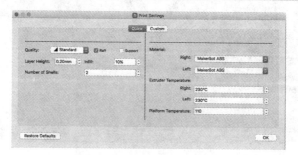

Most of the time, tinkering the menu options in the *Quick* tab of the *Settings* section should be sufficient to successfully print out a 3D model. But it is a good idea to explore the *Custom* tab if you want to have more ideas about the details of the 3D printing process. The *Custom* tab includes the list of nine options: *Device Settings, Extrusion Speeds, Infill, Model Properties, Multi-Material Printing, Raft, Supports and Bridging, Right Extruder,* and *Left Extruder.* Here, you will be able to view and change more options in each category, such as *Infill Density, Infill Layer Height,* and *Infill Pattern* under the *Infill* category.

Preview and Print Your 3D Model

Once you are happy with all the settings, you are ready to preview your model. This is useful because it allows you to see how the 3D printer will build your 3D model layer by layer. Click *Preview* on the menu bar. The MakerBot Desktop application will process your model and present the preview screen.

Using the slide bar on the left in the preview screen, you can examine the simulation of how the 3D printer will print your 3D model layer by layer. You can see how many layers will go into your 3D model. It will also provide you with an estimate of the printing time and the amount of the material required. Mark the checkbox *Show Travel Moves* if you want to see the paths that the extruder will take to build each layer. You may discover something that may cause a problem during the 3D printing process. In that case, you can go back to the 3D model and fix the issue.

If you are satisfied, click *Print* to send the job to the 3D printer. The 3D printer will start heating up the extruder (and the build platform if appropriate) for printing. If your computer is not connected to the Replicator 2X and you want to save the print job to take it to the 3D printer in an SD card, click *Export Print File* instead. Save the file on a SD card and then print from it directly on the Replicator 2X using the menu option *Build from SD* displayed on the screen. The exported file format will be .x3g.

Tips for Successful 3D Printing

How to Repair a Mesh Error in Your 3D Model

A previous section of this chapter explained that some digital 3D models are not 3D printable. However, you can easily create such 3D models using CAD software or a 3D scanner. Those 3D models may look fine when viewed on the computer screen. But they cannot be 3D printed because their geometry conflicts with what is possible in the real world. Therefore, these 3D models need to be transformed to watertight manifold meshes.

A mesh is a collection of vertices (a point), edges (a line that connects two vertices), and faces/polygons (a flat surface enclosed by edges, which is usually a triangle) that describe the shape of a 3D object.[18] For your 3D model to be 3D printable, all faces must be closed to form one or more solid and watertight entities. There should be no open holes, self-intersections, and inverted triangles in the mesh, for example.

Figure 5.4 shows a 3D model of the Stanford Bunny shown in NetFabb Basic, one of the popular 3D modeling software.[19] As you can guess from the big red triangle icon at the bottom right, this model is not watertight and cannot be 3D printed as it is. If you select the *Repair* menu option in NetFabb Basic, you can see the visual representation of the mesh. The red part signifies inverted triangles. The yellow lines indicate open holes. You can use 3D modeling software to perform repair tasks such as closing holes and fixing flipped triangles.

The simplest way to check if your 3D model is 3D printable is to use the free NetFabb Cloud Service available online at https://netfabb.azurewebsites.net/. Most of the time, this will do the trick. If you want to know more about mesh errors related to 3D printing, you can use 3D modeling software like NetFabb Basic, Meshlab, or Blender, and research each error. These applications will let you also perform more sophisticated manual repair to your 3D model.[20]

Troubleshooting Mechanical Issues

3D printing can fail for a variety of reasons. Sometimes, a model itself may have a faulty design. Other times, a 3D print job may fail due to some mechanical issues with your 3D printer. We reviewed measures to correct a 3D model file with a faulty design in the previous section. In this section, we will look at how to troubleshoot some of the common mechanical issues in the 3D printer. Below are the basic troubleshooting steps that you can take when your 3D print job fails.

- Re-level the platform.
- Clean the platform with rubbing alcohol and reapply the blue painter's tape.
- Unload and load the plastic filament.
- Check if the extruder is clogged, and if so, unclog it.

FIGURE 5.4

3D Model of the Stanford Bunny with Non-Manifold Geometry Issues,
Opened in NetFabb Basic

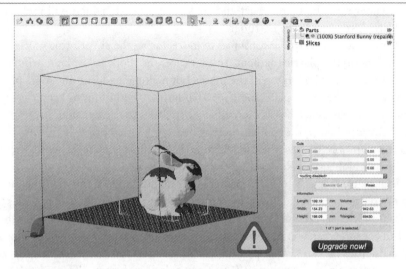

If the 3D printer does not respond at all after the print job is sent from the computer, the connection between the computer and the 3D printer may have been lost. You may need to restart either the 3D printer software application and the 3D printer—or both—to restore the connection. It may also be that the 3D printer is simply heating up the extruder and the build platform. This may take as long as thirty minutes, so you shouldn't expect the 3D printer to start moving its extruder and extruding plastic the moment you send the 3D print job to it.

Another common error in 3D printing is that the plastic layer does not stay on the build platform and instead sticks to the extruder. If this happens, try the following troubleshooting steps.

- Cancel the print job.
- Turn off the printer.
- Remove all plastic from the platform and the extruder. Be careful because the platform and the extruder will be very hot.
- Unload and reload the plastic spool to test if the extruder is clogged.

If the plastic comes out and drops vertically, everything is good. If it coils upwards, the extruder needs to be unclogged. Replicator 2X uses ABS filament only. If the clogging is relatively minor, one can unclog the extruder by feeding the cleaning filament through or using a thin wire to push out the ABS plastic stuck inside the extruder after it is heated up. If these steps do not resolve the clogging issue, the extruder must be taken apart and soaked in acetone, which will melt away the ABS plastic inside the extruder.

Sometimes, the extruder continues to move during the 3D printing process but stops releasing the plastic filament. In that case, the model must be reprinted. If the extruder is moving on top of the model but no longer adding any more plastic to the model, the build plate and the extruder may be failing to keep the right distance. In that case, the plastic will start sticking to the extruder itself rather than being applied to the model, thereby causing a failed print. If this happens, stop the print job, remove the model from the platform, clean the extruder, and try the print job again. Re-leveling the platform is also a good idea.

Make sure to check your 3D printer's user manual and troubleshooting guide. It is also recommended to join the user group if there is one. MakerBot provides the Replicator 2X User Manual and Troubleshooting and Maintenance Guide, which you can consult when you run into issues.[21] There are also active Google groups for MakerBot users at https://groups.google.com/forum/#!forum/makerbot-users and for MakerBot operators at https://groups.google.com/forum/#!forum/makerbot where you can see if other users experienced issues like your own and what solutions others suggested.

Commercial 3D Printing Services

Some library users may want their 3D model to be printed in a material that is not supported by your 3D printer. They may also need to 3D print something that exceeds the maximum build size of your 3D printer or that requires much more detail than what your 3D printer allows. In such a case, you can recommend some online 3D printing services such as Shapeways (www.shapeways .com/), i.materialise (http://i.materialise.com/), Ponoko (www.ponoko.com/), and Sculpteo (www.sculpteo.com/en/).

How Libraries are Using 3D Printing

Use Cases of 3D Printing at Libraries

3D printing can be used for prototyping a potential product idea. It can be also used for a craft project or for STEM education for children. Students and faculty at academic libraries would be particularly interested in prototyping. The 3D Printing and Fabrication Club at Oregon State University (OSU) is a great example of this. This club is supported by the OSU Valley Library and OSU College of Engineering and consists of students from all majors.[22] The club's Facebook page shows many projects that its members have worked on over the years. One of them is a 3D printed Omnipod case for insulin pumps, which is now being sold online at Shapeways with five designs and ten color options.[23]

Prof. Dr. Gene Shirokobrod, an adjunct faculty member at the Department of Physical Therapy at University of Maryland, Baltimore (UMB), School of Medicine, and Corey Fleischer, Discovery Channel's Big Brain Theory winning engineer, created a device called "ARC" that relieves tension in the neck and the back. Dr. Shirokobrod shared that they used 3D printing to create a prototype of the ARC device and refined the design at one of the Tech Brown Bag talks organized by UMB's Health Sciences and Human Services Library.[24] Their Kickstarter campaign raised over $7,000 in less than twenty-four hours,[25] and now the product is fully in production for sale.[26]

3D printing can also be used for a craft project either for academic or hobbyist purposes. After learning how to design a simple 3D model and operate a 3D printer, a staff member at my library designed a part for the old kitchen sink in his house when he could not find a replacement at a store. After a few trials and errors, he produced the part with the library's 3D printer and successfully used it to repair his sink. A graduate student also used the library's 3D printer for a similar purpose. He designed a 3D model for a small mousetrap device that will keep a mouse in place for his research project. Then he 3D printed this custom mousetrap device. Another user of the Innovation Space at my library designed and built a custom drawer knob for her vintage dresser with the library's 3D printer.[27] Recently, a professor who teaches anatomy inquired about where one can find proper 3D models for the human skull, scapular, and skull, and how to use the library's 3D printer to print them out. Those anatomical models can facilitate medical students' learning process by providing something that they can touch and examine without worrying about potential damage.

3D printing is also a terrific tool for STEM education. The Digital Harbor Foundation, a nonprofit organization that provides youth with a makerspace and hands-on, real-world learning opportunities, offers a variety of Maker Camp programs and school day field trips designed for first through twelfth graders.[28] In those programs, students learn about basic programming, 3D printing, and soldering.[29] One of the students who attended one of those after-school Mini Makers program, Jacob Leggette, was invited to the 6th and final White House Science Fair in 2016, where he had a chance to show off his 3D printed sticky mold and bubble wand to the president.[30]

There were two more inventions that utilized 3D printing at the 6th and final White House Science Fair. Using CAD software and a 3D printer, thirteen-year-olds Simon-Peter Frimpong and Maya Max-Villard, and fourteen-year-old Grayson Fast designed and built a functional prosthetic leg that allows an amputee to hike, manage uneven terrain, and even skateboard. Maya Varma, a seventeen-year-old student from California, developed an inexpensive 3D printed version of a diagnostic spirometer, a machine used to analyze lung health by having a patient blow into it. Her spirometer cost a mere $35 to produce but can diagnose chronic obstructive pulmonary disease, asthma, emphysema, chronic bronchitis, and restrictive lung disease with remarkable accuracy. [31] With this inexpensive and portable spirometer that people can use to monitor respiratory conditions, Varma also won the First Place Medal of Distinction for Innovation.[32] These examples show that 3D printing can be used as a great tool for STEM education.

3D Printing Projects

Organize a 3D Printing Demo and Petting Zoo Event

One of the most popular events a library can throw to promote its 3D printer is a 3D printing demo and petting zoo event. Many people are familiar with 3D printing, generally from news stories reported on the mass media. Still, a surprisingly large number of people have neither seen a 3D printer in action nor tried downloading or creating a 3D model to 3D print themselves. For this reason, it is always worthwhile to organize a demo and petting zoo event around the 3D printer at your library. Such an event also works as a terrific opportunity for promoting your library's new 3D printing services and other related learning events.

To organize a 3D printing demo and petting zoo event successfully, follow the steps below.

- Widely advertise the 3D printing demo and petting zoo event.
- Create and distribute promotional materials such as flyers, online blog post, digital and print signage, via the library's Facebook account to spread the word.
- Select several simple 3D models that can be easily customized and have been thoroughly tested for 3D printing. 3D print those models as examples using the library's 3D printer on the day of the event. A sample 3D model should be something small so that it can be 3D printed quickly, and attendees can take one as a souvenir. A library logo, a city symbol, or a key ring with people's initials are all good choices. If you choose to print a key ring with people's initials, have the file loaded on Tinkercad (www.Tinkercad.com/) on the day

of the event to show how you can easily swap out the alphabets on the key ring 3D model.

- Before the event, also prepare some larger models of various shapes and sizes. Print them in different colors and types of materials if possible. Keep the records of the printing time and the amount of filament used for each model. Create a sign that displays that information (see figure 5.5).
- On the day of the event, set up a PC with access to the Internet and a web browser. Display the Tinkercad website showing the various 3D models that you will be printing out. Arrange printed-out 3D models with signage presenting information such as how long each took to 3D print and how much plastic was used. Invite people to come and play with those 3D models and to ask questions.
- Have the 3D printer continue to print 3D models so that people can see the process in action. You could provide a list of 3D models that you are ready to 3D print on the spot and ask people to choose what they would like to see.
- Explain the basic mechanism of 3D printing and how it works to people at the event. Make sure to give interesting and fun examples of how 3D printing is already being widely used and what its future potential is.

FIGURE 5.5

3D Printed Gears Using MakerBot Replicator 2X, Displayed with Information about Material Type, Printing Time, and Cost

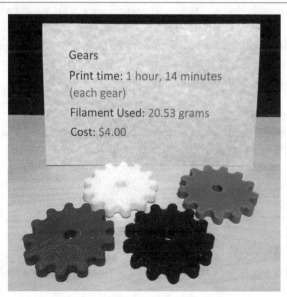

Gears
Print time: 1 hour, 14 minutes (each gear)
Filament Used: 20.53 grams
Cost: $4.00

- If your library offers 3D printing, 3D modeling, and other maker-related workshops services, workshops, or events, make sure to promote those so that people at the event will come back to try them.
- Make sure that people include their e-mail addresses in the guest book if they wish to be notified about future library events related to 3D printing. It is also a good idea to create a box into which people can drop their suggestions about what kind of 3D printing-related programs and events they would like to see the library organize in the future.

Turn Your Doodle into a 3D Model

Many people are not familiar with 3D modeling. Nor do they know how to use 3D modeling software to create or modify a 3D model on a computer. But understanding 3D modeling is an important step in using the 3D printer successfully. Anyone can draw a doodle. Inviting people to draw a doodle on a piece of paper and demonstrating how it can be transformed into a 3D model is a great way to introduce the concept of 3D modeling to people. People love to see their own doodles on a computer screen as a 3D model, and they are fascinated to see their doodles become solid objects printed out by the library's 3D printer.

Below are the steps to follow to organize a "Turn your doodle into a 3D model" event. To transform a two-dimensional doodle image on a piece of paper into a 3D model, we will use a website called "Doodle Fab" (www.doodlefab .ninja/) and a browser-based 3D modeling software Tinkercad (www.tinkercad .com/). Both are free. All you need is a computer with access to the Internet and a webcam, some thick Sharpie pens and papers, and a 3D printer. This program can be run either as a demonstration or a hands-on workshop where attendees participate in creating 3D models with their own doodles.

- Provide everyone with a thick Sharpie and a piece of paper.
- Ask participants to draw a doodle. Encourage them to draw something fun and simple like a star or the face of an animal.
- Make sure that the computer has a webcam attached so that it can read the image of people's doodles.
- Go to Doodle Fab at www.doodlefab.ninja/ on a web browser.
- Have attendees use the webcam to have Doodle Fab take pictures of their doodles so that it can convert the doodle image to an .svg (scalable vector graphics) file. Ask them to follow the directions on the Doodle Fab website.
- Ask attendees to save the .svg file and then to import it into Tinkercad.

- The 3D model automatically generated by Doodle Fab may have some unwanted parts. Show how to delete and modify part of the 3D model in Tinkercad. Go through step-by-step how people can delete certain parts and change the dimension of the model as well as its overall size.
- Once the model is ready, ask them to download it as an .stl file in Tinkercad.
- Open the .stl file in your 3D printer control software (e.g., MakerBot Desktop [www.makerbot.com/desktop]).
- Send the print job to the 3D printer. Make sure to scale the model to be small enough to print in a short time.
- Encourage people to create another doodle and go through the process again if there is enough time.
- Make sure to ask attendees if they have any questions and suggestions. Solicit any other feedback.

Host a 3D Modeling Workshop with Tinkercad

Tinkercad (www.tinkercad.com/) is among the easiest software that people can use to create a solid 3D model. It is browser-based, so there is no need to download or install any software. It is also free and quite straightforward to learn. By offering a Tinkercad workshop, you can help people become familiar with the basic concepts of 3D printing and the process of how to create and modify a 3D model by combining and subtracting several basic shapes such as a box, a cylinder, a pyramid, a sphere, a cone, and a tube.

For this project, you will need a computer with access to the Internet and a web browser. You can also run this project as two separate events, one about 3D modeling and the other about 3D printing the models created with Tinkercad.

- Create a lesson plan for a Tinkercad workshop.
- Seat attendees in front of computers with Internet access. Because Tinkercad is a browser-based 3D modeling software, people should be able to access Tinkercad online during the workshop.
- Explain the basic concepts of 3D modeling and how it relates to 3D printing.
- Provide links to several online repositories of 3D models such as Thingiverse (www.thingiverse.com/). Ask people to browse a few repositories.
- Encourage people to select a simple 3D model, download it onto the computer as an .stl file, and import the file into the Tinkercad website.
- Explain the controls in Tinkercad that people can use to view the model in different angles, move the model on the platform, and scale it to different sizes.

FIGURE 5.6

3D Model of a Keyring Displayed in Tinkercad

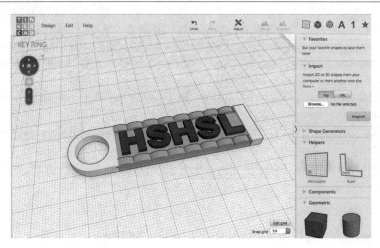

- Show more features of Tinkercad that allow people to adjust and modify the 3D model. Encourage people to try to use those features to edit the 3D model on the computer (see figure 5.6.).
- Ask people to build a 3D model using Tinkercad based upon what they have learned so far and help them along the way. Recommend Tinkercad's online tutorials at www.tinkercad.com/quests/, which people can follow step-by-step.
- Take a few successful 3D models that people created and show how they can be 3D printed using the 3D printer.
- Open those models in your 3D printer control software.
- Send the print job and print out the model.
- Pass around 3D printed objects once they are all printed out so that people can see how a digital 3D model can be transformed into a real-life object.
- Make sure to ask attendees if they have any questions and suggestions. Solicit any other feedback.

3D Print a Chemical Structure

This is a great project for students interested in science. It was originally posted at Instructables (www.instructables.com/), a website where people post and share their DIY projects. You can download full step-by-step instructions of this project at www.instructables.com/id/3D-Print-Chemical-Structures/.[33] A short summary of those steps follow. For this project, you will need a 3D printer and a computer with the access to the Internet and a web browser.

- Ask students to go to PubChem (https://pubchem.ncbi.nlm.nih.gov/), a website created by the National Center for Biotechnology Information. It provides information on the biological activities of small molecules.
- Encourage students to pick a relatively simple chemical compound that they would like to 3D print.
- Once they pick the chemical, have them write down the PubChem ID listed in the record.
- Ask students to go to the NIH (National Institute of Health) 3D Print Exchange. (http://3dprint.nih.gov/), a website that offers biomedical 3D model files.
- Once students log in to the NIH 3D Print Exchange, have them click *Create* in the top right corner.
- Ask them to enter the PubChem ID in the *Quick Submit.*
- After a few minutes, the students will receive an e-mail with the direct link to the 3D model file of the chemical compounds that they have submitted. Have them go to the link, view, and download the 3D model file in the .stl format.
- Show students how to open the downloaded 3D model file in 3D printer control software such as MakerBot Desktop (www.makerbot.com/desktop).
- Encourage students to open the file and to move, rotate, and scale the 3D model in the 3D printer control software.
- Once the model is ready, send the print job to the 3D printer.
- Once completed, pass the 3D printed chemical compound around so that students can see and experience how the chemical structure looks and feels.
- Have students discuss how the 3D model is different from its two-dimensional image and what is interesting about the 3D model of the chemical compound.
- Make sure to ask students if they have any questions. Solicit any other feedback.

Instruction on the Application of 3D Printing in Specific Subject Areas

Often students and faculty have heard about 3D printing and are curious to learn more. But they are not necessarily familiar with how it can be relevant to their areas of study and research. Librarians can provide a one-shot instruction, which highlights specific examples of how 3D printing technology is currently utilized to drive innovation in individual subject areas. Librarians can also offer a workshop with demonstrations and hands-on activities in 3D printing, so that students can experience how additive manufacturing works. Sometimes it is effective to combine both a lecture-style class with demo and hands-on activities.

Often you will see that just the experience of seeing the 3D printer in action is enough to prompt students to come up with many interesting ideas about how 3D printing could be used in their areas of study and research. An example of a one-time lesson that I developed specifically for graduate students in a physical therapy program is available online at www.slideshare.net/bohyunkim/3d-printing-and-physical-therapy.[34]

NOTES

1. "30 Years of Innovation," 3D Systems, www.3dsystems.com/30-years-innovation.

2. "3D Printing Process and Technologies," *Home Shop 3D Printing,* http://homeshop3d printing.com/3d-printing-qa/3d-printing-process-and-technologies/. See also "Processes" section in *Wikipedia, the Free Encyclopedia,* s.v. "3D Printing," https://en.wikipedia.org/w/index.php?title=3D_printing&oldid=719412123.

3. "MakerBot Replicator 2X," MakerBot, https://store.makerbot.com/replicator2x.

4. "ProX SLA Series," 3D Systems, www.3dsystems.com/sites/www.3dsystems.com/files/prox_sla_series_0313_usen_web.pdf.

5. "A Printed Smile," *The Economist,* April 30, 2016, www.economist.com/news/science -and-technology/21697802-3d-printing-coming-age-manufacturing-technique-printed -smile; "Stratasys Invents 3D Printing Again with Transformational, Market Disruptive J750 3D Printer (NASDAQ:SSYS)," Stratasys, http://investors.stratasys.com/release detail.cfm?ReleaseID=963214.

6. "Bioprinting Process," Organovo, http://organovo.com/science-technology/bioprinting -process/.

7. "What Is 'G-Code'?" *Ultimaker Wiki,* http://wiki.ultimaker.com/What_is_G-Code.

8. "Slicers and User Interfaces for 3D Printers," *EduTech Wiki,* http://edutechwiki.unige .ch/en/Slicers_and_user_interfaces_for_3D_printers.

9. For the explanation of mesh errors and problems in 3D printing, see Rich Borrett, "Creating Watertight Meshes for 3D Printing," Ponoko, http://support.ponoko.com/entries/20217167-creating-watertight-meshes-for-3d-printing.

10. "MakerBot Desktop," MakerBot, www.makerbot.com/desktop.

11. "Software and Drivers," Afinia 3D Printer, http://afinia.com/support/downloads/.

12. "Cura LulzBot Edition," LulzBot, www.lulzbot.com/cura.

13. "2016 Best 3D Printer Guide," *3D Hubs*, www.3dhubs.com/best-3d-printer-guide.

14. "The Make: 3D Printer Buyer's Guide," *Make: DIY Projects and Ideas for Makers*, http://makezine.com/comparison/3dprinters/.

15. Tony Hoffman, "The 10 Best 3D Printers of 2016," *PC Magazine*, April 11, 2016, www.pcmag.com/article2/0,2817,2470038,00.asp.

16. If the plastic goes upwards or does not go down in a straight line, the extruder is likely to be clogged and it needs to be cleaned.

17. "Glossary," s.v. "Raft," *RepRapWiki*, www.reprap.org/wiki/Glossary.

18. "What Is a Mesh?" *Blender 3D: Noob to Pro*, https://en.wikibooks.org/wiki/Blender _3D:_Noob_to_Pro/What_is_a_Mesh%3; and Rich Borrett, "Creating Watertight Meshes for 3D Printing," Ponoko, http://support.ponoko.com/entries/20217167 -creating-watertight-meshes-for-3d-printing.

19. "Netfabb Basic Download," www.netfabb.com/downloadcenter.php?basic=1.

20. The detailed instruction about how to use NetFabb Basic to check and repair a 3D model is found at Rich Borrett, "Self-Check Your 3D Designs with Netfabb," Ponoko, http://support.ponoko.com/entries/20181756-Self-check-your-3D-designs-with -Netfabb. A list of other software to repair 3D models is found at "Mesh Repairing Software on the Web," www.meshrepair.org/. Also useful are "3D Printing & Design Tutorials," Shapeways, www.shapeways.com/tutorials/; 3D Printing Tutorials & Tips, Ponoko, http://support.ponoko.com/forums/345643–3D-Printing-Tutorials-Tips; and Sean Charlesworth, "Bits to Atoms: 3D Modeling Best Practices for 3D Printing," *Tested*, March 19, 2014, www.tested.com/tech/3d-printing/460456-bits-atoms-3d -modeling-best-practices-3d-printing/.

21. *MakerBot_Replicator2X: User Manual*, MakerBot, http://download.makerbot.com/ replicator2x/MakerBot_Replicator2X_UserManual_Eng.pdf; *MakerBot_Replicator 2X: Troubleshooting and Maintenance*, MakerBot, http://download.makerbot.com/replicator 2x/MakerBot_Replicator_2X_Troubleshooting___Maintenance.pdf.

22. "About Us," OSU 3D Printing Club, https://osu3dprintingclub.wordpress.com/about/.

23. Oregon State University 3D Printing and Fabrication Club, www.facebook.com/ OSU3Dprinting/posts/1656231361283775.

24. Brown, Everly, "Tech Brown Bag at HS/HSL: 3D Printing in Health Sciences," *HS/ HSL Updates*, October 26, 2015, www2.hshsl.umaryland.edu/hslupdates/?p=1865.

25. "The ARC: Neck & Back Tension Relief Creates Perfect Posture," *Kickstarter*, www.kickstarter.com/projects/672590550/the-arc-neck-and-back-tension-relief-creates -perfe.

26. "ARC by Verve," www.goarcnow.com/.

27. "Innovation Space," Health Sciences and Human Services Library, University of Maryland, www.hshsl.umaryland.edu/services/ispace/.

28. "Tech Center," Digital Harbor Foundation, www.digitalharbor.org/tech-center/.

29. "Maker Camp 2016," Digital Harbor Foundation, www.digitalharbor.org/makercamp/.

30. Michelle Matisons, "9-Year-Old Representing Baltimore's Digital Harbor Foundation Dazzles President Obama with 3D Printing Expertise," April 18, 2016, *3DPrint.com.* https://3dprint.com/130082/jacob-leggette-white-house/.

31. Amanda Stone, "Science Fair 2016: Meet the Next Generation of America's Innovators," *White House Blog.* www.whitehouse.gov/blog/2016/04/08/science-fair -2016-meet-next-generation-americas-innovators.

32. "Intel STS 2017," *Student Science,* https://student.societyforscience.org/intel-sts.

33. "Entomophile. 3D Print Chemical Structures," *Instructables,* www.instructables.com/ id/3D-Print-Chemical-Structures/.

34. Bohyun Kim, "3D Printing/Scanning and Physical Therapy," June 19, 2015, www.slide share.net/bohyunkim/3d-printing-and-physical-therapy.

Raspberry Pi for Librarians

STEPHEN M. TAFOYA

When listing key items that go into a library media lab or makerspace, Raspberry Pi is often at the top of the list. Not much larger than a credit card, Raspberry Pi is something that looks like a component that was pulled out of a computer system (see figure 6.1). But don't let its size fool you. Raspberry Pi *is* the whole computer system—and a powerful one at that.

Because Raspberry Pi is affordable and flexible, these single-board computers are ideal for learning a new skill or building a DIY project that would be unimaginable without it. With Raspberry Pi, you can do everything from run a full open-source computer system, to automating your 3D print jobs with Raspberry Pi acting as a wireless server. It has the potential to be a gaming device running Minecraft and classic arcade emulators, and it is the perfect tool for teaching code to anyone.

These computers also encourage community collaboration because there is no one manual or right way to use it. In fact, Raspberry Pi is perfect for makerspaces because a majority of people who use it encounter problems along the way and need the help of others.

Stephen M. Tafoya is CHAOS Makerspace Manager at Rapid City Library.

Raspberry Pi Model B, with Its Many Ports and Connections

If you are thinking about adding Raspberry Pi to your makerspace, or maybe you have one already that is sitting on a shelf somewhere unused, then you have come to the right place. In this chapter, you will learn about all the components that make up a Raspberry Pi, the different models that are available for purchase and use, and how to get started with it. It will also explore examples of how other libraries have used Raspberry Pi, and wrap up by presenting you with several projects that you can easily implement in your library makerspace.

Introduction to Raspberry Pi

Raspberry Pi is what is known as a single-board computer (SBC); a complete computer system that is built on a single circuit board. The first single-board computer, the "dyna-micro," was created in 1976 and was the start of technological revolution that would pave the way for many of the electronic devices we use today. The challenge over the years has been the progression of creating a single-board computer that can run faster, fit in a smaller form factor, and, of course, cost less. This evolution took place as engineers were able to increase the density of the integrated circuits on the board.[1]

Although there have been many uses for single-board computers, few have earned the social acclaim of Raspberry Pi. Raspberry Pi grew out of a concern of several students from the University of Cambridge who noted that declining numbers of incoming students were choosing computer science as a major. What once was a promising educational endeavor in the 1990s had taken a back seat when the Internet bubble popped soon after the millennium.

Eben Upton, Rob Mullins, Alan Mycroft, and Jack Lang were students at the university who decided they needed to do something—anything—to stir interest in kids and teens who knew little or nothing about computer science. That something was to create an affordable computer that kids could program and tinker with to their hearts' content. In 2009, the Raspberry Pi Foundation was born.[2] Within several years, this $35 computer has revolutionized computational learning, and it has created a new generation of tinkering enthusiasts.

Today, there are several model choices of Raspberry Pi. Although each model falls under the $40 price point, the choice you make will be entirely based on what you want to do with your Pi. For example, if you wanted to 3D print and build a portable gaming system similar to a Gameboy, you would need to purchase the Raspberry Pi 1 Model A+ or the new Pi Zero to fit the build schematic. Or maybe you just want a Pi that people can use like a normal computer. Then you would be fine purchasing the latest and greatest Raspberry Pi 3. The current models available of Raspberry Pi are:

- Raspberry Pi 1 Model A+
- Raspberry Pi 1 Model B+
- Raspberry Pi 2 Model B+
- Raspberry Pi 3 Model B+
- Raspberry Pi Zero

To summarize differences in the versions of Pi without getting too technical:

- The Raspberry Pi 3 is the latest, greatest, and fastest system.
- Pi 2 is faster than 1.
- In Models A+ or B+, the letter refers to the size and inclusion of certain hardware components.
    - The Pi 1 Model A+ has fewer USB ports and no Ethernet connectivity.
    - The B+ models are stocked with several USB ports and include an Ethernet port.

Because each new iteration of Raspberry Pi tends to come in at the $35 price point, I highly recommend purchasing the Raspberry Pi 3 when getting started. Not only will you have the latest and greatest, but it includes onboard WiFi and Bluetooth connectivity. If you purchase a Raspberry Pi 2 or 1, you will need to include an additional WiFi dongle if you want access to wireless Internet.

The Raspberry Pi Zero is in a league of its own. This computer is smaller and costs only $5. Though it is not as fast as the Raspberry Pi 3, because of its size it serves a different purpose. It is meant to fit in spaces where no other Pi can go. Keep this in the back of your mind when you arrive at the point of next-level Raspberry Pi projects.

If you want to explore the details of each Raspberry Pi listed above, see www.raspberrypi.org/products/. When you click on a version of Raspberry Pi for more information, you will also find links to online redistributors where you can purchase them. (Note that the online distributor Element14 is good for those in the United States who want to purchase a Raspberry Pi, and the RS distributor is good for those who live in the United Kingdom. You can also purchase Raspberry Pi and various components from Amazon resellers, and websites like Adafruit .com and SparkFun.com. SparkFun generously gives discounts to libraries for many of their products).

Getting Started with Raspberry Pi

Now that you know a bit more about Raspberry Pi and where to buy it, let's list everything that must be purchased or gathered to get started with your Pi:

- Raspberry Pi
- WiFi dongle (necessary if you do not have a Raspberry Pi 3)
- keyboard (wired or wireless)
- mouse (wired or wireless)
- HDMI cable (OPTIONAL: HDMI to VGA adapter for older monitors)
- USB power source (any 5V 1a cell phone charger works)
- computer monitor or television
- SD card (regular size or Micro SD, depending on your Pi model) (size: 4 to 32 GB, Class 10)
- Mac or Windows computer with an SD card reader

There are many more components you can add to your Pi. The items listed here are the bare minimum for getting started with Raspberry Pi, and needed for the intro projects at the end of this chapter. It's probable that you may have access to many of these things already. But if you need to buy several parts from the list, I recommend purchasing a precompiled kit from Amazon (or Adafruit). On Amazon, search for "Raspberry Pi Kit." It will return kit results that range from $60 to $90 and include a variety of components like the SD card, charger, a Raspberry Pi case, and even the Raspberry Pi itself. Again, double-check to make sure the kit is compatible with the version of Raspberry Pi you want to use. (It usually says which Pi it is made for in the title or description.)

Once you have your Raspberry Pi kit compiled and ready to go, you need to spend some time working with the Pi so that when programming time comes, you have a solid foundation of its core basics. This involves learning how to install an operating system (which will be covered next), and reading the tips in the next section so you can convey important information to encourage participant (and Pi) safety and exploration. If you want, you can read the tips first, and then come back here to work through installing the Raspbian operating system.

Let's talk briefly about operating systems. There are numerous options for operating systems for Raspberry Pi. You will find some information on select systems at the Raspberry Pi website (www.raspberrypi.org/downloads/).

Let's explore some of these options.

- *Raspbian OS:* The main operating system associated with Raspberry Pi and functions in much the same way as a Windows, Mac, or Linux computer.
- *Ubuntu Mate:* A Raspberry Pi version of Linux Ubuntu.
- *OSMC:* Open Source Media Center—Similar to Roku or Apple TV.
- *Windows 10 IOT Core:* A trimmed down version of Windows 10 that lets you connect the Pi to home hardware systems.

Again, keep an eye out for these operating systems, and other ones you come across in your journey. They may spark inspiration for a new program or project.

We will begin by installing Raspbian using an interface called NOOBS (New Out of Box Software). This method is by far the easiest way of installing an operating system for Raspberry Pi on an SD card. I will summarize the overall steps of the installation process. However, the process for installing Raspbian tends to change over time. I'll briefly review the steps, but because they might be outdated in a year, you should frequently refer to www.raspberrypi.org/downloads/ for installation procedure and updates to the various operating systems. The page has a video tutorial you can follow along with as you install Raspbian with NOOBS.

To summarize the process:

- Format the SD card using an SD card formatting tool on your Windows/Mac computer.
- Download the NOOBS zip file.
- Extract the NOOBS zip file and copy to the SD card.
- Insert NOOBS SD card into Raspberry Pi and follow installation procedure.

That is the process in a nutshell. Expect to spend up to thirty minutes preparing, downloading, and installing this system on each Raspberry Pi you use. Once the system is installed, take some time to explore the Raspbian interface. Note the similarities and differences of Raspbian compared to Windows or Mac. Most of all, have fun!

Tips on Making the Best Pi Ever

So now you have your Pi and all its components. You've installed Raspbian, and you are ready to dive into some cool Pi projects. However, you may hesitate slightly. There is a nagging fear in the back of your mind: "Yeah, but what if I break it?"

Who could blame you? You grew up in an era of PCs that were constantly riddled with viruses. There was always the possibility of deleting a file required to run the operating system. If you accidentally spilled coffee on your laptop, there was a good chance it was done for. And who could forget the anxiety-inducing fear that your phone might shatter if you drop it? All of which are valid fears.

However, with Raspberry Pi, you are encouraged to fail. In fact, the Pi beckons you towards danger. Why? Because if you get a virus on your system, you can wipe that system clean and start over within an hour. Because if you delete a crucial file, you are hard set to then seek out your redemption song from the online Pi community. Because if you drop it, break it, or soak it in your coffee mug for seven hours straight, you can just get another one for the cost of lunch for two at your local diner. Put simply, the Raspberry Pi wants you to push it to its limits! Because this computer is geared towards kids, it's designed to be tough.

Don't be afraid of the Raspberry Pi, and tell your participants to not be afraid of Pi. Show them how to handle it properly, but also encourage them to hack their way forward into uncharted territory. How does one accomplish this? With these simple tips:

- *Before handling the Pi*, touch something metal to remove any static electricity from your body. This is called "grounding," and you do it prevent frying the circuit board with the electricity in your body.
- *When handling the Pi*, grip the circuit board by the sides. This also helps prevent any accidental zapping that could occur (remember, your body is a lovely conductive tunnel for electricity).
- *Consider purchasing a Raspberry Pi case*, or better yet, 3D print your own (see figure 6.2)! This leads to easier handling because the Pi has a protective shell around it.
- *When connecting your Pi*, always plug and unplug it by grasping the cord by the "neck" (the thick plastic that surrounds the plug head). Push in or pull directly out. Do not tilt your cable upon removal because you could snap the plug from the cord, or the port from circuit board.

If You Have a 3D Printer, You Can Create Some Cool Pi Cases

- *Finally, always plug in the power last.* This ensures that the Raspberry Pi recognizes all the connected components. Otherwise, you might need to start over.

Being adventurous yet safe with the Raspberry Pi won't give you the full Pi experience. Interacting with the thriving Pi community is often key to successful projects. If the primary purpose of Raspberry Pi is to teach the user about computers, then a natural response would be to share what you have learned with the community. Being a part of the Pi community likely means that there is someone out there that has completed a similar project to yours and may have already solved an issue you might be facing. And it is simply fun to be a part of a community whose members share the same passion as you. The Raspberry Pi Foundation offers a Facebook group (www.facebook.com/raspberrypi/) and user forums (www.raspberrypi.org/forums/). There is also a group at www.facebook .com/groups/librarymaker is an online community focused on makerspaces and libraries where you can interact with members of the library community to ask questions about Raspberry Pi and *anything* makerspace related.

To go one step further, seek out publications about Raspberry Pi. *Make Magazine* offers a detailed "Getting Started with Raspberry Pi" guide that is an excellent next step. And although there are numerous other publications about Raspberry Pi, the second resource I highly recommend is the *MagPi Magazine*.

The MagPi Magazine is usually a monthly publication, with a few specialty issues sprinkled in between. *MagPi* can be purchased from its website (www .raspberrypi.org/magpi/), or you might even find a copy at your local newsstand or bookstore. The great thing about *MagPi* is that you can get free copies in PDF format. Each issue of *MagPi* will immerse you in all things Raspberry Pi. The publication covers relevant Pi news, offers several project plans, shares personal stories of Pi fans, and more. It's free, so you can't go wrong at the price. If you find the publication helpful, then consider contributing via a subscription or a donation. It would make a great resource for your makerspace collection.

Your best bet for creating community around your Raspberry Pi program is on the home front. Offer introductory programs and projects in your space, or create projects at home and then share them with anyone who will listen. When you find people who are enthusiastic about what you are doing, provide them access so they can get their feet wet with Raspberry Pi.

Whatever community or resource you intend to use, be sure to share what you know—that's what this technology is all about. A few library specific examples are discussed below.

The Pi-brary

Raspberry Pi examples are a dime a dozen. Between the publications and online resources mentioned earlier, you will never be short of project ideas. However, we want to go straight to the source for our main audience: the library.

The library is an ideal platform for Raspberry Pi. The library already welcomes anyone in its doors. This is the stance of Raspberry Pi, too: everyone is welcome to play! Raspberry Pi and libraries go hand-in-hand.

Most of the projects mentioned in this section are "next-level," which means they require a solid foundation in Raspberry Pi basics and may involve additional hardware add-ons. These examples are meant to inspire advanced projects once you nail the basics of Raspberry Pi. The next section will outline some basic project ideas geared toward those getting started at the most basic level, to illustrate what is possible and relevant in a library setting.

The Denver Public Library (DPL) has employed several iterations of Raspberry Pi. It has hosted several Sonic Pi workshops where participants make music with code (we will tackle this in the next section; see also figure 6.3). This is a different approach to teaching and learning computational thinking that adds the element of music, which can be a draw for those who like music but may fear the idea of coding.

FIGURE 6.3

You Can Have Your Pi and Make Music with It, Too

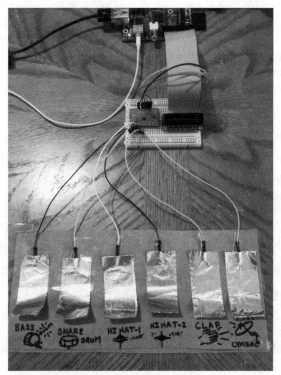

Photo by
Andrew Asquith.
Used with permission.

On a more practical note, DPL set up some Pis for functional service. Currently, it uses Pis to run event displays in its Community Technology Center using the Screenly software. This creates low-cost yet high-quality digital signage that is easy to manage and implement.

In DPL's ideaLAB makerspace, the staff had previously set up OctoPi to automate 3D print jobs on its LulzBot Taz 3D printer. This was during a time when 3D print jobs were accepted via its website, which allowed staff to print projects in a more streamlined manner. DPL has since discontinued this method of accepting print jobs, but confirms it was easy to set up and run the system.

DPL's first maker-in-residence is using a Pi to build a version of the Atari Video Music, the first commercially-available music visualizer. The idea is that when the project is finished, it will be hooked up to a screen in the ideaLAB that will allow patrons to connect and stream their music to the visualizer. Because the ideaLAB also has a recording studio, patrons on the outside looking in can catch a glimpse of the music being created in the space.

At the Arapahoe Library District, the staff host regular Raspberry Pi meetups. The program attracts a wide range of users, from beginner to advanced, who share their knowledge with one another. This library also implements digital signage using the Screenly software.

Sometimes there are projects that are not well-suited to libraries because of their complexity. In these instances, patrons can use the library as the ideal platform to share what they made at home. As an example, one library patron built a HAM Radio to IP Gateway, which is a Pi project that takes radio waves and transports them over the Internet; this allows a user to talk to anyone in the world with a similar device. The other is the popular open-source version of Amazon Echo.

A more reasonable next-level project is using a Raspberry Pi with some breadboards and LED lights that can be programmed to blink. Orlando Public Library and others offer this type of access to their Raspberry Pi systems.[3]

The Laramie County Library System used its Raspberry Pi with the Raspberry Cobbler connector to create an interactive drum machine.

At Colorado's Garfield County Libraries, one project of note was a program called Hacky Bird. Utilizing Scratch or the https://studio.code.org/ website, participants were prompted to code their own version of Flappy Bird. Then, with the Makey Makey microcontroller, the participants were challenged to create three different controllers using a variety of conductive materials (e.g., a metal percussive triangle, tin foil, and wires). The Raspberry Pi and Makey Makey work hand-in-hand.

These are just a few examples of what has been done with the Pi in a library setting. Join online communities, like some of the ones mentioned in the previous section, to keep an eye out for other Pi uses and ideas. If you can partner with school districts and educators, you can build useful projects like FM radios, weather stations, digital cameras, and so much more. But before you get that far, let's bring it back to the basics, both for you and the community of participants who may be new to Raspberry Pi.

Projects with Pi

Now that you have a solid understanding of what the Raspberry Pi is, and have collected all the necessary components required for it to function properly, it's time to dive into the projects. As mentioned earlier, many of the next-level projects require additional hardware. Most of the time these kinds of projects are rated above the beginner level. However, the five projects listed in this section are geared toward the absolute beginner, and they do not require additional hardware attachments beyond what was originally listed. Think of these activities as the foundation on which you can build up to next-level projects. One thing you will want to consider is the audience for each program. Although the Raspberry Pi can be used by both kids and adults, some projects require reading ability to progress through the tutorials. Keep this in mind when determining an audience for your program.

Now let's look at the first introductory project.

All About Pi

The All About Pi project is meant to teach participants about the Raspberry Pi, its components, and how they all fit together. Although it may seem like a futile exercise in setting up the device, this knowledge and hands-on practice is key to reducing users' tech anxiety, and it gives users a solid foundational knowledge of the Pi itself (see figure 6.4). Having this information and experience can lead users to projects they may not have considered because they didn't thoroughly understand the Pi.

FIGURE 6.4

By Diagramming the Pi, Users Learn the Parts of a Computer and How It Works

MATERIALS

- Raspberry Pi
- WiFi dongle (needed if you do not use a Raspberry Pi 3)
- keyboard (wired or wireless)
- mouse (wired or wireless)
- HDMI cable (optional; HDMI to VGA adapter for older monitors)
- USB power source (any 5V 1a cell phone charger works)
- computer monitor
- SD card (regular size or Micro SD depending on your Pi model) (size: 4 to 32 GB, Class 10)
- Mac or Windows computer with an SD card reader
- paper, pencils, and rulers

PREPARATION (forty-five minutes)

Depending on how many Raspberry Pi kits you have, set up as many stations as you have Pis available. Depending on how many participants you have in relation to Raspberry Pi stations, they may work alone or in small teams. In your setup, distribute all the items unconnected. Part of the program requires that participants figure out how to connect the Pi. Although optional, providing checklists could be handy so that users know which components are being used.

IMPLEMENTATION (one hour)

Let participants know that today they will be learning about the Raspberry Pi. Tell them that by the end of the class, the participant will be able to identify key components of the Raspberry Pi and to connect the device to all necessary components to make it a full-functioning computer system.

To begin, you could briefly share the purpose of the Raspberry Pi Foundation and define Raspberry Pi. Put simply, you could say that it is a computer much like a Windows or Mac system. You could also show them the Raspberry Pi website as a frame of reference for further research and additional ideas should they choose to explore Pi further.

Once you have discussed Raspberry Pi, give them some blank paper and pencils (and the item checklist if you made one). Have them sketch out, or even trace, the Raspberry Pi. As they go along, encourage the participants to map out the various components of the Pi (encourage them to Google "Raspberry

Pi diagram" for help). Besides the Ethernet and USB ports, the component that may be new to many are the GPIO pins sticking out of the board. You can share that those pins are used to connect to other hardware components, like a small LCD screen.

Then participants can then move into assembling the Raspberry Pi. You could demonstrate how to handle the Pi properly, using the tips mentioned earlier in this chapter. Give them upward of thirty minutes (more if you have them installing the Raspbian operating system) to complete their builds. Float around to assist as needed. When a team finishes early, encourage them to explore the Raspbian software and complete their diagram. Have them locate the system settings. Prompt them to change the computer's time or desktop background. Let them open Minecraft or some other preinstalled application.

Once all have finished successfully connecting their systems and have had time to explore, close out the day by having a brief conversation about their experiences. Let them share whether their journeys were hard or easy. Let them ask questions, and let them know about next-step projects and resources on Raspberry Pi. If you have follow-up programs centered around Pi, now would be the time to promote them.

REMIX

If time allows, a substep in the process would be to allow the users to install the Raspbian operating system on the SD card for their Pis. Point them to the website to get them started: www.raspberrypi.org/downloads/noobs/. You could also divide the groups into teams and have races to see who can connect their system and have it running the fastest.

Make Music with Sonic Pi

Creating music using Raspberry Pi is a nonthreatening and fun next-step program once the Raspberry Pi has been set up. Even if someone has no musical knowledge (or inclination, for that matter), creating music on Pi is more about sequencing instructions than knowing a musical scale. Speaking of sequences, this is a good activity to convey the message that a computer program, or the act of programming, is nothing more than an ordered list of detailed instructions. For anyone who has no coding experience, this is a great place to experience the concepts of programming first-hand (see figure 6.5).

FIGURE 6.5

You Can Code Games, Apps, and Even Music on Raspberry Pi

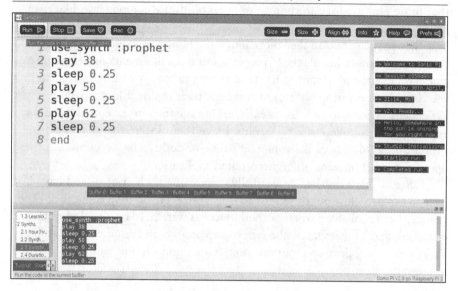

```
1 use_synth :prophet
2 play 38
3 sleep 0.25
4 play 50
5 sleep 0.25
6 play 62
7 sleep 0.25
8 end
```

MATERIALS

- Raspberry Pi setup with Raspbian OS preinstalled
- headphones or speakers

PREPARATION (forty-five minutes)

Again, have all the necessary Pi components compiled in stations. You can choose whether to use prebuilt stations or prefer the groups put them together as an optional first step (which helps solidify the concepts from the first project). The Sonic Pi software is already preinstalled on the Raspbian OS you have in your system. You should also find or create a sample of a song that can be coded and played using Sonic Pi (locate one from the online Pi community, YouTube, or create something original). If you have digital music experts or enthusiasts in your community, you could reach out to them and ask if they would be willing to host a short discussion and demo on digital music creation, regardless of whether they have used Sonic Pi.

IMPLEMENTATION (one hour+)

Have the individuals or groups boot up their Raspberry Pis. Hold a brief discussion on what Sonic Pi does, and show them a demo. From there, let the participants know that today they will be working through the basics of the Sonic Pi software at their own pace, and they are free to get creative at any point in the process once they've grasped the basics. Then, show them where the tutorials are located within the program at the bottom of the Sonic Pi window, and let them dive right in.

If you have worked through the tutorial yourself, you can set benchmarks for how far the group could progress together, or you can just let them go if this is a one-time program. Whether you're conducting a Sonic Pi program series or just a one-time event, you can schedule time at the end so that the group can see what was made at the various stations.

REMIX

You can explore the bigger picture of contribution via social media sites like SoundCloud. You can talk about the website itself and how to protect your work using Creative Commons licensing. You can show participants how they can find inspiration from similar enthusiasts from online sites. You can challenge participants to see if they can mimic their favorite tunes in a future program, or challenge them to create an original commercial jingle for a new product launch.

Pi from Scratch

The name of this project may be better suited for the "All About Pi" project, but it also works here because Scratch is a coding environment that is a staple on Raspberry Pi. If you are unfamiliar with Scratch, it will likely become one of your favorites once you interact with it. Scratch uses color-coded command blocks instead of coding language jargon to create games, apps, and short films. However, don't be fooled by Scratch's simplicity. Programs created in Scratch can accommodate advanced-level programming concepts, and many intricate projects can be created by stacking one colored block at a time.

Although Scratch can be accessed from any computer via a web browser and Internet connection, having Scratch on Raspberry Pi is complementary to the nature of Raspberry Pi being a learning machine. Plus, this version of Scratch does not require an Internet connection to run. Scratch will be an excellent precursor to the next project, which uses the Kano operating system, because Kano uses similar block-based coding environments.

MATERIALS

- Raspberry Pi setup with Raspbian preinstalled
- headphones or speakers

PREPARATION (thirty minutes)

It's not necessary to have participants assemble the Pi for the beginning of the program, but you can have them do so if you want. Besides setting up the stations, download and print out the "Getting Started with Scratch" guide and project cards for this program. Note that the version of Scratch on Raspberry Pi (version 1.4) is not the most current version of Scratch the company promotes. If you search the website for starter guides or project cards, you may get results for the current version of Scratch, and some features may not be available on the version you will be using. Bookmark the following links to access the appropriate guides:

- https://download.scratch.mit.edu/ScratchGettingStartedv14.pdf
- http://download.scratch.mit.edu/ScratchCardsAll-v1.4-PDF.zip

To prepare, complete one of the projects from the cards so you can demonstrate to your participants what can be done in Scratch.

IMPLEMENTATION (one hour)

Begin by having a brief discussion about what Scratch is—a computer coding language that uses color-coded blocks to create games, apps, and movies. Show the participants your demo project so they have an idea what to expect. Once you've done that, let them know they have access to the tutorial guide and a variety of project cards. Give them enough time to explore and complete projects at their own pace. If you plan to use groups for this project, limit them to two participants per Raspberry Pi station. At the end, discuss the projects. Let a few participants present their creations. Ask them if they thought it was hard or easy to code. Let them know they can continue to explore Scratch at home without a Raspberry Pi by visiting the Scratch website at https://scratch.mit.edu.

REMIX

Once your participants have a solid idea of how Scratch works, you can give them specific projects. Have a video game creation series. Have kids and teens create a promotional movie for the library's Summer Reading program using Scratch. When you get into using the GPIO pins to add hardware to your Raspberry Pi, there are Scratch coding blocks that activate hardware attachments (e.g., a breadboard with LED lights). These projects will require more time to complete. With Scratch, projects can be saved to a USB drive that participants can take with them and bring back to continue their work.

Minecraft Hacking with Kano OS

Although Raspbian is the main operating system that is associated with Raspberry Pi, it is by no means the only one. Kano OS is a free open-source platform for "exploration, creation, and play."[4] The system is designed to present information about the basics of computers and coding using a super-simple, self-taught approach using gamification. If you purchase the Kano Kit that's sold on Kano's website (which includes Raspberry Pi plus other components), you will get a printed booklet that walks users through the basics of the computer-building and coding processes. But you don't have to purchase the kit to gain access to the operating system—you can also access the digital version of the book on the website for free.

The great appeal of this software is that it allows users to hack and play Minecraft while learning how to code. Minecraft will be the focus of this project because of its mass appeal. Keep in mind that there are other gaming tools built into Kano besides Minecraft, and you can easily replicate and expand into future Kano programs (see figure 6.6).

FIGURE 6.6

Raspberry Pi Goes Hand-in-Hand with Minecraft

- Raspberry Pi setup or Kano Kit ($150 from the Kano website)
- SD card for installing and running Kano OS
- headphones or speakers
- optional Minecraft-themed crafts or other technology to occupy kids waiting their turns

PREPARATION (forty-five minutes)

As with the Sonic Pi project, you can have the stations preassembled, or you can have the participants assemble the Kano/Pi stations as a first step. However, you will need to install the Kano operating system ahead of time. I don't recommend making this step a part of this program (the practice is better suited for the "All About Pi" project). The process for installing the software is similar to that for Raspbian, but I've encountered more errors with Kano than I ever have with Raspbian. To get the Kano operating system, visit www2.kano.me/downloads and follow the steps for installing Kano OS.

IMPLEMENTATION (one hour+)

Since this program uses the Minecraft portion of Kano, you will draw a larger number of kids if you market it as such. It would be good to have a sign-up sheet or additional activities for participants waiting their turns.

To start the program, you can ask how many participants play Minecraft. Would any participants like to talk about something cool they made in Minecraft? Does anyone know how Mojang created Minecraft? From there, have a brief discussion about computer code and how it can empower people to make video games. Then transition into the fact that the participants are going to learn how to use code to hack Minecraft. Participants won't need much more motivation than that, just encouragement to build and discover, and to ask questions if they get stuck. Suggest teams take turns for each of the coding steps. Let them dive in and work at their own pace.

REMIX

Beyond Minecraft, Kano OS offers code hacking of other preinstalled programs like Snake and Pong, the ability to make music, and even the ability to program LED hardware. If Kano catches on in your library, you could provide access to Kano (or Pi) stations where users can plug in their own SD cards loaded with

Kano and continue their code-hacking journeys. Kano also has a safe embedded social media feature for tracking progress and contributing creations to the Kano community at large.

Google Coder Cloud Server

The final project uses Google Coder. This project turns Raspberry Pi into a machine that acts as a cloud server, which means a Raspberry Pi won't be plugged directly to a keyboard and monitor. Rather, the Google Coder environment is accessed from Windows, Mac, Chromebook, or additional Raspberry Pi system running on the same wired or wireless network. The purpose of Google Coder is to act as a coding playground for those learning or experimenting with HTML, CSS, and JavaScript. Half of this project focuses on hardware setup and half on software usage. It is a good example of how to create a solution to meet a real-world need.

MATERIALS

- Raspberry Pi setup
- Ethernet or WiFi connection
- additional computers

PREPARATION

I highly recommend letting participants work together to set up as many of these servers as you see fit (based on number of Pis available or the number of people attending this program).

Part one then begins with setting out the Raspberry Pi to build, and then using the additional computers so participants can install the Google Coder operating system on the SD card. Have the web link available so participants know where to go to find the instructions to download and install Google Coder. Once the Google Coder server is complete, you must then decide how you want participants to go about learning and tinkering with the web tools in Google Coder. Do you have books on HTML basics available? Do you want to bring in a local front-end web developer to give a short introduction to HTML markup language? Do you plan to utilize websites like codeacademy.com, freecodecamp.com, or w3schools .com so that participants can learn while coding in the Coder environment? The choice is yours, based on what feel will most help your participants.

Have a brief discussion about web (cloud) servers and allow participants to assemble the Raspberry Pi system. The participants will then use the additional computers to access http://googlecreativelab.github.io/coder/ to download and install the Google Coder operating system. When this is complete, have participants open a web browser (preferably Chrome) from their other computer stations and connect to one of the Coder interfaces via: http://coder.local/.

The first time a user connects to one of these systems, the Google Coder interface will prompt the user to create a password. Record these passwords. If multiple students will connect to one server, have them create a new project in the system, name it, and ask them to respect the other participants' projects by not deleting or manipulating them without prior consent.

REMIX

Once the Coder systems are running and the participants have started learning HTML basics, have them explore other Google Coder projects on the online repository at https://googlecreativelab.github.io/coder-projects/.

Additionally, you can extend your Coder program into a series by having participants focus on developing simple websites or apps. If you want, you could allow the Coder stations to be accessible outside of programming times. Because these environments are password protected, not everyone can access the tools. Beyond that, however, there is no additional security system to protect individual projects, so let users know that if multiple people access one Coder station, their work can be accessed or even deleted.

Conclusion

Now that you have reviewed the introduction to Raspberry Pi and several low-maintenance projects, it's time to make a decision. How do you proceed from here? Do you proceed at all? (Perhaps this isn't a good fit, or maybe you are ready to dive headlong into more projects.) Should you explore bringing in hardware components for more complex projects? And if so, do you have the resources and interest to complete them? If you saw minimal or no interest in Raspberry Pi from your community, maybe it will just become a personal project. But if the community shows interest, it may be time to explore *MagPi Magazine* for next-level Pi projects and information.

However you decide to proceed, remember that it is okay to take risks. It is also okay (and safe) to fail. This is how we learn. This is how we grow beyond the walls of current technological conventions and explore solutions for future problems. At the very least, you and your participants can say you created these awesome projects on a tiny computer the size of a credit card that cost only $35.

NOTES

1. *Wikipedia, the Free Encyclopedia,* s.v. "Single-Board Computer," https://en.wikipedia .org/wiki/Single-board_computer.
2. "The Making of Pi," Raspberry Pi Foundation, www.raspberrypi.org/about/.
3. "Tinkering with the Raspberry Pi," The Dorothy Lumley Melrose Center, http://tic.ocls .info/tinkering-with-the-raspberry-pi/.
4. "Kano OS," www2.kano.me/downloads.

ADDITIONAL RESOURCES

Publications

Make: Getting Started with Raspberry Pi (2nd Edition), www.makershed.com/products/make -getting-started-with-raspberry-pi-2e.

MagPi Magazine, www.raspberrypi.org/magpi/.

The Official Raspberry Pi Projects Book, http://swag.raspberrypi.org/collections/frontpage/ products/the-official-raspberry-pi-projects-book.

Raspberry Pi User Guide (3rd Edition), http://swag.raspberrypi.org/collections/frontpage/ products/raspberry-pi-user-guide-2nd-edition.

Online

Google Coder, https://googlecreativelab.github.io/coder/.

Kano OS, http://us.kano.me/.

MakerSpaces and the Participatory Library Facebook Group, www.facebook.com/groups/ librarymaker/.

Raspberry Pi Online Community, www.raspberrypi.org/forums/.

Raspberry Pi Products, www.raspberrypi.org/products/.

Raspbian OS and NOOBS, www.raspberrypi.org/downloads/noobs/.

Arduino for Librarians

JONATHAN M. SMITH

Arduino is an open-source platform for physical computing. It combines hardware and software into an approachable package that can sense the physical world (input), process it, and provide responses (output). Arduino is both a software platform, known as the Arduino IDE, and a hardware platform, in the form of the Arduino board. All manner of electronics—sensors, buttons, motors, and lights to name a few—can be connected to the Arduino board to enable it to interact with the physical world. Arduino is also a fun and affordable way to learn electronics, prototyping, and innovation. With it you can create flying autonomous drones, cat-feeding robots, weather stations, wearable light-up costumes, and much more.

This chapter offers a basic introduction to Arduino. It will introduce the common terminology you will run into and includes a few projects to help you get started. It is also recommended that you have an Arduino in hand as you make your way through the chapter and projects. Everything will make much more sense if you do!

Jonathan M. Smith is Director of Library Technology at Sonoma State University.

Before diving in, here's a quick explanation of the two biggest pieces of this physical computing package. The software that we'll be working with is the Arduino IDE (Integrated Development Environment), which is available as a free download. This is the programming environment that will run on your computer (Microsoft Windows, Mac OS X, or Linux operating systems) where you will type code. The other critical piece is the Arduino board. This is a piece of hardware comprised of a microcontroller circuit board with input/output pins for connecting with electronics. This will all make sense soon!

Major Arduino Boards Available

Because Arduino is open source, there are a variety of clones and Arduino-compatible boards available. Even Arduino itself makes several different boards with varying capabilities. For our purposes, however, this chapter will focus on the Arduino Uno because it is the most versatile and common board currently available.

Eventually, with some experience, you may find that the Arduino Uno doesn't quite fit the bill for a particular project. You may need something that offers more pins for a complex interactive display you are building. Or perhaps you would like something minimal that could be sewn into clothing. If you would like to learn about the main board options available from Arduino, see the Adafruit Arduino Selection Guide at https://learn.adafruit.com/adafruit -arduino-selection-guide/arduino-comparison-chart. For even more options see the SparkFun Arduino Comparison Guide at https://learn.sparkfun.com/ tutorials/arduino-comparison-guide.

It is also worth mentioning the SparkFun RedBoard. It is a slightly modified version of an Arduino Uno clone that is designed and manufactured by the electronics retailer SparkFun. The RedBoard is very similar to the Arduino Uno and can be used in place of the Uno in most situations.

Along with purchasing an Arduino, you will at the very least want to purchase a good-size breadboard, jumper wires, resistors, and LEDs. This can get you started with learning Arduino, and certainly programming LEDs can be a lot of fun! Given the option, I would recommend purchasing a starter kit. There are many options, which usually include a breadboard and enough electronic components (e.g., LEDs, resistors, buttons, and motors) to keep you occupied while exploring the capabilities of physical computing with Arduino. Just make sure you're also getting an Arduino (or Arduino-compatible) board along with those components!

Some online stores where you can purchase Arduinos and kits include:

- Adafruit (www.adafruit.com)
- SparkFun (www.sparkfun.com)
- Maker Shed (www.makershed.com)

How to Use the Arduino Board

Now you've got this nifty thing with pins and circuits on it (for the purposes of this chapter I'm assuming it's an Arduino Uno). Before you attempt to use it, let's take a closer look. If you orient the board so that you can read "Arduino Uno," the USB and power socket will be on the left with black pin headers along the bottom and top. The pin headers are where you will make connections between the Arduino and electrical components.

The Arduino Uno can be powered through either the power socket or the USB port. The power socket will work with an AC adapter (9 volts recommended). A USB charger or even your computer's USB port will provide enough power for the Arduino board—though not necessarily for everything you may want to connect to it. But don't worry, there are ways to provide additional power to those devices. If you happen to plug in both the power and the USB, the Arduino will draw electricity from the power socket rather than the USB.

Looking at the pin headers, start with the one on the lower left, labeled *Power*. You will see a label corresponding with each female connector on the header. Of particular interest are the pins 3.3V, 5V, and GND. These will be essential for completing the circuits you will create.

Next to that is the *Analog in* header. Note that while there are six pins, they are numbered A0 through A5. Computers begin counting at zero, not one. Get used to thinking like that! The *Analog in* pins can only read input—they do not output anything. They are designed for measuring voltage from 0 to 5 volts—which is translated to a range of 0 to 1,023. This is particularly useful for sensors that measure a range of values.

The headers across the top of the board are labeled *Digital PWM~*. These pins can be set to either input or output, and some can also simulate analog output. Most people are familiar with the idea of digital being on/off, true/false, or 1/0. That's the right idea—the digital pins can only read or output one of two values at a time, known to your Arduino as *High* or *Low* (as in high voltage—5V or low voltage—0v). But some of those digital pins can be set to simulate analog output! They accomplish this using Pulse Width Modulation (PWM). These (pins 3, 5, 6, 9, 10, and 11) are indicated on the board with a tilde (~).

There are also a few tiny LED lights on the board to convey important information. A single LED by itself near the right edge is labeled *On*, which is lit when the board has power. There is a group of three LEDs between the USB port and the Arduino logo. The *L* LED is connected to digital pin 13 and will light up when the signal is set to *High*. The *TX* (transmit) and *RX* (receive) LEDs will blink when data is sent to and from the board via the USB port.

Tips You Need to Know

Solderless Breadboard

In the early days, hobbyists would literally use a wooden board of the type you might use to slice bread for electronics projects. These days a breadboard is usually a plastic rectangle with a grid of holes into which wires and electronic components can be plugged. Each row has a strip of conductive metal hidden in it. Everything you plug into a particular row will be connected to each other, without the need to solder them together or use a wire to make the connection. Breadboards are great because they allow you to test out an idea, analyze, modify, and finally reuse all the pieces, because the connection isn't permanent.

Soldering

Although breadboarding is excellent for testing an idea, soldering can make the final version of the project permanent. (That's not quite true—when you get good at soldering you will be able to remove solder, but it isn't easy and certainly not the preferred method for prototyping). Soldering involves melting a filler metal (solder) with a soldering iron to join metal pieces, usually for the purpose of creating a circuit pathway. Soldering is a very useful skill if you will be making with electronics, but it won't be addressed in this chapter.

Programming Tips

Using Arduino will require coding—as in programming. But don't be intimidated. The basic format for an Arduino program (known as a "sketch") is fairly simple, and there are plenty of tutorials available to help you along and lots of code out there that you can copy. You've got nothing to worry about! Arduino is an excellent gateway to programming. Of course, the more familiar with it you become, the better you'll be able to understand what is happening and customize or troubleshoot your project.

Every Arduino sketch contains at least these two functions:

- void setup() is where you set things that need to be done once before the main part runs.
- void loop() is the main part of your sketch. This is where the instructions go, and as the name implies, they will repeat from top to bottom until told otherwise or the power to the board is cut.

Some syntax:

; (semicolon) Don't forget to end every line of code with it!
{ } (curly brackets) are used to contain blocks of code.

Comments are text within the sketch that are ignored by the Arduino. They are there to explain to humans what a section of the sketch does. There are two ways to comment in Arduino:

```
// single-line: the Arduino ignores this entire line
/* multiple-line:
you could
put a whole
paragraph here
*/
```

Libraries are external files that collect functions, often written to perform common tasks and used to simplify a sketch. They are included at the beginning of a sketch and look like this:

```
#include <awesomelibrary.h>
```

A *variable* is a stored value that you've named. If declared within a function, it can only be used within that function. But if declared outside of a function it is known as a *global variable,* and is usable throughout the sketch.

Electronic Components

These are the bits and wires that you will connect to the Arduino board for sensing and to perform all sorts of neat actions. Don't worry about memorizing this section; you can always refer to it later.

A quick note about polarized components. Sometimes a component is designed to function with the electricity flowing in a specific direction, and thus it matters how it is connected. If a polarized component is connected the wrong way, not only will it not function properly but it can be damaged or even destroyed. So how do you know? Polarized components will always be marked in some manner. LEDs will usually have one leg that is longer than the others to indicate the polarity. Other components may be marked with a + to indicate positive or a – to indicate negative.

A few common components:

- *Diode:* A semiconductor that only allows current to flow in one direction. A line may indicate the cathode (negative pin).
- *Infrared sensor:* This will detect an infrared signal, for example that from a TV remote or an infrared LED.
- *LCD:* Liquid Crystal Display, which can range from monochrome displays that only display a few characters to full-color, high-resolution screens. Useful for displaying information directly from your Arduino, some are designed to plug directly into a breadboard.
- *LED:* Light Emitting Diodes come in many different colors and there is even an RGB LED variety that changes color. Pay attention to the polarity!
- *Jumper wire:* These come with male and/or female headers for connecting the Arduino, breadboard, and components.
- *PIR motion sensor:* The Passive Infrared sensor is a common-motion detecting device.
- *Photo cell:* A small light sensor that changes resistance depending on the amount of ambient light.
- *Potentiometer:* A variable resistor that can control input and comes in many flavors—rotary (dials), soft (touch), and slide, to name only a few.
- *Resistor:* This limits the flow of electricity.
- *Servo:* This can rotate to a specific position.
- *Temperature sensor:* An analog temperature sensor that outputs an amount of voltage proportional to the ambient temperature.
- *Transistor:* A semiconductor that's used to switch or amplify current.
- *Ultrasonic range finder:* This is used to detect distance.

How Libraries Are Using Arduino

California State University, San Bernardino

The Innovation Lab in the John M. Pfau Library provides SparkFun Inventor's Kits based on the SparkFun RedBoard that students can use in the lab as an introduction to physical computing and Arduino programming. For advanced students, the lab has a collection of Arduino boards and compatible electronics such as sensors, LCD screens, and various components, along with plenty of breadboards and jumper wires to encourage prototyping. A couple of robotics kits are available as well. Several student groups have made the lab their home while working on Arduino projects such as an Arduino-controlled drone and a gate counter that uses an Arduino board and ultrasonic sensor.

St. Petersburg College

Librarian Chad Mairn shares that the Innovation Lab [Makerspace @ SPC] circulates Arduino starter kits and uses Arduino boards for a couple of projects housed in the lab. One project is a drone based on the ArduPilot platform. The Innovation Lab is also considering using an Arduino board for a RepRap 3D printer/laser cutter that's currently being built.

San Diego Public Library

Although the San Diego Public Library does not circulate Arduino boards outside of the library, it does use them in-house to support a number of events and projects. The library hosts a monthly Arduino meetup of community members at which participants will often work on projects together, teach a workshop, or present a "show and tell" of their latest projects. It has also hosted a "Week of Wearables" and monthly "Wearable Wednesdays" that focus on introducing students to wearable Arduino platforms Gemma and LilyTiny. These sessions involve sewing as well as programming, which according to Librarian Uyen Tran have been a great way to get girls involved in science, technology, engineering, art, and mathematics (STEAM). Arduino and Arduino-compatible boards are used by the Robotics Club (which meets every Saturday), a weeklong "Robotics Rule the World Robotics Camp," and the Entrepreneurs in Residence for various projects.

Arduino Projects

PROJECT 1 // Arduino Setup

To program your Arduino, you will need the Arduino IDE (Integrated Development Environment). In this project, you will set up the software and connect the Arduino board.

PARTS

- computer (running Windows, a Mac OS, or Linux)
- Arduino Uno

STEP 1

Head over to www.arduino.cc and click on the *Download* tab.

STEP 2

Choose the appropriate operating system and download.

- *Windows*
  - After it has finished downloading, run the application. (The file should be named something like, "arduino-1.6.9-windows.exe" with the number being the Arduino IDE version.)
  - Agree to the terms of the license.
  - On the *Components to Install* screen, you can choose whether to create any shortcuts. If not, leave everything else checked.
  - Choose the destination folder for the program.
  - Install.
  - (If a dialog asks whether to install a driver, be sure to approve.)

Connect your Arduino to your computer with a USB cable. The Arduino Uno will draw power from the USB connection. The green light labeled *PWR* on the board should come on, and the yellow light labeled *L* may start blinking.

- *Mac OS X*
  - After it has finished downloading, open the zip file to unpack the application. (The zip file should be named something like, "arduino-1.6.9-macosx.zip" with the number being the Arduino IDE version.)
  - You may have to go into your *Downloads* folder and drag the application named "Arduino" to the *Applications* folder.

- Connect your Arduino to your Macintosh with a USB cable. The Arduino Uno will draw power from the USB connection. The green light labeled *PWR* on the board should come on, and the yellow light labeled *L* may start blinking.

STEP 3

Now open the Arduino application. Because the Arduino IDE will work with many different Arduino boards, you need to tell it which board you are using. From the menu bar select *Tools*, then *Board*; assuming you're using an Arduino Uno you should select *Arduino/Genuino Uno*. (Genuino boards are exactly the same as Arduino—it's just a matter of branding. Arduino is marketed in the United States, whereas Genuino is marketed internationally.)

STEP 4

Select the serial port.

- *Windows*
  - From the menu select *Tools*, then *Port*, and then look at the list COM ports. If you're unsure which port to select, try disconnecting the Arduino, then look again at the *Serial Port* menu. The port that disappeared is most likely the one you want.

- *Mac OS X*
  - From the menu select *Tools*, then *Port*, and then select the port that begins with /dev/cu.usbmodem or /dev/cu.usbserial. If you're unsure which port to select try disconnecting the Arduino, then look again at the *Serial Port* menu. The port that disappeared is most likely the one you want.

Now you're ready to get started!

PROJECT 2 // Blink ──────────────────────────────

In this project, you will write your first sketch, which will cause the *L* LED on the Arduino board to blink.

PARTS

- computer with the Arduino IDE
- Arduino Uno

STEP 1

Connect the Arduino to the computer with the USB cable, and make sure that the correct board and port are selected (see Project One). It is possible that the *L* LED will start blinking even though you haven't uploaded a sketch (program) yet. That is because the Arduino will remember the last program that was loaded and automatically run it when it has power, and whatever was previously on the board (even if it is new) may have used pin 13.

STEP 2

Open the Arduino application on your computer. You may be presented with the last sketch you were working on. You are going to start a new sketch—click *File,* then *New.* The sketch will already have the basic format you will follow and should look something like this:

```
void setup( ) {
// put your setup code here, to run once:
}
void loop( ) {
// put your main code here, to run repeatedly:
}
```

Note the two basic functions mentioned earlier, as well as the curly brackets that will contain the code for that particular function. Each function here also has a one-line comment within the function. Those slashes at the beginning of the comment tell the Arduino to ignore that line.

STEP 3

Edit the code in the sketch window so that it matches the following:

```
void setup( ) {
pinMode(13, OUTPUT); // set digital pin 13 as an output
}
void loop( ) {
digitalWrite(13, HIGH); // turn the LED on
delay(1000); // wait for a second
digitalWrite(13, LOW); // turn the LED off
delay(1000); // wait for a second
}
```

What is happening here? If you recall, the setup() function is where you set things before the main part of the sketch runs. pinMode() is what you use to set up the individual pins on the Arduino board. As the *L* LED on the board is connected to digital pin 13, you are setting pin 13 to output.

Once things are set, loop() is where you list the instructions for the Arduino, which will run line by line until the end of the loop, then go back to the first line of the loop and repeat the process.

digitalWrite() is another built-in function (there are quite a few, which makes life a little easier). You can use this function to turn the LED on and off. First you give it the pin number (13), then you set the pin to either *High* or *Low*. *High* will output about 5 volts, whereas *Low* while LOW will output about 0 volts, essentially turning the electricity to the LED on or off.

While the Arduino is nowhere near as fast as your computer, it can still process instructions fast enough that if you didn't tell it to delay between turning the LED on and off, it would happen so fast that you wouldn't be able to see it. The delay() function counts in milliseconds, so 1,000 milliseconds will cause it to delay for one second.

STEP 4

The Arduino IDE has a handy feature that will compile your sketch and check for errors. At the top of the sketch window is a button that looks like a checkmark, which displays "Verify" when you hover the mouse-pointer over the button. Click the *Verify* button (alternately you can choose *Verify* from the *Sketch* menu). After a moment, if all is good, a message below the sketch will read "Done compiling" and there will be some feedback about memory. If there is a problem, the message area below will turn orange and provide feedback about the error(s).

At this point, it's probably a good idea to save your sketch if you haven't already. Select *File* from the menu, and *Save As*. Be sure to give it a meaningful name!

STEP 5

Once your sketch is error-free, it is time to upload it to the Arduino board and see what happens. Click the *Upload* button (next to the *Verify* button, represented by an arrow pointing to the right) and watch the *TX* and *RX* LEDs on the Arduino board flash as the compiled sketch is transmitted.

STEP 6

If everything went well, the sketch should start running immediately after it is finished transmitting to the board. In this case, the "L" LED should turn on for one second then turn off for one second repeatedly. Congratulations! Now, how might you edit the sketch to modify the blinking of the LED? Try changing the delay() so that the light stays on longer. What if you wanted the LED to flash a Morse code pattern?

PROJECT 3 // Traffic Light

In this project, you will take what you learned in Project Two, and use it to light three LEDs in sequence on a breadboard.

PARTS

- computer with the Arduino IDE
- Arduino Uno
- breadboard
- five jumper wires (male/male headers)
- three LED lights—one red, one yellow, one green
- three 330-ohm resistors

STEP 1

Assemble the parts you will need. The LED lights should have two legs, and because this project simulates a traffic light it will be more fun if you have one of each color—red, yellow, and green. Resistors are typically designed to provide a specific electrical resistance (except for variable resistors, which can be adjusted— like a dial). They come in a large variety of resistances, which are measured in ohms (Ω). Although LEDs have polarity, these resistors do not, so it doesn't matter in what direction you connect them.

STEP 2

Make the following connections between components (see figure 7.1):

- Use a wire to connect the 5V pin to the + (positive) rail on the breadboard.
- Use a wire to connect the GND pin to the – (negative) rail on the breadboard.
- Insert the end of each 330-ohm resistor into the – (negative) rail and the other end in the first column on the breadboard (perhaps labeled "A"). Leave a couple of rows space between each resistor.
- Insert each LED so that the negative side (shorter leg) is in the same row as the resistor—thus connecting the two components. The positive side (longer leg) should be in a row that currently isn't being used. To make it look like a

FIGURE 7.1

Breadboard View of a Circuit Diagram Illustrates the Connections for This
Three-LED Project (See Step Two for Details)

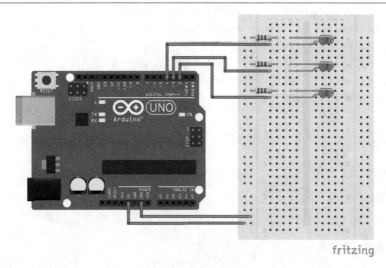

fritzing

This image was created with Fritzing, an open-source software tool for documenting electronics (http://fritzing.org).

traffic light, put the red LED on top, the yellow LED in the middle, and the
green LED on the bottom.
- Use a wire to connect digital pin 4 to the positive leg of the red LED by
  inserting the wire into the same row as the positive leg.
- Use a wire to connect digital pin 3 to the positive leg of the yellow LED.
- Use a wire to connect digital pin 2 to the positive leg of the green LED.

STEP 3

Now it's time to write the sketch! You could try to write it yourself based on what
you learned in the previous lesson, or copy what is written here.

```
void setup() {
pinMode(2, OUTPUT); // set digital pin 2 as an output
pinMode(3, OUTPUT); // set digital pin 3 as an output
pinMode(4, OUTPUT); // set digital pin 4 as an output
}
void loop() {
```

```
digitalWrite(4, HIGH); // turn the red LED on
delay(3000); // wait for three seconds
digitalWrite(4, LOW); // turn the red LED off
digitalWrite(2, HIGH); // turn the green LED on
delay(3000); // wait for three seconds
digitalWrite(2, LOW); // turn the green LED off
digitalWrite(3, HIGH); // turn the yellow LED on
delay(1000); // wait for a second
digitalWrite(3, LOW); // turn the yellow LED off
}
```

STEP 4

Verify the sketch.

STEP 5

Upload the sketch.

STEP 6

If everything went well the red light should turn on, pause for one second, turn off at the same time the green light turns on, pause for one second, turn off at the same time the yellow light turns on, pause for one second and repeat.

Did something go wrong? Double-check all your connections. Each LED should be part of a circuit, from the Arduino pin header (2, 3, or 4) to the LED, to the resistor, to the GND. Also check that you've haven't put the LEDs in backwards, because polarity does matter.

PROJECT 4 // Temperature Sensor

In this project, you will you use an analog temperature sensor to read the ambient temperature and display it using the serial monitor (see figure 7.2).

PARTS

- computer with the Arduino IDE
- Arduino Uno
- breadboard
- Analog Temperature Sensor—TMP36
- three jumper wires (male/male headers)

FIGURE 7.2

Note the Connection between ANALOG Pin A0 of the Arduino and the OUT (or Analog Voltage Out) Leg of the TMP36 Sensor

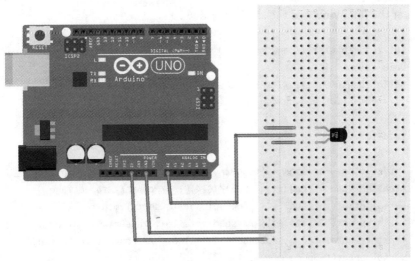

Image created with Fritzing (http://fritzing.org).

fritzing

STEP 1

Assemble the parts. This project introduces a new component, the analog temperature sensor. The TMP36 is a good sensor that is quite cheap and easy to find in online electronics stores. It has three pins—with the flat side facing you, from left to right they are: 5V in, analog voltage out, and ground.

STEP 2

Make the following connections:
- Use a wire to connect the 5V pin to the + (positive) rail on the breadboard.
- Use a wire to connect the GND pin to the – (negative) rail on the breadboard.
- Insert the temperature sensor into the breadboard so that each leg is in a different row. You may have to bend the legs a bit to separate them.
- Use a wire to connect the + (positive) rail to the same row as the 5V leg of the temperature sensor.
- Use a wire to connect ANALOG pin A0 to the same row as the middle leg of the temperature sensor.

- Use a wire to connect the – (negative) rail to the same row as the GND leg of the temperature sensor.

STEP 3

Enter the following into the sketch window:

```
int tempPin = 0; // analog pin 0 will be used to read the input
void setup( ) {
Serial.begin(9600); // set the speed to communicate with
// Arduino IDE so you can read the output
}
void loop( )
{
int reading = analogRead(tempPin); // get reading from temp sensor
float voltage = (reading * 5.0)/1024.0; // convert to voltage
Serial.print(voltage); // send voltage to serial monitor window
Serial.print(" volts, "); // send this text to serial monitor
float temperatureC = (voltage–0.5) * 100 ; // convert to Celsius
Serial.print(temperatureC);
Serial.print(" deg C, ");
float temperatureF = (temperatureC * 9.0 / 5.0) + 32.0;
// convert to Fahrenheit
Serial.print(temperatureF);
Serial.println(" deg F"); // send this text, then start a new line
delay(1000); // wait one second
}
```

What is happening here? Serial.begin(9600) starts the process for communicating from the Arduino board back to the Arduino IDE. 9600 is the baud—speed at which the Arduino and computer will communicate. analogRead() is used to get the input from the sensor, which is, of course, an analog sensor. To send the information gathered to the computer screen, use Serial.print() where the content of the parentheses is what is displayed in the serial monitor window (which is discussed in just a moment).

STEP 4

Verify and upload the sketch.

If everything went well, you won't see or hear anything from the Arduino board. The output is going to the serial monitor. Looking at the Arduino IDE, the upper-right corner of the sketch window is a button with a magnifying glass. If you hover your mouse over it, it reads "Serial Monitor." Click on this button to open the serial monitor. Every second a new line should appear with the voltage reading and conversion to temperatures that you wrote in our sketch. Awesome!

Did something go wrong? Make sure you have 5V and GND pins connected to the correct legs of the temperature sensor. Is the serial monitor displaying nonsense? Check the dropdown menu at the lower-left where the baud can be set. Make sure it is set to 9600.

PROJECT 5 // Room Occupancy Sensor

In this project, you will use a motion sensor to determine whether a room is occupied, and display the current state of the room using an LED light and the serial monitor (see figure 7.3).

FIGURE 7.3

Wiring May Look a Bit Different Depending on the Arrangement of the Pins on the PIR Sensor

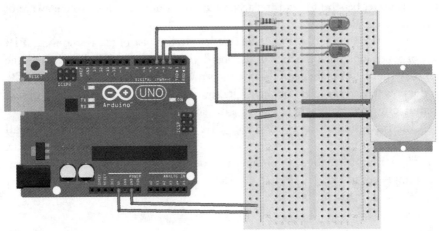

fritzing

Image created with Fritzing (http://fritzing.org).

PARTS

- computer with the Arduino IDE
- Arduino Uno
- breadboard
- one red LED light
- one green LED light
- two 330-ohm resistors
- seven jumper wires (male/male)
- one PIR sensor

STEP 1

Assemble the parts. This project introduces one new component—the passive infrared (PIR) sensor, sometimes called a PIR motion detector. This component works by detecting changes in heat radiating from objects in the viewing range of the sensor. If a person walks across a room that a PIR sensor is monitoring, the body heat leaves one area and moves to another and the PIR sensor detects the change. If a person enters a room and stands perfectly still, the sensor still detects her body heat but there is no change. This is why the lights in a room that are hooked up to a motion sensor will turn off even though you haven't left, and you do that funny dance to get them to turn back on (or is that just me?).

PIR sensors are fairly easy to find at electronics shops. I used a RadioShack Passive Infrared sensor, but Adafruit and Parallax also have a very similar product. SparkFun's is a bit different because the data pin is an open collector, but with a little adjustment it will work fine for this project as well. As with any components you purchase, be sure to read the accompanying information so you're aware of any idiosyncrasies.

The pins on the sensor should be labelled. In the case of the RadioShack PIR sensor, when looking at the back of the board (the front being the white dome—the sensor), the left pin labelled GND is the ground, the middle pin labelled VCC is the power, and the OUT is the digital output. Pay close attention as different manufacturers may put these pins in a different order!

The front side of the RadioShack PIR sensor also has a jumper—a small plastic bit that makes a connection between two pins that you can pull off with your fingernail to change which pins are connected. For this purpose, we want the jumper set to "Re_trig"—not "N_Retrig." Some PIR sensors also can adjust sensitivity, but this one doesn't.

Make the following connections:
- Use a wire to connect the 5V pin to the + (positive) rail on the breadboard.
- Use a wire to connect the GND pin to the - (negative) rail on the breadboard.
- Insert the PIR sensor in the into the breadboard so that each leg is in a different row. If the PIR sensor you're using has wires soldered to it, either plug it into the breadboard or use a male/male wire to do so.
- Use a wire to connect DIGITAL pin 2 to the same row as the OUT leg of the PIR sensor.
- Use a wire to connect the + (positive) rail to the same row as the VCC (power) leg of the PIR sensor.
- Use a wire to connect the - (negative) rail to the same row as the GND leg of the PIR sensor.
- Insert the end of each 330-ohm resistor into the - (negative) rail and the other end in the first column on the breadboard. Leave a couple rows space between each resistor.
- Insert each LED so that the negative side (shorter leg) is in the same row as one of the resistors.
- Use a wire to connect DIGITAL pin 3 to the same row as the positive leg of the red LED.
- Use a wire to connect DIGITAL pin 4 to the same row as the positive leg of the green LED.

Write the following into the sketch window:

```
int motionSensor = 2; // assign digital pin 2 to the PIR sensor
    int redLED = 3; // assign digital pin 3 to the red LED
    int greenLED = 4; // assign digital pin 4 to the green LED
    int roomState = LOW; // start with the assumption the room is empty

    void setup()
    {
    Serial.begin(9600);
    pinMode (motionSensor, INPUT); // set digital pin 2 to input
    pinMode (redLED, OUTPUT); // set digital pin 3 to output
    pinMode (greenLED, OUTPUT); // set digital pin 4 to output
    Serial.println("Room Available"); // send the initial message
    }
```

```
void loop( )
{
int motionDetected = digitalRead(motionSensor);

if(motionDetected == HIGH) { // if the sensor detects movement
digitalWrite(redLED, HIGH), // turn on the red light
digitalWrite(greenLED, LOW); // turn off the green light
if(roomState == LOW) { // check if the room had been empty
    Serial.println("Room Occupied"); // send a message
roomState = HIGH; // set to occupied for the next check
}
}
else { // if the sensor does not detect movement
digitalWrite(redLED, LOW), // turn off the red light
digitalWrite(greenLED, HIGH); // turn on the green light
if(roomState == HIGH) {    // check if the room had been occupied
    Serial.println("Room Available"); // send a message
roomState = LOW; // set empty for the next check
}
}

delay(2000); // wait 2 seconds to check again

}
```

So what's new here? If . . . Else statements! This is a common method in programming to check whether a condition is met before proceeding with the instructions—and if the condition is not met—it's necessary to tell it to do something else! But we've upped the ante by using Nested If statements. Yes, you can put an If statement inside an If . . . Else statement. Whoa!

In general, it looks something like this:

if (conditionA == TRUE)
Do this thing
if (conditionB == TRUE)
Do this thing
else
Do this other thing
If (conditionC == TRUE)
Do this thing

Why did we do this? Our goal is to send a message to the serial monitor about the state of the room. Is it occupied or available? The problem is that the PIR sensor continuously monitors for movement and would constantly output the current state. This would result in a bunch of messages in the space of a minute even if there had been no change in the room! The nested If statement checks to see what the previous state of the room was—that way, if a message has been sent about the room being available it won't be done again (and again, and again, etc.).

STEP 4

Verify and upload the sketch.

STEP 5

If everything went well a few things should happen. When the PIR sensor doesn't detect any motion the green light should be on and the red light off. Also, a message should print to the serial monitor that states "Room Available." When the PIR sensor detects motion the red light should be on and the green light off. Also, a message should print to the Serial monitor that states "Room Occupied."

Did something go wrong? Double-check all your connections. Pay particular attention to the pins of the PIR sensor as different manufacturers can put them in different places or use different colored wires.

Where to go from here? This project is a good example of a prototype—an initial proof of concept for a room occupancy sensor. Maybe you'd like to mount the sensor inside the room but place colored lights on the outside. How would you do that? Or perhaps you'd like the message being sent to the serial monitor to appear somewhere else, like a screen outside of the room or perhaps at a central location in your building. For a more advanced project, the Arduino could communicate with a website or mobile application—welcome to the Internet of Things! Maybe you'd like a security system where the motion triggers an alarm or a camera. With Arduino, the sky is the limit! (Well, not really, if you decide to build an Arduino-controlled drone!)

Lilypad, Adafruit, and More
Wearable Electronics for Libraries

MEGAN EGBERT

L ibraries that are looking for ways to combine STEM learning with art and creativity will embrace wearable electronics and the possibilities they bring for both programs and circulation. Whether you have an extensive background with making, or you are a newcomer to the movement, there is a place for you to get started with wearables. When librarians are introduced to e-textiles, also called soft circuits, many became enthralled with the concept of pairing technology and clothing. In addition to the benefits of cross-curricular learning, e-textiles offer a unique way to teach about circuitry by making the typically hidden parts of electronics visible. Through working with e-textiles, you will discover that wearable electronics allow you to combine an interest in technology with a passion for art in a way that will speak to many library patrons young and old.

In their 2014 article "Wearable Electronics and Smart Textiles: A Critical Review" Stoppa and Chiolerio group e-textiles and soft circuits under what they term *smart textiles*, which they define as "textile products such as fibers and filaments, yarns together with woven, knitted or non-woven structures, which can interact with the environment/user." Although the technology for many

---

Megan Egbert is Programs Manager at Meridian Library District.

components associated with smart textiles has existed for years, it wasn't until the 1990s, when MIT developed wearable computers (or microcontrollers), which would become the brain behind the projects that we started to see the scale of possibility.

In 2007, Leah Buechley released the LilyPad Arduino, the first commercially available microcontroller designed for smart textiles. Buechley recalls that "it was a great way to bust open the stereotypes associated with technology. That was one of my main reasons for wanting to make it commercial. It seemed like this was really a cool social disruptor" (Birch 2014). She knew from years of prototyping, experimenting, and teaching with smart textiles that this was a trend that would continue. and she recognized the need for some type of construction kit that could tie together e-textiles and hands-on learning: "The power of construction kits stems from the fact that they provide simple modules, the construction kit pieces, which can be combined in a multitude of ways" (Buechley 2006). The LilyPad proved to be successful in a variety of settings, and has helped learners of all ages engage with soft circuits.

Libraries were quick to embrace this new type of technology for a multitude of reasons. The rise of the LilyPad coincided with the time when many libraries were starting to explore makerspaces and maker programming. E-textiles are an innovative way to teach circuitry to users of any age, and add extension activities for circuitry projects like squishy circuits, circuit blocks, littleBits, and many others. Because they blend art and technology, e-textiles also offer a unique aesthetic that can help engage reluctant makers, including some girls who might not immediately be drawn to making. E-textiles allow libraries to offer programs or workshops that focus on fashion or art, but also teach about circuitry. This chapter will provide an overview of the major types of e-textile products on the market. It will also highlight areas to study before getting started with e-textiles. Finally, five different project examples of e-textile learning that could take place in your library will be presented.

Major Types and Brands Available

LilyPad/LilyTwinkle

The first version of the LilyPad, as mentioned above, was released in 2007 and utilized the Arduino platform. Arduino, a microcontroller platform that is inexpensive and open source, was developed by students and educators at the Interactive Design Institute in 2005 (Buechley 2006). The LilyPad was first constructed as a kit designed to teach e-textiles. It included sewable electronic modules including a temperature sensor, an accelerometer, and LEDs, as well as conductive thread. The mainboard itself was designed to be sewn onto a project and could be programmed in the Arduino environment. Since the LilyPad was originally released, several different variations of the main board have been produced, including the LilyPad Arduino USB (which does not require a FTDI board for programming) and the LilyPad Arduino SimpleSnap (which snaps to a protoboard on a garment). In addition, there is a LilyPad ProtoSnap that allows projects to be constructed without the use of a breadboard, and includes a LilyPad Simple Board with other LilyPad components like a buzzer, a vibration motor, an RGB LED, a button, a switch, five LEDs, a light sensor, and a temperature sensor. The LilyPad Arduino does not have a USB port on board, so it requires a FTDI breakout board to program it, unlike some other microcontrollers intended for use on garments.

Since the inception of the LilyPad Arduino, other accessories have been created, such as the LilyTiny and the LilyTwinkle. A LilyTiny is a miniature LilyPad board with limited functionality but minimal space requirements. A LilyTwinkle is a preprogrammed LilyTiny that will add twinkling LED lights to any LilyPad project. Both allow for further complexities in building LilyPad e-textile projects. (See Table 8.1.)

TABLE 8.1

LilyPad Specs

MICROCONTROLLER	ATMEGA168 or ATMEGA328V
Dimensions	50mm outer diameter, Thin 0.8 mm PCB
Input voltage	2.7–5.5 V
Digital I/O pins	14
PWM channels	6
Analog input channel	6
DC current per I/O pin	40 mA
Flash memory	16 kB (of which 2 kB is used by bootloader)
SRAM	1 kB
EEPROM	512 bytes
Clock speed	8 MHz

Listed on Arduino's website at www.arduino.cc/en/Main/arduinoBoardLilyPad.

- *Pros:* Several variations of the board allow customizing the board to a project; the LilyPad is washable and many projects can be found online
- *Cons:* FTDI breakout board is necessary since it has no USB port; limited flash memory in comparison to the Flora

Flora

The Flora, created by Adafruits Industry, is a round, Arduino-compatible board that can be sewn onto textile projects. Designed by "LadyAda" (whose real name is Limor Fried), it aimed to improve upon the LilyPad, which had already been released. It is smaller than the LilyPad, measuring only 1.8 inches in diameter. The Flora does not use FTDI headers, which can stick out and get caught on fabric, but instead has built-in USB support. It allows for a variation in power supply through an onboard power regulator ranging between 3V and 16V. Additional add-on sensors for the Flora include motion, direction, color, light levels, touch, and even a GPS module. (See Table 8.2.)

TABLE 8.2

Flora Specs

MICROCONTROLLER	ATMEGA 32U4 MICROCONTROLLER
Dimensions	45 mm round x 7 mm thick/ 1.8 inch round x 0.3 inch thick; weight: 4.7g
Input voltage	3.5–16 V
Digital I/O pins	8
Flash memory	28k
SRAM	2.5 kB
Clock speed	8 MHz

From adafruit.com.

- *Pros:* Ideal for larger projects, variety of input voltage, multiple sensors, built in USB support
- *Cons:* Fewer options for I/O

Gemma

The Gemma is also designed by Adafruits Industry and can be considered a bite-sized version of the Flora. Comparable to the size of a quarter, this microcontroller offers a smaller and versatile option for less intricate types of projects. The Gemma is not fully compatible with Arduino, which could add a few challenges, but it is still programmed in the same way as the Flora. (See Table 8.3.)

TABLE 8.3

Gemma Specs

MICROCONTROLLER	ATTINY85
Dimensions	Dimensions: 27.98 mm/1.1 inch round x 7.14 mm/0.28 inch high Weight: 3.29g
Operating voltage	3.3V
Input voltage	4V–16V
Digital I/O pins	3
PWM channels	2
Analog input channels	1
DC current per I/O pin	20 mA
Absorption	9 mA while running
Flash memory	8 kB (ATtiny85) of which 2.75 kB used by bootloader
SRAM	512 Bytes (ATtiny85)
EEPROM	512 Bytes (ATtiny85)
Clock speed	8 MHz
Diameter	27.94 mm

Found at www.arduino.cc/en/Main/ArduinoGemma.

- *Pros:* Small; inexpensive
- *Cons:* Not 100 percent Arduino-compatible; does not have a serial port connection for debugging; not intended for large projects

How to Use Wearables

Safety

There are very few safety concerns to be aware of when teaching e-textiles, which makes them an ideal maker activity for any makerspace or library. When working with e-textiles, versus other types of circuits, there is no concern about electrocuting yourself and the LEDs do not get hot enough to burn anyone. It is possible to short a circuit (usually caused by stitches that overlap), which could result in some smoke or sparks. Although the projects listed in this chapter have little risk of starting fires, always be aware of the potential damage your power supply could cause if a circuit shorts, and never work on a project while it is being powered. Always remove or disconnect the battery before making any alterations to your project. Prior to getting started with e-textiles, students should be comfortable using a needle, be provided with information about polarity, and be taught how to use a multimeter (a tool to diagnose circuits).

Tutorials

There are many tutorials that can get you started with e-textiles.

- SparkFun (www.learnsparkfun.com) has a tutorial for e-textiles that provides an overview on sewing with conductive thread, polarity, short circuits, flow within a circuit, and voltage, current, resistance, and Ohm's law. They can be found at https://learn.sparkfun.com/tutorials/e-textile-basics but they are specific to the LilyPad.
- *Sew Electric* is a book written by Leah Buechley and Kanjun Qiu that also has an online site at http://sewelectric.org/. Here you can find step-by-step project instructions as well as troubleshooting guides for the LilyPad.
- ETextile Lounge has a series of tutorials in a variety of formats, ranging from YouTube videos to Flickr photo streams. http://etextilelounge.com/.
- Adafruit also provides tutorials on a variety of wearable projects, especially for the Gemma and Flora. They can be found at https://learn.adafruit.com/category/wearables.

Programming

The following examples are projects that range in complexity from beginner to expert. Many e-textile projects do not require programming of any kind; however, if you are going to use a microcontroller for a project you will need to acquire some programming skills. All the microcontrollers discussed are Arduino-compatible, which means you can use the Arduino environment to program them. All Arduino programs are written in C languages, which are among the most widely used programming languages in the world. However, Arduino has many features that aren't typical of standard C languages, so it is often referred to as a dialect of C. If you don't have programming experience, don't let that stop you from getting started with e-textiles. Arduino has built-in example sketches in the Arduino software (IDE) and other tutorials can be found at www.arduino .cc/en/Tutorial/HomePage. Many e-textile projects will provide you with the code necessary to program the project. However, it is still advisable to familiarize yourself with the basics of Arduino programming so that you can make slight changes and alterations to your projects.

Tips and Tricks

Using Conductive Thread

There are a variety of types of conductive thread, which can be beneficial for different types of projects.

- **Plated thread** is a traditional nylon thread that is dipped in a conductive metal coating, typically silver.
  - *Advantages:* Slicker and less likely to tangle.
  - *Disadvantages:* Can't withhold head from soldering.
  - *Suitable for:* Small projects that require knots and/or where it is integral that the thread stay in place.

- **Stainless steel thread** is made entirely of stainless steel without any traditional nylon.
  - *Advantages:* Heat from a soldering iron won't damage the thread.
  - *Disadvantages:* Difficult to sew with, thicker, and more like twine. Hard to knot.
  - *Suitable for:* Large projects (more than a few feet) that require low resistance.

Conductive thread tends to fray, which can make it difficult to thread a needle. Needle threaders or beeswax can help with the threading process. Frayed stitches can result in a faulty circuit. If you find stitches are fraying, you can coat the entire length of thread with beeswax.

Insulation Techniques for Conductive Thread

When sewing with conductive thread, whether by hand or sewing machine, it is important to keep your stitches close together, but not overlapping. Because conductive thread does not have an insulating layer, it will cause a short in the circuit if you cross traces (positive and negative) with your thread. To prevent this, you can use a resistive layer such as fabric, fabric paint, or electrical tape between traces if you need to overlap.

In addition to insulating small sections of your project where traces might overlap, there are also ways to insulate your entire project once it is completed. Insulating the entire project allows for extended protection of short circuits that could occur when an item is folded, washed, or comes in contact with another conductive surface. For a full list of methods, see https://learn.sparkfun.com/tutorials/insulation-techniques-for-e-textiles. Some of these methods include a fabric liner, fabric paint, and stretch fabric glue. No matter which method you choose for your project, it should be fully complete and functional before you insulate it. Insulation will not be required for smaller projects like bookmarks that will lie flat, but is recommended for any projects that will move and/or bend.

Fabric Selection and Care

The type of fabric you select for a project can impact how difficult it is to sew and how long the fabric will hold up once the project is complete. Lynne Bruning, in her Instructables video "eTextiles: How to Select Fabric" (www.instructables .com/id/eTextiles-How-to-Select-Fabric/) suggests these things to keep in mind when selecting fabric to use for an e-textiles project.

Weave: Tight weave, fibers should hold together when pulled on
Weight: Medium weight, should hold its structure when bent

Once a fabric is selected, its care can also influence how long your project will last. Both the LilyPad and Flora microcontrollers are washable, but need to be powered off and have batteries removed before washing. Hand washing of garments is recommended to prevent loosening of stitches. In their 2015 book *Getting Started with Adafruit FLORA,* Becky Stern and Tyler Cooper provide tips for washing e-textile projects. They recommend that you hang or lie garments flat to dry, use lukewarm water with special hand-washing detergent, and avoid dry cleaning. Depending on what type of conductive thread you use, washing could impact the integrity of the thread. Silver conductive thread oxidizes over time, and washing can speed up that process. Stainless steel thread does not tarnish or corrode, so washing poses less of a hazard.

LEDs and Buzzers

Depending on the type of project you choose, you are likely to encounter LEDs (light emitting diodes) and buzzers. If you have never used them before, consider starting with squishy circuits. This is a great way to become familiar with these tools before trying to implement them into a textile.

LEDs turn energy into light and are found in objects all around us. They are a way to add light to your project. Here are some tips for using them:

- The positive side of a LED is called the anode and is marked by a longer leg. If you are using LEDs specifically intended for textile projects, it will be marked with a + (plus) sign.
- The negative side of the LED is called a cathode. It will have a shorter leg or be marked with a – (minus) sign.
- Current can only flow one direction, from the anode to the cathode. If you connect the anode side of an LED to the negative power source it will not work.
- There are multiple kinds of LEDs. RGB (red, green, blue) LEDs allow any color of the rainbow to be produced by blending primary colors. Flashing LEDs contain an integrated circuit that allows them to blink.

For more information about LEDs, read the tutorial at https://learn.sparkfun .com/tutorials/light-emitting-diodes-leds.

There are specific types of LEDs and buzzers for textile projects that can be easily sewn to fabric, however they are not mandatory to get started. Standard LEDs and buzzers can be used with projects as long as you have a way to fasten them to fabric. You can curl the legs of LEDs so conductive thread can be sewn to the cathode and anode. Alligator clips can allow for easy testing of your LEDs and buzzers before they are sewn into place. LEDs and buzzers are included in some kits, such as the LilyPad ProtoSnap, but they can also be purchased independently through Adafruit, Maker Shed, or SparkFun.

Sensors

A variety of types of sensors can be used with e-textiles, including temperature sensors, light sensors, color, UV, GPS, and motion sensors. Sensors allow a textile to detect a physical property and respond to it; for example, an outfit could start to light up as the surrounding light diminishes. Depending on what type of microcontroller you use, the available sensors will vary. If you are interested in using sensors in your projects, make sure to research what types are available for the type of microcontroller you choose.

Battery Holders

There are multiple types of battery holders that can be used for e-textile projects. Any battery holder you use for a project should include a way for it to be sewn or adhered to a fabric project. The CR1220 PCB Mount Battery (with Pins), sold through Kitronik, is a coin cell battery with a bin attached to it, which is intended for easy soldering or to lay on conductive paint. For many small e-textile projects, a pin can poke through thin fabric and conductive thread can wrap around it. LilyPad and Adafruit both offer battery holders. Depending on the project and type of battery needed, you should consider whether your battery holder needs to have a switch that allows the current to be turned off when you don't want the project to be active.

Time Commitment

Depending on what project you are leading, it is important to estimate the time commitment it will take to complete the project. You might also provide alternative projects for those who want a simpler task to complete. Several projects, like those featured in Emily Lovell's *Getting Hands on with Soft Circuits: A Workshop Facilitator's Guide* will provide you with an estimated time frame for a specific target audience to complete a project. For example, most of the projects she outlines are intended for eleven through seventeen-year-olds and will take around two hours. However, participants in your program will always have varying degrees of experience, so it is advisable to have the option of scaling the project so that it is harder or easier for participants. Although it can be time-consuming, the best way to determine the time commitment for a project is to first complete it yourself so you can judge how long it will take those you teach.

How Are Libraries Using Wearables?

Libraries that seek to design engaging programming for their patrons are already adopting wearables. Here are just a few ways that libraries are implementing this technology:

- circulating wearables (Google Glass, GoPros)
- circulating microcontrollers that can create wearables (LilyPad, Flora, etc.) or kits that allow patrons to create their own wearables
- hosting classes on sewing and other fabric arts
- facilitating programs on building wearables
- teaching about e-textiles and circuitry
- incorporating VR headsets into reference and circulation services and game development courses

Future of Wearables and Libraries

The Arapahoe Library, located in the Denver area, was one of the first libraries to provide Google Glass to their patrons. It believes that libraries are essential to expose people to new ideas, including technology, which it views as a way for people to test out things they would not otherwise be able to afford (Asgarian, 2014). Similarly, other libraries are beginning to offer patrons the same type of exposure to virtual reality (VR) headsets, and more. Libraries have always been about shared resources, especially those that are expensive and might only be of limited interest, and I believe the future of libraries and wearables will follow that same pattern. Libraries will, and should, continue to look for ways to introduce patrons to wearable electronics through programs, circulation, and new services.

Projects

LED Fabric Bookmarks

In-depth instructions for this type of project can also be found at: http://sew electric.org/diy-projects/bookmark-book-light/.

Description: Create a bookmark that lights up. This project can be scaled for participants who are not old enough to use a needle and thread by utilizing another conductive material like copper tape. Although this project doesn't necessarily create a "wearable," it does introduce the basics of e-textiles.

Time/Skill Level: One hour/Beginner

Supplies: Coin cell battery, coin cell battery holder (one with a switch is recommended); LED; conductive thread, paint, or tape; felt; scissors; needle; fabric; glue; paper; and pencils

INSTRUCTIONS

1. *Test battery and LED:* Before getting started it is important that participants understand how the LED and battery work, and that their ultimate goal is to connect the two with a conductive material to light up the LED. If you are using LEDs with long anodes and cathodes (versus the flat type designed to be sewn to a project) have your students hold the LED against the coin cell battery with the anode to the positive side, and the cathode to the negative side. If you are using flat LEDs, have participants temporarily connect the + and – sides using a temporary solution (i.e., paper clips). Once the LED has lit up, you can move on to the next step.

2. *Cut out fabric:* This step that can be done ahead of time if you are working with kids or students who are beginners. Felt works well for light-up bookmarks because it is durable enough to remain stiff as a bookmark, but soft enough for needles to pass through. Bookmark size can vary depending on how much fabric you have and participant preference.

3. *Design what the bookmark will look like:* I recommend having participants start by sketching out on paper how they want their bookmark to look. Where will the battery be? Where will the LED sit? Will there be a design element around the LED? Will it be, for example, the mouth of a dragon, or the eye of a butterfly? This is the fun part! Encourage them to dream, but set a reasonable time frame. If you spend too long on this phase you won't get the bookmark assembled within the hour.

4. *Attach battery holder and LED:* This stage will vary greatly depending on what type of LED and battery holder you are using. If the ones you are utilizing are intended for e-textiles (i.e., sewable) you can use a bit of fabric glue to adhere them to the fabric before sewing them in place. If you are using a pronged LED, you will need to poke the prongs through the fabric and then curl them (needle-nose pliers work best) so they can be sewn in place.

5. *Add design elements:* If you are adding decorations, whether by fabric or fabric paint, now is the time to do so. With the LED in place, participants should be able to decorate the bookmark without interfering with the place where the trace will need to connect to the battery.

6. *Create traces:* The ideal way to connect the battery and LED would be by sewing them together with conductive thread. (For a tutorial on sewing with conductive thread, see https://learn.sparkfun.com/tutorials/sewing-with-conductive-thread.) If your participants are young, you could also experiment with conductive paint or copper tape. Ideally, use a battery holder with a switch that allows you to fully connect the traces and control the light with an on/off switch. If you do not have access to battery holders with switches, you can leave one trace disconnected, and then connect it with tape when you want the bookmark to light up.

7. *Finish project:* Allow participants time to share their bookmarks and talk about ways LEDs could be added to other craft projects.

LED Cuff Bracelets

In-depth instructions for this type of project can also be found at http://alumni.media.mit.edu/~emme/guide.pdf.

Description: Create a bracelet that lights up with LED lights! Parallel circuits are introduced and participants will use more than one LED light.
Time/Skill Level: Two hours/Beginner
Supplies: Felt, scissors, coin cell battery, battery holder (switch not necessary), metal snaps, fabric glue or hot glue gun, conductive thread, needles, needle-nose pliers (if using LEDs with legs), measuring tape, paper, and pencils.

INSTRUCTIONS

1. *Test the battery and LEDs* (See the description of the LED bookmark project description above for instructions for this step.)

2. *Sketch out the bracelet design:* Have participants use paper and pencil to sketch out what their bracelets will look like. Introduce the concept of parallel circuits, and emphasize that all the positive sides of the LEDs must line up, as will the negative sides. Also, the concept of the prong snap and the hole snap will need to be explained. The hole snap, battery holder, and LEDs will be on the front side of the bracelet. The prong snap will be on the back side so it can attach to the hole snap when wrapped around a wrist. The circuit will need to connect when the bracelet is snapped.

3. *Cut fabric:* Have each person take a wrist measurement, then cut fabric two inches longer than that measurement.

4. *Glue on pieces:* Use a small amount of glue that won't interfere with areas where battery holders, snaps, and LEDs will be sewn in place. If you are using non-sewable LEDS with legs, use needle-nose pliers to twirl the legs of the LED so it can lie flat and the conductive thread can be sewn around it.

5. *Create the traces:* For a tutorial on sewing with conductive thread see https://learn.sparkfun.com/tutorials/sewing-with-conductive-thread. Using a needle and connective thread, create the traces.

6. *Test the bracelet:* This project should not need a switch because it will only light up when the bracelet is snapped.

7. *Decorate the bracelet:* Once the bracelet is functional, add any design elements around the LEDs, making sure they don't interfere with the conductive thread.

Light Locked Wallets

A kit for this project can be purchased at www.nycmakery.com/kits/light-up -lock-wallet-kit.

Description: A wallet that lights up when it is locked. Although this project is similar to the bracelet project, it is slightly more difficult because it requires conventional sewing skills.

Time/Skill Level: Two hours/Intermediate

Supplies: Piece of felt (About 4 x 5 inches or the desired size), regular thread, conductive thread, scissors, battery holder, coin cell battery, snaps, and sewable LED.

INSTRUCTIONS

1. *Sketch schematics for the wallet:* Lay your piece of felt flat. You will be working on what will become the inside of the wallet. The wallet will be created by

folding the piece in half once the inside portion is complete. Mark where you will fasten the prong snap and the hole snap, at opposite edges on the same side of the fabric. Make sure the LED is located around the middle of the wallet once it is folded, but is on the inside of the wallet (to create a glowing effect). The battery holder can be positioned anywhere inside the wallet. Once elements are in place, you can use a bit of glue to hold them down.

2. *Create traces:* As with the bracelet, connect traces between the battery holder, the snaps, and the LED with conductive thread.
3. *Test the circuit:* Fold the piece of felt in half and snap it shut. The LED should light up.
4. *Sew the wallet:* Keep the felt folded, and use regular thread to sew the sides together to create the wallet.
5. *Style:* Add a handle, decoration, or any element to customize the wallet.

Electrochromatic Circuits

A full tutorial can be found at https://learn.sparkfun.com/tutorials/21st-century -fashion-kit-electrochromatic-circuits or http://tinyurl.com/gmj02xg.

Description: Combine thermochromatic pigment with conductive thread and create something that changes color through electricity.
Time/Skill Level: Three hours/Advanced
Supplies: Scissors, conductive thread, needles, felt, thin fabric, paint brush, paper plate, fabric glue, fabric paint, thermochromatic pigment, power controller, polymer lithium ion battery.

INSTRUCTIONS

1. *Create a button:* Using felt and conductive thread, create a button. Cut out two matching pieces of a felt shape, one with a small hole cut out of its center. Choose where you want the button to sit on a piece of felt. Use conductive thread to sew from the power controller In+ to the side of your button, and the power controller In− to the bottom of the button's location. Create a long stitch underneath where the button will lie, and then sew the piece of felt with the hole on top of the stitch. Plug the battery in to test if the button is working, and then unplug the battery. When you are sure the button will work, stich the felt pieces in place with regular thread.
2. *Stitch a design:* Start by stitching from Out− a design or text, that you want to change color. Return the stitches by connecting to Out+.

3. *Thermochromatic paint:* Mix the thermochromatic pigment with the fabric paint, and paint a piece of thin fabric. Using fabric glue, adhere the painted fabric over the conductive thread design created in step two.
4. *Test:* When completed, you should see the text or design appear in white through the painted fabric.

Plush Game Controllers

The inspiration for this project can be found at https://learn.adafruit.com/plush-game-controller/overview.

Description: Using a microcontroller and conductive material, create a functional plush video game controller. No batteries required, but lots of sewing and some programming.

Time/Skill Level: Three hours/Advanced

Supplies: Flora, computer, felt, scissors, conductive thread, conductive fabric, heat-responsive iron-on adhesive, embroidery hoop (optional), embroidery marker, ruler, sharp blade, pins, and stuffing.

INSTRUCTIONS

1. *Create a circuit diagram and pattern for the controller:* Adafruit provides a free template for this project at http://learn.adafruit.com/plush-game-controller/ or you can create your own. Keep in mind that the Flora has eight pins, so you cannot use more than eight push sensors.
2. *Cut out controller buttons from conductive fabric:* Iron a piece of interfacing adhesive on to conductive fabric. Cut out a total of eight controller buttons. Remove the backing from the interfacing and then iron the controller buttons to a large piece of felt.
3. *Trace your connections:* Place the Flora on the large piece of felt and use an embroidery marker to trace each button to a pin on the Flora, making sure none of the paths will connect.
4. *Create your traces:* Use conductive thread to connect the buttons to the Flora along the connection paths you drew. The embroidery hoop can help you work on a single area without having to manipulate the entire piece of fabric. The thread can be sewn through the conductive buttons and then wrapped around a specific pin of the Flora.
5. *Code the Flora:* The code for this project can be found on GitHub (search "Flora game controller"), or if you have coders in your group who want to try to program the Flora themselves, have them give it a shot!

6. *Test the buttons:* Once the buttons are connected to the Flora, and it is connected to a computer, pushing the buttons should type letters in a text editor program.

7. *Sew the controller:* After the buttons are connected and working, create the controller. Keep the USB port to the Flora free so that it can easily be connected or disconnected from a computer. The controller will need a back and two sides as well as the front with the buttons. It can be customized as long as the circuits are protected and stay functional during construction. It can be sewn by hand or machine.

8. *Stuff the controller:* Leave a 2-inch opening in the top of the controller when you sew it together. Fill the inside with stuffing and then sew the gap closed.

REFERENCES

Asgarian, R. (2014). Arapahoe Library invests in Google Glass. *Library Journal,* 139(1), 1.

Birch, L. (2014, July 18). Leah Buechley: Crafting the LilyPad Arduino. *Make Magazine.*

Buechley, L. (2005). LilyPad Arduino: How an open source hardware kit is sparking new engineering and design communities. https://llk.media.mit.edu/courses/readings/democratized_LilyPad.pdf.

————. (2006, October). A construction kit for electronic textiles. In *2006 10th IEEE International Symposium on Wearable Computers* (pp. 83–90).

Foote, C. (2015). Far beyond makerspaces. *Internet@Schools,* 22(5), 12–13.

Peppler, K. (2013). STEAM-powered computing education: Using e-textiles to integrate the arts and STEM. *Computer,* 46(9), 38–43. doi:10.1109/MC.2013.257.

Peppler, K., & Glosson, D. (2013). Stitching circuits: Learning about circuitry through e-textile materials. *Journal of Science Education & Technology,* 22(5), 751–63. doi:10.1007/s10956-012-9428-2.

Stern, B., and Cooper, T. (2015). *Getting started with Adafruit FLORA.* San Francisco, CA: Maker Media.

Stoppa, M., & Chiolerio, A. (2014). Wearable electronics and smart textiles: A critical review. *Sensors* 14, 11957–992.

FURTHER READING

Bruno, Tom. (2015). *Wearable technology: Smart watches to Google Glass for libraries.* Lanham, MA: Rowman & Littlefield.

Buechley, Leah, and Qui Kanjun. (2013). *Sew electric: A collection of DIY projects that combine fabric, electronics, and programming.* Cambridge, MA: HLT Press.

Hartman, Kate. (2014). *Make: Wearable electronics.* Sebastopol, CA: O'Reilly & Associates.

Olsson, Tony. 2012. *Arduino wearables.* Berkeley, CA: Apress. http://site.ebrary.com/id/10603546.

Google Cardboard for Librarians

TOM BRUNO

What Is Virtual Reality and Google Cardboard?

Virtual reality, or VR, has been the Holy Grail of computer-technology enthusiasts for decades. Movies such as *Tron* and *The Matrix,* and the television show, *Star Trek: The Next Generation*'s Holodeck advanced the concept of being able to immerse oneself in a virtual computer-generated world and captured the public imagination. In science fiction, the idea of virtual reality as the future of entertainment appeared in Ray Bradbury's short story "The Veldt," where the antagonist is literally virtual reality's fourth wall come to life—thirty years before William Gibson's 1984 dystopian *Neuromancer.* It is therefore not surprising that generations of computer programmers and engineers have attempted to realize this goal.

In the 1990s the gaming and entertainment industry made a few early forays into VR with such devices as Nintendo's Virtual Boy and Sega's VR Headset, but in many cases the hype outstripped the actual product and the results were not terribly impressive—which made VR even less marketable to the general public. As a consequence, developers tended to treat virtual reality as nothing

Tom Bruno is Director, Knowledge Curation, and Innovation at The Westport Library.

more than a gimmick. The overall field languished until Palmer Luckey, a technology enthusiast and gamer, decided that crowdfunding his own VR platform was the only way to spur development. This platform, known as the Oculus Rift, became the basis for one of the most successful Kickstarter projects of all time, and ignited a virtual renaissance (pun intended) in the established gaming and entertainment industry.

At almost the same time as Google was launching its ill-fated Project Glass, it was also crafting a virtual reality platform of its own. Dubbed Google Cardboard, the device first made its appearance at the 2014 Google I/O Conference, where attendees found unassembled Cardboard viewers on their seats with instructions on how to assemble the device and insert their smartphones to view 360° content by turning the phone's display into a stereoptic split-screen. While Google Glass attracted mass derision from the tech sector and the public at large, Cardboard successfully flew under everyone's radar, at the same time slowly but surely insinuating itself into virtual reality circles as a cheap and easy entry point for enabling VR content. Especially when compared to the costs of acquiring a platform such as the Oculus Rift and outfitting a computer powerful enough to run the content, Google Cardboard is an absolute steal in comparison, and as such it makes the perfect low-cost introduction to the world of virtual reality for your library patrons.

This chapter looks at the various Google Cardboard viewers available to the public, including DIY versions, and review the various makes and models of compatible smartphones. It will also look at any special considerations you should be mindful of when organizing any activities or programming around Google Cardboard, and then will recommend some applications that can make the most of your Cardboard viewing experience. The chapter then presents several projects involving Google Cardboard that are suitable for a library or makerspaces: assembling devices from scratch, creating 360° virtual content and uploading it into Google Maps, or hosting a 3D virtual arcade.

Major Types, Brands, and Models of Cardboard Viewers

DIY Cardboard Kits

The easiest and cheapest way to acquire a Cardboard viewer is to assemble one from a premade kit. Until recently, Google did not sell its original Cardboard design to the general public, although it did make the full schematics available to anyone who wanted to try and build his or her own viewers from scratch (which will be discussed in the projects section that concludes the chapter). This left the market open for third-party providers to sell their own Cardboard-compatible viewers. Most of these products can be purchased for $15 to $20 per viewer. The same vendors usually offer slightly more rigid and durable designs made of silicone and plastic, which cost anywhere from $20 to $40. I am very fond of the Cardboard viewer kits sold by I Am Cardboard (www.imcardboard.com/), which sells viewers for both smaller and larger smartphone screens (the Cardboard and Cardboard V2.0 viewers, respectively). Kits arrive flat-packed as one piece and are easily assembled by matching numbered tabs to numbered slots, following instructions printed on the cardboard itself. Each kit is completely self-contained, with no additional external materials required to complete the device. Assembling a device from the sealed flat pack usually takes about five to ten minutes, and provides an excellent DIY activity for workshop participants while the instructor makes her opening remarks. Many Cardboard viewer vendors also offer options for bulk purchase or custom branding.

Some library patrons may also bring in their own Cardboard viewers, which they may have obtained through various promotions. For example, *The New York Times* recently sent viewers to all its subscribers as a way of introducing their new online articles that contain 360° video and VR content. Verizon partnered with Disney during the release of *Stars Wars: The Force Awakens* to release a series of Star Wars–themed Cardboard viewers in the fall of 2015. Do not be surprised if patrons bring these devices to a demonstration or workshop—they may be curious about how to use their viewers and are coming to the library for more information and instruction.

There are a couple of things to keep in mind when selecting a Cardboard viewer kit. One is whether you should purchase a kit with an NFC tag. NFC stands for *Near Field Communications*, which is a protocol that is built into most smartphones on the market today (frequently users must manually toggle it on in order for it to function). You may be familiar with new "tap to pay" smartphone features (such as Apple Pay for iPhones, or Samsung Pay for Samsung devices) that utilize NFC so that a phone can communicate with a pay kiosk. Similarly, the current wave of video games that employ collectible action figures, such as Disney Infinity, Skylanders, or Nintendo's Amiibo, use NFC to make the figures "talk" to the game. The NFC tags that come with Cardboard viewer kits, however, are slightly less sophisticated. Many of them simply instruct your smartphone to launch a certain application when the phone is placed within the viewer and within range of the NFC tag. Most of the time the app is the proprietary "home app" for the company. To be fair, many of these applications try to make it possible for a user to access all their Cardboard, 360°, or VR content through one hub, but given the extreme fragmentation of this still-embryonic market being forced to navigate from one master application to a user's desired content is clunky at best. Google has hinted that future iterations of Cardboard will be able to utilize NFC to configure specific phones to specific viewer models, thus potentially optimizing the Cardboard viewing experience, but at the moment the added value of that NFC tag is limited at best. If you are on a budget, you may want to consider eliminating it from your purchase.

Another important consideration is the viewer's ability to accommodate the ever-larger screen sizes of current smartphones. The original Cardboard viewer was released in June 2014. Since then screen sizes for mobile devices have increased significantly, and some recent phones do not fit in all Cardboard viewers. When you are purchasing viewers, check the specifications to see what size smartphones they can accommodate, and make sure that you have some viewers on hand for patrons with oversized smartphones or "phablets." For example, when I run Cardboard workshops I prefer to use the original Cardboard viewer from I Am Cardboard because of its DIY component and lower price. However, because this model does not accommodate newer iPhones or the Samsung Galaxy Note, I make sure that I either bring an additional smartphone or an oversized viewer that can be used for these devices.

A final important note about Cardboard viewers is that some of the kits use magnets to simulate a smartphone screen click, while others use conductive foam buttons. If you purchase a viewer that has magnets, please be sure to let your patrons know, because magnets can interfere with the operation of pacemakers and similar medical devices. Most kits will come with warnings to that effect, but always err on the side of more information in these situations!

View-Master Virtual Reality Viewer

In the fall of 2015, toymaker Mattel partnered with Google to resurrect the classic View-Master slide viewer by transforming it into a hard plastic, Card-board-compatible viewer instead. Instead of inserting one of the View-Master's iconic slide wheels, you place your smartphone inside the viewer. The same basic stereoscopic principle that made the View-Master so much fun for previous generations is still available from the Google Cardboard. Remember the old slide wheels? Mattel has also released a series of virtual reality content that uses the wheels in a clever manner: if users look at one of the slide wheels through the View-Master Cardboard viewer, an augmented reality image that's almost like a hologram will spring to life. Although this is currently no more than a gimmick, it is interesting to see Mattel and Google experiment with augmented reality, which Microsoft has attempted to lay claim to with its Hololens.

Although Google Cardboard is primarily focused on delivering a low-cost means of entry into the virtual reality market, I will review a couple of augmented reality Cardboard applications in the project section of this chapter to demonstrate that the Cardboard viewer is theoretically just as capable of delivering an augmented reality experience as it currently does with virtual reality.

Samsung VR Gear and Other Viewers

The fact that the Cardboard viewer ultimately relies on a smartphone to power the virtual reality experience leads to the obvious conclusion that the smartphone vendors themselves must be interested in cashing in on this brand-new market with enormous growth potential, and not surprisingly, this has been exactly the case. It is beyond the scope of this chapter to cover all of these developments, as these viewers are proprietary and are usually only designed to work exclusively with certain makes and models of smartphone, whereas the purpose of this chapter is to present as many ecumenical and open options for the purposes of library instruction. Nevertheless, as proprietary virtual reality devices such as the Samsung VR Gear or HTC Vive become more common, library staff may be asked to help support such devices. Therefore, I will mention one such proprietary viewer, the Samsung VR Gear.

The Gear VR, which is compatible with Samsung's Galaxy S7, S7 Edge, Note 5, S6, and S6 Edge, is a $99 headset with its own accelerometer, gyroscope, and proximity-based sensors that enhance the existing capabilities of a smartphone. It also comes with a built-in control pad that allows the user a wider range of VR interactivity than merely pointing and clicking (it is also possible to connect an actual gamepad or controller via Bluetooth). Samsung has partnered with Oculus to deliver an already impressive and growing array of virtual reality content through the Oculus application, including 360° video, including movies and television programs optimized for 3D viewing, and of course games. The net effect of a headset such as the Samsung Gear VR is to provide a virtual reality experience somewhere between that of Google Cardboard and the full-blown immersion possible with the Oculus Rift or similar dedicated VR consoles, and it will probably continue to fill a market niche for people who would like to do more than dabble in virtual reality but who aren't ready to commit to purchasing their own Oculus Rift—as well as top-end personal computers capable of running it.

How to Use Cardboard

Downloading the Google Cardboard App

Although it is not necessary to download the Google Cardboard app to use your Cardboard viewer, the officially supported app from Google provides an excellent introduction to Google Cardboard and virtual reality. Also, although proprietary app-based hubs can be more of an impediment than a helpful resource, the Google Cardboard app is perhaps the least offensive of the lot, because it is less interested in selling you additional virtual reality content than providing a safe and manageable entry point into the VR milieu.

The Google Cardboard app contains a simple tutorial for using and navigating the interface, a point and click flying tour through the 3D renderings of Google Earth, a virtual tour guide via 360° photos of a selected point of international interest (e.g., the Palace of Versailles), a gallery of three-dimensional art objects, and viewers for users' own video and photo content, which allow you to browse your files visually and watch them using the viewer. There is also a virtual reality "featurette" included with the Google Cardboard app that showcases the immersive potential of virtual reality. In its initial release, the app's featurette was a walk through a windy animated forest, followed by another nature-themed Arctic Adventure, which lets you run with the wolves, fly with the seagulls, and try your hand at some deep-sea fishing (watch out for whales!).

The Cardboard app discovers any additional VR content you may have downloaded and makes it accessible through its portal. It also tries to make it easy for you to discover additional Cardboard-compatible virtual reality content, with a delimited search link to the Google Play store as well as a link to YouTube's 360° Video Channel. What the app doesn't do, however, is make it easy to switch among VR apps, which means even when using the Google Cardboard application, you will still need to remove your smartphone from the viewer and manually change the application anytime you wish to try another program. This is one of the more frustrating aspects of Google Cardboard, because when working with a touch screen it is very easy to launch a VR application only to click back out of it by accidentally handling the phone or its screen in a way that causes it to toggle modes, switch programs, or set off another of the myriad smartphone functions that are triggered by movement or touch.

Locating VR Applications, Games, and Content

Although the Google Cardboard application and other proprietary viewer hub applications attempt to offer curated virtual reality content that is suitable for or compatible with your viewer, the best way to find new VR applications and other content is to search for them directly, either in the Google Play store for Android phones or the Apple Store for iPhones. Keyword searches using the terms "VR" or "cardboard" tend to yield the most results, although you may want to try using other terms such as virtual or augmented reality as well. It is possible to do the same kinds of searches on YouTube for VR video content, although it is very important to point out that as of the time of this writing that YouTube does not currently support Apple smartphones for VR or Cardboard content.

Because the Cardboard enthusiast community is still relatively small (although it is growing fast), places like /r/googlecardboard and /r/AndroidVR on Reddit can be excellent resources for recommendations and reviews. Online magazines devoted to computers, technology, and gaming will often come up with curated "Top Ten Apps for Cardboard" articles; although this can be a great way to discover new content, be mindful that reviewers are often cutting and pasting from other articles and may not note that a free VR game or app that looks interesting is just a thinly veiled advertisement for a more expensive paid version of the app. Although this is not a problem exclusive to the Cardboard app market, it can be particularly frustrating as an instructor when you find a particularly promising app, only to learn on the third subsequent run that it locks up unless you pay for the full version!

Creating Your Own VR Content

If you are a developer, this chapter is probably not the best resource for you to create your own VR games or applications for Google Cardboard. That said, Google does have a Cardboard Design Lab tutorial app available in the Google Play store that walks developers through best practices for designing virtual reality applications. Gaming enthusiasts may also attempt to hack Cardboard so that it can play normal video games on the 3D viewer. This is often done by using some kind of software or application to serve as the "middleware" between the original game and the desired virtual viewing platform. One of the most popular middleware conversion platforms is called Trinus VR. Again, using Trinus to play conventional two-dimensional video games in virtual reality is well beyond the scope and intent of this chapter; truly dedicated individuals should be able to find inspiration and ample resources online.

For most of us, however, creating VR content will be centered on recording 360° photos or videos for playback on a Cardboard viewer. There are several ways to do this: some involve applications that modify or process the images taken by conventional smartphones or other digital cameras and convert them into a VR-friendly format, while others involve using specialized hardware, such as the GoPro Jump rig or the Ricoh Theta series of 360° cameras. Therefore, the chapter will review both methods of creating this kind of VR content later in this chapter.

Tips You Need to Know

Smartphone Requirements

Although there is no simple rule of thumb for determining minimum hardware requirements because of the complexity and fragmentation of the current smartphone market, Google Cardboard requires at the very least a smartphone with a built-in gyroscope to function; older smartphones that only have an orientation sensor will not work. For the best viewing experience, it is recommended that your phone screen's resolution be at least 1080 × 1920 in CSS pixels and the screen size itself be larger than 4.5 inches. Also, phones older than three years may not be able to run Cardboard or VR apps without glitching or crashing—and some older phones may not even launch them at all.

iOS versus Android—Which Mobile Platform Works Best?

There is, however, an answer as to which mobile platform currently supports Cardboard and VR content the best: the Android OS, hands down. This should not be surprising, as Google Cardboard and the Android operating system are both designed by Google. Consider as well that Google Maps and Google Earth are also (obviously) Google properties, as is YouTube, so it is more than a happy accident that the optimal Cardboard viewing experience will come from an Android phone. In fact, at the time this chapter was written, YouTube still does not support the Cardboard viewing option for iPhones, although there are unofficial iOS apps (such as in360Tube) that can provide a viable workaround in the meantime. Another factor is that there are simply more Cardboard and VR apps being developed for the Android OS, which means that it can be difficult to find the iOS equivalent of certain Cardboard applications in the Apple Store.

All of this is well and good if you are providing a demonstration of Google Cardboard and you can choose the best device for the experience, but the fact is that when you are running a Cardboard class or workshop you are going to see a lot of iPhones among your participants. You are also going to see quite a few older Android phones that may not be able to run Cardboard or can only run some of the VR apps with difficulty. How best can you manage a mixed group of smartphones, with wildly varying makes, models, and years?

One way is to ask people in advance what smartphones they intend to bring—you could even suggest minimum recommended versions of phones and operating systems, but then you run the risk of turning away people who might enjoy the program even if they can't run the Cardboard or VR apps on their own smartphones. In the past, when I've known I'll see a mix of smartphone types, I am careful to highlight applications that I know exist on both the iOS and Android platforms, even though this sometimes means passing up an opportunity to show off the latest apps. Knowing which smartphones your attendees plan to bring can also give you an idea of how much troubleshooting you'll need to do during your demonstration, class, or workshop, or whether you'll need to ask your participants to double up on the smartphones that function without any difficulty.

Another solution is to bring extra smartphones to your program. This is often easier said than done, because even if you have used phones you can co-opt to this purpose, you still need to make sure that they meet the minimum technical requirements for Cardboard viewing. If your library asks for smartphone donations, that might be one way to procure an extra phone or two; you can also try buying them online or checking used-game stores, which often sell last-generation smartphones at deeply discounted prices. I bring my retired Samsung Galaxy S5 smartphone to my workshops along with my current phone; despite having a cracked screen, the older phone can still run Cardboard viewer apps without any problems.

Managing Memory, Data, and Power

There's no delicate way of putting this, so I'll be blunt: VR applications are huge. Even the simplest of games or short simulations will range between 50 and 100 megabytes on your phone, and the Google Cardboard official app itself weighs in at 199 Mb! Putting together an introductory assortment of VR apps can easily fill up your phone, so keep this in mind when planning your Cardboard viewer program. If you are running a class or workshop where participants will be running VR apps on their own smartphones, consider sending a list of apps for them to download before coming to the event. Not only does this allow people to jump right into the action without waiting for apps to download, but depending on your library or venue, the local WiFi might be sorely taxed by an entire classroom of participants attempting to download a bunch of large VR applications. Even worse, people may have to use their own mobile data to download apps on the spot—I've blown through my cell provider's data caps on more than one occasion when I was running a Cardboard event and the local WiFi was too slow for me to use on-site. This also brings up an important point about the venue: if you have any control, try to stage your Cardboard event in an area of the library or building that either has an excellent WiFi signal or, at the very least, the best possible cellular service.

Another consideration for running Cardboard apps is power. Virtual reality will drain your smartphone's battery as quickly as playing a high-end video game or using your mobile GPS for turn-by-turn navigation. Obviously, it is difficult to use your phone while it is plugged in for charging, so it is imperative that you bring a fully charged smartphone to any demonstration, class, or workshop. This is something that you might want to mention to your participants if they will be bringing their own devices. At least be sure to provide ample facilities for recharging phones (provide a conveniently-located power strip or a cell phone recharging station if your library has one).

User Input for VR Applications—Bluetooth Controllers and Other Options

Currently the default user input for Google Cardboard apps is the button click. Depending on the Cardboard device, this click is simulated either by the motion of a magnet on the side of the viewer, which the smartphone's magnetometer registers as a click, or the physical pressure of a conductive button that actually touches the screen. If you pair a Bluetooth mouse with your smartphone, it is also possible to simulate the Cardboard button with a left mouse click. You can also pair other Bluetooth devices such as input controllers and gamepads to your smartphone, but whether these controllers will be supported varies from application to application.

An interesting take on the problem of providing additional user input to the Cardboard app environment is Realiteer's GermBuster VR game, which provides instructions on how to assemble your own hand trigger with cardboard and a trackable QR Code, which the smartphone's camera can follow and replicate the user's hand motions inside the game. In doing so, Realiteer blurs the lines between virtual and augmented reality by using the latter to enhance the former. It will be interesting to see if other developers follow suit and take advantage of the smartphone's onboard camera in a similar fashion.

Other VR Options?

Although there are other options in the works, with Sony's PlayStation VR shipping in October 2016, and the Microsoft HoloLens now being distributed to developers. Currently the only virtual reality platforms available to libraries and patrons are represented by higher-end PC setups, such as the Oculus Rift and the HTC Vive, and those powered by smartphones, like the Cardboard viewer and other proprietary devices such as the aforementioned Samsung Gear VR. Although this chapter will not discuss PC-based virtual reality (such as the Oculus Rift), it is perhaps important to note that many VR programs originally developed for higher-end platforms are now being adapted as smartphone apps to supply content to the burgeoning mobile VR market. In fact, the Samsung Gear VR headset was developed in partnership with Oculus, so it literally functions as a hybrid bridge between the cheaper Cardboard-based viewers and the PC-based platforms.

How Libraries Are Using Google Cardboard

Google Cardboard has been generating a slow but growing crowd of followers in library circles. Indiana University has been using Google Cardboard to view photo spheres of a virtual tour of the campus's nineteen branch libraries in Google Street View. The Westport Library has taken 360° photos and videos of its MakerSpace, and has documented its annual Maker Madness overnight event using a Ricoh Theta S spherical camera. Other libraries have introduced Cardboard during tech petting zoos that expose users to a range of applications, and other similar events. Recent publications in the library technology and public library circles have lauded the potential of Google Cardboard, but even as public interest in virtual reality increases there appears to be some reluctance in library circles to embrace and explore Cardboard.

Perhaps librarians, still feeling somewhat jaded about being co-opted as early-adopter cheerleaders for Google Glass, are not ready give Google another free pass. Unlike the ill-fated, experimental Glass, Cardboard is running a stealthy grass-roots initiative that has succeeded because it hasn't attempted to sell itself. Instead, since its release at the Google I/O conference in 2014, Cardboard has been allowed to grow organically, and it has only begun to percolate up into the broader public consciousness. Now that a full spectrum of virtual reality platforms has evolved, it will be interesting to see what libraries make of them, how they will support them, and—perhaps most important—how they will integrate them into the patron experience over the coming years.

Projects

Build Your Own Cardboard Device
A DIY/Maker Project for Teens or Adults

One of the most fun things about Google Cardboard is that patrons can actually build the viewer by themselves, which makes it a perfect DIY activity for a library or makerspace. Whenever I run a Cardboard workshop, I still prefer to use kits that require some assembly, so that participants get a chance to do hands-on experiential learning.

There are several ways to approach building a Cardboard device:

1. *Buy a Cardboard kit that requires assembly.* I've discussed some of the Cardboard viewing options earlier in this chapter, and of the ones mentioned I still prefer I Am Cardboard's basic VR kit (www.imcardboard.com/cardboard.html), which comes with precut cardboard components, lenses, magnets, an NFC tag (optional), Velcro strips, and a rubber band. Assembly consists of lining up numbered tabs and slots, and can usually be completed within five to ten minutes, which leaves plenty of time to use the device and explore various applications. (Note that at the time this chapter was written, there are increasingly fewer options available for these kinds of kits, as many companies that previously offered DIY assembly kits—such as DodoCase—now only offer viewers that are designed to be assembled as quickly and easily as possible. It is for this reason that I hope I Am Cardboard continues to offer its basic VR kit, which will keep this option available for DIY Cardboard enthusiasts.)

2. *Build a Cardboard device from scratch.* Although Google is more than happy to point you in the direction of several different vendors that sell a premade, preassembled Cardboard Viewer, and includes a link that to a page where it sells its own device, Google also provides detailed instructions for building a Cardboard viewer from scratch (see the "Build It Yourself" section at www.google.com/get/cardboard/get-cardboard/). Google's official instructions include specifications for all of the necessary components (e.g., lenses), for those who want to purchase parts from other sources. Such a project will require you to print out the templates of the various Cardboard components, mount them to a sheet of cardboard, and cut them to specification. If you're planning such an activity, make sure to restrict it to participants who are old enough to use X-Acto knives or similar cutting tools. There is an excellent step-by-step article by *Computerworld* (www.computerworld.com/article/2881175/emerging-technology/

diy-build-your-own-google-cardboard-vr-viewer) where the author follows Google's instructions to build his own Cardboard viewer using a pizza box. (I've always had a mind to build a foam version of the Cardboard viewer, although I'm not sure if an all-foam build would be sturdy enough).

3. *3D print a Cardboard viewer.* Not surprisingly, there are myriad templates for Cardboard viewers on Thingiverse and other repositories for 3D printing models. Because an all-plastic viewer would be more rigid and inflexible than a cardboard build, you should make sure to select and download a template that will fit your make and model of smartphone. Also, you will not be able to 3D print your lenses, so they will need to be purchased separately and added to the final build. The same is true if you are going to add a magnet for a button or make one out of conductive foam. There are a few online guides to help you 3D print your own Cardboard viewer, (e.g., https://a113dp .com/3d-print-google-cardboard/).

4. *Build an old-fashioned stereopticon.* This last option was inspired by a recent Google Cardboard workshop I ran, where one of the participants brought a nineteenth-century stereopticon from her library's historical collection. To our surprise, not only did the viewer accommodate a smartphone, but the device worked with Cardboard or VR content! You can find a simple but excellent guide to making your own stereoptic viewer at WikiHow (www.wikihow .com/Make-a-Stereoscope).

Google Cardboard Workshop
How to Host a Cardboard VR Demonstration and Hands-On Workshop for Tweens, Teens, or Adults

Once you have your Cardboard viewers either purchased or assembled (or have built one from scratch), you are ready to host your own Cardboard VR demonstration. Please bear in mind the caveats explored earlier in this chapter covering all the various considerations regarding device compatibility, mobile device operating systems, as well as best practices and guidelines about memory, data, and power. Again, I recommend polling your audience in advance, not only so that you can see what kinds of smartphones they will be bringing, but also to give them a list of Cardboard or VR applications they should download in advance so that they will not need to spend time and precious data trying to get them on the day of the demonstration/workshop. Knowing who is bringing what will also alert you as to whether you'll have to have extra devices on hand, just in case, or whether participants will need to share devices for the event; this is often the case when offering this kind of program to younger kids, as not all of them may have fully functioning smartphones yet.

As I mentioned previously, the way I usually organize my Cardboard demonstrations/workshops is to start by assembling the devices as a group activity. Even if you choose to do the same, with the New York Times, Verizon and other companies giving out Cardboard devices, it is likely that you will have people who will want to know how to use their specific device to view VR or Cardboard content, so try to at the very least familiarize yourself with these kinds of viewers beforehand. I also like to have a couple of my own devices ready to go and already running one of the following VR/Cardboard applications so that people who are having difficulties getting the content to run on their smartphones can jump right into the action and follow along without having to worry about troubleshooting their problems during the workshop.

Once everyone is ready to start viewing VR content, you should choose what introductory content you'd like to explore. Although there is an Official Cardboard App available for both Android and iOS, the respective apps differ slightly in terms of functionality and content. Although this is mostly unavoidable, as the two mobile platforms are slightly different themselves in terms of supporting virtual reality viewing, it makes for uneven instruction and some confusion on the part of your workshop participants. That being said, Google tends to update this application with new content on a regular basis, so it is worth exploring with your audience, albeit with the caveats just mentioned.

One of my favorite "starter" VR applications is Tuscany Dive, which is a virtual walkthrough of a villa in Tuscany. Although the graphics are somewhat on the simple side, the illusion of motion is quite compelling, as the viewer will move in whatever direction the participants look until they bump into an obstacle. Be sure to caution your participants to be mindful of their surroundings as they use this app, because they are very likely to want to wander in whatever direction the simulation is taking them. One of the reasons I'm so fond of this app as an introduction to VR is that it keeps things simple—the interface is easy for kids, adults, and seniors to figure out, and because the motion never goes faster than a stroll the possibility of vertigo or motion sickness is reduced. Even though there are more detailed simulations out there, Tuscany Dive remains a tried and tested introduction to the wonderful world of virtual reality, especially because it remains free and available for both the Android and iOS platforms.

For those who are willing to brave a little motion sickness, there is also the Dive City Rollercoaster, which is another simple but free VR/Cardboard app. Again, although there are more detailed and complex ride simulators available, many of them are larger and of significant download size, and can be either paid apps or "freeware," which requires the viewer to pay at some point in the process of running the app. The goal of your workshop should be to provide as many different examples of virtual reality as possible, so I would recommend opting for smaller and free apps whenever you can, and suggesting other richer paid content if your audience expresses interest in further viewing.

A good example of a simple cross platform Cardboard game would be Germ-Buster VR, which is basically a point-and-shoot simulator where you aim a stream of bubbles at various germs which creep up at you from all directions. One of the more interesting aspects of the GermBuster game is that it also comes with instructions for creating your own augmented reality hand trigger that allows you to aim the bubble gun using your hand, which is tracked by the camera in your smartphone (see the previous section on user input for more about this innovative blend of VR and AR in one application).

Finally, I like to complete my whirlwind tour of VR apps with the short but creepy horror app called Sisters, in which you keep looking around a room during a dark and stormy night as a series of scary events unfold before your eyes . . . or, as it turns out, right behind you! Based on the frightened screams of workshop participants, Sisters is a great example of just how immersive virtual reality can be, and how much potential VR has to transform the entertainment industry as a whole.

If time permits, you can incorporate any or all the remaining projects into your Google Cardboard workshop, although I've found that simply getting a group up and running with a handful of applications can provide enough material for an hour-long demonstration.

Create Your Own Cardboard Content
Learn How to Use Cardboard Camera and Other Applications to Create 360° Photos and/or Video

One of the most useful aspects of Google Cardboard is its ability to view 360° photos (or Photo Spheres) and videos. Until recently, cameras capable of shooting such footage, such as the Ricoh Theta S or the GoPro Jump, were prohibitively expensive., However, for creating 360° pictures Google's new Cardboard Camera app allows you to create and view your own Photo Spheres by just using your smartphone's camera in a special form of panorama mode. For extra immersion, the resultant 360° image is combined with a short loop of recorded ambient noise as well. Although Google has not released an iOS version of this application, there is a functionally similar app called Optonaut that was still in free beta at the time this chapter was written. 360° video is still more challenging to capture with anything other than specialized equipment, although it is probably only a matter of time before this function is possible using your smartphone camera.

Cardboard Virtual Tours
Using Google Cardboard with Google Maps

Creating 360° photos and posting them online is one way to add virtual-tour content to the Internet, but Google has already been busy creating an entire virtual world with the Google Street View function within Google Maps. When Cardboard was first introduced, it was possible to toggle from Street View directly into a stereoptic format for Android devices. While this easter egg still exists, because it is cumbersome to switch back and forth between regular and stereoptic views (especially with your smartphone mounted inside a viewing device), Google released a stand-alone Google Street View app for both Android and iOS. Not only does the Street View app allow you to browse existing Photo Spheres created by Google and others, but it allows you to create, manage, and upload your own to Google Maps as well, or curate and manage them privately.

Thrills, Chills, and Spills
How to Host a Google Cardboard Game Night

Although there's no way to compete with the Oculus Rift or the HTC Vive in terms of virtual reality gaming entertainment content, such rigs are still extremely expensive to outfit and maintain, whereas some quality VR games can be played for the cost of a smartphone and a viewer (and sometimes a nominally app fee) on Google Cardboard. To this end, you could curate a selection of Cardboard games, with each ready to play on a different device, so that it is easy for people to move from station to station and play as many games as possible. Unfortunately, for the time being, there's a profound lack of parallel development between Android and iOS platforms most profoundly, with the result that the following list contains Cardboard/VR games, most which are mostly only currently available for Android in the Google Play Store. The following lists iOS gaming apps where available:

1. *GermBuster VR* (Android and iOS)
2. *Sisters* (Android and iOS)
3. *VR Crossy Road* (Android and iOS) A great 3D take on the addictive one-button mobile gaming app. Because many kids are familiar with the original Crossy Road, this is an excellent gateway application for VR.

4. *Swivel Gun! VR Log Ride* (Android only) The premise is entertaining enough—a pirate-themed virtual log flume—but creators Pixels of Eight up the ante by giving you a cannon that you can point and shoot at various stacks of barrels set up along the route, making this one of the more absorbing Cardboard/VR game apps I've demonstrated for participants.

5. *Proton Pulse* (Android only). A 3D version of the popular "breakout" genre of video games, Proton Pulse has a slick retro feel to it as you tilt your head to keep the ball in play to bounce against a series of virtual bricks. The gameplay starts slowly and seems deceptively easy, but then ratchets up quickly in difficulty. Whatever the future of VR gaming is, it is almost certainly bound to be more exhausting than its 2D analog!

Legos in the Library

MEGAN LOTTS

O ne of the most interesting parts of my daily routine as the art reference
librarian at the Rutgers University Art Library is to see what transpired
overnight at its Lego Playing Station. On some days, it appears as if a
group of young children have been let loose at the table and have scattered Legos
everywhere, including on the floor. On other days, I find elaborate models that tell
stories about our patrons—their lives, their imaginings, and their dreams.

Although the Rutgers University Art Library has only acquired 300 pounds
of Legos thus far, the LEGO Group itself has manufactured over 400 billion
colorful Lego bricks since 1958, which comes to about sixty-two Lego bricks for
each person on earth. Approximately 19 billion Lego pieces are produced per
year, 2.16 million are molded every hour, and 36,000 every minute.[1] In 1990, the
LEGO Group was one of the world's top-ten toy manufacturers, and in 2009 it
had reached number five in sales. In 2014, Lego beat out longtime leading toy
manufacturer Mattel to become the world's largest toy company.[2]

Megan Lotts is Art Librarian for Reference and Instruction Services at Rutgers, the State University of New Jersey.

Legos are ubiquitous in twenty-first century culture, and are commonly found in all types of libraries and makerspaces. Active learning and engagement are concepts that are prevalent in many institutions of learning, and Legos are a tool that embraces creative and explorative types of self-driven learning. Legos are being used by professionals to help children learn about emotions, by veterinarians to find creative solutions to their patients' problems, and, on one memorable occasion in 2013, by thirty-two master builders to create a 23-ton, 5.3-million-brick replica of a Star Wars Lego X-Wing fighter in New York City's Times Square.[3] Creative possibilities with Lego bricks are limitless, and these toys are changing the world in many different areas, including libraries and makerspaces. This chapter will provide tips, ideas, projects, and links to materials that can help you incorporate active learning via Lego play easily and affordably into your organizations, libraries, and makerspaces.

A Brief History of Legos

The LEGO Group was founded in Billund, Denmark, by Ole Kirk Kristiansen in 1932. In 1934, the company adopted the name "LEGO," formed from the Danish words "LEg GOdt" ("play well"). Later it was realized that in Latin the word means "I put together."[4] But it wasn't until 1949 that LEGO created the Automatic Binding Brick with four and eight studs.[5] In 1958, the LEGO stud-and-tube coupling system was patented and became what is known today as "the brick."[6] Please note that for the purposes of this chapter, I have only briefly touched on the history of the LEGO group and its many subsidiaries. However, if you would like to know more, visit the LEGO Group History web page at the LEGO website, or view the film *A LEGO Brickumentary*.[7]

Where Are Legos in Modern Times?

Legos can be found everywhere, and many individuals are using these toys in creative and innovative ways. There are individuals on Etsy (a global online community of makers who curate and sell unique items) who use Legos to make jewelry, clothing, wallets, keychains, and many other Lego-themed creations. Further, users of Pinterest (a visual bookmarking tool used to discover, save, and share creative ideas) can find creative ways to use Legos, such as building a Lego car powered by a balloon, finding creative ways to prepare for a Lego-themed party, helping children to learn math, and so on. Lego has a large presence on social media sites such as Facebook and Twitter. For instance, users can learn more about Legos on the Brick Fanatics website (www.brickfanatics.co.uk/) and Facebook page (https://www.facebook.com/brickfanatics/), United Kingdom–based sites that cover Lego news as well as reviews of Lego sets, books, and games. Legos are used by internationally known artists such as Nathan Sawaya, Ai Weiwei, and Olafur Eliasson. Legos are also found in the movies. In 2014, *The Lego Movie* grossed over 257,756,197 million dollars in the United States; the sequel, *The Lego Movie 2*, is due for release in 2018.[8] Remarkably, you can even find Lego octopi, dragons, and scuba gear washing up on the shores of the Cornish coast in Britain. These Legos are from the *Tokio Express*, a container ship that was hit by a rogue wave in 1997, and lost its cargo of sixty-two containers, one of which was filled with nearly 4.8 million Legos.[9] However, the simplest way to find out about Legos is to google the word "Lego," which will return over 200 million results discussing, using, or promoting this toy.

Major Types/Brands Available

Types of Lego Bricks

When it comes to Legos, there are four major types, and many styles and sets. The traditional brick was introduced in 1949. In 1969, the LEGO group introduced DUPLO, a series of larger bricks designed for children five and under.[10] In 1977, Lego began creating plastic rods and parts that made it easier to build more complex movable models; it named this line Lego Technic in 1984.[11] LEGO MINDSTORMs came to fruition in 1998, and included software and parts that can be used to create programmable robots.[12] Finally, in 2001, Lego created BIONICLE, which is a line of Legos that shares similarities with Lego Technic, which was targeted at children aged five through sixteen.[13] After being discontinued in 2010, Bionicle was reintroduced in 2015 as a new Lego line called Hero Factory.[14]

When it comes to Lego knockoffs, there are multiple brands available on the market, including Mega Bloks, Kre-o, Sluban, Wange, Nanoblock, Playmobil, and Star Diamond.[15] Some individuals choose to 3D print their own Lego bricks. However, it should be noted that this can be a risky endeavor; it is important to be aware of copyright issues and violations of registered trademarks before printing Legos. Many of the brick brands mentioned above can sometimes be hard to find, because some of them can be purchased at much lower prices. However, not all knockoff brands will work well with Legos. When purchasing Lego bricks from eBay, Craigslist, or at a garage sale, make sure you know what you are getting.

How to Use Legos

Legos can be used in a variety of ways, such as making the prescribed model using provided directions, or simply to create an individual's own abstract designs. Legos have been used as a medium for learning team-building skills in science, technology, and education, to make artworks, or for general free play. Playing with Legos is known to be a fun experience that makes individuals happy. Having them in your library or makerspace can provide an opportunity for many individuals to play and learn using materials they might not otherwise have access to, or cannot afford. Legos can also be an all-inclusive medium, and a great way to collaborate with others and to build community partnerships. To learn more about ways to use Legos, consider looking for ideas on Pinterest and Lego social media sites.

Free Play

One of the quickest and easiest ways to engage individuals with Legos is to place a pile of Legos in a public space and let individuals indulge in free play however they wish. This provides patrons opportunities to mix and match Legos, add to other models, and collaborate with other individuals working at the table. This also enables model makers to leave their creations on the table for other library patrons to see.

Many libraries, museums, and other organizations have more structured ways of creating free play, such as providing specific times or events in which the Legos are temporarily brought out. Lego clubs can be popular among people of all ages, and offer a great way for younger patrons to interact with older patrons. To put it simply, a box of Legos can be enough to bring together a daily, weekly, or monthly Lego club whose members will learn more about how to be creative, how to make and innovate, and how to engage with people in a community setting.

Team Building

Whether you are looking to create a community or enhance patrons' team-building skills, Lego play is a great option. Think about hosting weekly challenges that individuals can enter as a team, or potentially come together to work on as a group. You can also consider looking into Lego Serious Play (LSP), which is a methodology that was created to enhance innovation and business performance. LSP can be customized to work with groups of individuals from your library communities or with employees working within the library. LSP encourages critical thinking, team-building skills, and innovation, which can be beneficial when performing both library research and the everyday tasks of working in a library.

Designing, Prototyping, and Building

Legos can be found widely used in the fields of science, technology, and engineering. LEGO MINDSTORMS can be used to create programmable robots, as in the collaborative project between the Houston Public Library and Citizens Schools. The website LEGO Engineering presents information about the many ways teachers can bring Lego-based engineering to students, including a variety of ideas for challenges, lesson plans, and organizing Lego workshops.

In one example from 2014, UNICEF developed a reusable "LEGO-inspired brick that doubles as a food storage container and building material."[16] The bricks are packed with rice and water and distributed to individuals who have experienced a natural disaster. Once the contents are used, the bricks can be filled with materials such as sand or water and used to build a shelter, similar to how someone might build with Lego bricks. In another example, a video of a disabled turtle getting a wheelchair made from Legos went viral in early 2015, and the world was introduced to the veterinarian who conceived the solution, Dr. Carsten Plischke. Plischke explains that he used six pieces of his son's Lego bricks, as well as tortoise-safe glue, allowing the tortoise to move more easily after a metabolic bone disease rendered it unable to bear the weight of its shell.[17] However, the tortoise can move more easily now thanks to his Lego wheelchair. Both examples are simple yet brilliant uses of Legos in science and engineering. In makerspaces, projects like these can help inspire individuals to solve problems and develop their own ideas when they sit down at a table of Legos.

Teaching and Learning

In-depth information about Legos as a learning tool can be obtained at the LEGO Education website. This site provides ideas for using Legos to teach students of all ages, specifically those in preschools, and elementary and middle schools. In addition to ideas for LEGO MINDSTORMS, there are also ideas for projects like Storystarter, which engages students in writing, language, and reading. There is also more information about "BuildMe emotions," which are Lego blocks designed for preschoolers to learn more about recognizing and understanding emotions.[18]

Legos are used widely in higher education. In early 2015, the Rhode Island School of Design (RISD) announced its collaboration with LEGO Education, a division of the LEGO Group based in Billund, Denmark. The RISD course covers "the interplay between digital and analog modalities—looking at how these forms of engagement can most productively inform each other".[19] In a press release about the collaboration, RISD Interim President Rosanne Somerson stated, "LEGO Education and RISD share a deep commitment to learning through making; and to story-telling, problem-solving, and connecting. We are natural partners, and I'm excited to see what we can make and build together!"[20] At the Massachusetts Institute of Technology (MIT), students and researchers use CityScope, a 30-by-60-inch Lego model of Kendall Square in Cambridge, Massachusetts as a device on which to project data.[21] With CityScope, an "urban observatory," individuals can learn more about flows of traffic, goods, people, energy, and how people live and work in a city.[22] Although toys are not something associated with higher education, the previous examples show how Legos can be used as a tool for data collection and scholarly research.

Creating Art

Many artists use Legos as their medium. In August 2015, I visited the exhibition *The Art of the Brick* by Nathan Sawaya at the Franklin Institute in Philadelphia. The exhibition included stunning renditions, re-created in Legos, of well-known pieces of art such as the heads of Easter Island, *The Vitruvian Man* (1490) by Leonardo da Vinci, and *The Scream* (1893) by Edvard Munch. Sawaya also exhibited a room of hyperrealistic Lego sculptures that were photographed by Dean West, including a red dress, worn by a model, which was made entirely out of Legos.[23]

The Danish-Icelandic artist Olafur Eliasson is known for his use of Legos in many of his community-based, site-specific artworks. From May 29 to October 12, 2015, Eliasson exhibited "The Collectivity Project" at the High Line in New York City.[24] The High Line is "a 1.45-mile-long linear park in New York City that was built in Manhattan on an elevated section of a disused New York Central Railroad spur called the West Side Line."[25] The installation consisted of white Lego bricks that featured an imaginary cityscape conceived and designed by the public. This project invited individuals to play and create in a community setting, and was similar to projects the artist has previously completed in public squares in Tirana, Albania (2005), Oslo, Norway (2006), and Copenhagen, Denmark (2008).[26]

Tips You Need to Know

Legos in libraries can be a concept that is foreign to many individuals. Legos can be noisy, which many patrons would rather avoid when visiting a library. It is also necessary to consider the location of the Legos and the kind of signage and information to be provided to library patrons about the Legos. Although most (but not all) patrons will understand or appreciate Legos in the library, the tips below about getting started with Legos will help ensure a positive experience for all.

Acquiring Legos

Acquiring Legos can be expensive, but it does not need to be. The cheapest way to get Legos is to crowdsource them by asking for donations. You can send out an e-mail to your library staff, or consider putting up a poster or blurb on your social media sites requesting Legos for your library. You can also purchase Legos more affordably on eBay, Craigslist, or at garage sales; however, this is something you will want to work out with your administration, because these venues are probably unusual suppliers for many libraries. You can also purchase kits from the LEGO Group, but these can be expensive. However, one benefit to buying kits directly from Lego is that you know what you are getting. When purchasing Legos from eBay, Craigslist, or garage sales, you are most likely to get mixed bags of pieces, which may not always be useful if you have specific projects that you want to accomplish. However, if you are just looking to create a space for general Lego play, then the mixed-bag variety will work well.

Noise

Legos can be loud when they are dropped on the floor, and the players can be even louder when collaborating or having fun. Consider having your Legos in an area where they can be seen, but are also contained to minimize any disruptive noise. A room with a glass wall or many windows can be an ideal place—patrons can see individuals playing and creating with Legos, but not hear the noise that can accompany this type of play. If you choose to keep the Legos in an open public space, place them on a rug or in a carpeted area so that the noise is dampened when they are dropped on the floor. Further, if you are locating your Legos in an open public space, do not place them near the quiet area. If you do, however, consider buying a supply of earplugs for patrons to use if needed.

Where Are You Keeping the Legos?

When installing Legos in your library, you need to carefully consider the location. This is in part because of the noise, as mentioned previously, but also because of the potential for theft. Do not hide the Legos in a corner, but be mindful of the foot traffic in the location and the type of patrons who will be sharing the space. You want patrons to be able to see the Legos, because not all patrons will be aware there is a Lego playing station at the library. However, if you do not want the Legos to be a disruption for patrons visiting the library, you may wish to consider placing the Legos close to a service point, such as a reference or circulation desk. This can help with noise from the players, as some patrons are likely to be quieter if library staff is in the area. Further, placing the Legos in the proximity of library staff will also ensure that the staff will be on hand to answer any queries the patrons might have. Finally, as anything placed in a public space has the potential to go missing, situating Legos close to service points will help prevent theft. However, it is important to recognize that a few Legos will inevitably go missing when placed in an open public setting.

Cleaning the Legos

Legos can be cleaned in a variety of ways. You can visit to the LEGO "Customer Service" web page for useful tips on cleaning bricks under the topic "sanitizing and washing your LEGO bricks."[27] Although it might be tempting to use your washing machine or dishwasher to clean the bricks, both the LEGO Group and I advise against this. I have found the best method is to clean them in a large container such as a bucket or storage tote, using soap and water. After soaking the Legos for an hour in soapy water, drain the water and place the Legos in a thin layer on a clean towel, sheet, or blanket. Drying Legos can take time, depending on the location. A sunny location, perhaps outdoors, is ideal. However, if you dry Legos outdoors, make sure you remove any debris that may find its way into the Legos, such as twigs or leaves. Legos also retain water in their cavities. Shaking the Legos or moving them around will help drain the excess water and lessen the drying time. If you are drying Legos in a sunny area, they should take no longer than a day to dry. However, drying them on a cold day in winter might take as long as two to three days. Finally, to further enhance cleanliness of the Legos, consider providing hand sanitizer to your patrons. This provides an additional way to help keep the Legos clean while also helping the players maintain hygiene.

Good Signage

It is important to provide good signage for a Lego playing station, particularly when the station is located in a public space. Information to be featured on signage can include contact details for staff who can answer the patrons' questions, as well as a request for further Lego donations to help expand your library's collection at no cost. You can also consider offering patrons an opportunity to post to social media, by featuring a hashtag or a link to social media sites where your patrons can share their comments or ideas and pictures of models they make in your library. Signage can encourage individuals to take pictures of the models they make, rather than the Legos themselves, which discourages theft. Further, you might consider creating a comment box with pens and paper as a way for individuals to leave comments anonymously and provide feedback for assessment.

Theft

The prospect of theft is inevitable when something is placed in a public space. Legos are fun and inviting, and it can be very tempting for individuals to take their creations home. To help prevent theft, it would be advisable to select the location with care, as previously noted. Is the area you are considering for your library's station a potential high theft zone? Are there staff members around who can monitor the Legos carefully? Do you use humorous signage that discourages theft? If there are items from your Lego collection that are expensive or indispensable, make sure to keep those in a separate container that you only use for special events or build activities.

How Libraries are Using Legos

Public Library Projects

Lego Block Parties ————————————————————————————————————

Legos are used in public libraries in a variety of ways. They are commonly used for block parties, family Lego events, science, technology, engineering, arts, and math (STEAM) learning events, as well as in many makerspaces. Block parties are events where individuals come together to play with Legos at a specific time and place. At the Radnor Memorial Library in Wayne, Pennsylvania, as many as fifty patrons, from toddlers to teens under the age of fourteen, show up for the block party on the last Sunday of each month from 1:30 to 3:00 p.m.[28] Lego block parties can be a space for individuals to play, have fun, and engage with other members within their communities.

Lego Junior Makerspaces

In 2014, the Association for Library Service to Children (ALSC) and LEGO Systems, a North American division of the LEGO group, announced that they would work together to bring Junior Maker Spaces to libraries across the country. As stated in the press release, junior makerspaces are areas that provide an opportunity for children from ages four through six to create and make.[29] Over 750 libraries nationwide received a tool kit that included 10,000 Lego bricks, an activity guide, and an inspirational poster.[30] This project was inspired by the hope that play and the use of imagination would encourage young children to become makers, sharers, and innovative problem-solvers.

Lego Robots

The Houston Public Library has been using LEGO MINDSTORMS to interact with its teen community. As stated on the Lego website, "LEGO MIND-STORMS is a programmable robotics construction set that gives you the power to build, program, and command your own LEGO robots."[31] In one instance, the Houston Public Library partnered with Citizens Schools to create a ten-week afterschool LEGO MINDSTORMS program for sixth graders. Each week, the Library transports the materials needed for the program, including Lego kits and laptop computers, to the middle school. The librarians begin by providing information on how robots are used in the real world, and then students work in groups of three or four to create their own robots. At the end of the ten-week program, the participants present their work to their parents and their peers.[32] Through this collaboration, the students learn more about the library, as well as how to innovate, make, and share ideas. The library also further integrates itself into the local community and teaches teenagers how to become creative problem-solvers and team players—while the teens themselves get to build a robot.

Academic Library Projects

Finals Stressbusters

Although toys might not be considered to have a place in higher education, today, Legos are found in many academic libraries. Perhaps the most common use of Legos in college libraries is during the finals events usually known as "Stressbusters." During this event, Legos are often left out for patrons to help them slow down, take a break from their studies, and maybe even make new friends. In December 2015, the Walter Library at the University of Minnesota offered free snacks, Legos, and making events for patrons to participate in during stressbusting season at the end of the semester.

Legos and Instruction

For its Open Access week in October 2015, the Cabell Library at Virginia Commonwealth University (VCU) used Legos to help students better understand the benefits of open access. Legos were left out in the library for five days for students to build, create, and remix in collaboration with library employees and patrons. From this event, patrons also had an opportunity to work together and learn as a community, which can be beneficial to any library or college campus. Although VCU purchased its Legos specifically for this project, it has future plans to use Legos in more creative ways.

Stop-Motion Films

In Denmark, the Copenhagen University Library has created a stop-motion movie in which it uses Legos to introduce new students and patrons to the library system. The video is roughly two minutes and fifty-nine seconds long, and teaches viewers about "the basic need-to-know stuff like locations, opening hours, course literature print, wifi, etc." as well as a bit more about what can happen at the Copenhagen University Libraries.[33] Using toys like Legos that are popular in modern culture can be a great way to connect with students in a playful and humorous way.

Training Sessions ——————————————————————————

In the United Kingdom, University Campus Suffolk (UCS) introduced Lego Serious Play (LSP), a methodology created to enhance innovation and business performance, into its academic and library support training sessions with their students. In addition, I have used LSP as a method to teach 245 academic library faculty and staff more about teamwork, the power of making, and the potential for makerspaces in academic libraries. I also installed the Rutgers Art Library Lego Playing Station in the summer of 2014 as a means to connect with students from the Rutgers community via active learning techniques aimed at teaching them more about information literacy and the possibilities in an academic research library.

Projects

Free Play/Pop-Up Play/Stressbusters ——————————————————

You do not need much to start a pop-up, free play, or Lego stress-busting event. Ideally, you would need somewhere between 40 to 60 pounds of Legos, which is equivalent to roughly four or five 5-gallon buckets full of Legos. However, a shoebox full of Legos will suffice for two or three people to create something and have a good time. You would need to consider who might be using your Legos. For instance, it would be inadvisable to put out a pile of Legos for "Toddler Story Time" afternoons, for which age-appropriate tools such as Duplos or Mega Bloks would be better suited. You will also need a table, chairs, signage, and containers to hold the Legos. If you do not have a table to use, you can try putting down a sheet, blanket, or mats to provide a space in which Legos can be easily picked up after your event. Although you can consider using social media to publicize your Lego event, Legos sell themselves—if left in a space, they will attract players and model-makers. Finally, you should think about noise levels and consider placing your Lego play event in a carpeted area that is suited to hosting noisy events. Ultimately, however, all you need to host Lego free play are some Legos, a table and chairs, and patrons.

Building a Full-Time Lego Playing Station ——————————————

Building a full-time Lego playing station in your library is like creating a pop-up free play Lego space. You will need Legos, a table, chairs, and some signage. You will also want to come up with some programming and outreach ideas to engage the community. Further, attracting good publicity can help boost awareness of the Lego-playing station. Make sure you have your station located in a visible area, because patrons who see people playing with Legos will often be inspired to explore the possibilities offered by the library. When creating your full-time station, ask yourself what your goals are. Whom are you trying to engage, and what types of events might be of interest? For instance, consider starting a weekly or monthly club. Think about who might be potential partners or which organizations might be interested in using the Legos for special events. Plan contests or activities around the Legos, such as a "create your own character" coloring contest, a "build the best library ever out of Legos," contest, or a "build the tallest tower with the least number of Legos" contest. Use social media and advertising to help boost your play station's presence, and post pictures of patrons using Legos on your social media sites. But make sure to get patrons' permission and keep in tune with your library's photography policies. In short, building a full-time Lego playing station is not particularly different than a pop-up free play event, with the exception that it provides individuals with access to materials that they might want to use any time the library is open.

"Create Your Own Character" Coloring Contest

If you are looking for an inexpensive and creative way to engage your patrons' interest, and you do not have funding to purchase Legos, you can consider hosting a "create your own character" coloring contest. All you need for this contest are black-and-white printouts of a Lego character, coloring tools such as crayons, markers, or colored pencils, and some publicity. In fact, you do not have to make this a contest, but incentives can often help draw participation. Ideally, you will need a wall, a bulletin board, or some type of flat space where you can display the entries; you can also create a digital collection of the entries for your library's website or social media pages. When selecting your blank Lego character for printing, make sure you are aware of copyright issues; cite your image if necessary. Further, consider accepting digital submissions from those patrons who like to create and color, but are unable to physically make it to the library. If you want to help boost the number of participating patrons, consider partnering with a local school or organization that might be interested in a contest of this nature. Finally, if you choose to make it a contest, find some local judges or patrons who can provide unbiased judgment. If you are not able to provide prizes, you can perhaps consider purchasing or making award ribbons.

Best Library Contest ───

To engage your patrons about Legos and to learn more about their needs and wants, I recommend hosting a "create your own library out of Legos" contest. To start this contest, you would need a Lego playing area, which (as noted previously) can be a permanent or temporary space. Think about how long you want to run your contest and how you will promote it. Ideally, you should leave your Legos out for the entire run of the contest, thus providing access to patrons any time the library is open. Further, you will need to consider how individuals will submit the models they have created for the contest. Will they submit digital images or physical models? How will you archive them for posterity? Will there be prizes for the contest, or will bragging rights and a picture in a library media story be reward enough for patrons? Alternately, there is perhaps no need to have winners; instead, a digital collection of images created by participants can be hosted on the library website or social media pages. An event of this nature can also be an opportunity to reach out to users who are not able to come to the library, because they can use their own collections of Legos at home, and submit a digital image. Regardless of how you choose to run or display the creations made in the contest, you will assuredly learn more about your patron's needs and wants by assessing their models. Figure 10.1 shows a group of students from a Rutgers Mason Gross Visual Arts Printmaking course who entered a "create the best library ever" contest hosted by the Rutgers University Art Library.

FIGURE 10.1

Mason Gross Printmaking Class

Photo by Megan Lotts, 2014. Used with permission.

Creating a Lego Stop-Motion Movie

Creating a Lego stop-motion movie may seem like a daunting task, but it can be easily accomplished with a device that captures video, a tripod, a computer, free software used to create your movie, a small-to-medium learning curve, an idea for a story, and some Legos.

Before you begin this task, it would be advisable to do some initial research on existing stop-motion movies to get an idea of the different types of software available and to select what would work best for your needs. Consider writing a script and creating a storyboard so that you have an idea of what your film might look like. Run some initial tests to make sure you have all the equipment you need, that it is in proper working order, and that you understand how to use the software you will be working with. The Copenhagen University Library created a two-minute and fifty-nine-second-long video using an iPhone 5, the free stop-motion app iMotion, and a MacBook. It took roughly sixty hours to create the film, which cost around $75 to purchase the Legos featured in it.[34] Further, you should ensure you check out Lego stop-motion movies on YouTube, where you will find not only good examples but also many short films on how to create your own Lego stop-motion film.

Lego Workshops and Lego Serious Play

If you are looking to build community, enhance teamwork skills, or creatively solve a problem, you can consider hosting a Lego workshop. This could be for patrons of the library, employees who work for the library, or local organizations who are looking for a lively experience. You can either hire a professional Lego Serious Play (LSP) facilitator or visit the LSP website to learn more about the process. Alternately, you may consider creating your own workshop from scratch, using ideas from Pinterest, such as a competition for creating a Lego balloon-powered car to go the farthest, building the tallest tower with the fewest number of pieces.

For a workshop, you can either use a hodgepodge of Legos that you have already acquired for your library or makerspace, or purchase LSP Lego kits from the LEGO Group directly. The number of Legos needed depends on the number of participants in a workshop. You will want to have enough Legos so participants have many different pieces to choose from. But don't provide so many that the participants will feel overwhelmed by too many choices. I have found that a workshop can ideally accommodate eight to twelve participants, depending on the space in which it is held. It is necessary to have enough room for individuals to work solo as well as in groups, and to move around the room to view each other's creations. There is no one formula for hosting a Lego workshop. It is necessary to keep in mind that you will learn on the go, and figure out what works best for your library or the space that you are using.

In the fall of 2015, I took a 6,000-mile road trip with 100 pounds of Legos in my car to visit twenty public academic research libraries to facilitate Lego workshops based on the LSP methodology. My assistant and I worked with 245 academic library faculty and staff to learn more about creative problem-solving, innovation, and teamwork via active learning exercises using Legos. Activities from this workshop included creating and drawing a library superhero, building models that depict who you are in your home or work life, what makes your library awesome, and what challenges you face at work, and finally, working in groups to build a model of the "best library ever." Throughout the workshop, participants were invited to share their models and ideas, and to work together more cohesively as a team (see figure 10.2). To learn more about LSP in practice and the #LeGOMAKE study, the reader is encouraged to read my article, "On the Road, Playing with LEGO, and Learning about the Library, Part Two."[35]

FIGURE 10.2

Image from #LeGOMAKE Tour Workshop

Photo by Megan Lotts, 2015. Used with permission.

Conclusion

Legos offer the means to build a low-cost pop-up or permanent station in your library or makerspace that encourages creative thinking, teamwork, and innovation. Legos can help patrons embrace the ideas of community and bring together different groups of individuals who might not have the opportunity to otherwise connect with each other. Active learning with Legos can be used for activities for children as well as adults, and be a great way to encourage interaction and teamwork amongst patrons of all ages. Legos can comprise a three-dimensional language that uses hands-on active learning to communicate and build critical thinking skills, while also being a mode of activity that makes people happy. Although you do not need a lot of money to get a Lego movement going in your library or makerspace, you will need time and space.

Implementing a culture of creativity in your library encourages lifelong hands-on learning. Makerspaces encourage patrons to try new ideas and create new solutions in a self-driven learning environment. Legos can be a catalyst for building bridges and making connections with patrons from local communities. These connections can lead to a greater understanding of what is possible in a library or makerspace and how the act of making can help embrace a culture of creativity. If you are looking for an inexpensive, easy-to-use, easy-to-manage, colorful, fun, and active learning tool for all ages, consider adding Legos to your library or makerspace.

NOTES

1. Jesus Diaz, "Everything You Always Wanted to Know About Lego," June 26, 2008, http://lego.gizmodo.com/5019797/everything-you-always-wanted-to-know-about-lego.
2. Jacob Davidson, "Lego Is Now the Largest Toy Company in The World," *Money*, September 4, 2010, http://time.com/money/3268065/lego-largest-toy-company-mattel/.
3. Angela Watercutter, "This 23-Ton, 5.3-Million-Brick X-Wing Is the Biggest Lego Model Ever," *Wired*, May 23, 2013, www.wired.com/2013/05/largest-lego-x-wing/.
4. Tine Froberg Mortensen, "LEGO History Timeline," www.lego.com/en-us/aboutus/lego-group/the_lego_history.
5. Ibid.
6. Ibid.
7. *A LEGO Brickumentary*, directed by Kief Davidson and Daniel Junge (2014), DVD.
8. *Internet Movie Database*, s.v. "The Lego Movie," www.imdb.com/title/tt1490017/.

9. Nicholas Reilly, "Lego Is Still Washing Up on Britain's Shores, Almost 18 Years after Falling Off a Container Ship," *Metro*, January 3, 2015, http://metro.co.uk/2015/01/03/lego-is-still-washing-up-on-britains-shores-almost-18-years-after-falling-off-a-container-ship-5008359/.

10. Tine Mortensen, "Timeline 1960–1969," www.lego.com/en-us/aboutus/lego-group/the_lego_history/1960.

11. *Wikipedia, The Free Encyclopedia*, s.v. "Lego Technic," https://en.wikipedia.org/wiki/Lego_Technic.

12. Tine Mortensen, "Timeline 1990–1999," www.lego.com/en-us/aboutus/lego-group/the_lego_history/1990.

13. *Wikipedia, The Free Encyclopedia*, s.v. "Bionicle," https://en.wikipedia.org/wiki/Bionicle.

14. ———, s.v. "Hero Factory," https://en.wikipedia.org/wiki/Hero_Factory.

15. Jayvee Fernandez, "Lego Knock-Offs You Should Check Out," http://81ist.ph/site/articles/8-lego-knock-offs-you-should-check-out-105.

16. Tafline Laylin, "UNICEF's Clever LEGO-Inspired Bricks Provide Food, Water, and Shelter to Disaster Victims," *Inhabitat.* http://inhabitat.com/unicefs-amazing-lego-inspired-bricks-carry-food-and-water-to-disaster-victims/.

17. Kimberly Yam, "Tortoise Gets Wheelchair Made from Legos, Skates Around Like a Pro," *Huffpost Good News.* January 12, 2015, www.huffingtonpost.com/2015/01/12/tortoise-lego-wheelchair-_n_6458142.html.

18. "LEGO Education," https://education.lego.com/en-us.

19. "Rhode Island School of Design Kicks off Collaboration with LEGO Education," PR Web, January 14, 2015, www.prweb.com/releases/2015/01/prweb12438576.htm.

20. Ibid.

21. Craille Maguire Gillies, "Lego: Can This Most Analogue of Toys Really Be a Modern Urban Planning Tool?" *The Guardian*, December 18, 2014, www.theguardian.com/cities/2014/dec/18/lego-toys-urban-planning-tool-architects-mit.

22. Ibid.

23. "Nathan Sawaya's Hyper Realistic LEGO Sculptures Photographed by Dean West," *Designboom.* www.designboom.com/art/in-pieces-nathan-sawayas-hyper-realistic-lego-sculptures-photographed-by-dean-west/.

24. Olafur Eliasson, "The Collectivity Project," *High Line Art,* http://art.thehighline.org/project/olafureliasson/.

25. *Wikipedia, The Free Encyclopedia*, s.v. "High Line (New York City)," https://en.wikipedia.org/wiki/High_Line_%28New_York_City%29.

26. Eliasson, "Collectivity."

27. LEGO Customer Service. Sanitizing and Washing LEGO Bricks. wwwsecure.us.lego.com/en-us/service/help-topics.

28. Abbe Klebanoff, "Block Party: Legos in the Library," *School Library Journal*, July 1, 2009, www.slj.com/2009/07/programs/block-party-legos-in-the-library/#_.

29. Ison, Joanna, "ALSC and LEGO Systems Partner to Create Junior Maker Spaces," *ALA News*, July 15, 2014, www.ala.org/news/press-releases/2014/07/alsc-and-lego-systems -partner-create-junior-maker-spaces.

30. Ibid.

31. "What Is LEGO MINDSTORMS?" www.lego.com/en-us/mindstorms/support.

32. Rachel Stout, "Hand in Hand: Teens, Tech, and Community Engagement," *Young Adult Library Services* 13, no. 2 (2015).

33. *Welcome to Copenhagen University Library*, directed by Christian Lauersen, Copenhagen University Libraries, 2015. www.youtube.com/watch?v=kgABWpEhY5A.

34. Christian Mortensen, *The University Library Brick by Brick—A LEGO Library Movie*. https://christianlauersen.net/2015/09/08/the-university-library-brick-by-brick-a-lego -library-movie/.

35. Megan Lotts, "On the Road, Playing with LEGO, and Learning about the Library, Part Two," *Journal of Library Administration* 56, no. 5 (2009).

littleBits, Makey Makey, Chibitronics, and More
Circuitry Projects for Libraries

WENDY HARROP

lthough electricity and circuitry have always been a part of the school science curriculum, they have not historically been found in libraries, whether school or public. But with the integration of makerspaces and libraries, they now are. Several circuitry kits have become must-have components in library and school makerspaces, and for very good reasons. They are straightforward, user friendly, and offer immediate success, which keeps users engaged and motivated. But the look of circuit kits has also changed—students are learning about electricity through a variety of conductive materials—circuit stickers, conductive ink and paint, magnetic circuit components, and more. This has opened doors for students to explore and create a wide variety of projects incorporating circuits and electricity.

What Are the Major Brands Available?

Two of the more popular circuit kits are Makey Makey boards and littleBits kits. These have quickly become mainstream equipment in makerspaces. One of the

Wendy Harrop is Learning Resource Teacher at Summit Elementary School at Oconomowoc School District.

reasons for their success is that they are very versatile—students both young and old can find ways to use and learn from these kits. Applications range from the very basic to very advanced programming.

Makey Makey

Let's start by looking at the Makey Makey kit by JoyLabz (see figure 11.1). One of the products biggest advantages is that it is inexpensive, priced at about $50.00 per kit. If a school or library is developing a makerspace on a small budget, this is a great starting point. The Makey Makey kit comes with everything you need to get started—the board, seven alligator clips, six wires, and a USB cable to connect to your computer. Makey Makeys can be run off any computer with a USB port, regardless of the operating system. The Makey Makey board allows users to replace buttons on their keyboards with everyday objects (anything from fruit to Play-Doh). This allows users to interact with the computer by touching these objects to complete a circuit. For young learners, this is a high-interest, hands-on method to learn about circuits and conductors. JoyLabz provides many online programs that allow students to play sounds, games, and more using whatever conductors they choose (even high-fiving a classmate).

FIGURE 11.1

Makey Makey Kit by JoyLabz

To get started, the board needs to be connected to a computer using the USB cable. It will be readily apparent that the board is receiving power, because a green light will begin blinking if it is connected correctly. One wire needs to be connected to "Earth" on the board, and the user needs to stay in contact with that wire. Other wires can be connected to the desired ports on the Makey Makey board (all clearly labeled with the name of the key on the keyboard to which they correspond). When the other end of that wire is touched (while still in contact with Earth), the circuit is closed, and that key is activated. There are several fun and engaging programs already online that set each key to play a different sound or control a character in a game. Within minutes of opening the box, a student can be using the Makey Makey piano or drum set to create music by touching objects that are connected to the various keys.

Students who understand basic circuitry can take the Makey Makey to the next level by integrating it with Scratch on their computers. Rather than using the precoded programs provided by JoyLabz, students can write the code themselves for what they want their Makey Makey to do. They can program a project to play music and sound effects, or even to record their voices to provide narration at the touch of a button (or banana, or whatever). Students can use the graphite from their pencil as their conductors, allowing them to bring pencil sketches and drawings to life by attaching a Makey Makey and writing code in Scratch. This is also perfect for creating interactive posters, displays, and board games.

More advanced programmers can use the back side of the board, which gives options for controlling additional keys on the keyboard and mouse controls by using Arduino Leonardo firmware. But users need not have any experience with Arduinos to be able to use the Makey Makey. The back of the board can also be run in Arduino Mode, which allows it to run motors and LED lights, among other add-ons.

littleBits

Another type of circuitry kit rapidly making its way into school and library makerspaces is littleBits. littleBits are magnetic circuit components that are color coded for specific purposes (input bits, like buttons or switches, are pink; power source is blue; output bits, like motors and buzzers are green; etc.) Pieces can be magnetically joined together to make a variety of circuits to be used independently or to power something else.

FIGURE 11.2

littleBits Magnetic Circuit Components

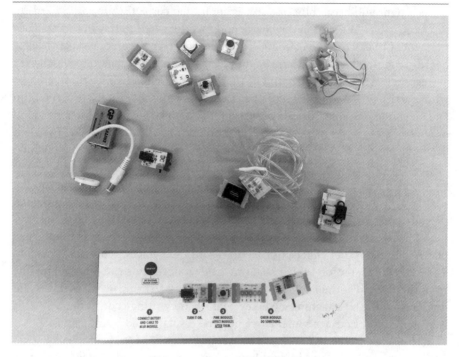

The littleBits Base Kit, the simplest place to start, contains ten basic bits and a thirty-page book of ideas and activities to accomplish with them (see figure 11.2). There are add-on kits, larger kits, and even a Pro Library, designed specifically for schools and makerspaces, which comes with 304 bits, accessories, and a reference book to help get you started.

To get started with a littleBits creation, a power bit (which is always blue), is required—these can be connected to 3V coin batteries or 9V batteries, depending on the kit and the bit being used. From there, the bits will vary based on what the circuit is intended to do. Will the circuit turn on a light, buzzer, fan, or motor (green bits)? Will it go on with a switch, a button, or a light or sound sensor (pink)? Are longer wires needed (orange)?

The designers behind littleBits are very much in tune with what their users want to do and what other products they are using. This has resulted in littleBits creating a bit that is a Makey Makey, and another that can be programmed with Arduino software, a Lego brick adaptor, and Scratch extensions.

Snap Circuits

For those wanting to explore the many different parts of more elaborate circuits in a way that is very accessible, even for young learners, a great starting point is Snap Circuits, by Elenco (see figure 11.3). There are several different Snap Circuits base kits, containing anywhere from thirty to one hundred parts that all snap on to a plastic base board.

Snap Circuits by Elenco

Kits come with a book of hundreds of project ideas and instructions, but it is also very easy for students to create projects of their own design once they understand the basics of the circuits (see figure 11.4). Elenco also offers accessories, upgrade kits, and student/teacher guides to go with the kits. Snap Circuits projects from their instruction book are easy enough for makers as young as seven or eight years old. However, the individual snap components are a bit more complex, involving resistors (components designed to regulate the flow of the electricity in the circuit) and capacitors (components that control and filter the electrical flow, such as the radio transmitter piece of the Snap Circuit kit). Using the various components to create electrical designs outside of those in the book is better suited for older users.

FIGURE 11.4

FIGURE 11.4

Students Snap Pieces Together to Complete Circuits

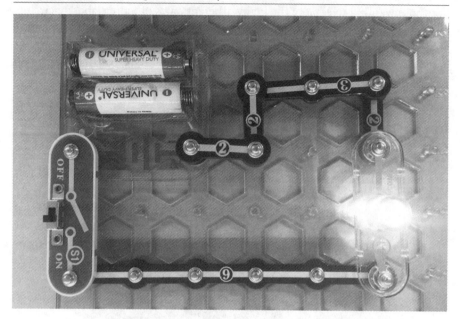

Chibitronics Sticker Lights

Chibitronics produces a product called Circuit Stickers—adhesive LED lights, which can be combined with coin batteries and copper tape to create circuits, and adhered to surfaces for several uses. Circuit Stickers are a great way to teach simple and parallel circuits, as well as switches. There are printable templates available online, and the kit comes with a book of these same templates as well. It guides users through the placement of all the elements of the circuit to make it successfully light up. One benefit to using Circuit Stickers over the traditional circuit kit, which involves bulbs, bulb holders, batteries, battery holders, and wires, is that the components are easier to place because the copper tape is adhesive. The basic kit contains a roll of the copper tape, a few coin batteries, a book of instructions and templates, and a few pages of the LED stickers (see figure 11.5). There are also add-on kits for more advanced users. These contain lights that blink, fade, or pulse like a heartbeat; light and sound sensors and timer stickers to add on to circuits.

FIGURE 11.5

Chibitronics LED Sticker Circuits

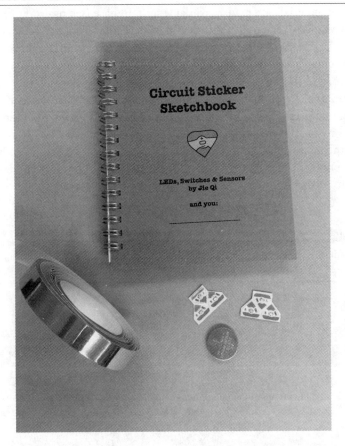

Circuit Stickers can be integrated into many subjects. The most obvious use for them would be for a science unit on circuitry, to demonstrate how a circuit works, and to show the necessary components to make the lights illuminate (imagine the impact of an assessment that allows students to demonstrate on paper how to create a functional circuit rather than one in which you are labeling parts of a diagram). The LED stickers are also great for creating interactive artwork, posters, and diagrams that light up when a part of it is pushed, or that use a sensor to create light when someone turns the page or opens a flap.

Conductive Materials

Conductive materials are readily available for purchase (see figure 11.6). Copper conductive tape is very useful for creating interactive displays, posters, games, and artwork. It is also useful for making nonconductive materials able to conduct electricity. Copper tape pairs well with the Makey Makey to make everyday objects conductive, and thus controllable through the Makey Makey board.

There are also conductive paint and conductive pens that write in the conductive paint. Users can paint or draw in the conductive paint and then connect their lines to a battery and a bulb or some other output device to "electrify" their writing and painting. The most popular manufacturer of these products is a company out of England called Bare Conductive. It also produces accessories to help the user integrate the conductive paint into larger projects.

FIGURE 11.6

Basic Conductive Materials to Help Students Explore Circuitry in the Library Makerspace

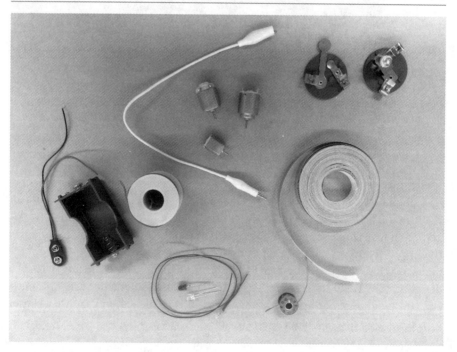

How to Use Circuitry Kits

For students to be able to successfully use circuitry kits, they need to understand the necessary components of an electrical circuit—the power source, the positive and negative terminals of the battery and the output item, the path of the electricity, the concept of open and closed circuits and of conductors and insulators. Circuitry kits are a great way to explore these, but without some introduction to the idea, students are likely to become frustrated if they are not able to make anything happen.

At the very least, students need to understand the basic components needed to create a complete electrical circuit:

- power source (battery, USB plug, electrical cord)
- output device (lightbulb, motor, fan, buzzer, etc.)
- conductive path

If you want students to apply circuitry to their projects, they would also benefit from understanding a bit more in-depth information:

- conductors versus insulators
- open versus closed circuits
- series versus parallel circuit
- resistors, transistors, and capacitors (what they are, what they do, and how and when to use them)

To facilitate exploration and understanding of circuitry, the aforementioned kits would be sufficient. Students can use the kits to learn about electricity and circuits, and to experiment with changing various components to test the impact on the circuit. It is also important to have a selection of different materials, both conductive and insulating, to use in testing the flow of electricity. Makerspaces should also be stocked with wires of different lengths (those with alligator tips on their ends are helpful for young children) and gauges. Spaces should also have a variety of battery holders, LED bulbs, mini light bulbs, bulb holders, and switches. All of these can be found easily and purchased for very reasonable prices online.

There is value in introducing the concept of electricity and circuitry just by exploring and testing materials, but there are also wonderful ways to introduce the information in a whole-group demonstration. One of the most entertaining, engaging, and effective ways to demonstrate circuitry with a large group is with the Makey Makey. Using something very accessible, like the Makey Makey Piano program online (http://makeymakey.com/piano/), facilitators can start with a basic circuit, using one conductive object (a paper clip, a strip of foil, a wire) to complete the circuit, demonstrated by piano notes playing from the computer. Then facilitators can add themselves into the circuit, showing that the electricity is now traveling through their bodies to complete the circuit, so that electricity is flowing, and the piano is still playing. One by one, kids can be added to the chain by holding hands, touching elbows or fingers, thus extending the circuit and still making the piano play. The group can explore by letting go of each other's hands to demonstrate open circuits, high-fiving to close a circuit, and touching hair or clothes instead of skin, to demonstrate conductors versus insulators. Kids find this activity mesmerizing, and they walk away from it able to explain what variables need to be in place for them to play the piano. (And as a side note, adults are equally impressed, which makes it a great activity for open houses, demonstrations, and presentations.) Once they understand the basics, they will be able to explore the circuitry equipment with more success and troubleshoot without frustration if their circuits don't work. There will be some students who will always choose to defer to the instruction books when they build circuits with the kits, but other students will immediately take off with the concept and start thinking about what kinds of robots and machines they can build. and what they want them to do.

With the growth in popularity of these kits, there has also been a rise in compatibility between the components in circuitry kits and some of the more popular coding programs such as Scratch and Arduino. Once students learn to write basic code in these programs, they can plug in creations they've made from the kits and control them with the code. This allows them to add sound; control when motors, lights, or other output items turn on and off; or add programmed responses to sensors included in their circuits.

Tips and Troubleshooting

With any circuitry project, students will know immediately whether they have successfully created a circuit. If they connect all the components and do not see results (e.g., the bulb doesn't light up or the motor doesn't go on), there are a few questions to guide them through when they try to find the problem.

- Does the battery work, or is it dead? Students can test the battery in a circuit you know works, or even test the battery and the bulb/motor without any other components to ensure that it works in that setup.

- Does the output component work? Is the bulb burned out, or does the motor turn when it is in a different circuit? These can be tested as described above.
- Is there a break anywhere in the circuit? This could be a physical gap or just a connection through an insulating material rather than a conductive material.
- Is there a short circuit anywhere in the electricity flow? Is there a path for the electricity to follow but no output, thus creating an increase of flow of electrons causing heat and possibly depletion of battery power?
- Is the path of the electricity flowing from positive to negative through the circuit? Switching the direction of the battery often fixes this problem. Most of the components in the kits will clearly indicate which side of a component is positive and which is negative, so that users can check the path.

Much of the learning about circuitry and how to correctly set up a circuit can take place during the troubleshooting stage of a project. Students will develop a deeper understanding of how electricity flows in a circuit by following the path and checking each part of the circuit to be sure it is working.

In addition to kits, there are many materials that complement the circuit kits and are easily available and inexpensive. Once the students have their circuits working, it's important to them to have things to "run"—makerspaces should have a variety of motors, batteries, and battery holders; bulbs and bulb holders; and wheels, axles, propellers, wires, and other conductive materials. It's also helpful to have things like boxes, blocks, and Legos to build objects that will contain the motors, lights or wheels.

> **TIP** For younger students, LED bulbs and coin batteries are very useful—they are inexpensive, versatile, and easy to integrate into projects..

How Libraries Are Using Circuit Kits

One of the benefits of circuit kits like the littleBits, the Snap Circuit kits, and Makey Makeys, is that they are perfect for freely exploring. All come with books of suggested projects and step-by-step instructions. The support websites for these various kits also have extensive galleries of tutorial videos and additional project ideas. This makes them extremely useful for school and library makerspaces, especially for short events like Maker Nights at public libraries, family STEAM Nights at schools, or pop-up makerspaces. The kits can be placed out on the table with the books, and families or students can just walk up and explore.

Public libraries that don't have dedicated makerspaces are often hosting Maker Nights. These are periodic events where patrons of all ages are invited to drop in and make something. In addition to providing a variety of building materials for use in design projects, these nights often feature Legos and circuitry kits. Schools that don't have dedicated makerspaces are starting to develop mobile makerspaces—carts on wheels that contain a variety of kits, materials, and tools. Sometimes these carts are "themed"—a circuits cart might contain only circuitry kits and materials, whereas a creativity cart might be made of design materials. It might make sense just to offer bins and boxes of all sorts of materials. One advantage of the mobile makerspace cart is that a teacher can move it into the classroom and use it within a lesson, integrating making into the curriculum in a very organic way. This is not just limited to science lessons. Teachers and students can create activities that have an interactive answer board that will tell them if they choose the right answer. For example, students can create a math fact review using a Makey Makey kit and balls of playdough. Using Scratch, they can design a question-and-answer game and program it so that the responses to each question are color coded. Then, when the correct color of playdough is touched, the computer will respond with a cheer or a certain tone, but if the wrong playdough is touched, it will not make a sound, or it will buzz, or say "try again" or give similar feedback.

In a formal makerspace, circuitry can be used as part of a design challenge. When creating a design challenge, you don't want to set too many restrictions or create too many rules, so your challenge could be something along the lines of "design something that either lights up or has a part controlled by electricity." This leaves the choice of materials, circuits, and types of object wide open for students, allowing them to work at their own comfort and to think creatively about how to solve the problem. Students who need more guidance can use the kits and the instruction manuals to help them be successful, where students who have a greater understanding of circuitry and conductivity can use components from the kits or separate materials to create something of their own design. This is truly individualized learning.

Projects

Interactive Models

MATERIALS NEEDED

- Makey Makey
- computer

- Scratch coding program
- variety of design materials (cardboard, Model Magic, Paper, Dough, etc.)

At some point in their school careers, all students have designed a diorama, a model, or a display. With circuitry kits, those projects can become interactive, increasing student interest and engagement in the project and enhancing the end product. Although there are limitless variations on this project, and it could easily be adapted for any subject, the project explained here is a second-grade animal-research project.

To Create Interactive Models: Have students build a model of an animal using Model Magic, dough, or other materials of their choosing. Connect the Makey Makey board to the model, using one wire and keyboard connection for each sound desired. Ensure that the circuit is complete by following the path starting with Earth on the Makey Makey board and flowing through the model and back to whomever is holding the wire connected to Earth.

On the computer, log in to Scratch (scratch.mit.edu) and click on "Create" to start a new project. For each desired sound, add one "Control" block (brown) and one "Sound" block (purple). Scratch has a library of prerecorded sound files, or new sounds can be recorded and added to the user's library. If the Makey Makey is connected to the space bar, then the brown block chosen should be set to specify that "when the space bar is clicked" the designated sound will be played. Hold on to the wire that is connected to Earth, and touch the part of the model that is connected to the desired part of the Makey Makey board. This should cause the sound file to play.

Instead of sounds, students could also record narration or music to be played when the model is touched.

Light-Up Board Games

MATERIALS NEEDED

- copper tape
- Circuit Stickers or LED lights
- coin batteries
- posterboard or cardboard

Student understanding can be assessed using an interactive question-and-answer board.

To Create Interactive Board Games: Create a game mat/board on cardboard or poster board. Write questions on cards or stickers attached to the game mat.

Create a circuit using copper tape and a Circuit light sticker (LED bulbs work as well if Circuit Stickers aren't available). There should be a separate circuit running to each of the questions. Create windows or tabs with possible answers, which are folded up until the question is asked. When the tabs are up, the circuit is open and the LED is dark. The correct answer should have copper tape on the back of it as well, so that when it is pushed down it closes the circuit and causes the light to illuminate. When the correct one is pushed down, it closes the circuit and makes the sticker light up. This is a great way for students to review or for teachers to assess learning.

These board game projects can be used with any subject material simply by changing the types of questions and answers involved, and making them appropriate for students of different ages studying many curricular areas.

Interactive Artwork with Paper Circuits

MATERIALS NEEDED

- copper tape
- painting or drawing materials
- conductive ink (Bare Conductive Electric Ink/Paint)
- graphite pencils
- clear tape
- coin batteries (3V)

Although visually impressive, paper circuits are versatile and simple to create. They are a great way to synthesize art and technology without the need for large kits. Students will need to decide if they want their circuits to be a part of their design (using copper tape, graphite pencils, or conductive ink) or if they want it to be hidden by running the copper tape on the backside of the paper.

Place the bulbs and secure them with clear tape. Trace the path of the circuit, deciding where the battery will go.

> **TIP** It works best to have the battery on a folded-down corner or a cut-away "window" of the paper. Then the circuit can be turned on by folding the paper back down to touch the battery to the circuit.

Before creating the actual work of art, it is important to place the circuit by adhering the copper tape to the circuit path or creating a thick, heavy line of graphite or conductive ink. Once the circuit is created, students can design the rest of the piece, using regular materials. To test the circuit, attach the battery, paying attention to the polarity of the LED and the polarity of the battery. When the circuit is closed, the bulbs should illuminate.

Beginner Robots with littleBits

MATERIALS NEEDED

- littleBits
- variety of recycled materials to create robots
- batteries
- Anything can be made into a robot by adding a moving or automated part to it. Using the various output bits in a littleBits kit, students can be introduced to robotics in an easy and creative way. The integration of littleBits into this project allows for many possible types of robots.

To Create littleBits Robots: Build a robot with some part that will be controlled with a circuit to either light up or move. Design and materials don't matter, and the task can be as simple or as complicated as desired. Attach the green (output) bit of choice to the robot so that it performs the desired task; for example, when the motor is turned on, it will make the robot's pennant spin around, or when the sensor picks up sound, the robot's head will light up. Use the magnetic connectors on the bits to attach (at the very least) a blue power source bit and (if needed) orange wire bits to extend the reach of the bits, and a pink input bit with a sensor or a button to turn the circuit on and off.

Illuminated Greeting Cards

MATERIALS NEEDED

- cardstock or paper
- copper tape
- wire
- coin battery (3V)
- LED mini-lights

To Create Illuminated Greeting Cards: Design the outside of the card with whatever materials and decoration are desired. Poke a small hole where the light(s) will go and affix the LED mini-bulbs by using clear tape on the back to hold the leads in place. Note which lead is the shorter and which is the longer.

Connect the leads to where the battery will go with copper tape. The rough side of the battery will need to end up in contact with the shorter lead on the LED bulb. Tape or glue a flap to the inside of the card that will hold the battery and a short length of copper tape that runs under the taped down side of the coin battery. This will close the circuit when pressed down to the tape already on the card, and will be the switch on the circuit.

> **TIP** A 3V coin battery will provide enough power to illuminate three LED mini bulbs. If your design calls for more bulbs than that, you'll want to include more than one battery in the circuit or wire them in separate circuits.

Whether in a formal makerspace, a public or school library, or a pop-up or mobile makerspace, circuitry kits are versatile, easy, and relatively inexpensive tools that allow users of all ages to create interesting and engaging projects.

RESOURCES

1. *Electric Circuits: Basic Concepts of Electricity,* www.allaboutcircuits.com/textbook/direct-current/chpt-1/electric-circuits/.
2. Electric Paint 50 ml. Bare Conductive, www.bareconductive.com/shop/electric-paint-50ml/.
3. Learn—Chibitronics, http://chibitronics.com/learn/.
4. littleBits: Electronic Building Blocks for Creating Inventions Large and Small, http://littlebits.cc/.
5. Makey Makey Classic How-To, http://makeymakey.com/how-to/classic/.
6. Snap Circuits | Electronic and Educational Toys, www.snapcircuits.net.
7. "What Is a Circuit? Learn at SparkFun Electronics," https://learn.sparkfun.com/tutorials/what-is-a-circuit.

Computer Numerical Control in the Library with Cutting and Milling Machines

ROB DUMAS

What Is Computer Numerical Control?

As makerspaces appear in more and more libraries, computer numerical control (CNC) is fast becoming one of the cornerstone technologies of the maker movement. CNC is the technology behind all sorts of electronic tools found in makerspaces, and the process by which machine tool hardware is automated using computer software. Numerical control first appeared in the mid-twentieth century, when manufacturers fitted manually operated machines to move according to instructions on paper tape or punch cards (Olexa, 2001). Today, USB cables and flash memory are used to transmit or store the instructions, but the idea remains the same: using computers, a thing cannot only be made precisely, but because the instructions are stored on a computer, that thing can reliably be made *over and over.*

Rob Dumas is Librarian at Chicago Public Library.

Software and Hardware

The key to CNC is in how the software will turn the many lines, curves, and shapes in a design into a language machines can understand. Machines don't understand what a "rectangle" is, but they can understand certain instructions, such as "lower the blade," "move this far along the X axis," "move that far along the Y axis," "turn off the laser," and so forth. These encoded instructions are called *G-code* and it's the fundamental language of CNC. Fortunately, the software used today will turn a design into G-code automatically, so there probably won't be a need to edit G-code by hand any time soon.

Software

Most hardware comes with software to control it, for example, Silhouette Studio, Cricut Design Space, Inventables Easel, and Full Spectrum RetinaEngrave. These apps will often allow users to create designs, but they're generally pretty basic and often specific to the hardware. An illustration program will allow instructors to teach one design program that can be used on several different kinds of hardware and can create files in Scalable Vector Graphic (SVG) format. I recommend Inkscape, which is free, open source, runs on Windows, Linux, and Mac.[1] Inkscape can be downloaded from inkscape.org, but any comparable app (e.g., Adobe Illustrator) that can generate SVGs will suffice.

Hardware

Electronic cutting machines such as Silhouette Cameo or Cricut Explore are great tools for a new makerspace, because instructors can host all sorts of craft classes with them: personalized decals, holiday cards, party invitations, tote bag iron-ons, even screen printing . . . the list goes on and on! There are many different materials for use with cutting machines, but cardstock, adhesive vinyl, and iron-on vinyl are the areas on which to focus when starting out.

> **TIP** Stock up on transfer paper, extra blades, cutting mats, tote bags, cardstock, and colored vinyl. When users get tired of cutting, replace the blade with a special pen and the cutting machine becomes a plotter.

Laser cutters (e.g., the Full Spectrum Hobby Laser) can be expensive to buy and require ventilation, but the results speak for themselves. Laser cutters are used most commonly with acrylic, balsa wood, and cardstock. Using a laser cutter, users can make jewelry, Raspberry Pi cases, name tags, and more.

> **TIP** Stock up on acrylic (two-layer acrylic is great for making name tags), make sure the laser is calibrated correctly, well-ventilated and the material is safe to laser.

Milling machines such as the Woodcraft CNC Piranha FX, Carverlight, Shapeoko, Carvey, Showboat, or Carbide Nomad allow users to take a block of material and carve out portions with great precision.

> **TIP** Milling machines can be loud when running, so make sure the space can handle some noise. Stock up on wood and extra milling bits.

3D printers such as the Up! Mini, LulzBot, Taz 5, MakerBot Replicator, or Dremel 3D IdeaBuilder work like milling machines, but in reverse: instead of removing material from a solid piece, they draw an object in plastic from the bottom up. (See chapter 5, A Librarian's Guide to 3D Printing.)

Important Tips

Necessary Resources

- *Computers:* The first word in CNC is "computer," so it's necessary to have computers with Internet access and proper software installed (see above).
- *Instructional time and open hours:* The instructional portion of a class should run between thirty minutes and one hour, depending on how much work the class is. Be sure to leave adequate time for students to complete their own projects, or provide open hours during which they can work on their projects.
- *Expectations and Examples:* It's important to provide clear expectations in your instructions, so students understand what they are making. It also helps to have an example of a finished design as an instructional aide so students can see how a design becomes a real-world object.
- *Supplies:* Stock up on adhesive vinyl, iron-on vinyl, transfer paper, acrylic in various colors, cardstock, and wood blocks, because these are the most common materials used in the classes discussed below.

Weighing Choices

It is important to consider space requirements when setting up a makerspace. Machines should be spaced far enough apart to prevent crowding when in use, because students often like to watch the machines work. It's also important to remember that some machines that make truly amazing things may be bulky, noisy, or require ventilation. Carefully weigh the positive and negative aspects of each tool. Consider how much design time versus production time a class will take.

Be Clear

Always be clear about your expectations.

Crash!

Without proper preparation, it's possible that a machine will move in a way that is harmful to the machine itself, tools, or materials. For example, if a machine isn't positioned correctly, the tool might move along its axis until it bumps into its limit; this is called a *crash* and it means a mistake has been made somewhere. When a tool experiences a crash, safely put it back in position and double-check all settings and positions.

Ooh . . . Shiny!

When a machine finishes, examine the product carefully for flaws *before* removing it. You can always repeat the job, but once you take something out of a machine, you'll never find the original starting position.

Safety First

Hardware manufacturers work hard to ensure their products are safe, but safety procedures must still be followed. (See chapter 4, Safety and Guidelines in the Library Makerspace.)

Explore

In a makerspace, it's important to cultivate a culture of exploration and collaboration, rather than a rigorous adherence to the steps outlined in the class lecture.[2] It's common for enterprising students to come up with something new by changing the process to suit their needs or methods.

How Libraries are Using CNC

Many libraries with makerspaces are teaching classes in design and production using CNC tools to explore the role of libraries in makerspaces and as a place to teach maker technology to the public, using 3D printers, laser cutters, electronic cutting machines, and more. Some of these libraries include:

- 4th Floor at Chattanooga Public Library, Chattanooga, Tennessee
  chattlibrary.org/4th-floor

- The Studio at Anythink, Thornton, Colorado
  www.anythinklibraries.org/thestudio

- Maker Lab at Chicago Public Library, Chicago, Illinois
  www.chipublib.org/maker-lab

- Make @ HCPL at Harris County Public Library, Houston, Texas
  www.hcpl.net/content/make-hcpl

- D. H. Hill Library Makerspace at North Carolina State University, Raleigh, North Carolina
  www.lib.ncsu.edu/spaces/dh-hill-makerspace

- Make Central at Michigan State University, East Lansing, Michigan
  www.lib.msu.edu/makecentral

Projects

Laser-Cut Name Tag

Goal: In this project, students will create an engraved name tag using a laser cutter and sheet of acrylic.

Audience: This project is recommended for ages thirteen and up.

Notes: This is a great project for staff, patrons, or anyone who'd like to create a personalized name tag. For this project, it's important to use two-color acrylic[3]; for the best results, use sheets with a white bottom layer (e.g., green on white, blue on white, red on white, etc.).

MATERIALS NEEDED

- computer with Inkscape and RetinaEngrave installed
- sheet of 1/8-inch-thick two-color acrylic
- laser cutter (in this case, a Full Spectrum Engineering 40W laser cutter), connected to the computer via a USB cable
- pin for the name tag

INSTRUCTIONS

1. Start a new Inkscape document, then open the Document Properties (Ctrl+-Shift+D). Under the Page tab, set the Default Units to **inches (in)**, set the Orientation to **Landscape**, set the Page Size to **11" wide** and **9" tall**, and close the Document Properties window.
2. Choose the Rectangle tool (F4) and create a rectangle 3" wide by 1.5" tall. Select the rectangle using the Select tool (F1), then click the circular gripper at the corner of the rectangle and drag it about ¼" to create a rounded corner.
3. Open the Fill and Stroke panel (Ctrl+Shift+F) and set the Fill to **None** (X), then click the Stroke Paint tab, click **Flat Color** (the square next to the X) and set the RGBA sliders to **R=0, G=255, B=0, A=255**. Now click the Stroke Style tab and Set the Width to **0.01 in**. This will be the *cut line*, or the edges of the name tag.
4. Select the Type tool (F8), choose a font and size and type your name. Repeat to add a subtitle (such as a job title). All text should fit inside the rectangle just created. Check your spelling.
5. Using the Select tool, click on the text object and, as in step three, set the fill to *yellow* (**R=255, G=255, B=0, A=255**) and the stroke to a solid *blue* line (**R=0, G=0, B=255, A=255**). These will be the *etch fill* and *etch lines*, respectively.

6. Use the Select tool to select both the green name tag box and the text object. Using the Align and Distribute palette (Ctrl+Shift+A), click the **Center on Vertical Axis** button, followed by the **Center on Horizontal Axis** button. This should center the name in the middle of the name tag.

7. The laser cutter doesn't understand text (only shapes and solid colors), so it's necessary to turn the text into shapes. Select your name using the Select tool and from the menu, select **Path > Object to Path**. It might look like nothing's changed, but Inkscape has turned the text into the outlines and shapes of the letters.[4] Select everything on the page (Ctrl+A) and group all the objects. (Ctrl+G).

8. The design phase of our tag is now complete. Now save it in a format the laser cutter can read. From the menu, select **File > Save As . . .** and save the name tag as an SVG (*.svg) on the desktop.

The name tag is now ready to be made by the laser cutter. The next part of the project uses the 40W laser by Full Spectrum Engineering and its accompanying RetinaEngrave software.

The reason the name tag was designed using different colors for the various lines and shapes is that the cutter differentiates "layers" based upon their color, so we must tell it to use low power/high speed on our yellow area and blue lines (to etch our name into the acrylic) and use high power/low speed on our green line (to cut through the acrylic).

1. Place the two-tone acrylic into the laser cutter, position the red dot at the top-left of the acrylic and calibrate the beam using the spacer.[5] Close the lid of the laser cutter.

2. Open RetinaEngrave; after it connects, home the laser using the **Home** button in RetinaEngrave's toolbar. The red dot will represent the top-left corner of the job, so use the arrow keys to move the red laser dot to the spot on your acrylic where you want the job to start.

3. RetinaEngrave works like a printer in Windows, so in Inkscape, use the **File > Print** menu, choose the RetinaEngrave driver, click **OK/Print** and switch from Inkscape to RetinaEngrave.

4. In RetinaEngrave, set the order, speed, power, and number of passes for the vector layers, using the Control Panel palette. Set the blue layer (**Order: 1; Speed: 100; Power: 20; Passes: 1**), followed by the green layer (**Order: 2; Speed: 20; Power: 100; Passes: 1**).[6]

5. Click the **Raster Engrave** tab at the top-left, then go to the Control Panel palette and drag down the B/W Threshold slider until the border disappears, but the letters remain.

6. Choose **Raster then Vector** from the drop-down menu at the top of the screen. Double-check the design's positioning using the **Run Perimeter** button (the one with four arrows pointing outward). If everything looks satisfactory, click the **Play** button to start the job. The laser will first move rapidly left and right, etching (or *rastering*) the yellow fill. Once that's done, the laser will move quickly to lightly cut (or *vector*) the blue line around the letters, before finally moving slowly around the green line, cutting the name tag out of the acrylic.

7. Before removing the acrylic from the machine, check these carefully:

   – *Did the etching remove the top layer completely?* Did it leave the lower layer color visible everywhere we saw yellow in the SVG?

   – *Did the laser cut all the way through the acrylic along the green line?* We may need to play with the speed or power settings, depending on what make and model laser we're using, but sometimes we won't *quite* get all the way through the material. This can happen if your laser isn't focused, calibrated, and homed; if your optics are dirty; if smoke isn't quickly vented in the cutting chamber; if your laser tube is nearing replacement; or if your acrylic is outside of its stated tolerances. If the green line didn't cut all the way through, go back to RetinaEngrave, set the blue line to **0 passes,** select **Vector Mode** from the dropdown, and run your job again.

8. When it's all done, remove the acrylic from the machine, glue the pin on the back, and wear it with pride!

Milled Wooden Phone Stand

Goal: Students will create a simple smartphone stand using a milling machine and block of wood.

Audience: This project is recommended for ages thirteen and up.

Notes: This is a good project for small groups that demonstrates how CNC is used in milling. Make sure to observe safety procedures and be aware that the mill can be noisy.

MATERIALS NEEDED

- computer with Internet access, and Inkscape and the Easel driver installed
- block of ½" thick bamboo plywood
- cutting machine (in this case, a Shapeoko 2) with a wood bit installed and connected to the computer via a USB cable
- sheet of sandpaper

1. Start a new Inkscape document, then open the Document Properties (Ctrl+-Shift+D). Under the Page tab, set the Default Units to **inches (in)**, set the Orientation to **Landscape**, set the Page Size to **11" wide** and **9" tall**, and close the Document Properties window.

2. Choose the Rectangle tool (F4) and create a rectangle 4" wide by 2" tall. Select the rectangle with the Select tool (F1), then grab the circular gripper at the corner and drag it a bit to create a rounded corner.

3. Open the Fill and Stroke panel (Ctrl+Shift+F) and set the Fill to **None (X)**, then click the Stroke Paint tab, click **Flat Color** (the square next to the X) and set the RGBA sliders to **R=0, G=0, B=0, A=255**.[7] Now click the Stroke Style tab and Set the Width to the width of the bit (so if using a ⅛" bit, set the Stroke to ⅛"). This will be the edge of our phone stand.

4. Repeat steps one and two, but make the shape 3" wide by 0.5" tall. The Fill should be a **Flat Color** and the RGBA sliders should be set to **R=128, G=128, B=128, A=255**. This will be the slot in which the phone will rest.

5. Use the Align and Distribute panel (Shift+Ctrl+A) to center the shapes on both the vertical and horizontal axes.

6. From the menu, select **File > Save As . . .** and save your name tag as an SVG (*.svg) on your desktop.

7. Easel is a web app, so open a browser, go to easel.inventables.com, and sign in. Inside Easel, click **File > Import SVG**, choose the SVG file just created, and click **Open**. This will place the design on the workspace.

8. Select all objects (Ctrl+A) and move the design up and to the right a bit, away from the corner (and away from where the clamps will go on the machine). Make sure **Use Tabs** is checked in the Cut/Shape palette. This will leave several small "tabs" connecting the design to the board, so that the piece of wood you're cutting doesn't move while the mill is running. (You can easily detach them by hand when finished.)

9. Set the Material to **Bamboo**, the Bit Size to ⅛" (or the width of the bit being used) and choose **Recommended** for the Cut Settings. Click **Show Toolpaths** to generate the paths the mill will take.

10. Place the bamboo plywood board in the Shapeoko and clamp it down securely. Double-check all settings, turn on the milling spindle and *slowly* turn it up, then click the **Carve** button in the top-right corner of Easel to start milling the project.

11. When it's all done, the stand will still be connected by several tabs. Remove the block from the machine and carefully break the tabs, freeing the stand from the rest of the block. Sand the edges with sandpaper to smooth them out and show off your new phone stand!

Business Hours Decal

Goal: Students will create a decal they can put in a window to advertise their business hours to passersby.

Audience: This project is recommended for ages thirteen and up.

Notes: This project is great for owners of small businesses who want to make decals. Remember to reverse the decal before cutting it, so it can be mounted on the inside of the window.

MATERIALS NEEDED

- computer with Inkscape and Silhouette Studio installed
- cutting machine (in this case, a Silhouette Cameo), connected to the computer via USB cable
- cutting mat
- sheet of adhesive white vinyl, 11" wide by 9" tall
- sheet of adhesive transfer paper, 11" wide by 9" tall

INSTRUCTIONS

1. Start a new Inkscape document, then open the Document Properties (Ctrl+-Shift+D). Under the Page tab, set the Default Units to **inches (in)**, set the Orientation to **Landscape**, set the Page Size to **11" wide** and **9" tall**, and close the Document Properties window.
2. Select the Type tool (F8), choose a font and size you like, click on the page, and type your business name (e.g., Bob's Burgers).
3. Repeat step two to create text boxes for the days of the week and for the business hours. To make sure the text lines up as intended, use the Align and Distribute palette (Shift+Ctrl+A) to make sure the text boxes are correctly aligned and evenly distributed. Make sure all text fits on the page with ¼" of extra space at the margins.
4. Because the decal will be mounted on the inside of the window, we need to flip the text backwards to make sure when we cut the decal, the sticky side faces the window. Select everything (Ctrl+A), group it together (Ctrl+G), flip it horizontally (H), and ungroup (Shift+Ctrl+G) the objects.
5. To turn the editable text boxes into shapes the cutter can understand, select each text box and choose **Path > Object to Path** from the menu (or press Shift+Ctrl+C).
6. Choose **File > Save As . . .** from the menu and save the design as an SVG (*.svg) file on the desktop. This will be your original, editable file.

7. Some cutting machine software understands SVG natively, but Silhouette Studio doesn't, so save another copy in Desktop Cutting Plotter (*.dxf) format. In Inkscape, select **File** > **Save a Copy . . .** from the menu and save a second copy of the file on your desktop as a DXF file. In the dialog that pops up, uncheck **use LWPOLYLINE type of output** and click **OK**.

8. Switch to Silhouette Studio and open the DXF file just saved. Position the design at the top-left of the canvas and resize it so that it's about 10.5" wide by 8.5" tall. Click the **Cut Settings** button in the toolbar, choose **Vinyl** from the Material Type, and check **Return to Origin** under Advanced > Feed Options.

9. Smooth the vinyl onto the cutting mat, leaving no air bubbles, and load it into the cutting machine. Set the cutting machine's blade to the height recommended by the software for vinyl (usually 1 or 2) using the blade setting tool built in to the Cameo.

10. Click the **Send to Silhouette** button in the toolbar, followed by the **Start** button in the palette it brings up. The cutter will start working on the job.[8] *Note:* Never stick any fingers into the machine while it's working.

11. Unload the cutting mat from the cutting machine and carefully remove all unwanted vinyl from the backing sheet, leaving only the decal portion on the backing.

12. Carefully peel the transfer paper off its backing, then carefully smooth the transfer sheet on top of the decal, pressing firmly, and leaving no air bubbles.

13. To mount the decal on a window, slowly peel away the backing sheet, leaving the decal attached to the transfer paper. Carefully place the decal on the window, smooth it on, and then slowly peel back (not up) the transfer paper.

Personalized Cat Decal

Goal: Students will trace an image, personalize it, and create a decal from it.
Audience: This project is recommended for ages thirteen and up.
Notes: This is a great introductory project, because students enjoy making decals that express their personalities. It also teaches several important concepts: vector design, adding, and subtracting vectors from one another, image tracing, and CNC basics. For this project, we're using Inkscape to create a cat shape, then put our name into the design and cut it out as a decal.

MATERIALS NEEDED

- computer with Internet access, and Inkscape and Silhouette Studio installed
- cutting machine (in this case, a Silhouette Cameo), connected to the computer via USB cable

- cutting mat
- sheet of adhesive vinyl, 11" wide by 9" tall
- *Optional:* a sheet of adhesive transfer paper, 11" wide by 9" tall

INSTRUCTIONS

1. Inkscape can trace images, but a photo won't give a nice, clear shape, so we need to go online and find a high-contrast *silhouette* of a cat that we can easily vectorize. Search Google Images (images.google.com) for "cat silhouette" and choose an image that is large, high contrast, and free of watermarks. Save it to the desktop.

2. Start a new Inkscape document, then open the Document Properties (Ctrl+-Shift+D). Under the Page tab, set the Default Units to **inches (in)**, set the Orientation to **Landscape,** set the Page Size to **11" wide** and **9" tall,** and close the Document Properties window.

3. Select **File > Import . . .** from the menu, pick the image just saved and click **Open.** Inkscape will present a dialog; choose **Embed, From File** and **None (auto),** then **OK.** Resize the image so it fits between the document margins.

4. Select the imported image and open the Trace Bitmap window (Shift+Alt+B or **Path > Trace Bitmap . . .** in the menu). Set **Scans** to 2, click **Grays** and check **Remove Background** before clicking **OK** and closing the Trace Bitmap window. At first, it might look like nothing happened, but if we click on the object and move it, we'll see that Inkscape has created a new vector object. (We might need to ungroup the new object to get just the outline of your cat.) Once we're happy with the tracing, we can delete the original imported image.

5. Select the Type tool (F8), choose a font and size you like, click on the page and type your name. Position the text inside your cat shape and turn the text into outlines (Shift+Ctrl+C, or **Path > Object to Path** in the menu).

6. Ungroup the outlined objects (Shift+Ctrl+G, or **Object > Ungroup** in the menu) and select the first letter in your name. Hold down Shift and click on the cat outline to select both. Choose **Path > Difference** (or press Ctrl+ -) to "subtract" the letter from the cat's shape. Repeat for each other letter.[9]

7. Choose **File > Save As . . .** from the menu and save the design as an SVG (*.svg) file on the desktop. This will be the original, editable file.

8. Some cutting machine software understands SVG natively, but Silhouette Studio doesn't, so save another copy in Desktop Cutting Plotter (*.dxf) format. In Inkscape, select **File > Save a Copy . . .** from the menu and save a second copy of the file on the desktop as a DXF file. In the dialog that pops up, uncheck **use LWPOLYLINE type of output** and click **OK.**

9. Switch to Silhouette Studio and open the DXF file just saved. Position the design at the top-left of the canvas and resize it so that it's about 10.5" wide by 8.5" tall. Click the **Cut Settings** button in the toolbar, choose **Vinyl** from the Material Type, and check **Return to Origin** under Advanced > Feed Options.
10. Smooth the vinyl onto the cutting mat, leaving no air bubbles, and load it into the cutting machine. Set the cutting machine's blade to the height recommended by the software for vinyl (usually 1 or 2) using the blade setting tool built in to the Cameo.
11. Click the **Send to Silhouette** button in the toolbar, followed by the **Start** button in the palette it brings up. The cutter will start working on the job. *Note:* Never stick any fingers into the machine while it's working.
12. Unload the cutting mat from the cutting machine and carefully remove all unwanted vinyl from the backing sheet, leaving only the decal portion on the backing.
13. Carefully peel the transfer paper off its backing, then carefully smooth the transfer sheet on top of the decal, pressing firmly, and leaving no air bubbles.
14. To mount the decal, slowly peel away the backing sheet, leaving the decal attached to the transfer paper. Carefully place the decal, smooth it on, and then slowly peel back (not up) the transfer paper.

T-Shirts I and II

Goal: Students will create a personalized t-shirt using the vinyl cutter and iron-on vinyl.
Audience: This project is recommended for ages thirteen and up.
Notes: T-shirt classes start out like decal classes, but they use iron-on vinyl instead of adhesive. Because there are two ways of using the vinyl, this class offers a great opportunity to show student improvement and progress. Just as important, though, are the amazing t-shirts people make and the smiles they wear. With these classes, everyone gets to walk out feeling like a fashion designer. Both classes start off similarly, but go in different directions. I recommend teaching T-Shirts I and, if students respond well, trying T-Shirts II.

MATERIALS NEEDED
- computer with Inkscape and Silhouette Studio installed
- cutting machine (in this case, a Silhouette Cameo), connected to the computer via USB cable
- cutting mat

- sheet of iron-on vinyl, 11" wide by 9" tall
- clean, ironed t-shirt
- clothing iron and ironing board
- butcher paper
- smooth board at least 10" wide by 12" tall (T-Shirts II only)
- screen-printing frame with screen installed, at least 10" wide by 12" tall (T-Shirts II only)
- screen-printing squeegee (T-Shirts II only)
- acrylic screen-printing fabric ink (T-Shirts II only)
- painter's tape or masking tape (T-Shirts II only)
- latex or nitrile gloves (T-Shirts II only)
- plastic spoon (T-Shirts II only)

INSTRUCTIONS

By this point, we're familiar with the steps to create decals, so we'll start off much as we did in the Business Hours Decal (steps one through ten) and Personalized Cat Decal (steps one through twelve) classes, but with a few minor differences. Whether teaching T-Shirts I or II, remember to flip the design backwards before cutting it (as in step four of the Business Hours Decal project) so the design faces up through the clear backing.

T-Shirts I

1. After removing the vinyl sheet from the cutting machine, carefully remove from the clear backing all the vinyl we *don't* want to see on the finished shirt.
2. Smooth the t-shirt onto the ironing board and carefully place the vinyl sheet on the shirt, vinyl side down. Place a sheet of butcher paper on top of this sheet.
3. Iron the decal onto the t-shirt using medium heat (no steam). Keep the iron moving and turn it down if the sheet wrinkles severely. Check the edges of the decal to make sure it's adhered to the t-shirt.
4. When the decal has adhered to the t-shirt, remove the butcher paper and allow the sheet to cool for a minute. When it is warm to the touch, carefully peel the clear backing off the decal.

The t-shirt is safe to wash; use cold water and turn the shirt inside out before washing. The vinyl is not permanent, but can be ironed back on. For a more permanent solution, we turn to our other class.

T-Shirts II

As with T-Shirts I, we start off much as we did with the Business Hours Decal (steps one through ten) and Personalized Cat Decal (steps one through twelve) classes; however, instead of ironing the design right onto the t-shirt, we're going to iron it into a screen-printing frame to create a template we can use to permanently ink multiple shirts. *Note:* remember to flip the design backwards before cutting it.

1. After removing the vinyl sheet from the cutting machine, carefully remove from the clear backing all the parts we *do* want to see on the finished t-shirt.
2. Put the screen-printing frame on the ironing board and carefully center the vinyl sheet on the screen, vinyl side down. Place a sheet of butcher paper on top of this sheet.
3. Iron the decal onto the screen using medium heat (no steam). Keep the iron moving and turn it down if the sheet wrinkles severely. Check the edges of the decal to make sure it's adhered to the screen.
4. When the entire decal has adhered to the screen, remove the butcher paper and allow the sheet to cool for a minute. When it's warm to the touch, carefully peel the clear backing off the decal. Give the screen a few minutes to cool off completely.
5. Using painter's tape or masking tape, block out the space between the edge of the vinyl and the edge of the frame. Make sure there are no gaps in the overlap.
6. Wrap the cutting board in butcher paper, then put it inside the t-shirt to keep the ink from going all the way through to the back. Make sure the shirt is placed smoothly on the cutting board, and put it on a flat surface.
7. Carefully position the screen-printing frame in the center of the t-shirt.
8. Put on rubber gloves and open the screen-printing ink. Using the plastic spoon, drop a small dollop (1 to 2 teaspoons) of ink along one of the inside edges of the frame. Spread it evenly along the edge.
9. Put the squeegee in the ink at a 45° angle, hold the frame still, press firmly, and draw the squeegee swiftly to the other end of the frame. Look for anywhere the ink might have missed and, if it did, repeat.
10. Lift the frame off the t-shirt carefully and hang the t-shirt up to dry (thirty to forty-five minutes). Thoroughly wash the remaining ink from the frame and squeegee using soap and water.

Once dry, the t-shirt will be safe to wash and should permanently retain the imprint of the design. The frame is a template and can easily be used to make more shirts.

NOTES

1. Inkscape for Mac requires XQuartz (xquartz.org).
2. Safety procedures, however, should always be followed.
3. Two-color acrylic is a sheet of colored acrylic with a thin layer of differently colored acrylic on top.
4. Check all spelling before doing this step, because the text will be indelible from here on.
5. The spacer should just slip between the last lens and the acrylic.
6. Due to a bug in Inkscape, you might see an extra color layer in the list; if so, just set its number of passes to 0.
7. Easel differentiates what depth to cut which shape by the shade of gray (so a shape in black means "cut all the way through," whereas white means "don't cut at all").
8. If the cutter cuts too deep or not at all, or if the vinyl moves, stop the job using Silhouette Studio or the pause button on the cutting machine.
9. Some letters of the alphabet, like A, B, or O have an "inside" part that may not be connected to the rest of the design. You can either reconnect these pieces by drawing connecting shapes and using **Path > Union** to "add" them to the design, or you can use transfer paper after cutting the decal. We will use the latter method.

REFERENCE

Olexa, R. (2001, August). The father of the second industrial revolution. *Manufacturing Engineering, 127*(2).

Robotics in Libraries

ANTONIA KRUPICKA-SMITH

Do you want to introduce robotics at your library but don't know where to start? Do you work with a limited budget and worry that you don't have enough funding to introduce robotics? Are you concerned about not knowing what you are doing? This chapter will provide you with examples that illustrate that you can do it! It is full of tips and tricks for how to begin, what you need to get started, and where to find what you need. It will also describe some common pitfalls that can set back your robotics program. Finally, it will share detailed program and project guides to help you hit the ground running. It runs the gamut from making wobblebots with grade schoolers, to teaching robotics concepts to teenagers using LEGO MINDSTORM EV3 and Cubelets, to showing adults what programming a robot looks like and how a humanoid robot really works. After reading this resource, you should be well on your way to introducing and growing robots at your library.

Antonia Krupicka-Smith is Innovation Catalyst and Programming Librarian at Pikes Peak Library District.

What Is Robotics?

Robotics can mean different things to different people, but the simple definition of robotics is the use of computer-controlled robots to perform manual tasks. The concept of robotics is relatively new. The term was coined by Isaac Asimov in 1941 (www.dictionary.com/browse/robotics). Robotics can be done in a formal classroom setting or in a more creative setting like a makerspace. Robotics includes two elements: building and programming. To some patrons, robotics will mean coding and programming an already-built robot; these patrons will be disappointed if this isn't what they encounter during a library program or in your makerspace. To other patrons, robotics means building an actual robot—putting together batteries, wires, motors, and casings to build the physical robot. It is important to decide the approach your makerspace will take; this will help you determine the focus of your programs and help you to effectively allocate funds, staff time, and effort. When you decide, make sure that you have the necessary resources.

Major Types Available

Companies have tried to make using their products as easy to use as possible by offering kits for classroom and group settings. A selection of the most common and easily accessible kits are listed below. (Some of these will be discussed in greater detail later in the chapter.) Most of these are available as educator packs or offer educational discounts.

- Cubelets and MOSS—Available on modrobotics.com in educator packs
- LEGO MINDSTORMS EV3—Available on www.mindstorms.lego.com
- Ozobot—Available on ozobot.com as classroom kits
- Sphero—Available on sphero.com in educator packs
- Dash and Dot—Available on makewonder.com as both classroom packs and school packs
- Finch Robot—Available on finchrobot.com with an education discount

How to Use Robotics in Libraries

The first step in introducing robotics in a library is to believe that any library can do robotics! Whether your library has a dedicated makerspace with tools (e.g., soldering irons, laser cutters, CNC machines, and 3D printers) or is a library with only three public computers, you can offer robotics. The key is to identify which element of robotics you would like to support, coding or physically building robots, and allocating resources towards that choice. Start small. Your community's excitement will grow and demand will increase.

Coding and Programming Robots

To support coding and programming robots, you will need to provide access to different platforms. There are many free or very low-cost coding platforms available online, such as Scratch, which are not intimidating and will be easy to teach to your youngest patrons. This does not mean that only children should learn and use Scratch. When it comes to robotics, there are no age limits. The following project guide should get you thinking about what would be required to start a coding- and programming-centered robotics program at your library.

Coding and Programming Robotics Project Guide —————————————

RESOURCES NEEDED

- *Computers with Internet access.* These must be equipped to download, or be predownloaded with, one or more coding platforms. (A full list of free and low-cost platforms can be found in the resources section of this chapter.)
- *A physical robot.* When teaching coding, it is helpful to have a physical robot that patrons can use to check out their code. It is not necessary to have a robot for every patron; in truth, it can be advantageous to stick to one or two different robots that can be coded using a wide variety of platforms.
- *Instructional time and open hours.* To get patrons excited about learning how to code, it is important to demonstrate how to code using your chosen platform. Teaching both introductory and intermediate classes will help patrons to become comfortable working with code and prepare them to create their own code for a physical robot. One way to encourage staff to lead robotics classes is to bring in a professional to lead a staff training session. Reach out to local companies and colleges—it's a great way to build partnerships and to help prepare staff to launch a robotics program. Many of these people are so passionate about what they do that they can't wait to share their knowledge!

Building Physical Robots

To build physical robots at your library, you'll require resources. What you will need depends on the depth of the proposed programs. For children and tweens, you can simply buy an electric toothbrush from a dollar store and use the motor and battery casing to create simple vibration-focused robots. Or, for more ambitious projects, you can use tools such as laser cutters, 3D printers, and CNC machines to build the gears and casings to house purchased batteries and motherboards. The program's scope is up to you, based on patron demand and your staff's comfort level. A basic project guide for starting with a simple robot-building program follows. From there, the sky is the limit!

Building Physical Robots Project Guide

RESOURCES NEEDED

- *Materials.* This type of robotics is very materials-heavy. Finding and purchasing each of the components needed to build the robots will be the most time-consuming and costly part of this type of programming. The components required to build a robot should be mined before beginning a project. Depending on how adventurous your patrons and staff are, you can find parts everywhere! Simple motors can be found in cell phones that can be acquired cheaply through donations, and electric toothbrushes can be bought inexpensively at a dollar store. Many parts can also be purchased at reasonable prices on websites such as Amazon.com.
- *Background information.* With this type of programming, education is in the why and what of the build. Creating instructional material for patrons is important so that they understand why each component is needed and how it functions.
- *Training staff to teach using inductive and deductive reasoning.* To make creative-based programming successful, staff must encourage exploration rather than just giving directions. This may come naturally to some staff members, but might be very difficult for others. Training staff to use prompts in a creative program setting will bring you one step closer to encouraging an environment of exploration.

Using this project guide will help create an "environment of making," which is just as important as having the physical space to create robots. Once this environment is achieved, patrons can't help but make amazing things!

Robotics Tips

Things to Avoid

The biggest pitfall when starting a robotics program at your library is trying to launch an extensive program at the beginning. Choosing—and keeping—your focus will make your program much more successful in the long run. It may be tempting to start out by trying a little of everything because you aren't sure what will work or what your patrons will like. However, keeping your focus and putting your resources behind one goal will best serve your patrons.

Second, avoid getting distracted by the newest gadget out on the market. There are hundreds of current Kickstarter campaigns focused on technology and creating the next big thing that will solve every problem. Stick with what has worked for a few years rather than jumping on a newer process that may still have bugs and might cause more headaches than success. Finally, don't force staff to begin robotics programming before they're ready. Train your staff first and help them to locate more information before forcing them to lead a program in front of fifty scary parents during the summer. You'll achieve more success when your staff are just as jazzed as your patrons.

Tried and True Methods

First, determine if participants' expectations line up with what you will be providing. It's easy to disappoint them if they have the wrong ideas about what programs will cover and which supplies will be provided. Make your program descriptions simple and easy to understand. Always tell participants what to expect at the beginning of the program so that they understand exactly what you will provide.

Next, remember that simplicity is always best. Make simple robots. Code robots to do simple things. Provide simple instructions and outline simple goals. Breaking down big scary concepts into steps that are easy to follow will eliminate the risk of making complex concepts more complicated.

Finally, create an environment that will encourage your patrons to have fun. Allowing patrons to make mistakes and figure out solutions is much more beneficial than forcing them to follow a monotonous process.

Have Materials to Get Started Making Simple and Complex Robots

The route you decide to take your library's robotics program will determine what you should always keep on hand, but the most common materials needed for robotics are:

- *Coin batteries:* You can never have too many coin batteries. They can be expensive, so buy in bulk.
- *Motors:* Find a good source for your motors and stick with it. Any kind of motor will do, but in simple robotics the most common is a vibrating motor. Get creative and think about everything in our world that vibrates, which might help you to figure out good and cheap sources for vibrating motors.
- *Wire strippers:* Get a universal wire stripper and keep it close. Everything runs on positive and negative leads, so you will need to expose a good deal of wire while building robots.
- *Tape (Double-side foam and electrical):* Both double-sided and electrical tape are useful when building robots. Double-sided foam tape saves space and holds parts in place when a vibrator motor is shaking everything around. The electrical tape is for safety. Sometimes there will be exposed wire leads on connection points and a little electrical tape will make sure everyone is safe.

How Libraries Are Using Robotics

No matter their population, size, location, or budget, libraries are introducing robotics programs. You are not the only librarian who wants to start or grow one. Regardless of size, location, or funding, the most common approach to robotics in libraries is to focus on the youth population, using kits to build robots that are programmed with Scratch or various other free platforms. Those libraries that have designated staff and/or an area such as a makerspace will be able to launch robotics programs more easily. But regardless of library size, patrons and communities resoundingly support robotics. Community demand is high for this type of programming so let's get started by looking at some sample projects!

Projects

The next section will provide program plans for three different types of robotics programming: making simple robots, programming or coding robots, and programming with humanoid robots.

Making Simple Robots

Simple robots are characterized by being unprogrammable. This is not to say that they aren't programmed, but rather the programming cannot be changed. Here are some simple robotics programs that you can offer in your library.

Simple Robot 1 // Bristlebots

Goal: In this program, patrons will be attaching a vibrator motor and coin battery to the back of a brush to move it across a surface.
Audience: This program is intended for ages six and up. (Younger children can be accommodated with adult assistance.)

MATERIALS NEEDED

- brush heads (toothbrush heads work very well)
- coin battery
- vibrator motor (small motors from inside cell phones work best). Note that it is important to purchase motors with leads attached.
- double-sided foam tape
- single-sided tape

TOOLS NEEDED

- scissors
- wire stripper (you may need to expose more wire on the leads for better contact with the battery)

INSTRUCTIONS

1. Prep all your materials. If using a toothbrush, you will need to cut the head from the toothbrush handle. For the vibrator motor you will want to use the wire strippers to expose about a half inch of raw wire on both the positive and negative leads.

2. Attach the vibrator motor with a small piece of double-sided foam tape to the back, flat side of the toothbrush head closest to the handle.
3. Cut a half-inch piece of double-sided foam tape and affix to the flat side of the toothbrush head closest to the top of the brush.
4. Place the negative wire lead on the double-sided foam tape and place the negative side of the coin battery on top of the lead. The piece of tape should now be holding the coin battery in place with the negative lead wire making contact with the negative side of the battery.
5. Take the positive lead wire and place it on top of the coin battery. Once the wire makes contact, the motor will begin to vibrate. Hold the wire in place with a small piece of single-sided tape.

The bristlebot is complete and will begin vibrating across the surface.

Take it one step further: Have patrons experiment with ways to control their bristlebots. Trimming the bristles can make the bot change directions. Try adding more weight in the front or back of the bots by layering on more tape. This will also manipulate the direction that a bot will go as well as control its speed.

Challenge: Create racing tracks for patrons to race bots against each other. Then ask patrons to think about real world problems that can be solved with bristlebots or similar robots.

Simple Robot 2 // Wobblebots/Wigglebots

Goal: In this program, patrons will attach a motor, battery case, and drawing implements to an object such as a cup. By doing this, the cup will move in circles across a sheet of paper to create circle designs.

Audience: This program is intended for ages six and up. (Younger children can be accommodated with adult assistance.)

MATERIALS NEEDED

- large plastic cups (used CDs, DVDs, or sections of foam pool noodles can also be used)
- AAA battery case with leads
- motor (small motors from inside electric toothbrushes are suitable); if using parts from electric toothbrushes, their battery cases and batteries can also be used

- two AAA batteries
- electrical tape
- three markers
- craft stick
- clothespin
- piece of craft paper
- *Optional*: Googly eyes

- scissors
- wire stripper (you may need to expose more wire on the leads for better contact with the battery case and the connectors on the motor)

1. Prep all your materials. If using an electric toothbrush, you will need to remove the battery, battery case, and motor from the handle of the toothbrush. You may also need to rework the wiring for it to work for the project. For the traditional battery casing, use the wire strippers to expose about half an inch of raw wire on both the positive and negative leads.
2. Attach the battery case to the flat bottom of the cup using electrical tape by using a single strip of tape across the top side of the case.
3. Take the positive and negative leads from the battery case and wrap around the connector points on the bottom of the motor. Put the batteries in the case to ensure that you have connected the leads with the corresponding connector points. If the motor turns on, take the batteries out to turn off the motor and secure the connection points with electrical tape.
4. Attach the motor to the bottom of the cup next to the battery case using electrical tape.
5. Attach the three markers to the inside of the cup at three opposite points to create "legs" for the bot to stand on. Optional: Affix the googly eyes to the side of the cup and draw on a face.
6. Affix the craft stick to the clothespin with electrical tape and clip onto the rotating pin of the motor. This will create the weighted affected need to make the bot wobble/wiggle.
7. Remove caps on the maker and place on sheet of craft paper. Put batteries into the case.

The wobble/wigglebot is complete and will begin moving across the surface.

Take it one step further: Have patrons begin to experiment with ways to control their bots. Try changing the positioning of the markers. This will make the bot change the size and shape of the circles. Have patrons try to add or remove weight on the rotating pin of the motor. This will change the speed of the bots.

Challenge: Have patrons think about real-world problems that can be solved with wobble/wigglebots.

Simple Robot 3 // Design Your Own Robot!

Goal: In this program, patrons will be taught the simple concepts of what a robot needs: power, a sensor, and a motor. They will then be challenged to think of a real-world problem that a robot could solve and then build it!

Audience: This program is intended for ages six and up. (Younger children can be accommodated with adult assistance.)

MATERIALS NEEDED

- power sources (battery cases with batteries, coin batteries)
- motors (vibrator motors, spindle motors)
- creative materials on which to place the power sources and motors onto (boxes, brush heads, cups, and CDs or DVDs)
- electrical tape
- double-sided foam tape
- single-sided foam tape
- miscellaneous craft materials (googly eyes, markers, craft sticks, craft paper)

TOOLS NEEDED

- scissors
- wire stripper (you may need these to expose more wire on the leads for better contact with the battery)

INSTRUCTIONS

1. Explain simple robots to the patrons. Talk about the three main elements needed for a robot: power, a motor, and a sensor. Introduce the idea that robots can do things to make the world an easier and better place. Have patrons brainstorm something that a robot could do to solve a problem.
2. Have the patrons draw out a plan for their robots and list what materials they may need to create their bots. Ask them what materials they have and explain that their bot can't require anything that they don't have on hand.

3. Let them build their bots! Assist where needed with the construction, but not with the concept.
4. Have them test their robots and then explain to the group what problem their bot was intended to solve and whether it succeeded.

Take it one step further: Have the patrons experiment further depending on if their bots were successful or not. Brainstorm ways to make it better. Think about other materials that would have been useful to make the bot more successful. Ask if there is anything that already exists that already solves the problem or challenge they were trying to solve.

Simple Robots 4 // Premade Buildable Robots

As noted earlier, there are a very large number of premade buildable robotic kits available that claim to be the best. I will highlight two well-known kits that have been available for some time. In no way do I sponsor these kits or have I been paid to promote them.

Both robots can be programmed to allow patrons to learn coding. Therefore, these products offer crossover options to integrate building physical robots and learning to code and program them.

▧ Cubelets and MOSS

Cubelets and MOSS are both available through Modular Robotics, which is based in Boulder, Colorado. Per the company's website,

> Cubelets are magnetic blocks for children age 4+ that can be snapped together to make an endless variety of robots with no programming and no wires.... Each Cubelet has a tiny computer inside of it and is a robot in its own right. Each Cubelet in the kit has different equipment on board and a different default behavior. (https://www.modrobotics.com/press-kit/)

There are three different categories of Cubelets: Sense Cubelets, Act Cubelets, and Think Cubelets. The way that each Cubelet is magnetically snapped together will determine what type of robot you have created, as well as what your robot will do. According to the company website, "MOSS is a block-based robot construction system. Each block is a different part of a robot and combining those blocks in different ways yields a ginormous variety of robots" (https://www .modrobotics.com/press-kit/). "Both Cubelets and MOSS can be programmed, but programming is not required to create functional robots. Programming uses either a free app or through free programming platforms such as Scratch and C" (www.modrobotics.com).

Goal: In this program, patrons will learn how to build robots through simply magnetically connecting preprogrammed blocks.

Audience: Ages four and up.

MATERIALS NEEDED

- The number of Cubelets you need will depend on how many patrons will be participating. A group, which can include up to four patrons, will need at least three Cubelets. MOSS is sold in a kit format; one kit can make hundreds of different robots.

INSTRUCTIONS

1. Have patrons work in groups of up to four people.
2. Start off by explaining what each of the Cubelet and MOSS blocks does. Understanding what each part does helps patrons to understand how the blocks work together.
3. Lead your patrons through Cubelets Challenges, Part I, and Cubelets Challenges, Part II, which are available for free from modrobotics.com. Once patrons have completed these challenges, they will have a better understanding of how Cubelets work together.
4. Modrobotics.com has full curricula available for teaching MOSS in an organized class.

Take it one step further: Encourage your patrons to try programming their robots using either the Bluetooth Cubelet or Scratch with MOSS.

Challenge: What real world problems can patrons solve by building and programming either Cubelets or MOSS?

■ LEGO[1] MINDSTORM EV3

LEGO MINDSTORM EV3 is an all-in-one product that allows your patrons to build robots using the LEGO building blocks they're already familiar with, and teaches programming on a free platform designed to work directly with MINDSTORM EV3. Each kit contains everything needed to begin building and programming (www.mindstorm.lego.com).

Goal: Patrons will build and program robots to complete challenges provided via the free programming platform.
Audience: Ages ten and up.

MATERIALS NEEDED

- One kit for each group of up to four patrons
- An individual tablet, laptop, or computer for each patron works best. The free software must be downloaded on each device.
- The challenge mat that comes with each kit

INSTRUCTIONS

1. Ensure that the free programming platform is downloaded on each computer.
2. Have each group follow the instructions included in the software to build the robot they would like to create.
3. Have patrons work on learning the software and completing the challenges.

Take it one step further: This is a great program for a club or multiple sessions because patrons can leave and then start up where they left off when they return.
Challenge: Can participants use the skills they've learned to build and program their own robots to fix problems that they see in the real world?

Learning to Code with Robots

Learning to Code with Robots 1 // Dash and Dot Robots ───────

Dash and Dot are available through Wonder Workshop. Per the Wonder Workshop website "Dash is a real robot, charged and ready to play out of the box. Responding to voice, navigating objects, dancing, and singing" (https://www.makewonder.com/dash). Using various apps, kids and adults can create new behaviors for Dash and learn simple coding. There are numerous apps available for all ages that teach simple robotics and encourage individuals to create independently. Per the Wonder Workshop website, "Dot is the brains of a robot" (https://www.makewonder.com/dot). Dot is the top of Dash. Dot does not move, but can be used to play different games that teach coding through various app platforms.

For library settings, educator kits can be purchased that include multiple Dashes and all that is needed to maintain the robots. You will need to provide a tablet or app-enabled device to control the robots (www.makewonder.com).

Goal: Program Dash to complete a specific maze.
Audience: All ages.

MATERIALS NEEDED

- at least one dash robot and tablet for every two to three patrons
- tape to make a maze on the floor

INSTRUCTIONS

1. Ensure that the Wonder programming app is downloaded on each tablet.
2. Connect each Dash through Bluetooth with the designated tablet.
3. Have patrons work through using the simple programming app to guide Dash through the maze.

Take it one step further: Try out other available apps to see what else you can make Dash and Dot do.
Challenge: Try one of the many challenges and curriculum lessons available on the Wonder Workshop website.

Learning to Code with Robots 2 // Sphero Robots

According to the creators of Sphero SPRK Edition:

> There's no rule that says learning shouldn't be fun, or that playing can't be valuable. If there is, we created SPRK Edition to break it. We know that kids love Sphero, so we turned that love into learning and creation. SPRK makes the skills of the future approachable and practical. And most importantly, fun.
>
> The SPRK app experience lets you give your robot the orders with visual blocks representing code—[a] C-based language called OVAL. Immediately see the connection between the program you created and how the guts of your Sphero work and react. Sphero SPRK Edition will inspire a love of robotics, coding, and STEM principles . . . all through play. (http://store.sphero.com/products/sphero-sprk-edition)

Goal: Control Sphero through a maze over multiple obstacles.
Audience: Ages eight and up.

MATERIALS NEEDED

- One SPRK Sphero and tablet for every two to three patrons
- Materials to make a maze with obstacles

INSTRUCTIONS

1. Ensure that the correct apps are loaded on the tablet.
2. Connect the SPRK Sphero with the tablet using Bluetooth.
3. Don't forget to aim your SPRK Sphero before driving!

Take it one step further: Now code your robot to complete your maze!
Challenge: Work through the numerous lessons available on the SPRK Sphero
education website.

Learning to Code with Robots 3 // Finch Robots

Finch Robots were developed by Birdbrain Technologies LLC. The Finch was
designed to support STEM and computer science education. Finch works with
over twenty different programming languages or environments and fully supports
all the languages. The Finch robot website (www.finchrobot.com) provides detailed
lessons and assignments for the Finch and is a wonderful resource for support as
patrons learn and build programs for the robot.

Goal: Learn to program the Finch robot.
Audience: Ages five and up.

MATERIALS NEEDED

- Finch Robot
- laptop (with the programming languages and environments downloaded or
  with the ability to download)

INSTRUCTIONS

1. Open finchrobot.com.
2. Select which software you would like to learn and use. Open that language
   on the laptop and have patrons go through learning the language and doing
   the lessons.

Take it one step further: Try a new language!
Challenge: Use what you have learned to program the robot to move through a maze.

Programmable Robots

Programmable Robots // NAO and Pepper Robots

NAO, Pepper, and Romeo are all humanoid robots created by Aldebaran, a SoftBank Robotics company. Each robot serves a slightly different purpose and are all intended to be used differently. According to the company's website (www .aldebaran.com/en/cool-robots), NAO was the first humanoid robot created by Aldebaran and is intended to be a fully programmable tool. Pepper was developed as an emotional companion and can analyze emotions and is being used for a number of functions including greeting customers in stores. Per the manufacturer, "Romeo is a platform for exploration and aimed at developing new technologies and solutions to help people with reduced mobility" (ald.softbankrobotics.com/ en/robots).

In the realm of libraries and makerspaces, NAO is a great fit to help support programming, testing, and development of new applications. Connecticut's Westport Library has used NAO. The library purchased an NAO robot and used it to teach two levels of programming to introduce people of all ages to robots through public interactions with the robot. It held two levels of programming classes to teach the public about Choregraphe, a programming platform associated with the NAO robot. The library also arranged open lab times for the public to try out different applications that they had coded themselves on the NAO robot. An area was set up where the public could see the robot in action and learn more about robotics (Lewis, 2015).

Conclusion

Adding robotics to your makerspace may be in your future! By planning where you want to invest your resources, asking your patrons about their interests, and encouraging your staff to try something new, you will create a robotics program for your library in no time. There is a fit for any library's size, budget, and strategic goals. Now that you have the tips, tricks, and ideas, get started!

Resources

Robots

- Cubelets and MOSS, www.modrobotics.com
- LEGO MINDSTORMS EV3, www.mindstorms.lego.com
- Ozobot, www.ozobot.com
- Sphero, www.sphero.com
- Dash and Dot, www.makewonder.com
- Finch Robo, www.finchrobot.com

Programming Platforms

Every robot mentioned in this chapter has a free programming software associated with it to be used either on a desktop or as an app. The following list of software only touches on the surface of what is available.

Free

- *Scratch* (scratch.mit.edu): Scratch is "a programming language that makes it easy to create your own interactive stories, animations, games, music, and art—and share your creations on the web" (https://www.facebook.com/scratchteam/about/?entry_point=page_nav_about_item&ref=page_internal).
- *Code.org* (code.org): Code.org is "a nonprofit whose goal is to expose all students to computer programming."
- *Codeacademy* (codeacademy.com): Codeacademy describes itself as "an education company. ... committed to building the best learning experience inside and out."
- *BlueJ* (bluej.org): BlueJ is an Integrated Development Environment for Java, developed mainly for educational purposes, but also suitable for small-scale software development.
- *CodeAvengers* (codeavengers.com): Code Avengers takes a fun approach to learning JavaScript.
- *SQLZoo* (sqlzoo.net): SQLZoo's goal is to help users "learn SQL using: SQL Server, Oracle, MySQL, DB2, and PostgreSQL."
- *Hackety Hack!* (hackety.com): Hackety Hack teaches the basics of programming.
- *RubyMonk* (rubymonk.com): RubyMonk teaches the "syntax, idioms, and even the philosophy behind effective Ruby use in an interactive, Codeacademy-like interface" (http://alternativeto.net/software/rubymonk/).

Low-Cost

- *Treehouse* (teamtreehouse.com): Treehouse teaches web design, development, and iOS.
- *Lynda.com* (Lynda.com): Lynda provides training on computer-related subjects.
- *CodeHS* (codehs.com): CodeHS is a "comprehensive program for helping schools teach computer science."

NOTE

1. LEGO® is a trademark of the LEGO Group of companies, which does not sponsor, authorize, or endorse this chapter or book.

REFERENCE

Lewis, J. (2015). Libraries are for making: robots. *Young Adult Library Services,* 13(2), 25–26.

ADDITIONAL RESOURCES

BirdBrain Technologies LLC. (2010–2016). *About Us.* www.finchrobot.com/about-us.

Modular Robotics. (2016). *Modular Robotics Press Kit.* www.modrobotics.com/press-kit/.

Robotics. (n.d.). *Dictionary.com Unabridged.* www.dictionary.com/browse/robotics.

Softbank Group. (2016). *Cool Robots.* www.aldebaran.com/en/cool-robots.

Sphero. (2016). *Press Kit.* wwwsphero.com/press.

Wonder Workshop. (2016). *Media Kit.* www.makewonder.com/about.

Drones in the Library

CHAD MAIRN AND KRISTI SEFERI

Drones are becoming very popular with hobbyists, pilots, photographers, makers, and consumers. They are also known as unmanned aerial vehicles (UAVs), quads, and quadcopters, but throughout this chapter, drones will be the primary term used. There are autonomous drones that fly using a predetermined path thanks to Global Positioning System (GPS) technology, can be steered manually by a radio-controlled transmitter, or can be controlled while having photographic and video images displayed to First Person Viewer (FPV) goggles and/or a tablet or smartphone, so the pilot can see exactly what the drone "sees." Many of the same electronics that are incorporated into today's tablets or smartphones, like accelerometers, gyroscopes, and GPS, can also control drones in flight.

There certainly is not a shortage of both good and bad information on drones in a variety of international news stories. Just recently, officials believe that a drone hit a passenger airplane in London (Hume 2016). Luckily, no one was injured. Consequently, anti-drone systems are being developed to keep drones away from

Chad Mairn is Librarian/Innovation Lab Manager at St. Petersburg College. Kristi Seferi is a mechanical engineering student at St. Petersburg College.

aircraft and other sensitive equipment where they could cause serious harm, perhaps even death. Some people believe that drones with cameras are a violation of privacy, but United States citizens are protected under the Fourth Amendment from unreasonable searches and seizures, For the most part, capturing drone video several hundred feet above the population will not clearly identify people, so their privacy seems to be secured somewhat. Regardless, drones are seeing explosive growth, and the achievements of this technology will be highlighted throughout this chapter.

There are practical applications for drone use that go beyond hobbyists who fly just for fun. As mentioned above, drone operators can capture aerial photography and video, and provide an interesting perspective on a landscape, construction projects, a sporting event, a boat speeding through the water, a realtor's guided house tour, or whatever else a creative mind wishes to accomplish. First Person View (FPV) goggles or headsets can control drones in flight while displaying video right to the operators' personal screens. Drones conduct search and rescue missions. They can monitor and spray crops and even deliver packages. The University of Leeds was awarded a grant to study and eventually develop "self-repairing cities" where a collection of drones and robots will inspect, monitor, and repair roads and streetlights as needed (Passas, 2015). There is also growing interest in racing drones, and the St. Petersburg College Innovation Lab [Makerspace@St. Petersburg College], in partnership with the Engineering Club, recently built one and programmed the flight computer to improve the drone's flight controls. A GoPro video camera was also added to the drone. This chapter will discuss what was necessary to accomplish this first build.

Drones are not only fun, but can also lead to career opportunities. According to the Association for Unmanned Vehicle Systems International, drones are expected by 2025 to create more than 100,000 jobs and generate an "economic impact of $82 billion" (AUVSI, 2013). Thanks to forward-thinking companies, services like Amazon's Prime Air, which delivers packages via drones, this will become a reality once regulations can be sorted out. Drones can help move products between warehouses to free up traffic on highways in the United States. Dispatch is a company that is starting to deliver products by a fleet of autonomous vehicles that can drive on sidewalks, which will help eliminate some of the local traffic issues cities face throughout the world. Drones can augment security cameras by patrolling larger spaces like parks and power plants from above, because of their bird's eye views of the surrounding area. Journalists, filmmakers, and photographers are starting to use drones to shoot beautiful videos from the air, capturing views rarely seen before. Drones can also capture footage of dangerous areas like war zones and natural disasters. No matter how far drone technology takes our society—and what is being seen now is just the beginning—remember that it should be a tool to make our lives easier and better.

This growing interest in drones in both the private and public sectors prompted the Workforce Institute at St. Petersburg College to partner with the UAS Training and Certification Center and a local aviation group to provide Private Pilot Ground School training, online courses, and certifications for drone owners. The introductory course addressed appropriate drone use, Federal Aviation Agency (FAA) airspace regulations, and weather. It also covered the process to petition the FAA for a "Certificate of Waiver of Authorization" (COA) for commercial drone operators in low-risk, controlled environments (Tucker, 2015).

History

In 1898, Nikola Tesla demonstrated the first radio-controlled boat at the Electrical Exhibition in New York City. The boat was powered by batteries and the radio controlled the switches that worked the propeller, rudder, and lights (PBS, 2000). There was not much interest, however, in this type of radio-controlled technology until later in the twentieth century, when the military started to experiment with guided bombs. During the Space Age, scientists and engineers began to refine rockets and pushed society into a future that now continues to experiment with guided aircraft (e.g., drones).

Hobbyists built remote-controlled planes. Rockets could be controlled from the ground while flying near or in outer space. In the 1960s hobbyists started to add one-shot cameras to their drones to capture breathtaking pictures from above. Today, extremely high-definition 4K cameras are connected to drones and capture stunningly beautiful aerial photographs and video. Cameras with 360° views are becoming more affordable, so it is likely that those devices will soon be attached to drones. These videos or still pictures can be experienced in 3D via virtual reality headsets like an Oculus Rift or Google Cardboard, and added to other media using programs like Unity.

Throughout the twentieth century, the military employed drones to accomplish reconnaissance and bombing missions. It was only when drones started to make their way into consumer markets that we saw an explosion in growth and innovation, and regulations started to make their way into the picture.

Regulations

The FAA uses the term "Unmanned Aircraft System" (UAS) to refer to drones and similar aircraft. At the time this chapter was written, these aircraft had to be registered before they could be flown legally outside. Registration costs $5 and can be completed online at www.faa.gov/uas/registration. If drone owners do not register their UASs, they may face civil and criminal penalties. Because the registration process is inexpensive and straightforward, there is no excuse for not registering a drone.

All owners who wish to fly their drones commercially and within the National Airspace System must submit a Section 333 exemption as well as registering their drones. If an aircraft weighs more than 55 pounds, is operated outside the United States, is owned by a trustee, or if the owner uses a voting trust to meet citizenship requirements for the United States, it cannot be registered online, and the owner must submit paper forms. Libraries should play a role in educating the public about drone regulations just as they have informed and helped the public make sense of other emerging technologies such as e-books, e-mail, social media, and privacy rights.

Major Types, Brands, and Models of Drones Available

When it comes to building drones, things can get extremely complicated. You may encounter a unique situation that no earlier hobbyist has documented. You might need to come up with a solution when dealing with multiple components that interact with each other. The best thing for a beginner to do is buy an inexpensive "ready-to-fly" drone kit from a local or online retailer. Use the inexpensive drone as a trainer. Once you've mastered flying it around, you can dismantle everything and learn how all the parts are connected.

The most popular and trusted drone brand is DJI, which is considered the best in the drone industry. The company has developed the iconic quadcopter frame that many companies attempt to re-create. The DJI's advantages are that it is incredibly reliable, built with quality parts, and user-friendly. The main drawback to a DJI is its high price. It can cost anywhere from $500 to over $1,000, depending on the model and its features. (To learn more about the DJI drone, visit www.dji.com.) However, many companies based in China have begun to produce versions at a fraction of the DJI's cost. Many of these drones have generic names and are inexpensive, ranging from $30 to $100. The drawback to these generic drones is that their quality is atrocious. They may short out or may not be able to fly through any kind of light wind. A hard landing may damage one or more of their components.

How to Use Drones

Drones are improving because of the availability of advanced lithium polymer (LiPo) batteries, motors, and flight-controlling software. The LiPo batteries are lighter and have more power, so drones can fly longer and go further. Flight controllers, which function like a computer's central processing unit (CPU), are the brains of a drone—and they are getting smarter. The flight controller receives power from the batteries, and instructions from the radio-controlled transmitter. It also receives data from the gyroscopes to help with leveling, from the accelerometers to measure velocity and direction, and from the GPS to detect its position in space. Programming the flight controller requires attention to detail and a few simulated test flights. Radio-controlled transmitters usually have many channels, which means they can control different actions like throttle, pitch, roll, and more.

A drone can also act like a flying web server by sending back data in real time, We will soon start to see drones being used in mobile advertising campaigns. If drones do not violate the United States Fourth Amendment, then one day they may monitor segments of the population from the air and report back in real time. Ads can then be displayed on consumers' mobile devices, or offers will auto-generate based on their locations when they enter stores, and thus provide added bonuses to encourage impulse buyers.

Flying a drone is exciting, but it requires patience to master piloting skills. Serious pilots will be glad that they put in the time to learn how to fly correctly and safely. Again, be sure to register a drone before flying it. According to FAA regulations, a drone is only allowed to fly 400 feet above the ground, and it must remain within eyesight during flight. Some radio-controlled transmitters will not stay in contact with a drone beyond a certain distance, so it's important to understand the drone's capabilities so it does not get lost or crash. Do not fly drones near airports or highly populated areas and keep them away from other sensitive places like power plants. Do not fly a drone when the weather is bad. Gusts of wind can make it difficult to fly a drone, and some have even knocked them swiftly to the ground. Avoid flying drones at night unless they are equipped with bright LEDs or other safety lights.

Necessary Skills and Tools Involved in Building a Drone

Programming the flight computer requires mastery of basic skills (e.g., downloading and installing firmware). Beyond that, a knowledge of basic coding and an understanding of computer logic will prove useful, although these are not completely necessary to configure and program a drone's flight computer. Attention to detail is crucial when running simulated flight maneuvers via the programming interface to get the flight controls just right. It can be just as frustrating to program the flight computer as it is to learn to fly the drone, but the learning experience is richer when the flight computer is programmed so that its characteristics can be tested and retested before flying the drone. To see a video of the flight computer being programmed, visit http://j.mp/FlightComputer.

Understanding the safe way to use tools is also vital. Knowing how to use a razor knife, a soldering iron, and various electronic components properly is key, or serious injury can occur. Using a magnifying glass and working in good lighting will make it easier to identify the drone's parts. Keep the various parts in a logical order on a clean table during the build, because trying to find misplaced small parts can be time-consuming and infuriating.

Soldering is an essential skill for building drones and working on other electronics projects; however, if the person building the drone is not comfortable doing this type of work, there are some motors that use simple plugs. Soldering is the process of joining two or more metal pieces together by melting the solder (i.e., a low melting alloy) to fill the connecting joints. Battery wires, for example, are soldered to the circuit board (see figure 14.1). It is difficult to remove or reposition these wires after they are soldered, so pay close attention when doing this. Serious burns can occur because the tip on the soldering gun must be extremely hot to melt metal, so use soldering irons with extreme caution. A quick search on Amazon.com or on hobbyist websites will list several good soldering irons and kits. The kits are helpful because they usually come with a manual to help users learn the fundamentals of soldering. A soldering kit is a great addition to any hobbyist's basic computer-repair kit, and it is worth the time to learn how to use one correctly. A variety of library makerspaces have started to offer soldering classes, and these are a great learning opportunity for the public.

Schematics are line drawings that demonstrate how an electronic circuit's components, are connected. They are written in symbols (e.g., this schematic of a resistor ⊐▭⊏), so being able to read basic schematics is useful, but not absolutely necessary. However, if you want to understand every part of your drone and how all the components work together to make it fly and transmit data, then

FIGURE 14.1

Soldering Motor Wires to Drone Frame

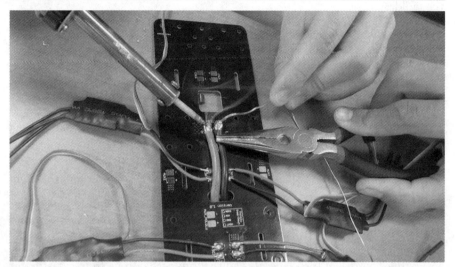

Photo courtesy of Chad Mairn.

it is a good idea to spend some quality time learning basic schematics. To learn more about reading schematics and for some good examples, visit https://learn .sparkfun.com/tutorials/how-to-read-a-schematic. Building your own drone is a fun experience, and, if it needs repair or basic maintenance, you will know exactly what to do, because you built it from the ground up.

Step-by-Step Assembly of a Drone

Once you are comfortable with the hobby, it is time to move into the world of do-it-yourself (DIY) drones. People can create high-performing drones at a fraction of the cost of commercial drones. A drone can be designed for any purpose and a well-built DIY drone can perform better than some of the top brands at a fraction of the cost. With every new industry, there are pioneers who reinvent the wheel. With drones, the hobbyist community is changing everything from the quality of parts to the laws and regulations on drones that Congress passes.

Before building a drone, it is important to decide why you are creating it in the first place. Consider what is being added to the drone (e.g., a camera), because that will add weight that may impact its flying capabilities. When designing and building your first drone, you may get carried away and purchase unneeded tools and gadgets, so be sure to sketch out your design idea and stick to it throughout the build process.

Decide how many motors are needed and how large the drone will be. The more motors used and the larger the size of the drone, the more expensive and complicated the build. DIY drones can range anywhere between a small, three-motored "tricopter" to a large, heavy-lifting eight-motored "octocopter." The simplest and most common drone is the four-motored drone, called a "quadcopter," because of the user-friendly features four motors offer. Most quadcopters have similar build plans. Basically, start with a frame, add a power distribution board, solder in your battery lead, solder in your electronic speed controllers, plug your motors into the electronic speed controllers, plug your electronic speed controllers into your flight computer, and then finish off by plugging the receiver into the flight computer. This may sound complicated, but if the build is approached logically, then it becomes obvious what parts need to get power and signals by working together with the other parts.

The frame of any drone is important because it houses the equipment. The structural integrity of the material is all that protects a drone from catastrophic failure. Frames come in many different shapes and sizes. They are generally made from high-grade polyurethane. Frames are usually modular, so in the event of a crash, parts of the frame can be switched out on demand. Make sure to plan ahead and purchase a frame that has a large enough fuselage (i.e., main body of the drone) to accommodate all the components and wiring that must fit inside.

The Power Distribution Board (PDB) powers the drone. The battery leads and Electronic Speed Controllers (ESC) are directly soldered into place on the PDB. Before purchasing a PDB, make sure it has a high ampere rating (an ampere, abbreviated as A, is a measurement of electric current). Amp rating is important because the motors and ESCs draw power from the PDB. If the amps being drawn are higher than the maximum amperage the board can handle, it will cause a short that will immediately damage the drone. For example, if the drone has four motors with a maximum 20-amp draw, then the PDB must be able to handle a maximum amperage of 80 for the motors to operate at peak performance. A general recommendation is to purchase a PDB that is rated for over 100 amps even if the drone does not require that much power. Four ESCs and a battery lead will be soldered to the board, which usually has clearly marked areas showing where the soldering should occur. The battery lead will most commonly be an XT-60 cable because most batteries are now discharged with XT-60 connectors.

The next step is to choose the ESCs and solder them to the PDB. One ESC is needed for every motor, and the amp rating must either match or exceed the maximum possible amperage of the motors. For example, if the motor can hit 20 amps at peak performance, then the recommendation is to purchase ESCs that can handle 20–25 amps. The ESCs perform two functions: providing power to the motors and dictating how fast the motors can spin. An average ESC will have a positive and negative battery lead, a receiver cable on one side, and three 3.5 mm gold female connectors on the other side. The battery leads will always be black for ground and red for positive, and the recover cable will always be bundled together whereas the 3.5 mm connectors will always have identical female connections.

After building the frame and soldering four ESCs to the PDB and the XT-60 battery lead, it is now time to focus on the motors. Motors come in different sizes and ratings. The sizes are measured in millimeters (mm) and the performance rating is measured with rotations per minute or (KV). Choosing a motor for a specific need is key. Large motors will burn through batteries quickly, but although small motors are efficient, they perform to a lesser degree. Motors come in every size, shape, and color. You can find both high KV motors and low KV motors that are small and large. When planning the build, calculate how much the drone will weigh to decide how large of a motor to use. A racing quadcopter, for example, will use small motors, 20–23 mm in diameter with a high KV rating of over 1,200. If building a stable photography drone to perform decently while being efficient, larger motors that are 35–44 mm with a KV rating of 600–900 are preferred. The larger the motor and higher KV, the more motor thrust. A drone weighing 100 grams requires four motors with a total maximum thrust of 200 grams. Thus, each motor must have at least 50 grams of thrust once it's pushed to peak performance by the user.

A simple equation to keep in mind is the total weight of your entire drone multiplied by two. Then divide that amount by the number of motors on the drone and that is the minimum amount of thrust needed to power each motor. Remember that every single part of the drone is serving a specific purpose, which will dictate the quality of the parts needed. Once the motors are screwed into place on the drone, there will be three cables with 3.5 mm gold male connectors that will need to be plugged into the corresponding female connectors on the ESC. When testing the motors, it is possible to change the orientation of the spinning by unplugging two of the three connectors and switching them.

Along with the motors, propellers are needed to fly the drone. Always test motors first without propellers to avoid accidents. Propellers come in a wide variety of lengths, weights, and materials. Small six-inch plastic propellers are efficient, but flimsy. Large carbon fiber propellers will create large lift, but they will drain the batteries quickly. Frame specifications will determine the exact size propellers that the drone will require.

Flight controllers are the "brain" of the drone. The receiver and ESCs are directly connected to the flight controller. The controller takes input from the receiver and makes the drone operate. Without a flight controller, the signals would not be able to control anything. Flight computers range in price and functionality. At first, the simpler the better. It is possible to upgrade in the future for more advanced motor features. ESCs have specific wires that plug right into the flight computer, and the flight computer will have pins that take the wires in a specific order. Each is labeled, and it is not difficult to connect everything together. Although some flight computers require extremely small soldering for the pins, it is easier to purchase and work with a pre-soldered version.

The most common flight computer is the Naze32. It is inexpensive and easy to program. A computer is required for programming the flight computer. When deciding on a flight computer, make sure to do some research and compare various functionality such as battery voltage monitoring, motor outputs, and configuration software. The flight computer usually has two sets of pins and a micro-USB connector. One set of pins is for the ESCs to plug into and the other set of pins is used to connect to the flight receiver. The micro-USB cable is used to connect the flight computer to a computer for programming purposes. There is also an arrow on the flight computer dictating which direction it should point while mounted inside the drone. While programming the flight computer, it is possible to change the orientation (i.e., front and back) of the drone. Basic computer skills are needed to install the required firmware and settings on the flight computer. There are countless guides and tutorial videos available online covering the setup and function of the flight computers.

The last two components needed in addition to a battery are a transmitter and receiver. These usually come in a set, and they determine how input is directed to the drone and how the drone receives said input. Transmitter and receiver combos range from $60 to over $500. Transmitters (see figure 14.2) work by sending radio commands to the receiver. Radio frequencies are amazing! A high-end transmitter can send a signal that can be accurately picked up several miles away. The radio frequencies are measured in gigahertz (GHz). There are three radio frequency ranges that hobbyists are legally allowed to use: 1.2 GHz, 2.4GHz, and 5.8GHz. Video transmissions are restricted to 1.2GHz and 5.8GHz, and 2.4GHz is used for controlling the drone. There are pros and cons for using either 1.2GHz or 5.8GHz when transmitting video. The first, 1.2 GHz, offers extreme range, up to 20 miles with the proper setup, but the video quality is not great. 5.8 GHz sacrifices range—only up to 1000 meters—over clear transmission, but the video quality is much better. The latter is mainly used by hobbyists, whereas 1.2GHz is primarily used for commercial and scientific purposes because it offers a longer range.

Turnigy Radio Transmitter

Photo courtesy of Chad Mairn.

Be careful when choosing the transmitter and receiver combination because many of the more inexpensive versions are not for multicopter drones, but are for hobbyist planes and helicopters instead. When first setting up the receiver, plug in the binding antenna that is supplied and then proceed to plug all the connectors from the flight computer into the corresponding pins on the radio receiver. Once everything is plugged in, follow the instructions that came with the transmitter/receiver to execute the binding procedure (i.e., linking the drone to the transmitter) because most receivers are not the same.

When choosing a transmitter, it is important to purchase one with six or more channels. Channels are different inputs that can send maneuver and other instructions to the drone. The more channels the transmitter and receiver have, the more capabilities the drone will have. Switches that toggle different items on the drone like LED lights or retractable landing gear can be used. After the transmitter is bound to the receiver and wired to the flight computer, it is almost time to fly the drone.

Hobbyist drones use LiPo batteries to power all the equipment, so it is vital to purchase the correct battery. The difference between LiPo batteries and AA batteries is the chemicals used inside. LiPo batteries are based on lithium polymer chemistry, which give the batteries extremely high-energy densities. A battery with a higher energy density will be able to hold more energy than an AA battery of the same weight. Therefore, LiPo batteries are commonly used with radio-controlled aircraft and drones. There are a few things to consider when choosing a battery for the drone. For one, the discharge cable must match the connector that was soldered to the PDB. If a male XT-60 battery lead was soldered to the PDB, then a battery with a female XT-60 discharge cable is needed to make a circuit.

The next specification to look up is the capacity of the battery. The representation of how long it can provide energy is measured in milliamp hours (mAH). The larger the number, the greater the battery's capacity. However, the higher the capacity of a battery, the heavier it is, and this will impact the drone's flight capabilities. When purchasing the drone motors, be sure that the retailer provides thrust data. The thrust data will show the maximum current draw of the motors and ESCs compared with different propeller sizes. Pay attention to how much amperage the drone will draw, then choose a battery with the amp discharge that is required. Make sure to account for the maximum possible amp reading of the motors in case of any emergency where the thrust will be held to maximum output. Chargers for these batteries should also be bought from reputable dealers and resellers since low-quality chargers can destroy batteries. Always carry batteries in LiPo safe bags, and never leave a charging battery unattended. Figure 14.3 shows the parts of a drone.

The frame is built, everything is installed and soldered into place, and the battery is plugged in. Before flying, it is important to perform a preflight test. Make sure there are no wires obstructing the path of the propellers and that the motors are tightened onto the booms and completely torqued. Then give the motors a test by removing the propellers and pushing the throttle stick forward. If everything performs correctly, then it is time to fly. Reattach and tighten the propellers and find an open field to test the new DIY drone. When building your drone, keep in mind it may crash and prepare for that eventuality by giving wires extra length to be pulled, and fastening all the important equipment tightly—but not so much that it would break if it was put under strain. The impact should be taken by the frame, not the components inside. (See figure 14.4 for completed drone.)

Basic Flight Skills

- *Roll:* Push the right stick to the left or right. Literally rolls the quadcopter, which maneuvers it left or right.
- *Pitch:* Push the right stick forward or backward. Tilts the quadcopter, which maneuvers the quadcopter forward or backward.
- *Yaw:* Push the left stick to the left or to the right. Rotates the quadcopter left or right, and points the front of the copter in different directions and helps with changing directions while flying.

FIGURE 14.3

Complete Drone Parts

Photo courtesy of Kristi Seferi.

FIGURE 14.4

Completed Drone

• *Throttle*: Engage by pushing the left stick forward. Disengaged by pulling the left stick backward. This adjusts the altitude, or height, of the quadcopter.

Tips You Need to Know about Drones

One thing is certain. New drone pilots will crash their drones a few times, but the more they fly, the easier and more natural it will become. Find friends who have been flying drones for a while, watch them fly, and ask for constructive feedback. Learning to fly a micro-drone may be the way to go before trying to fly a larger, more expensive model. There are also flight simulators to help prepare a new pilot to get the feel of flying a drone. For example, HELI-X is a professional radio-controlled helicopter flight simulator that offers a free trial at www.heli-x .info/cms. There are also apps (e.g., Indoor Heli Sim 3D, shown in figure 14.5) that are decent flight simulators. Nevertheless, the best practice is to learn to fly an actual drone.

Practice is the best preparation for flying. After you have become familiar with the radio-controlled transmitter and how it controls the drone, it is a good idea to find a place outside with plenty of space with a soft area to land or crash the drone. Choose a day when there is good visibility and minimal wind resistance. If the drone is not programmed to auto-land, be sure to practice landing

---

FIGURE 14.5

Indoor Heli Sim 3D Simulator

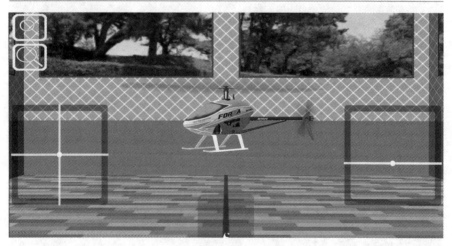

Photo courtesy of Chad Mairn.

in a safe area, preferably a grassy field where there are few people present. When landing or crashing the drone, it is important to turn off the throttle completely so that the blades and motors don't hit the ground while they are still spinning, which would do some serious damage to the drone and whatever it hits on its way to the ground. Create landing zones to practice precision when landing the drone. Regarding flying drones, the adage that "practice makes perfect" is particularly applicable.

There are laws that every drone operator should be familiar with before flying. It was mentioned above that drones need to be registered with the FAA. A plethora of websites go into detail about various regulations for flying drones. There are three key points. One, don't fly a drone above 400 feet. Two, never let the drone out of sight when flying. And three, try to stay away from populated areas in case the drone crashes.

Some things will be learned accidentally. For example, never plug the LiPo battery into the receiver without the antennae attached. Make sure to charge LiPo batteries on a fireproof surface and keep the batteries away from other flammable items in case they self-ignite. Be sure to read the owner's manual to make sure you turn on all the components in the correct order. And, spend some quality time testing the drone's controls such as direction, flight angles, and lift from the ground with weights on it before the drone is several hundred feet in the air or by using a simulator. Disconnect the battery whenever moving the drone so that the throttle does not accidentally engage and cause the motors to spin and potentially, risk injury.

Be smart and safe when building and flying drones. Pay special attention to spinning propellers because they can easily injure humans, animals, and property. If the plan is to test something new, remove the propellers first. Once it works as planned, put the propellers back on and use the drone safely. Don't forget to charge batteries in nonflammable areas and keep water away from them. Having a fire extinguisher nearby is a great idea, too!

Libraries Using Drones

In 2014, the University of South Florida Libraries introduced a plan in place that allowed students to check out drones for school-related projects. Library officials expected to be eligible for a Certificate of Waiver or Authorizations (COA) to do drone research, but "General Counsel for the FAA issued a legal interpretation that education is not a government function under COA guidelines," and the program was temporarily dropped (Roldan, 2014). The library continues to work with FAA officials to figure out a solution and hopes to make this service a reality in the future. Libraries are places of discovery and learning, so making drones available to patrons for a variety of reasons seems a natural extension to that discovery and learning process, but the regulations need to be finalized before that happens.

With the introduction of proposed commercialized drone delivery projects like Amazon Prime Air, it seemed that the next logical step would be to offer an Inter Library Loan (ILL) delivery service via drone. However, as far back as 2013, an Australian textbook company named Zookal was already thinking of using drones to deliver textbooks and other school-related items (Welch, 2013). To lessen privacy concerns, Zookal drones were designed without cameras, but they included what is now becoming a common feature on many drones, anti-collision technology, so that the drones would not crash into objects while delivering items.

Fast forward a year or two, and there were quite a few online joke videos showing Amazon Prime Air crashing to the ground and then having people steal the package before the buyer could retrieve it. These jokes raised serious issues regarding drone delivery. Zookal seemed to have it figured out because its drones would never land. Instead, they would hover over the spot where a buyer asked to have the package delivered and the drone would wait until the buyer tapped a button on her smartphone that would then release a package. A quick review of the Zookal website does not mention its proposed drone delivery program, so at the time this chapter was written, there was no confirmation whether this program was approved or not. With any potentially disruptive technology, it can take several years before it is fully understood and appropriately utilized, but it is clear that drones are here to stay and have the potential to make society better.

In early 2015, the Seminole Community Library at St. Petersburg College in partnership with the Innovation Lab [Makerspace@SPC] invited drone expert Donny Klotz to do a workshop. Klotz discussed the variety of drones available to consumers, showed how to assemble the popular Phantom 2 Vision + drone, and reviewed what is involved in the preflight checklist to a group. Some of the items mentioned in the preflight checklist were to

- Check the drone for any noticeable damage.
- Verify battery levels are full.
- Determine if the flight area is clear of potential hazards (e.g., people or power lines).

- Turn on the camera.
- Set the throttle to zero.
- Hover for a moment at a few feet to check various flight controls and stability.

Klotz fired up the drone and demonstrated maneuverability and other drone flight controls on the campus soccer field and later showed the participants how to edit the video on his tablet that the drone captured. The video from that day can be viewed at http://j.mp/iLabDrone.

As Klotz confirmed in this workshop, drones are becoming very popular with hobbyists, pilots, photographers, makers, consumers, and with journalists. For example, Tim Pool used two drones to cover the dangerous Gezi Park protests in Turkey for *Vice* magazine in 2013. Pool said that he sees drones as "democratizing the news, allowing individuals to report live news in a way only the largest broadcasters could ten years ago" (Demmons, 2015). Klotz confirmed Pool's statement a few months later when he located a dog being swept off a Hawaiian cliff with his drone video. Klotz's drone video was viewed more than 40,000 times in one week and the story was featured on *Inside Edition*, The Weather Channel, *The Atlanta Journal Constitution*, and more.

Google's Project Loon is using drones to provide Internet access to remote places on earth. Libraries have been providing Internet access to people for decades, and it seems that those serving rural areas could benefit from Project Loon or similar projects. Drones can deliver resources to natural disaster victims. Because drones are also helping collect data for research projects, it makes sense to invite libraries to participate in archiving photographs and videos captured by these research drones and to provide mechanisms to find and use these files.

Projects

Libraries have long been known for discovery and learning. Thanks to the makerspace movement, a library can provide an initial spark for an idea that may eventually flare into an intellectual flame. People can now visit their local library makerspaces and gain hands-on experiences with bleeding-edge technologies that they probably would not have access to otherwise. They can take what they have learned in these programs, and through various project workshops hosted at their libraries, further their education at other institutions that offer drone programs and degrees. Lifelong learning is a vital component for the continued success of libraries and makerspaces are just another tool to achieve it.

Create a Drone Community

When the Engineering Club at St. Petersburg College/Seminole Campus did not receive funding to create its own drone, the Innovation Lab [Makerspace@ SPC] saw a huge learning opportunity and consequently created a partnership with the club to build a drone in the library. The Innovation Lab purchased, with a college-provided grant, all the drone parts as well as a GoPro video camera and then offered a collaborative space in the library to build the drone. All these drone parts, including the GoPro, cost less than $350. Building the drone was a rewarding experience for everyone involved, and it opened even more possibilities for the library to begin experimenting with other drone projects and workshops in the library.

"How to Build a Drone" Workshop

Because staff kept good notes in our community notebook highlighting what worked and what did not work during our first drone build, we were prepared to conduct a hands-on "How to Build a Drone" workshop with a group of eager hobbyists in the library. Learning how all the parts work together to build a drone is important, especially for someone interested in owning a drone, either for a hobby or a professional opportunity, because a drone can be fixed and modified more easily for a variety of different tasks with knowledge of precisely how it was built in the first place. As mentioned above, soldering can be dangerous; so, offering a brief workshop on the basics of soldering would certainly be a good idea so that potential drone builders understand how to do it correctly before trying it on a drone or another electronic project.

This workshop can be taught in two ways. In one, participants build a drone in a group with one set of parts taught by a group leader. In the second, they would purchase their own parts from a Bill of Materials and take home the drone that they built themselves. If a camera is not included, the cost of materials would be a little over $150. This workshop works best when taught in two sections: one section to identify and organize the parts and to do the actual build, and the other section to cover how to program the flight computer and the receiver. It can take time to learn how to use the Cleanflight Configurator application to unlock the full potential of many flight computers and receivers, but it is a gratifying experience to learn firsthand how a drone's flight controls are programmed. Cleanflight.com has information about Cleanflight Configuration, including all documentation.

An "Advanced Drone Building" workshop could review how to add a telemetry function to demonstrate how drones can transmit real-time data such as battery levels, wind speed, GPS coordinates, height, speed, and motor temperature back to the operator on the ground. Being able to generate, read, and analyze this data while making quick decisions from that data is important not only in a school, but in professional environments as well.

"Introduction to Drone Flight" Workshop

Flying a drone is not easy at first, so libraries might offer a drone flight school workshop, similar to the previously discussed workshop offered by expert drone operator Donny Klotz. The workshop should cover current FAA rules and regulations, drone safety, and explain what equipment and software are involved in flying a drone. Although the theory of flying techniques can be taught indoors, flying a drone inside can cause damage to the building and serious injury can occur if not done properly. Therefore, it is best to hold the workshop in a large space outside to give participants hands-on experience flying a drone,

Note that if participants wish to fly a drone at this workshop it is a good idea to ask them to bring their FAA registration certificates. The registration fee is $5 and can be completed online at https://registermyuas.faa.gov.

However, part of the workshop could walk the participants through the registration process. They will likely select "Model Aircraft," because the majority of the participants would fly for noncommercial and/or other non-hobby purposes. Once a profile is created, a unique registration number will be assigned and that number will then apply to any drone owned by that one individual for years. Another registration is required after three years. Before obtaining the registration number, the owner must select that they have read and understood the "Acknowledgement of Safety Guidance" section, which is a good way to reiterate all the safety guidelines they learned in the first part of the workshop (e.g., fly below 400 feet and within visual line of site; do not fly over people, stadiums, or near airports; do not fly under the influence, etc.). Every drone must have the registration number marked in a visible place; because a registration number is assigned instantly after payment is received online, this could be covered in the workshop as well.

"Alternative Drone Technologies for Aerial Photography and Videography" Workshop

Multiwii is software designed for the popular Nintendo Wii video game controller that includes gyroscopes and accelerometers, and can now be used to control drones. Visit www.multiwii.com to learn about and download this powerful software. Multiwii can also be uploaded to many Arduino circuit boards, or an already built ArduPilot circuit board, which is based on the Arduino open-source electronics prototyping platform, can be used. An autopilot drone powered by the ArduPilot Flight Controller can transmit real-time data back to the operator, including photographs and video. The customizable Arduino sketch (as the program is known), which can be edited using the Arduino Integrated Development Environment (IDE), will also demonstrate how Arduinos are programmed for these types of projects and will hopefully inspire other possibilities for using drones and Arduinos. The Darien Public Library in Connecticut offered a workshop on building an ArduPilot, which they configured to execute a "hands-free flight plan around a neighboring Civil War cemetery getting footage with a GoPro" in the library's media lab (Blyberg, 2013).

"Drone Buying Guide" Workshop

Drones are gaining popularity because they are becoming more affordable and are easier to set up and use. This workshop can help participants figure out what their options are if they are considering a drone purchase. For example, First Person View (FPV) drones are very popular with hobbyists. The three basic FPV components are the camera, the video transmitter, and the video receiver. FPV setups can fail, so knowing how to safely fly a drone manually is essential and participants should have an opportunity to learn this in a library workshop.

There are plenty of ready-made drones and DIY models that can be controlled and viewed via FPV goggles or touchscreen displays, and it is a good idea to spend time researching the various options. The "Drone Buyers Guide" workshop can also use a Show-and-Tell format where the library shares its own drones and encourages others to bring in their personal drones, so that people can learn about the various types. To read detailed reviews of FPV goggles and to learn more about this technology, visit www.dronethusiast.com/the-ultimate-fpv-system-guide.

Drone racing is becoming extremely popular, so much so that it's developing into a live sport. Racing drones are basically very small and light with extremely powerful motors that allow the pilot to make fast turns with lightning precision. Many drone racers use FPV goggles because they are more intuitive controlling the drone through various obstacles and at faster speeds. Spectators can find the signal being used to transmit the drone's video to the pilot so that they too can experience the race with their own FPV googles. Future films, other race events, or even space travel may one day allow people to experience this type of entertainment using their own FPV goggles. (The drone that was described in detail earlier in this chapter is a basic race drone, but we are interested in taking it a step further and trying to build another one without a camera attached so the focus can be on speed and maneuvering it.)

Conclusion

Without a doubt, drones have entered the consumer marketplace, and more people are becoming interested in learning to fly. It is not difficult to imagine a society that has many autonomous and nonautonomous drones, robots, and other objects working together to help make the world a better place. The Internet of Things (IoT) brings all of this into a different light too. Many of the IoT devices are static. Drones are not, so they can include a variety of sensors to allow them to conduct sophisticated measurements for various meteorological research, for example, and to accomplish many other tasks. There has even been talk of creating an "Internet of Drones" where drones can be connected to the Internet to follow other connected devices to help them to finish a specific job.

Drones are on their way to becoming a ubiquitous technology and many people are discovering this at their libraries. Again, the library makerspace is a perfect place to share drone and other emerging technologies with patrons, to help them become well-informed citizens and responsible users of technology.

Complete Drone Part List

- Turnigy 9X Nine9-Channel Transmitter with Module and Eight-Channel Receiver (Mode 2) (v2 Firmware), $59
- AfroFlight Naze32 Rev5 Acro FunFly Controller, soldered version (Horizontal Pin), $20

- Turnigy 9XR Safety Protected 11.1V (3s) 2200mAh 1.5C Transmitter Pack, $14
- Zippy Flightmax 2100mAh 3S 35C LiPo Pack, $12
- Turnigy E3 Compact 2S/3S LiPo Charger 100–240V (US Plug), $12
- Power Pack E kit (Racing MINI Quadcopter), $99. This setup is designed to be used with a 3s LiPo battery but is also rated to be used with 4s with smaller props installed. Pack includes:
    - four motors—Emax 2204 2350 kv (CW threaded)
    - four ESCs—BL Heli 12 amp (XT-30—connectors)
    - four propellers—6 x 4.5 CW
    - four propellers—6 x 4.5 CCW
    - one battery lead—XT60
    - one FT Allen driver (2.0 mm)
    - one Custom Flite Test LiPo bag
    - four M5 lock nuts (CW threaded)

- FT VersaCopter 280 V2 Quad Kit (Power Pack E Racing Mini Quadcopter), $158. Kit includes:
    - one top VersaCopter plate
    - one bottom VersaCopter power distribution plate
    - two carbon fiber booms
    - four aluminum motor mounts
    - two aluminum boom brackets
    - one Delrin structural casing
    - one Delrin backside antenna/battery lead
    - one ten-pack 30-mm screws
    - one ten-pack 25-mm screws
    - two FT battery straps
    - twelve 4-inch black zip ties
    - two 8-inch black zip ties
    - one grommet
    - one FT sticker

- GoPro HERO Starter Bundle, $150. Bundle includes:
    - one GoPro HERO, 1080p30 and 720p 60 video. (records audio with the built-in microphone)
    - two SanDisk Ultra 32 GB Ultra Micro SDHC UHS-I/Class 10 cards with adapter

– one Wasabi Power Extended Battery for GoPro HERO
– one AmazonBasics Head Strap Camera Mount for GoPro

REFERENCES

1. Association for Unmanned Vehicle Systems International (AUVSI). (2013). Economic impact of unmanned aircraft systems integration in the United States. www.auvsi.org/auvsiresources/economicreport.

2. Blyberg, John. (2013, March 25). Library "maker" program. *DIY Drones.* http://diydrones .com/forum/topics/library-maker-program.

3. Demmons, Chris. (2015). "Innovation Lab Brings Drone Expert to Seminole Campus." *Sandbox News,* February 2015. https://sandbox.spcollege.edu/index.php/2015/02/innovation-lab-brings-drone-expert-to-seminole-campus.

4. Hume, Tim. (2016, April 2017). Investigations launched after suspected drone strikes passenger jet in London. *CNN.com.* www.cnn.com/2016/04/17/europe/london-heathrow -drone-strikes-plane.

5. Passas, Jennifer. (2015, 29 October). Cities of the future might rely on drones to repair themselves. *PSFK.* www.psfk.com/2015/10/cities-of-the-future-university-of-leeds -drones-self-repairing-cities.html.

6. PBS.org. (2000). Tesla—Master of lightning: Remote control. Directed by Robert Uth. *PBS.org.* www.pbs.org/tesla/ins/lab_remotec.html.

7. Roldan, Roberto. Library Drone Plan Hits Turbulence. (August 28, 2014). *The Oracle.* www.usforacle.com/news/view.php/845153/Library-drone-plan-hits-turbulence.

8. Tucker, Fred. Want to fly a drone? SPC offers training in growing industry. *St. Peters- burg College Blog.* November 4, 2015. https://blog.spcollege.edu/engineering/spc-drone -training.

9. Welch, Chris. (2013, October 15). Zookal will deliver textbooks using drones in Austra- lia next year. *The Verge.* www.theverge.com/2013/10/15/4840706/zookal-will-deliver -textbooks-with-drones-in-australia.

ADDITIONAL RESOURCES

Drones, quadcopters, UAV's, FPV photography and flying, www.droneflyers.com/.

15 best drone training colleges, http://successfulstudent.org/15-best-drone-training-colleges/.

Unmanned aircraft guidance, http://knowbeforeyoufly.org/.

Unmanned aircraft systems: Frequently asked questions, www.faa.gov/uas/faq/.

Unmanned aircraft systems (UAS) registration,www.faa.gov/uas/registration/.

Library Hackerspace Programs

CHAD CLARK

Rise of the Hackerspace

In recent years, there has been a surge of interest in making, from DIY and crafts to hacking, 3D printing, and electronic tinkering. This has been accompanied by the emergence of community spaces offering public and shared access to resources where individuals can pursue DIY projects. These spaces have been interchangeably referred to as hackerspaces, makerspaces, TechShops, and FabLabs. Although there are no standard guidelines to create a hackerspace, they generally stand by a set of "hacker ethics." Values include "freedom, in the sense of autonomy as well as of free access and circulation of information; distrust of authority, that is, opposing the traditional, industrial top-down style of organization; embracing the concept of learning by doing and peer-to-peer learning processes as opposed to formal modes of learning; sharing, solidarity, and cooperation."[1] The exact way a hackerspace functions is often determined by its members. Above all else, hackerspaces are motivated to recognize and value individuals who take action and relish getting things done, similar to the philosophy of a "do-ocracy."[2]

Chad Clark is New Media Manager at Highland Park Public Library.

The word *hacker* is often misapplied to describe law-breaking, information theft, privacy violation, and other black-hat activities. In this chapter, I do not use it in this sense of the word, but in its original meaning: a person who rearranges and repurposes the objects and systems around her to satisfy her curiosity and create new meaning.[3] To many of those inside the maker movement, the terms "hacking" and "hacker" are fundamentally about blocked entrances.[4] Whether they refer to the traditional act of programming to circumvent existing systems, or the act of working with physical parts, there is a basic understanding that "hacking" refers to activities that involve making existing objects do something unexpected.

In schools, universities, and libraries in the United States, hacking has begun to be embraced as a culture of making. It can be supported in diverse ways and can motivate individuals to understand systems at a deeper level. Also supporting this culture of making are new educational environments (e.g., The Maker Education Initiative, San Diego Central Library's Fixit Clinic), conventions (e.g., Maker Faires, and lower-profile maker gatherings), shared working spaces (e.g., hackerspaces, makerspaces), local meetups and events (e.g., XOXO Festival, Ars Electronica) and online forums where tremendous amounts of knowledge are exchanged (e.g., Creative Applications Network, Instructables).

Why Hackerspace Programs in the Library?

Makers and hackers are creating an emerging culture of "learning by doing" that is shifting how future workers learn to innovate.[5] They are seeking spaces that support a new user/learner experience. By providing physical hackerspaces or hackerspace-related programming, libraries can play a role in the development of future systems that will support lifelong learning.

Of course, there is precedent for public libraries creating and tailoring programming and services to meet the needs of the children and families they serve, and this relatively newer trend towards making and hacking is no different. In a post on the ACRL TechConnect Blog, Nicholas Schiller reasoned that hackers and libraries in fact already share many of the same values. Schiller refers to library education and technology advocate Char Booth's distillation of the Library Bill of Rights into five core values: access, freedom, advocacy, inquiry, and openness. He contends that these core values compare closely to those of the hacker, which include sharing, openness, collaboration, and the hands-on-imperative.[6] With regard to access to information, public openness, freedom, sharing, and collaboration, libraries and hackers appear to be on the same wavelength.

Librarians know that libraries have always played a role in supplying their communities with information that will allow them to modify their environment. Hackerspaces in libraries are primary locations for building community and exploring new ideas. Although many libraries have begun offering tools for digital-content creation, hackerspace programs have the potential to reorient the library towards even greater user engagement, collaborative creative activity, and participatory learning.

Types of Hackerspace Programs

Hacking does not necessarily involve working with code, computers, or technology. Hacking projects can integrate any combination of high- and low-tech materials and processes. No matter what type of hackerspace program you choose to organize, it should always be clear that its goal is to spark curiosity and, if all goes well, create new meaning. The most successful hackerspace programs reinforce the idea that our world is malleable and that the devices and spaces we interact with everyday can be repurposed and modified to create new experiences. The act of hacking can take on many different forms. This section reviews some of the major types that can work well in libraries.

Hacking with Code

Learning and working with computer languages are entry points to understanding systems at a deeper level. Making computers behave in unintended and creative ways, regardless of how simple or complex they may be, satisfies the hacker requisite of learning by doing.

Three popular entry-point programming languages considered rewarding by many experienced coders are Python, Ruby, and Scratch. Once comfortable with these, many progress to more challenging languages like Perl, C++, and JavaScript. Some languages require learners to be confident typing on a keyboard, whereas others like Scratch are visual and require good hand-eye coordination for image manipulation. First programming languages should be easy enough for beginners to understand and have strong online support communities. Both Python and Ruby work well as a first programming language because they are higher-level languages, meaning they are closer to a natural spoken language. Scratch works well because it's a visual language that uses color-coded blocks on a stage. All three are supported by many dedicated online forums.

Hacking Old Hardware

Hacking can include tinkering with a goal of understanding how something works; therefore, tearing apart old hardware works perfectly as a hackerspace activity. For some, the discovery phase of hacking doesn't click with software because they can't *see* it. With hardware, however, you make a change and you can immediately see the results. During the deconstruction of an object, an amazing amount of discovery occurs. Hackers discover, learn, and innovate through deconstruction. It is also an extremely inexpensive activity. Programs can be designed around taking apart unwanted computer keyboards, PC towers, old tablets or smartphones, and other items that would otherwise be donated or discarded.

Physical Computing: Arduino, Raspberry Pi, Wearable Computing, E-Textiles, LEGO, and Robotics

Physical computing, in the broadest sense, means building interactive physical systems by using software and hardware that can sense and respond to the real world. Physical computing workshops and events in libraries that use sensors and microcontrollers can include learning how to make handmade art, design, or DIY hobby projects. Various versions of the Arduino microcontroller are the foundation of literally thousands of projects created by makers worldwide. Arduino runs on an open-source development environment. RaspberryPi and BeagleBone (both of which run on Linux) are two other popular physical computing platforms that allow users to make computers that drive both functional and creative projects.

Popular items for hacking electronics with the Arduino include:

- Parallax robots
- Spakfun Redbot
- Particle Photons
- Feather Bluefruit LE
- ESP8266
- Wave Shields
- WiFi Shields
- RGB LCD Shields with I2C
- GPS Logger Shield
- SD Logger Shield
- NeoPixels
- SparkFun 6 Degrees of Freedom IMU Digital Combo Board

The number of educationally focused companies that are providing robot kits designed to introduce basic programming and physical computing is growing rapidly. Here is a list of kits that libraries have used with success:

- The Finch
- Hummingbird Robotics Kits
- Sphero 2.0
- Ollie
- mBot Robot Kit
- Romibo
- Cubelets
- Ozobot
- Dash & Dot
- WowWee MiP Robot
- Roboblock
- LEGO MINDSTORMS
- LEGO WeDo
- GoGo Board

Wearables are another popular type of hacking that some refer to as "crafting electricity." Wearables are clothing and accessories that incorporate computer and electronic technologies. The open-source hardware company Adafruit offers FLORA, a fully-featured wearable electronics platform. The Arduino LilyPad Kit is another set of sewable electronic pieces designed to help build soft interactive textiles. No-sew DIY hacks can also be performed with stitch adhesive and rivet kits. Searching for the terms "Clothing Hacks" or "Fashion Hacks" on Pinterest will pull up a ton of ideas.

How to Plan Hackerspace Programs in the Library

The maker movement is largely driven by peer-to-peer learning. Making and hacking activities can generally be characterized as informal and ad hoc. Information and directions aren't necessarily provided by an expert or a teacher, as the process is exploratory and participants learn from each other. That said, there are certainly basic skills and strategies that will allow library staff to host successful hackerspace programs.

- When it comes to hacking, there is a tradition of starting with something that already exists and modifying it, and this translates to a solid instructional strategy as well. Plan your programs around the process of deconstruction, but be open to new avenues discovered by participants.
- Reach out to other libraries to build on their experiences with the programs you're implementing.
- Use the resources provided by companies producing these tools. Most are eager to assist libraries in bringing these programs to fruition.

- Because hackerspace programs are at their roots problem-solving programs, some participants are bound to get to a point in a project where the logic or activity becomes difficult for them to define. Many will be ready to stop once they can't figure it out. Be prepared to provide general support and motivation, to facilitate teamwork and problem-solving. Be prepared to act as a sounding board, fellow brainstormer, and timekeeper.
- Successful hackerspace programs often incorporate exhibitions. Planning opportunities for participants to present to parents is important. It helps participants to organize their thoughts if they know that when they finish their projects, they'll have to explain what they've accomplished to someone else. Actively encourage participants to not simply sit by while a system does its work, but to hack the technology and, most importantly, to share what they learn.

Tips You Need to Know about Hacking Programs in the Library

In many ways, it's not the programming that is key—it's how learning generates socialization that counts. Think of the librarian as a facilitator, rather than librarian as an expert. As a facilitator, your role is to create a welcoming environment in which people feel encouraged to imagine new ideas and bring them to life through creative hands-on explorations. Rather than directly instructing, your focus as a facilitator is to provide a safe and inviting space in which makers can experiment and learn from their own explorations. Before you begin hackerspace programming ask yourself a few questions—are you set up to empower participants to think, to challenge, to explore, to discover? Do your hackerspace programs encourage participants to say, "I can do this!"? Learners of all ages need trust and permission to act.

Here are tips that will help regardless of the type of hackerspace program you wish to implement:

- You may choose to give participants the ability to use soldering irons, saws, glue guns, things that are quite dangerous. Soldering irons, solder, tip cleaners, wire strippers, wire snips, and helping hands are required tools for running successful soldering workshops. If you are concerned about the use of soldering in your library, there are solderless solutions available as well. These alternatives use breadboards and wire that is inserted to the breadboard to make electrical circuits. Safety should be paramount in maker activities.

- Work areas should be ventilated, fire-resistant (if need be), well-lit, and conceived in a fashion that allows groups of patrons to work together safely on projects. Although most activities carry a low risk of danger, there are some activities that present more possibility for risk. Speak with your administrators to gauge their comfort level with the activities that you are considering. A release form to be signed by participants can confirm they are aware of and consent to any possible hazards encountered in your making programs.
- A popular way to gain comfort and experience with physical computing is with Trinkets, which are small and economical Arduino variants used for electronic prototyping. Trinkets allow users to learn from simple projects, programming code examples, and tweaking them to make them unique.
- You do not need to have expertise in a specific area; rather, collaborate with the participants to seek out answers. Be prepared to exploit the teachable moments that naturally occur during hacking to expose the underlying math, science, and engineering principles involved.
- Emphasize process over product and that it is okay to fail. Hackerspace programs should value experiential learning (learning by doing). Avoid dictating step-by-step instructions. It is better to advise participants to try and figure out how to do it by themselves, asking other participants, or researching it using the library's resources. Choose to celebrate the fact that participants are doing, not simply taking home some shiny object that they've made.
- Hackerspace programs should be interest-driven, so kids or adults will themselves choose what projects or challenges they're going to do. Often with kids you will find that if you tell them what to do or how to do it, they quickly lose interest.
- Hackerspace programs do not necessarily have to take place in a designated area. Making can happen anywhere depending on your time, financial considerations, and space. Like all library programs, it is important to provide a space where participants know that they can be safe, be creative, and have autonomy no matter what part of the library that may be.
- Kids are experts at things like Minecraft, so try to have kids teaching classes and encourage them to teach each other and to share their knowledge and what they've learned. Kids can also teach us—they know more about Minecraft, for example, than we do, and we should encourage them to share this online so other people can benefit from their knowledge.
- You don't need an electrical engineering degree to start hacking electronics. There are many intuitive guides that demonstrate how to wire, disassemble, tweak, and repurpose everyday devices quickly and easily. Hacking-based websites and books provide full-color illustrations, photos, and diagrams that

feature fun, easy-to-follow projects. With the right amount of confidence and intuition it is best to discover along with your patrons how to hack sensors, accelerometers, remote controllers, ultrasonic range finders, motors, stereo equipment, microphones, and FM transmitters.

- A dollar store is a major source of useful objects to hack. Find the aisle with the electronic stuff: flashlights, fans, solar toys, illuminated cooling laptop bases, and so on. It's amazing what can be bought for under a dollar. Often you will find motors and arrays of LEDs for a lower price than you would pay for the raw components from a conventional supplier. Supermarkets are another source of cheap electronics. Good examples of useful gadgets are cheap computer speakers, mice, power supplies, radio receivers, LED flashlights, and computer keyboards.

- It may take some effort to show your administration why hackerspace programs belong in the library. There are a number of articles that have been published, and more research is being done all the time on the benefits of making and makerspaces. You can also try hosting community events such as "Open Hack Nights," to let your community know the library is interested in maker activities. Invite local makers to come and exhibit and give patrons a chance to learn about making. Use photos and statistics from these events to make the case for expanded maker activities at your library.

- Try to identify the niche your hackerspace or hackerspace programming fits into. Show marketability: Create a solid "who we are and what we offer" statement on your website, and pick your logo and hackerspace colors for consistency. Encourage kids to Tweet and share photos. Do outreach. If you just offer access and nothing else, the people that use your hackerspace will be very self-selected.

- It would benefit most hackerspace programmers to get their local schools involved. Libraries can provide opportunities for teachers who are considering introducing similar programming at their schools to learn for themselves and gain firsthand experience.

- Reach out actively to local businesses and the community at large. You may be surprised to find how many free donations you will gather, and just how much amazing talent will come out of the woodwork. Anyone from HVAC experts to ex-NASA scientists may be part of your community. If they are aware of your hackerspace programming, chances are they will investigate.

- Start out by looking up your local makerspaces. Who else in your library community is doing this work? Look on http://hackerspace.meetup.com/. Who else in the community at large is making? If there are not any other established makers, then turn to local businesses, organizations, and professional groups to see if they are interested in joining forces.

- Don't overlook the partners within your organization. Your IT staff, the tech-savvy librarians or staff around you are your greatest allies. Whether you need help with 3D printers, rebooting the wireless network, or just creating the double-sided print job needed to make Minecraft paper art, your colleagues may be your closest emergency relief.
- Many hackerspace programs work well for families. Consider holding hackerspace programs on a Saturday or Sunday, depending on the days and times your library is open to support families.

How Libraries Are Implementing Hackerspace Programs

Libraries are implementing hackerspace programs under the auspices of coding events, DIY crafting activities, 3D printing, hackathons, physical computing workshops, and so much more. As a result, a mixture of different learning opportunities is being created. For example, the concept of responsible digital citizenship weaves quite naturally into many hackerspace programs, even if it is not explicitly stated. Libraries such as Innisfil Public Library are cultivating a hacker ethic in their strategic plans by integrating technology into their services and spaces, and building technological confidence.[7] This section reviews some of the hackerspace programming events that are reshaping the boundaries of libraries services.

Fixit Clinics

Libraries such as San Diego Central Library and Oakland Public Library are partnering with a group called Fixit Clinic to organize and host all-ages do-it-together (D.I.T) repair events at the library. Fixit Clinic's mission statement reads as follows: "Education, entertainment, empowerment, elucidation, and, ultimately, enlightenment through guided disassembly of your broken stuff." "While the primary objective of Fixit Clinic is to demystify consumer technology and empower people to disassemble and repair their broken stuff, the secondary, somewhat surreptitious goal is to improve science and technology literacy in the population overall, so we can choose officials to make good policy decisions," says Peter Mui, who founded the Fixit Clinic in 2009.[8]

For its Fixit Clinic events, The San Diego Central Library helps pair passionate and dedicated individuals from the community who are comfortable using their hands to help participants troubleshoot and repair small items. They encourage community members to bring broken electronics, appliances, toys, etc. for assessment, disassembly, and possible repair. San Diego Central Library coordinator and youth services librarian Laura Anthony calls this process a disassembly education. "It's more about the experience of taking it apart to see what's working and what's broken about it" says Anthony.[9] In the process, participants gain an understanding of how their products work.

Hour of Code

Hour of Code is an annual event held in December during Computer Science Education Week in which many libraries are beginning to participate. Hour of Code was created in 2013 to encourage students to learn computer science and advocate for more schools to teach it. Librarians are well positioned to run Hour of Code activities because they most likely already have the computers and Internet access needed to run these programs. The Denver, Colorado, and Chattanooga, Tennessee, public libraries are two of many public libraries that have hosted successful Hour of Code events. High-profile code days or code weeks like Hour of Code offer gateways for exposing learners to coding and to apps like Hopscotch, Daisy the Dinosaur, Tynker, Scratch, ScratchJr, and Lightbot Programming Puzzles.

Coder Dojo

Coder Dojo is a volunteer-led, global movement of free coding clubs for young people. Libraries are beginning to host Dojos, where young people between seven and seventeen learn how to code, develop websites, apps, programs, games, and explore technology in an informal and creative environment. Volunteers share their coding expertise with the participants and mentor and motivate them through the learning process. To seek out or start a CoderDojo group in your area go to coderdojo.com.

Brooklyn's Central Library hosted a CoderDojo Maker Party for teens and tweens interested in coding and making. This event included hands-on multimedia tech activities, including coding with Scratch and web page building. Denver Public Library hosted what they called "Open Code sessions with Coder Dojo" where they invited participants to bring in their own projects. Volunteers and experienced coders were on hand to help debug code or provide ideas to take projects to the next level. Denver Public Library also makes it possible for participants to show off their creations on a big screen. Like many successful hackerspace-like events, this model of programming is not necessarily a formal class but rather a community building event to help kids and teens expand their creativity as they apply their technical skills in a friendly and supportive atmosphere.

Hackathons

- **Chattahoochee Valley Libraries** hosted an event called Hack the Library in 2014. The winning team was Girl Scout Troop 50132, who won over judges with their app Badge It Up, which allowed them to track the badges they earn electronically and find books and resources in the library to help them earn those badges.
- **DC Public Library** hosted an Accessibility Hackathon. For this a group of young adults with disabilities were mentored through the stages of entrepreneurship around the process of innovating new adaptive technologies. The hackathon was led by a group of participating developers in a series of events related to DC Week, a citywide tech festival that brings together developers, government, and nonprofits.
- **The Cupertino Library** hosted CU HACKS, a tech-centric campout of sorts that allows high school and early college-age residents to compete at the library. Hackers were given roughly a thirteen-hour window to combine their critical thinking, technical planning, and coding development skills to produce applications directly relating to a specific prompt. Cupertino Library limited this free event to 150 teenagers aged fourteen through nineteen. "CU HACKS is an innovative program that establishes the library as a place that engages teens in creating projects that make a positive impact on the lives of teens in the Cupertino community," says Eno Schmidt, president of the Cupertino Library Foundation.[10]

Hackerspaces in Libraries

- **The Danbury Hackerspace @ the Innovation Center** is a hackerspace and coworking facility that is connected to the Danbury Library.
- **Maker Jawn** is a hackerspace that provides space for community members in North Philadelphia Free Libraries. At Maker Jawn, self-directed experimental and experiential learning is promoted through a focus on creativity, critical thinking, and skill-building. Maker Jawn embraces a hacker ethic by striving to "expose youth and adults to materials, encourage them to engage in playing and tinkering, and to further collaborate with their peers and Mentors."[11]

- For an extensive list of Maker-Hacker-Lab Spaces and Events both in and outside of libraries, see the shared Google Doc at http://bit.ly/26UcGLe.

Projects

MIT App Inventor 2: <HelloPurr/>Tap the Kitty, Hear Him Meow: Building My First App

The tablets and smartphones that we use today to consume entertainment and information are black boxes to most of us. To the average person, creating the apps that run on these devices appears inaccessible and the systems within in them inexplicable. MIT's App Inventor 2 is an ideal platform for introductory hackerspace programming because it demystifies all of this. It is a free visual drag-and-drop tool for building mobile apps on the Android platform. In short, users can design the interface of an app using a web-based graphical user interface builder, then specify the app's behavior by piecing together "blocks" as if they were working on a puzzle.

HelloPurr is a simple app that can be built in a very short time using MIT App Inventor 2. In this activity participants create an app that displays a picture of a cat that meows when you touch it and purrs when you shake it. HelloPurr is a useful way to help participants learn the basic components of MIT App Inventor 2 and take it in their own directions. If all goes well participants gain a less passive and more creative relationship to these devices.

Setting up App Inventor 2

MIT App Inventor 2 is a cloud-based tool, which means you can build apps right in your web browser. If you don't have an Android phone or tablet handy, you can still use MIT App Inventor 2. MIT provides an Android emulator, which works just like an Android but appears on your computer screen. Users can test their apps on the emulator and still distribute the app to others, even via the Play Store. To use the emulator, you will first need to install some software on your computer.

Introducing MIT App Inventor 2

The MIT App Inventor 2 platform consists of basically two parts: the Designer and the Blocks Editor. In the App Inventor Designer users select the components for their apps. In the App Inventor Blocks Editor, they specify how the components should behave. App Inventor programs are typically broken into multiple sessions as follows:

- selecting components for your app
- adding media (sounds and images) to apps
- assembling blocks that define the components' behavior
- testing apps with App Inventor's live testing
- packaging the apps and downloading them to a phone

Tutorials, forums, and supplementary learning resources can all be found at http://ai2.appinventor.mit.edu/.

Hackasaurus

Described as an "open educational resource," Hackasaurus was developed by the Mozilla Foundation and allows its users to hack their favorite websites by changing their text and photos. Hackasaurus helps teens hack through tools that make it easy for youth to explore, remix, and redesign the web. By turning on Hackasaurus "X-Ray Goggles" on almost any website, users can view the code and remix the individual parts of the web page, including photos, subject headings, and body paragraphs. They can then publish their version of the site and share the link with others to view and further remix.

Hackasaurus can serve as an effective platform for hackerspace programming in libraries and works great for mini library-sponsored hackathons. By deconstructing and remixing websites, participants become critical producers, rather than passive consumers, of web content. Participants can spend a relatively short amount of time using Hackasaurus to make something unique and then turn their completed makes over to a friend who can then remake it and create something new.

Minecraft Community Hack

Minecraft is an extremely popular video game designed to make things out of virtual blocks. Minecraft generates a distinctive world filled with mountains, rivers, hills, and lakes. Blocks can be attached to one another to quickly produce structures. Using Minecraft as a community participation tool for public space design is an excellent way to introduce hacking. Minecraft Community Hacks can be effective ways to bring the young and old together. Illinois's Highland Park Public Library hosts an after-school club where participants work together and make connections with local historians and archivists to reimagine prominent pieces of their community.

Toy Hacking

Toy Hacking is a fun and playful way to learn how circuits work and a relatively easy way to put together a hackerspace program in your library. Workshops can be held that use electronic toys rescued from thrift stores and garage sales. Participants carefully and safely take the toys apart to learn how they work. They explore both the simplicity and complexity of these toys. Participants get a firsthand look at unique circuits and can learn how to identify inputs, outputs, and power.

Toy hacking is a creative reverse engineering project—learning how something works by taking it apart—then making it new. This activity inspires experimentation and exploration. Toy hacking uses electronic toys that are accessible to everyone and inexpensive. It is also an opportunity to recycle and use up cycle parts that would otherwise end up in a landfill.

Art Bot

An art bot is a DIY robot that wobbles across a piece of paper, creating drawings as it moves. This is a beginner-level project that requires no robotics experience. For a typical art bot program, participants hack apart small devices with motors inside (e.g., electric toothbrushes) and repurpose the parts to create personalized art-creating creatures that scribble, scrape, sing, or splatter. Building an art bot is a laid-back and easy project for both librarians and participants to begin to explore with electronic circuits, playing, and tinkering. Science Buddies (http://bit.ly/10xfbtV) is one of many places on the web to find lesson plans and examples of art bot projects.

Hacking with Python

Like any other skill, coding becomes more relevant when learners can use it in a way that is meaningful to them. Here are two introductory activities that use the computer programming language Python:

How to Make Snowflakes with Python Turtle

Participants create a landscape of snowflakes using Python Turtle. Along the way you will learn how to think in sequences, use loops to repeat a sequence, use the random module, and how to use functions.

Create a Virtual Magic 8-Ball

Participants create a virtual Magic 8-Ball, a mystical, fortune-telling device that answers yes/no questions. Explore textual programming and begin learning sequence of instructions.

Hacking with Scratch: Digitally Interfaced Book with Paper, Graphite, Makey Makey, Scratch, and Imagination

The free, visual programming language Scratch is another option for introducing hackerspace programming. Scratch is designed for kids to remix culture via computer programming. Version 2.0 is browser-based and features a library of more than 8 million projects you can play, explore, remix, and reuse for your own purposes. It is a real programming language with an enormous community built around it. Great for animation, game design, and storytelling.

In the language of computer science, "Scratching" means reusing code that can be beneficial and effective for other purposes and easily combined, shared, and adapted to new scenarios. This is a key feature in Scratch—the "remix," in which users can download and build upon public projects uploaded and developed by other users. It also gives credit to the participant who built on the original work and to the participant who created the original program. Simply prompting participants in hackerspace programs to remix projects is a fun way to get started with Scratch.

More components can be added to push Scratch outside of its normal use. A great example is the National Writing Project's *Digitally Interfaced Book: Paper, Graphite, Makey Makey, Scratch, and Imagination.* Directions can be found on its website (http://bit.ly/1m8jsZc).

Outro

Neil Gershenfeld, a professor of media arts and sciences at the Massachusetts Institute of Technology (MIT), maintains that the real importance of hackerspaces (MIT calls its Fab Lab) lies in the value created and communities exposed when hackers share their experiential stories about hacking. Hackerspaces anchor communities of people who use their skills for the benefit of the public and each other. Though it's useful to make high-end tools like 3D printers accessible to all, it's disadvantageous to see tools as an answer. Being a maker and a hacker is a mindset, not a tool.

Libraries are among the fastest-evolving learning spaces and should be continuously reshaping themselves to fit their communities' needs. Libraries have an opportunity to prepare the next generation of innovators by designating learning spaces for making, hacking, and coworking. The future of technology will be largely determined by end users who will design, build, and hack their own devices, and our mission as librarians is to inspire, shape, and support these communities.

NOTES

1. Vasilis Kostakis, Vasilis Niaros, and Christos Giotitsas, "Production and Governance in Hackerspaces: A Manifestation of Commons-Based Peer Production in the Physical Realm?" *International Journal of Cultural Studies* (2014): 1–19.
2. "Do-ocracy," *Noisebridge*, www.noisebridge.net/wiki/Do-ocracy.
3. Ben. A. Yagoda, "A Short History of 'Hack,'" *The New Yorker*, March 6, 2014, www.new yorker.com/tech/elements/a-short-history-of-hack.
4. "Is It a Hackerspace, Makerspace, TechShop, or FabLab?" *Make Magazine*, May 2013, http://makezine.com/2013/05/22/the-difference-between-hackerspaces-makerspaces -techshops-and-fablabs.
5. Kathleen Constanza, "Millennials Who Blaze Trails in the Innovation Economy," Remake Learning, March 24, 2016, http://remakelearning.org/blog/2016/03/29/ millennials-who-blaze-trails-in-the-innovation-economy/.

6. Nicholas Schiller, "Hacker Values ≈ Library Values," ACRL TechConnect, November 13, 2012, http://acrl.ala.org/techconnect/post/hacker-values-%E2%89%88-library -values.
7. Debra Mann, "Cultivating a Hacker Ethic: Digital Citizenship at the Innisfil Public Library," *Webjunction*, October 9, 2014, www.webjunction.org/news/webjunction/ cultivating-a-hacker-ethic.html.
8. Camilla Brinkman, "Education, Empowerment and Enlightenment through Guided Disassembly of your Broken Stuff," *MIT News*, February 7, 2012, http://news.mit.edu/ 2012/education-empowerment-and-enlightenment-through-guided-disassembly -of-your-broken-stuff.
9. Paul Sisson, "Fixit Clinic Gives New Life to Broken Stuff," *San Diego Union Tribune*, January 9, 2016, www.sandiegouniontribune.com/news/science/sdut-fixit-clinic-library -2016jan09-story.html.
10. "Hackathon for Teens June 20th at the Cupertino Library," Cupertino Library Foundation, http://cupertinolibraryfoundation.org/hackathon-for-teens-june-20th-at -the-cupertino-library/.
11. "Maker Jawn," YOUmedia Network, http://community.youmedia.org/site-spotlights/ makerjawn.

Part III
Looking Ahead

Mobile Makerspaces

KIM MARTIN, MARY COMPTON, AND RYAN HUNT

What's a Mobile Makerspace?

Throughout the earlier chapters of this book, you have learned about the maker movement, makerspaces, and a variety of maker tools and technology. This chapter will talk about mobile makerspaces, and what can happen when you take all the excitement of a makerspace and put it on the road.

So, what is a mobile makerspace? Basically, it's a miniature makerspace that's built into a vehicle, usually the back of a truck or a revamped bus. These mobile spaces can take many forms depending on your own individual needs. A mobile makerspace may, for example, be used primarily as a mobile workshop with tools and workstations where people build, create, and innovate inside the vehicle itself. Imagine walking onto a bus, where instead of seats, you see workbenches and stools; instead of school bags, kids are wearing tool belts and safety goggles. Tools hang from pegboard, and craft supplies line the wall in color-coded storage containers.

Kim Martin, Mary Compton, and Ryan Hunt are Cofounders at The MakerBus Collaborative, Southwestern Ontario, Canada.

A mobile makerspace may favor relaxed seating over workstations and may be used primarily as an inspiring community space where kids and adults can gather and brainstorm project ideas. Although a vehicle like a van or a bus can make a great classroom, workshop, or community space, they can also be pared down and used primarily for the transportation of maker equipment to other spaces (particularly if you are working with a smaller vehicle). Sometimes individuals choose to focus entirely on equipment storage, portability, and modularity. As our examples will show, most mobile makerspaces incorporate elements of all of these functionalities to varying degrees—the allocation of storage space and usable space becomes a fine balancing act, shaped chiefly by what you choose to prioritize and by how creative you can be in your use of space. Many different versions of mobile makerspaces exist, and this chapter will introduce you to several of those, as well as providing you with tips and tricks to get your own mobile makerspace started. But first, let's start with a quick discussion of why you might consider "going mobile" in the first place.

Why Go Mobile?

Before taking on the task of creating a mobile makerspace (and believe us, it's no small undertaking!), you should be aware of the pros and cons of such a project. The first thing to think about is why you might want to go mobile in the first place. Here are a few reasons to get you started:

1. *People are fascinated with mobility.*
   Historically, people are fascinated with mobility, and mobile information spaces in particular. The bookmobile is perhaps the most well-known of these, built to take books out to the public, and to provide library access to those who might not be able to get to the stationary branches in person. In addition to bookmobiles, there are also libraries on bikes (known as "book bikes") that encourage people to read in parks, gardens, and city streets.

2. *You have a small library.*
   Makerspaces take up space—there's no getting around it. Though there are many ways you can work maker technology and tools into a small library, sometimes having a mobile addition to that library is necessary for your users to be able to make good use of the tools you have available.

3. *Your library caters to a large population located over a wide geographical area.*
Many libraries these days are experiencing cutbacks, and this often means that
one branch must provide access to information for a very large area, which
can make it difficult for everyone in that area to access the stationary library.
A mobile makerspace can help with this, by allowing maker tech to be shared
with the public from a variety of locations (parks, shopping mall parking lots,
and farmers' markets, to name a few).

4. *You are excited about making, and want your community to be as well!*
Taking making on the road is a great way to showcase library offerings to
the public! Not only can your vehicle be a great advertisement for the library
system, but it can also be a place where new users first learn that your library
is supporting makers, whether through workshops, lending of maker tools,
or lessons on various equipment.

If any of these reasons apply to you, or if you have other reasons to go mobile,
this chapter will be a great first step in helping you gather your thoughts.

SO, You're Thinking of Going Mobile?

Thinking that a mobile makerspace is the way to go? There are several different
things to consider before taking the leap. This section will outline three key things
to do before making the move to mobile.

1. *Gather a core team*
Looking at a makerspace from the outside, it might seem that the most important things to begin with are technology: 3D printers, scanners, laser cutters,
and so on. However, none of these things run without what is truly the most
valuable part of any makerspace: people! Some of your staff may already be
thinking about this new venture. That's great! But early on you will need to
establish a core team to take your project forward. Try to find people with a
variety of interests and talent, because so many skills are needed to create a
mobile makerspace project. Ideally, you'll need someone with project management experience, someone to help fund-raise, someone to do research, and at
least a few folks who like to work with their hands. Obviously, it might not be
possible to find folks with all these skills; if this is the case the best thing to find
is people that are passionate about the project. The passion to create a mobile
makerspace for the community will help a few interested folks to become a
dedicated team. So . . . how do you find these folks? In your community.

TALES FROM THE ROAD 1 // MEET OTHER MAKERS

Paul can (and will) pick you up by the neck. He is a large man both in stature and in creativity and is just one of the numerous fascinating people we have met on the road with the MakerBus. Paul is a hobbyist designer of custom spacesuits and is a member of the OpenLuna Foundation—an open-source, volunteer-driven, space mission. With backgrounds in engineering and fabrication, Paul helped us to transform our barely functional 1989 school bus into Canada's first mobile makerspace. With the body of a Norse Viking, the mind of an engineer, and the heart of a poet, people like Paul are the cornerstone of the maker movement.

2. *Engage your community*

Along with your core team of makers (or makers-to-be) you will need to work with your community to find out what people need, what people want, and what gaps a mobile makerspace might be able to fill in your local area. The people who might be interested in working with your mobile makerspace will differ from community to community, but here's a list of possible places to chat with before starting your project:

a. Your local library: This book has shown that libraries are great places for making. Reaching out to your local branch is a great way to let your community know about your project.

b. Tech companies: Whether they build electronics, or build websites, there's a good chance that your local technology companies are interested in promoting making and hands-on education throughout the community. You might consider looking to them for ideas, sponsorship, or offers to work with them on an event.

c. Schools: Depending on what the goals and intended audience of your makerspace are, working with local schools can help to get your project moving. STEAM (Science, Technology, Engineering, Arts, Math) education is being emphasized in both primary and secondary schools, but many schools do not have the space or the resources to properly address this new style of learning. Your mobile makerspace can travel from school to school, helping to ease some of this burden.

3. *Be financially prepared*

Perhaps the most stressful side of your mobile makerspace project will be finding a way to finance it. There is a wide variety of mobile makerspaces (see below), largely because some of them have private funding and others are self-funded passion projects. Either way, you will need to make many decisions about what vehicle to buy, what technology to include, and what you want to do with the end result. But before you can make any of those decisions, you need some money to get started. Here is a list of possibilities to get you started:

Funding Possibilities

1. Local organizations (Rotary Clubs, community associations) might have some money to donate
2. Larger library grants, such as those offered by the Knight Foundation
3. Province or statewide granting schemes
4. Private library funding (Friends of the Library, donations)
5. Crowdfunding campaigns require a great deal of work, but can really pay off
6. Larger corporations (Verizon, Lego) often donate in dollars or in-kind
7. Local companies with an interest in making will often donate in smaller amounts, which can add up fast!

Having a good amount of available cash when starting the project is a must. The vehicle will often be the largest up-front cost, but the technology and tools, together with all the materials, staff costs, and money for fuel will add up quickly. The following section talks about expenses for which you should be prepared.

Planning Your Financial Route

What type of vehicle you purchase and where you get it are entirely up to you, as determined by your budget. Every mobile makerspace will be different, because every population will have different needs, and every maker team will have different goals. In addition to the vehicle itself, however, there are other costs to keep in mind as you move forward:

Gas

Every single time you hit the road in your mobile makerspace it will cost you money. It might not seem like much at first, but fuel costs add up quickly and must be factored into the cost of the project. You might consider working this expense into the grants you apply for, or into the cost of visits if you are charging patrons to use the mobile makerspace. You might also want to talk to local gas stations, and see if they are willing to sponsor you in gas in return for some mobile advertising.

Insurance

Insurance companies do not always know what to do with a maker classroom on wheels, and this can often mean you pay *a lot* to be covered. You'll need insurance to drive the vehicle (and for some vehicles, a special driver's license), and liability insurance to cover any accidents. Your insurance needs will also depend on what you plan to do in your mobile makerspace. If you anticipate transporting people, you'll need another type of insurance altogether. If you will only be transporting equipment, make this clear to your insurer, because this can help keep your costs down.

Retrofitting

Unless you are extremely lucky, no vehicle you purchase will be a ready-to-roll makerspace, so you'll need to set aside some money for the changes you want to make. Because a retrofit can run the gamut from completely stripping an old school bus to building an organizational system in a cube van, costs should be worked out prior to making your purchase. One tip to remember is that this can be done in phases. Work out what is essential to get your mobile makerspace on the road. What projects will you take with you? What tools and supplies are necessary for those projects? Then get the interior of your vehicle organized to carry them. Establish a small budget to get you through this first step. The needs of your space will change over time as you get to know more about your community of makers, and this way you won't spend a fortune on a set up that you may want to change within a year.

Maintenance

Depending on where you live, and how much you must travel with your mobile makerspace, you'll have to be prepared for proper vehicle maintenance. Ensuring that the vehicle you find is in proper working order before you purchase it is a good way to avoid some of the costs of maintenance, but having a small pot of money set aside for unexpected parts and labor is always a good idea. Get to know a good mechanic, and make sure you get yearly safety checks, in addition to oil changes, tire rotations, and so on. Depending on the age of your vehicle, you'll also want to be ready for annual emissions tests, which can cost a bundle if you don't take proper care of your vehicle from the get-go.

TALES FROM THE ROAD 2 // IN THE DRIVER'S SEAT

If you can't drive your mobile makerspace it isn't very mobile. For MakerBus cofounders Kim Martin and Ryan Hunt, building a mobile makerspace meant learning how to drive a standard transmission. Mobile makerspaces have a way of pushing everyone involved to learn new skills—from learning to weld to finding ways to make DIY funnels at the side of a road, be prepared to learn unexpected skills if you plan to start a mobile makerspace.

Although all these costs may seem overwhelming, if you are aware of them in advance you will be prepared to start your project on the right . . . tire. If you have a large grant or another source of funding, you can pay to have the retrofitting done for you, and insurance might not be such a burden. But it is also possible to make a little money go a long way, if you and your team are willing to put in time and labor to make it happen.

What Goes Inside?

As you've learned from the other chapters in this sourcebook, there are many different options for what you could include in your makerspace. We spoke earlier about the need to ensure that you meet your community's needs, but you also need to guarantee that your team is enthusiastic about the tools and technology in your makerspace so that their own passion and curiosity can intrigue patrons. Some key tools that are found onboard existing mobile makerspaces include:

- 3D printers and scanners
- portable laser cutters
- vinyl cutter
- virtual reality headsets

- tablets and laptops
- Makey Makeys, Raspberry Pis, and Arduinos
- hot glue gun
- hand tools
- soldering equipment
- button maker
- label maker

In addition to these tools, you'll want to have a variety of supplies on hand to help your makers get crafty. Many of these can be found at garage sales, secondhand shops, or dollar stores. Another way to get the community involved is to ask for donations—people are usually happy to help, and eager to get their little-used supplies out of their basements! Ask for

- LEDs, batteries, and magnets
- tape (all kinds)
- Lego, K'nex, or any type of building blocks
- conductive thread, yarn, wool
- sewing and knitting needles
- paper, paper, and more paper
- craft supplies (popsicle sticks, pipe cleaners, felt, googly eyes)
- variety of fabric
- scissors

The great thing about a mobile makerspace is that you can change what it has on board every time it goes out. If your library does not have storage capacity for these extras, however, you will need to be more careful about what you want to keep inside, and make sure that you have a great storage system to remain organized.

Being mobile also means you might like to have some things that a permanent makerspace might not need. We personally have a stockpile of magnets to display our visitors' artwork in the MakerBus. Lots of spaces use pegboard for storage, and there are a great set of hooks you can 3D print from thingiverse .com to get organized. If you have a truck, cube van, or bus you will likely have all-metal walls and ceilings—why not take advantage of the possibilities of an ever-changing space?

What Happens Inside?

Once you've set up your mobile makerspace, and you have the tools and supplies needed to get making, what's next? How do you use this space to the best of your ability? This section will propose several ways that people might use your space, and how you can plan programming for your new audience of makers. Figure 16.1 shows makers at work.

As you may have realized by now, there might not be very much room inside your mobile makerspace. Many mobile makerspaces are simply ways of getting technology and tools from one place to another—and that's just fine. If you do have room in your vehicle to invite people inside, however, you'll want to determine a few things. First, you'll want to think about how you manage the flow of people through the space. Will you take small numbers in and run programming in the space? Or will it be more of a demonstration area for people to tour? Whichever you plan, it's best to do a couple of test runs with family and friends to get some feedback on how they feel about the space. You might want to consider setting a maximum number of people that can be in your space (we have a sign on the MakerBus that says "No more than twelve makers at a time) to prevent traffic jams or the space feeling overcrowded."

FIGURE 16.1

Young Makers Using littleBits to Create Circuits

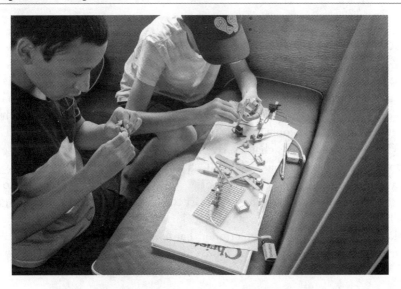

Second, you'll want to think about the furniture in your space. At first, it may be best if the furniture is movable and your layout can be changed from visit to visit. Furniture that doubles as storage is key (e.g., stools that can store hand tools, and desk space on top of cabinets). You want people to be able to come in and use the makerspace without having to move too much around to get comfortable.

Third, and most important, be aware of who is going to be using your space. Think through any accessibility needs your audience may have, and be prepared for them. Being mobile isn't just about the vehicle—it's also about being able to set up activities in meaningful places in your community. Though ramps and lifts can be costly, you can always consider using the exterior of your mobile makerspace to accommodate more people. Make sure to be prepared to provide activities that are accessible to those that might have trouble navigating the vehicle, and to design projects that incorporate the natural environment of the areas you intend to visit.

Obstacles

No matter how much you plan or prepare, you are going to experience some unexpected obstacles in your travels with your mobile makerspace. Below are a few questions that we have personally had to confront during our three years with the MakerBus.

Who Is Going to Drive the Mobile Makerspace?

When we first purchased a bus, we had to seek volunteers to drive it. Our bus has a manual transmission, and it is large—and at first, we weren't prepared to take this on. Finding drivers proved to be very difficult, and we felt we were relying too much on certain people to show up and drive the bus to where we needed to be. Of the authors of this chapter, Ryan was the first (and so far, the only) of us to volunteer to drive the bus. He has been immensely helpful, but there are still many times we could do with a few other folks willing to drive around town. There are a couple of ways you could skirt this issue, of course. You could get a much smaller vehicle, like the pickup trucks used by the University of Ottawa's MakerMobile, or you could get a trailer that hooks up to vehicles people already drive, which may make them feel more comfortable about helping.

Where Are You Going to Park?

Finding room to park your mobile makerspace can also prove quite difficult. Libraries located in urban centers often don't have ample or affordable parking, and those in the surrounding areas may not have enough space for a large vehicle to park. Make sure to find out where you might be able to park ahead of time—this might even impact the vehicle you choose to purchase. You can also ask local shopping malls or schools if you can occupy a few parking spots. Offering some advertising or pop-up maker events is a great way to persuade them to give you some space.

How Are You Going to Power Your Space?

Any makerspace that is going to use computers, 3D printers, microprocessors, or a vinyl cutter will need electricity. Although some newer vehicles contain power outlets, running anything off them for very long will kill the battery, so you will need to be prepared with other options. Currently we check in with the places we will be visiting to ensure that there is a power supply we can connect to with our 100- or 50-foot extension cords. Although this is clearly not a good permanent solution, we have yet to encounter a situation where this isn't possible. If you foresee that it might be an issue for your community, you will need to invest in a power generator for your mobile makerspace.

TALES FROM THE ROAD 3 // WHAT GRAD SCHOOL DOES AND DOESN'T TEACH YOU

Most graduate programs don't teach you how to weld or strip paint, but you might be surprised how well grad school can prepare you for creating a mobile makerspace. Clear communication is key to starting any project—being able to explain your crazy idea in a way that connects with other people will be essential to getting your project off the ground. Draw on grad-school skills like researching, synthesizing data, and putting ideas into words and create a pitch for your mobile makerspace. Be clear about what problem you will need to solve, why your community needs a mobile makerspace, and how you will go about making a difference.

Examples of Mobile Makerspaces

There are many examples of mobile makerspaces, and the numbers just keep on growing. People are quick to realize the potential of shared space for creating, and that the access that can accommodate wider communities increases when these spaces are put on wheels. Below you will find five different examples of mobile makerspaces, each with different audiences and tools, but all with the same desire to spread creativity and hands-on education.

1. FryskLab | www.frysklab.nl/
   FryskLab is a mobile FabLab based in the Netherlands. The project started in 2013 and is the first library-operated mobile makerspace in Europe. The team at FryskLab works hard to re-center the importance of the public library through the maker movement and hands-on education. They work with schools, small companies, and surrounding villages to provide access to technology and to stimulate digital literacy.

2. SparkTruck | http://sparktruck.org/
   SparkTruck was started in 2012 by a group of Stanford students who were interested in making. They refer to themselves as an "educational build-mobile" and spent two summers travelling across the United States inspiring students to make. Since then, the team has worked to build up teacher support, and has developed design-based learning experiences for classroom integration. There are some great instructional posts and a short movie about the project on its website.

3. MakerMobile | https://engineering.uottawa.ca/Maker%20Mobile
   The Faculty of Engineering at the University of Ottawa boasts the Maker-Mobile—a bright red cube van packed full of technology. Containing 3D printers, scanners, laser cutters, and Arduinos, the MakerMobile visits schools, libraries, and community centers in Ottawa, allowing engineering students to do public, educational outreach during their time at university.

4. The MakerBus | www.makerbus.ca
   The MakerBus of London, Ontario (figure 16.2) was Canada's first mobile makerspace. This retrofitted 1989 school bus carries everything from high-tech maker tools like 3D printers and scanners, to low-tech supplies like scissors and tape. The team worked closely with the London Public Library in their first summer, visiting all sixteen branches as part of the TD Summer Reading

FIGURE 16.2

The MakerBus Readies for an Event

Eureka! program. Team members have recently trained the teacher-librarians of their local school board on various maker-technologies to help facilitate the shift from school libraries to the learning-commons model. In addition, they have a whole lot of fun popping up at festivals, museums, and cultural events to help get everyone excited about making.

5. **Arts and Scraps** | **www.artsandscraps.org/**
   The folks at Arts and Scraps were making long before the maker movement became a phenomenon. Their project started in 1989, when they formed a nonprofit for crafting in a basement of the First Lutheran Church in Detroit. Since then, the project has flourished, and amongst its many achievements is the Scrapmobile—a 26-foot bus designed by the Ford Motor Company and funded by Humana Insurance. This bus brings tons of craft supplies to schools and communities around Detroit. But the best part is that all of these supplies are donated, recycled materials from local companies! The Scrapmobile is loaded with craft material from string to stickers, lets visitors pack a brown bag of goodies for only $1, and encourages everyone to start making.

The Importance of People

No matter how much funding you find, or how decked out your mobile makerspace ends up being, nothing will work unless an awesome group of people is involved. Assuming you already have assembled that great core team we spoke about earlier, you'll need to get to know a variety of different makers, educators, communicators, and volunteers. Here are a few tips for working with them.

Makers

Everyone makes *something*. The people on your core maker team likely have some serious maker talent, or at least an intense curiosity to learn more about making. In addition to these folks you will want to connect with people who build and create things that aren't offered by your core team. These folks can help in a variety of ways: they can volunteer their time to teach their skills, they can help you generate ideas for new workshops and demos to take place at your mobile makerspace, and they can help connect you to other makers in your community. Chances are that many members of your library staff have making skills in their back pockets (your children's librarians, for example, have been making well before the term was popularized). Invite them to get involved in planning, and share the excitement of your new mobile makerspace with them. The more people invested in the project from the beginning, the more likely it will be to succeed.

Educators

In addition to libraries, schools and universities are other places where makerspaces and hands-on learning are thriving. Connect with your local school community, where you will find teachers with a wealth of information that they are eager to share. You'll also find another audience for your mobile makerspace—many schools, like libraries, are underfunded and would benefit immensely from the access you can provide. Educators and their students are a great way to build community.

Students

Young children, teenagers, adults, and seniors are all makers and all have their own stories to tell. Although younger generations have been raised with technology that some older adults might still be growing accustomed to, this often means that youth are likely to teach their elders lessons, often without even knowing they are doing so! The excitement they have for making is trumped only by the fabulous questions they ask. If you ever want to test a new maker tool or lesson on anyone, having a great group of children to create with will give you an audience full of honest answers and unbridled enthusiasm. Teenagers are often portrayed as hard to engage, but piquing their curiosity with maker technology is a great way of getting them involved. Working with teens who have an interest in making can also lead to peer-to-peer learning, and partnering up a teenaged maker with a group of younger learners can have great results. Finally, never forget that people don't stop being students just because they have graduated from high school! Adults are just as curious about new technologies as their younger counterparts, and are often eager to share their expertise.

Volunteers

Volunteers are essential to a mobile makerspace. They can lend their time, knowledge, and passion to the project. Although volunteers are an invaluable resource, you should also be aware that it takes time and energy to train and coordinate volunteers, and that any volunteer who works with the public should go through the proper safety checks. Keep in mind that your volunteers invest their own time and energy to a mobile makerspace and the projects that grow from it. In return for their time and energy, be sure to let your volunteers know how great they are by organizing get-togethers and parties in their honor. Including your volunteers in decision making about the project, and ensuring they know where the project is headed will help to keep their morale high. Finally, remember that it is important to be well organized to maintain and communicate with your pool of volunteers.

Lessons Learned

Before concluding this chapter on mobile makerspaces, we wanted to add a short personal account of lessons we've learned through running the MakerBus. These lessons revolve around three main themes: time investment, commitment to the project, and answering the eternal question, "What exactly do you do?"

Time Investment and Commitment

Of everything we've had to invest in our mobile makerspace, time has been the most important. Since buying the bus, we've had to deal with everything from simple e-mails and phone calls, to teaching ourselves to weld, creating a make-shift gas siphon, and even building a 3D printer. Although operating a mobile makerspace requires some library-related skills (time management, marketing, fund-raising), other competencies will be necessary, so you need to find a team that is willing to go above and beyond to see the project through. If your library has funding or sponsorship for a mobile makerspace, we recommend that at least one person works full time on this project for the first year, to get it up and running, to purchase and install the tech, and to create programming for the space. The connection with the physical library will help to spread awareness and promote these programs, which is a major benefit of having a library team backing a mobile makerspace.

The library management who approve this project need to know that this is no small commitment. At minimum, the mobile makerspace team should be planning ways to extend programming and outreach efforts for five years. Maker tech and digital literacy tools will obviously change over that period, but the amount of money, labor, and creative power that will go into your project means that anything less than a five-year plan might not be worth starting in the first place.

Answering the Question "What Exactly Do You Do?"

Librarians are excellent planners, so chances are that you and your team will have set up great plans for outreach, programming, maker activities, and potential partners. That said, the maker movement is still a new concept to many, and you will need to be prepared to field many, many questions about what you do on your mobile makerspace, what use it is to the community, and what it means to make. There are many great resources listed throughout this handbook on making and the maker movement, but the role of your own makerspace will depend on your community, and the partners you find.

Conclusion

We hope this chapter has given you all the information you need to start planning a mobile makerspace. Our focus on the importance of people, the awareness of how much time you will have to devote to the project, and issues you'll need to consider ahead of time should make you much more prepared than we were when we first purchased the MakerBus! Remember that every library is different, and therefore every makerspace will be as well. Use this space to grow your library offerings, communicate your goals to the community, and drum up a new awareness in the unique positions librarians are taking in the changing world of information literacy. As you begin to construct your mobile makerspace, be excited, be confident, and be ready—this might well be the biggest maker project you ever take on!

Note: The authors of this chapter own and operate a mobile makerspace, The MakerBus, located in London, Ontario. We have written this chapter using our own knowledge and experience as a guide, but have done our best to be inclusive of what many library-operated mobile makerspaces will need. The "Tales from the Road" stories, together with the Lessons Learned section, provide a glimpse into our own experience, which undoubtedly will be different from any you choose to undertake. Each mobile makerspace is unique, and there is no right way to go about creating one: you just do the best with what you have!

RESOURCES

Attig, Derek. (2016). *Bookmobility.* http://bookmobility.org/.

Bowler, Leanne. (2014). Creativity through "maker" experiences and design thinking in the education of librarians. *Knowledge Quest, 42*(5), 58.

Craddock, IdaMae Louise. (2015). Makers on the move: A Mobile makerspace at a comprehensive public high school. *Library Hi Tech,* 33(4).

de Boer, Jeroen. (2015). The business case of FryskLab, Europe's first mobile library FabLab. *Library Hi Tech,* 33(4): 505–518.

Elton, Cassandra I. (2015). Breaking down invisible barriers: Using bookmobiles to facilitate library outreach in urban and suburban communities. *University of Iowa SLIS Journal.*

Gierdowski, Dana, and Reis, Daniel. (2015). The MobileMaker: An experiment with a mobile makerspace. *Library Hi Tech,* 33(4), 480–496.

Moorefield-Lang, Heather Michele. (2015). When makerspaces go mobile: Case studies of transportable maker locations. *Library Hi Tech* 33(4), 462–471.

Purpur, E., Radniecki, T., Colegrove, P.T., and Klenke, C. (2016). Refocusing mobile makerspace outreach efforts internally as professional development. *Library Hi Tech,* 34(1), 130–142.

Sustainability
Keeping the Library Makerspace Alive

SHARONA GINSBERG

After all the hard work of planning and developing your makerspace, you want to ensure it won't be a passing fad that is short-lived and unable to sustain itself into the future. There are a number of important elements to consider when planning for your makerspace's survival and success. Most obviously, you will need to have models in place for ongoing financial support. Just as important, however—if not more so—is considering how you will maintain momentum and interest in the makerspace once the initial novelty dies down among your patrons and your colleagues. Finally, as with anything else in library world, keeping up with trends, new developments, and current best practices can make a big difference to the makerspace's continuing maintenance and growth.

Financial Considerations

Whether you've settled on an expensive, high-tech makerspace with lots of machinery, a smaller mobile model with cheaper supplies, or something in between, you

Sharona Ginsberg is Learning Technologies Librarian at State University of New York at Oswego.

will eventually need more funds to keep your project going. Undoubtedly, you will need to replace equipment or parts. Many types of making require consumables: 3D printing filament, skeins of yarn, batteries, fixatives such as glue and tape, and so on. Supplies sometimes go missing and must be repurchased, or you may want to expand into new areas in the future. You will need to consider a staffing model. To cover all these costs, you can either explore options for charging your patrons a fee or alternatives to help you limit expenses.

Charging Patrons

A 3D printing fee is the prime example of a model in which patrons might be charged a small amount to help cover costs. Many public and academic libraries ask patrons to pay either by weight or by the amount of time their print will take; fees tend to range from 5 cents per gram to 25 cents per gram, or from 5 cents per minute to $5 per hour. Some models also combine both type of fees, such as charging 20 cents per gram plus $1 as a flat fee for printing.[1] Although libraries might be uncomfortable about charging patrons for services, there is precedence for this option: many libraries already charge patrons a small fee for making photocopies or printing documents. Charging for the use of a 3D printer can be a natural extension of this model: you are not asking the patron to pay for access, but to pay for consumable supplies. Generally, fees can be kept low and affordable.

Another method of handling the costs of consumables is to have patrons directly purchase these supplies. North Carolina State University Libraries' D. H. Hill Library Makerspace (NCSU Libraries) has patrons buy items such as a spool of filament, fabric, or electronics components, which are then theirs to keep and use as much as they would like. As a result, patrons don't need to pay a fee each time they would like to work on a project.[2]

This type of model can be applied beyond 3D printing to any equipment in the makerspace, especially anything that makes use of consumables. The following are some questions you may want to ask yourself when setting prices and policies:

- *Who has access to this equipment, and will all groups pay the same amount?* At an academic library, will you charge faculty the same as students? If the library is at a public university, will members of the general public be allowed access, and will they pay the same fee? At a public library, will you allow use by nonresidents, and if so, what will you charge them? What about children versus adults?

- *Will there be a minimum fee or flat fee in addition to any fees determined by supply use or time?* For instance, at my library, any 3D prints under $1 are rounded up. This policy takes into account the labor of 3D printing, because staff put time and effort into setting up prints and monitoring them. A minimum or flat fee might also be appropriate to compensate for wear and tear; as an example, running a Silhouette Cameo electronic cutting machine often means doing damage to a cutting mat, which will eventually need to be replaced. A flat fee can be especially useful if you want to encourage more thoughtful use of machines, or if staff are involved in the printing process and need to be compensated for their time.

- *What are the fees meant to cover?* This question will go a long way in helping determine what makes sense to charge. In charging for 3D printing, are you merely setting out to recover the costs of filament, or does that money also need to cover repairs and replacements? Will the money be used to fund any other makerspace equipment, supplies, or upgrades?

- *These questions address the needs of the library and the makerspace, but a fee model should acknowledge the needs of patrons as well.* How financially comfortable are your patrons, and at what point will fees become an unacceptable barrier to using the makerspace? At what point will fees discourage experimentation and exploration? Can you compensate for this in some way (e.g., first use is free, use is free during special events, adopting a sliding scale for payment, and so on)?

It's perfectly acceptable to change a model as you learn more about your community members and how they use the makerspace. You may set out to provide 3D printing for academic purposes, then discover students mainly employ the service for personal use. You might find out ambitious entrepreneurs are starting businesses using the equipment in your space. Would these situations change your plans for fees?

Another fee-based model you might explore, especially if your makerspace holds workshops or if your program tends to be event-based, would be to charge patrons for supplies used during an event. You might hold a crocheting workshop and ask that attendees each pay for a skein of yarn and a cheap crochet hook, which will cover all supplies needed. This approach has the added benefit of allowing patrons to take home their projects, because they now own the equipment; it may also be a good choice for a situation in which a library has received a grant to purchase initial equipment, but needs to find a way to continue funding consumable supplies. Though having patrons simply recoup the costs of a workshop will not provide much wiggle room for activities and tools beyond these workshops, it's a workable model, and could be used in conjunction with other policies.

Finally, if it makes sense for your library, you might choose to charge patrons for makerspace membership, similar to the way independent makerspaces and hackerspaces function. These collectives often ask members to pay dues to keep the space going. Membership fees could be implemented in different ways, such as family memberships. A public library may choose to charge membership fees for nonresidents but not for residents, or an academic library may charge members of the public but not students. It's worth considering what kind of barriers this approach sets up, and—as with the fee-based model mentioned above—you may want to incorporate some ways to lower these barriers, such as charging on a sliding scale or allowing open use of the space during special occasions.

Beyond Fees

Although charging patrons to recover costs is, in some ways, the easiest way to handle funding, it's not always ideal. As mentioned earlier, it may set up various roadblocks and discourage patrons from using the space and equipment. It may also not be feasible in certain situations; it's simpler to charge a small 3D printing fee to college students than to K–12 students, for example. Even if you do adopt fees in some cases, they may not cover all the costs associated with the makerspace. As such, it's useful to explore alternate options to pursue instead of or in conjunction with fee-based models.

One of the most effective ways to keep costs reasonable and to make it more likely the library can handle the financial aspects of a makerspace without needing to charge fees is to keep costs low to begin with. A dedicated physical location with high-tech machinery that requires training and staffing is only one type of makerspace model. There are many viable smaller approaches, such as mobile makerspaces (maker kits, maker carts), pop-up makerspaces, and maker events or workshops. These alternatives often lend themselves to smaller, cheaper equipment and eliminate the need for staff who must be constantly present. They provide the added benefit of letting you start small and build your equipment gradually, which provides a valuable opportunity to collect feedback and carry out assessment to tweak your future plans and purchases. It's much better to start with a small stash of equipment that you can supplement over time than to buy a bunch of equipment up front that ends up not being used because it's not a good fit for your community.

Your local community is your absolute best resource in the challenge of keeping your makerspace alive and growing. Some ideas of how to get your community to help with funding include the following:

- *Form partnerships with local maker organizations.* Many areas have independent makerspaces, hackerspaces, or hobbyist groups (such as amateur radio groups, knitting groups, robotics groups, and so on). Invite these people into mutually beneficial partnerships with your library. Hold a workshop or event for which the local makerspace or hobbyist group will bring its own supplies and trained makers, and the library provides the space and promotion, helping raise the makerspace or group's profile to attract new members. Or, simply agree to share costs. Allen County Public Library in Fort Wayne, Indiana, partnered with TekVenture, a maker organization looking for a home, to set up TekVenture Maker Station, a makerspace in a trailer in the library parking lot. This makerspace operated successfully for a number of years, so much so that TekVenture was able to move on to its own permanent location, and the Allen County Public Library was able to develop its own Maker Labs.[3] Another excellent example of a partnership is Brooklyn Public Library's work with BRIC Arts | Media | Bklyn, a local nonprofit arts and culture organization.[4] Rather than allocating money for staffing and training, Brooklyn Public Library collaborates with BRIC, which acts as the library's "lead media education partner," teaching workshops in exchange for being offered library space to operate a TV studio.[5]

- *At an academic library or a school library, start an official club.* Student organizations generally receive some funding, and this budget often renews each year. This steady source of money works well for purchasing consumable supplies and carrying out any necessary repairs or replacements. Leadership looks great on a resume; encourage students with an existing interest in your makerspace to join you in getting a club founded.

- *Ask for and encourage donations.* When I was starting a maker program in my library, a librarian donated her old sewing machine. It's likely both library staff and patrons will have things to offer if you seek them out. Think creatively about what you might use in the makerspace when considering what to ask for: broken appliances to take apart and tinker with, spare tools like screwdrivers and pliers, duct tape, craft supplies, batteries, buttons, old clothing or leftover scraps to reuse in new fabric arts projects, and so on. Upcycling is the process of using old, often "junk," materials to create something new and valuable. Donated materials can be excellent for upcycling projects. Libraries often accept food donations in exchange for eliminating fines in "Food for Fines" programs; try carrying out this type of program, but ask for makerspace donations instead. You might also start a "junk box" at home, in your office, or in various parts of the library, and encourage other library staff to do so as well. You may surprise yourself with what you find a creative use for such materials, and with how much ends up in a box once it exists.[6] There may be local businesses or other corporate donors who you can interest in your makerspace; maybe the local hardware store has some equipment they can give the library in exchange for being listed as a makerspace sponsor. A fabric store might want to sponsor a series of maker workshops focused on textile arts. Companies with specific interests in the maker movement (SparkFun, Adafruit, etc.) might also be good sponsors.[7] Explore all possible connections and interested parties. At universities, alumni are also an excellent source of potential funding and interest.[8]

- *Consider crowdfunding.* Crowdfunding is a method of fundraising often carried out online where many people each make small contributions to add up to a large total. Sometimes, those who donate are offered a small perk or reward for their contribution (such as a postcard, a t-shirt, having their names listed in a prominent location, etc.). Perks often increase in value and desirability based on how much a person donates. Other crowdfunding models do not offer perks other than the satisfaction of helping. If you have a community already invested in the project, it may be willing to give a small amount of money to help, because sustaining the makerspace can directly benefit their own interests. You may even uncover unexpected connections, as librarian Colleen Graves found when a friend who worked at Microsoft got others at the company interested in supporting Graves's crowdfunding campaign.[9] Useful sites for setting up crowdfunding campaigns are Kickstarter (www.kickstarter .com), Indiegogo (www.indiegogo.com), GoFundMe (www.gofundme.com), and DonorsChoose (www.donorschoose.org). On Kickstarter, projects must be fully funded by a deadline in order for the project's creator to receive any of the money.[10] Indiegogo offers this option, as well as a "flexible funding" option in which project creators can receive whatever funds have been raised by the deadline even if they have not reached their goal.[11] GoFundMe does not require deadlines, so contributions can be received at any point.[12] DonorsChoose is particularly useful for K–12 makerspaces, as the site is designed for funding the needs of public school educators and all donations are tax-deductible.

Project creators ask for supplies that DonorsChoose will purchase and send to them if the project is fully funded. If not, creators are free to repost their project and try again.[13] (Check out maker librarian Diana Rendina's useful blog post with tips for creating a DonorsChoose project: http://renovated learning.com/2014/09/29/5-tips-for-creating-donorschoose-projects.) Although it was not connected to a library, The Possible Project (TPP) is a great example of successful makerspace crowdfunding. TPP is an intensive after-school program for high schoolers that teaches students how to make and sell their own products using STEAM and digital fabrication skills. TPP ran a successful Kickstarter campaign to purchase a laser cutter, offering donors perks of custom, unique items that would be created by their teen makers, such as a laser-engraved phone case, a laser-cut water bottle, and more.[14] It ended up doing so well it exceeded their fundraising goal.

Once you have some supplies, use them to their fullest. Practice thinking like a maker: just because something is broken or a project failed doesn't mean the materials themselves are now worthless. I keep a box of failed 3D prints and extra bits of prints, such as rafts and supports. Recently, a student was fascinated by these and asked to take them to her art therapy class to reuse them in projects. Many had interesting textures and could be used as stamps with paint or ink; others could be built on further with clay, or pieces could be glued together. What seemed like junk was, in actuality, the beginnings of a new maker project. Save your scraps, tinker with broken equipment, and reuse everything you possibly can.

Grants and Budgets

Grants are most useful when creating a makerspace, as they are generally one-time endowments and are more suited to initially building up your space and equipment. However, you can also explore the possibility of grants to support ongoing operational expenses. They may be able to help keep you going or help you expand just enough to ignite your community, increase the visibility of the makerspace, and make some of the above-mentioned options even more feasible. Useful places to begin your search are Grants.gov (www.grants.gov), GrantForward (www.grantforward.com), and Demco (www.demco.com/goto?grants).[15] It's also a good idea to do research on what grants other libraries have received for makerspace projects.[16]

Finally, there is always the option of the library itself funding the makerspace's continued life. Though it may be challenging to set up a separate budget just for the makerspace, you can think creatively about which existing budgets might support the work. For example, at my library, we felt our maker work was a natural extension of our existing Learning and Information Commons (LINC), so it made sense to allocate some of the LINC budget to maker supplies. There might be a special projects budget or library technology budget you can use, or—especially if you are planning workshops and/or events—you might draw from a programming budget. The maker program at NCSU Libraries has been able to make use of a library services budget, as well as a budget comprised of technology fees paid by students as part of their tuition.[17] Fayetteville Free Library was able to reallocate money toward the makerspace by carrying out constant, meaningful assessment of library services; through this process, they discovered they were spending a large amount of money on databases patrons were not using and did not value. Instead, they gathered and provided access to similar low-cost, authoritative material, putting the money into making and STEAM efforts that patrons saw as more valuable and relevant.[18]

Additionally, it's important to consider the fiscal year when you put in your requests for funding.[19] Think about how your library works: is it more likely to grant such requests at the beginning of the fiscal year when there is more money in the budget? Or perhaps people are more open to requests late in the year when they are trying to spend out existing budgets?

Sustaining Interest and Momentum

Many maker tools have a definite "wow" factor, especially those that incorporate newer and less accessible technology like 3D printing. It's not particularly difficult to get people initially interested in these activities, and it's likely that you will experience some buzz and excitement when beginning a makerspace. The real challenge crops up in maintaining the momentum and interest as the makerspace loses its novelty and becomes more of a fixture in the library. The absolute best (and most important) way to sustain the energy of your makerspace is to focus on building a community around it. Integral to community building is ensuring your makerspace is well-tailored to your patrons and their specific needs.

Understand Your Community

Creating and stocking a makerspace should be like doing collection development. Although it's important to have a balanced collection, patron needs, interests, and circulation habits are essential to deciding what materials the library should purchase. The same should hold true for makerspace building and maintenance. Additionally, as with a collection of books and media, the makerspace and maker supplies should be periodically evaluated. Ask questions about whether you are meeting needs, what those needs are, and whether the cost of maintaining the makerspace is worth the current benefits.[20] The most effective way to perform this assessment is to ensure you are talking to—and paying attention to—your community members.

When setting out to create the maker program at my library, I held a series of focus groups to gather information about the existing maker interests and equipment on campus. I wanted to know what needs were already being met, what needs still existed, what strong interests or passions were important to my community, and what people might want to see from this type of project. From this information, I was able to set objectives for my maker program, which helped to inform my purchases and approach. Other good ways to gather data could be examining the nonfiction circulation records,[21] holding open town hall meetings, asking for feedback with surveys or comment forms, having a suggestion box,[22] calling for comments on social media, and so on. Fayetteville Free Library, the first library to start a makerspace,[23] considers its maker program a community-led effort. The library is merely a facilitator, providing a support system, structure, and a resource system. The program is driven primarily by community members' interests and passions.[24] Teacher librarian Colleen Graves noticed that patron input led to a measurable difference in her maker program's success; the program did significantly less well the year it was primarily directed by her own decisions, as opposed to students' input and choices.[25]

A 3D printer or laser cutter might not be the right fit for every community. Patrons from an area less focused on technology, for example, might be more excited about hands-on activities.[26] If you ensure you are building toward what your patrons care about and value, it will be easier to avoid a sharp decline in interest after people have gotten past their initial excitement. This type of assessment should be an ongoing process to be truly successful, rather than something that's only carried out at the beginning of a makerspace project, especially as patron populations and interests change over time—students and faculty come and go, people move in and out of an area, people discover new hobbies, and so on.

Another important consideration is what niche you would like your makerspace to fill, and where it fits into the making ecosystem of your school or community.[27] If your area already has independent makerspaces, makerspaces at other institutions, hobbyist groups, maker equipment in other departments on campus, and so on, it might not make sense to set out to replace or duplicate these.

Duplication can create unnecessary conflict, and will also leave patrons without a clear idea of the purpose of your space, which can threaten sustainability. Therefore, determine what role the library makerspace will play. Are you providing access to equipment not available elsewhere? Will the library makerspace serve as a gateway or jumping-off point, where people can be introduced to new tools and ideas that they can explore at a more advanced level at the local independent hackerspace? Does the library work in partnership with the local museum makerspace, offering services geared toward adults and teens, while the museum is aimed at children? The answers and correct approach will vary depending on what your local making ecosystem looks like, but it's important to find where the library makerspace fits, and to clearly convey that purpose to patrons.

Embrace Your Community

The way you represent and promote your makerspace can also affect its longevity. As with the rest of the library, the makerspace should welcome a diverse population and be accessible to those with disabilities. Consider how you might encourage diversity with the following suggestions (and beyond):

- *Take care with advertising.* Recently, author Shannon Hale tweeted a photo of a flyer from her local library advertising a robotics event that declared, "No girls allowed." Hale's eight-year-old daughter was put off by this.[28] Although libraries do face the challenge of engaging young boys, this approach is not the best way. Focus on inclusion, rather than exclusion, and ensure that any promotion for the library makerspace or events is welcoming. If you find it necessary to plan gendered events, balance them well; don't declare that sewing events are for girls, while robotics is for boys. Be aware of the needs of transgender patrons or those who do not identify with the gender binary by explicitly welcoming them to events (e.g., "This event is open to anyone who identifies as a woman, including trans women" or "People of all genders are welcome.").

- *Offer supplies and furniture appropriate for people with disabilities or for those with limited dexterity and mobility.* For example, make sure some workspaces are at a height appropriate for those in wheelchairs. Purchase assistive equipment, such as an OttLite Magnifier, ergonomic crochet hooks and knitting needles, left-handed scissors, and so on. Be certain the entrance to your space is accessible and easy to navigate.

• *Consider writing and publicizing a code of conduct for your space or program.* Although you may have created a list of guidelines or policies, a code of conduct is useful for explicitly stating what behavior is unacceptable in your community, defining that behavior, and outlining the reporting procedures and consequences to help members of marginalized groups understand that they will be safe. The group Geek Feminism has an excellent example of a community code of conduct, and has also provided a public domain sample document to help others get started.[29] Individuals who experience harassment, bullying, and threats cannot always take for granted that they will be welcome and safe, so expressly stating these details can go a long way toward helping create a positive, diverse community.

• *Don't forget about neurodiversity.* People on the autism spectrum or with conditions such as Tourette Syndrome or ADHD have much to contribute to the maker movement, but can face unique challenges that neurotypical patrons may not. As an example, autistic people may become overwhelmed by too much sensory input, and it could be useful to have a quieter, calmer area of the makerspace to help them feel secure. Think about how to celebrate the wide range of strengths and learning styles that come with neurodiversity.[30]

Build Your Community

Although the word "makerspace" has a strong sense of physical place to it, the concept goes beyond a location; a thriving makerspace is more about the community of makers who use the space to collaborate, share, and form relationships. Below are some ideas to get you started building a strong community of makers that will help sustain your makerspace into the future.

• *Focus on collaboration and partnerships with members of the community your library serves.* At a university, this may include students, staff, and faculty, as well as residents of the local city or town. At a public library, this will include the wide array of patrons the library serves. At a K–12 school, this includes not only the students and staff of the school, but parents as well.[31] Who might have interesting skills or ideas to share? Involving others will help get them excited about the makerspace. Some examples of successful partnerships include maker-in-residence or artist-in-residence programs. Rochester Public Library has run a program called "Caution! Artist @ Work!" in which local artists are invited to work on their art in the library, sharing skills and information with interested patrons. In exchange, the artists receive either a stipend or use of the library's display cases to promote their art.[32] Carnegie Library of Pittsburgh employs creative mentors to guide makerspace users and to share their own maker skills.[33] These types of programs help the makerspace develop as a vibrant place where connections can be made. Fayetteville Free Library runs an enormously successful volunteer program that drives the development of their maker program. Allowing the project to be community-driven and staying consistently informed about the community's goals and aspirations have been among the most important factors in the library's success. The library has created a form that asks patrons what they love to do, what they are passionate about, and if they would be interested in sharing their knowledge with neighbors. This form is available all over the library, and staff members are encouraged to offer it to patrons any time they recognize an opportunity. Through this method, the library receives a huge amount of community feedback and engagement; roughly 40 percent of all their programming is community-led.[34]

- *Create a badging system for skills and collaboration.* Digital badging is a credentialing framework in which participants earn badges (online images that contain information in the form of metadata) to demonstrate that they have learned a skill or completed a project.[35] This can also be done with a low-tech approach; for example, Fayetteville Free Library offers "Maker Passports" in which patrons can collect stamps. Makers might earn badges for completing training to use certain machines or to learn certain skills, or they might be awarded a badge for helping share skills and teaching others. When setting up a badging system, make sure you consider what behavior you are rewarding and what you are encouraging patrons to learn.

- *In a school setting, look for ways to work together with instructors to incorporate making into the curriculum.* Science and Math departments are obvious collaborators, but seek out ways to partner with teachers of all subjects. Students might explore making in English, Writing, or Language Arts contexts by writing maker journals about their projects,[36] or writing and recording podcasts. Many different classes and disciplines could incorporate students making stop-motion animation or green-screen videos. This past semester, I worked with an art professor at my university to incorporate Arduinos and Makey Makeys into a fantastic course that merges computer programming with art.

- *Make use of "secondary promotion."* Because it established strong partnerships with local organizations, Cleveland Public Library has enjoyed the benefits of the additional advertising carried out by these other groups.[37] This additional marketing can also be useful in reaching individuals who ordinarily would not see promotional materials from the library. Another way to encourage "secondary promotion" is to have patrons make use of their own social media accounts, rather than putting everything on the library's social media accounts. For example, rather than snapping photos of makers' creations and uploading them to the library's Facebook account, ask patrons to upload photos or videos to their own accounts and tag the library. Not only does this encourage a greater sense of participation and ownership, but the shared media will be viewable by friends of the patron who might not be following the library's account, and potentially spark more interest in the makerspace and its offerings. By observing what patrons share, you might also gather valuable information about what interests and excites patrons.

- *Develop an environment that's welcoming, safe, and low pressure.* Libraries already work toward this, so continue the effort in your makerspace. Encourage experimentation and even failure; rather than being stressful, emphasize that failure is an opportunity for learning and growth. Additionally, not everyone will feel comfortable jumping into making right away. Make it clear that anyone is welcome simply to visit and watch or spend time in the space; it's likely that after spending time watching others, those who are more hesitant will be motivated to try making on their own.[38]

- *Build a library-wide maker culture with internal promotion.* Though you may not turn every library employee into a hardcore evangelist for the makerspace, it's important that all the information, know-how, and excitement isn't limited to only one or two people. Get others involved within your library (and within your school, if you are at a K–12 or academic library), and aim for this involvement as early in the process as possible.[39] Ensure that reference librarians, circulation staff, student workers, and others who work at a public-facing desk can answer questions about the makerspace or maker program, its purpose and goals, and the supplies and policies. Invite staff to maker events specifically aimed at them,[40] planned during times that will fit into their schedules— lunch, breaks in the academic calendar, slower times of the year, and so on. Work with supervisors to encourage them to allow time for staff to attend these events. At a school library, invite teachers and administrators to join you for coffee before school, or ask for fifteen minutes during a staff meeting to share updates on the maker program and perhaps even demo a new tool.[41] Fayetteville Free Library stresses strong internal relationships in the library built on deep trust and understanding. Executive Director Sue Considine says that the library's thriving maker program would not work without these relationships. Rather than attempting to get others excited about an existing makerspace they have no part in, provide everyone with an equal opportunity to talk about where the project is going and to offer their ideas. Fayetteville holds regular meetings (forums) that all library staff attend; assigned note-takers record the proceedings of meetings for those who cannot be present. These forums include discussions of content, programming, and services, as well as peer-to-peer training to ensure all have the same level of general knowledge.[42]

Keeping Up with the Movement

Part of sustaining your library makerspace is, of course, keeping it fresh and staying up to date with trends and new ideas in the maker movement. Because of the pace at which changes occur in the movement, the Internet and social media are often the best platforms to turn to for information. Fortunately, there is a lot available online; some recommended resources are listed below.

Of course, because things do change quickly, this list will inevitably become outdated—and it certainly isn't an exhaustive list—but it can at least serve as a jumping off point. Attending conferences where makerspaces are a topic—or where interesting vendors might be found—is also a great idea, whether they are large national conferences or smaller regional ones. Look into library conferences, technology conferences, education conferences, and so on.[43]

Social Media

Facebook Groups
- Makerspaces and the Participatory Library
  www.facebook.com/groups/librarymaker

- Library Entrepreneurship and Maker Services
  www.facebook.com/groups/startup.library

- Technology Training and Libraries
  www.facebook.com/groups/215892381802232

- School Library Makerspaces
  www.facebook.com/groups/427832880731312

- Vermont Libraries as Makerspaces (not just relevant for Vermont, despite the name) www.facebook.com/groups/441719939268502

Google+ Communities
- Maker Ed https://plus.google.com/u/1/communities/108516741770696736815

- Makerspaces https://plus.google.com/u/1/communities/114363838456755905212

- STEM on Google+ https://plus.google.com/u/1/communities/110555615319066448343

- School Makerspaces https://plus.google.com/u/1/communities/100654515662223353477c

Twitter Hashtags
#makered
#makerspace or #makerspaces
#makeredchat
#makerchat
#elemaker
#librarymakers
#STEM or #STEAM[44]
#GirlsinSTEM or WomeninSTEM[45]

Twitter Lists
- Technology News https://twitter.com/makerbridge/list32s/technology-news

- Makers/Hackers https://twitter.com/makerbridge/lists/makers-hackers

- Maker/Hackerspaces https://twitter.com/makerbridge/lists/maker-hackerspaces

- Three-D Printing https://twitter.com/makerbridge/lists/three-d-printing

- United Makerspaces https://twitter.com/ETIBerlin/lists/united-makerspaces

- Important 3DPrinting Geeks
  https://twitter.com/PARTcloud_net/lists/important3dprintinggeeks
- Play Meets Education
  https://twitter.com/fork_do/lists/playmeetseducation
- Arduino Enthusiasts
  https://twitter.com/Arduin024x7/lists/arduino-enthusiasts
- Makers to Follow
  https://twitter.com/make/lists/makers-to-follow
- Make Hack Play
  https://twitter.com/brasst/lists/make-hack-play
- Find more at https://twitter.com/makerbridge/lists or check the lists of
  interesting people you follow.

Blogs and Websites
- MakerBridge: especially focused on libraries and schools
  http://makerbridge.net
- Make It @ Your Library
  http://makeitatyourlibrary.org
- Adafruit
  https://blog.adafruit.com[46]
- Active Learning: run by Kristin Fontichiaro, founder of Michigan Makers
  www.fontichiaro.com/activelearning
- *Make Magazine*
  http://makezine.com
- Maker Ed
  http://makered.org/blog
- Create, Collaborate, Innovate: run by Colleen Graves, a high-school maker
  librarian
  https://colleengraves.org
- Renovated Learning: run by Diana Rendina, a middle school maker librarian
  http://renovatedlearning.com/blog
- Worlds of Learning: run by Laura Fleming, a high school maker librarian
  http://worlds-of-learning.com

- Invent to Learn
  http://inventtolearn.com/blog

- Expect the Miraculous: run by Andy Plemmons, an elementary school maker librarian
  https://expectmiraculous.com[47]

- The Library as Incubator Project
  www.libraryasincubatorproject.org

Listservs and Mailing Lists

- Library Makerspace
  https://lists.ufl.edu/cgi-bin/wa?A0=LIBRARYMAKERSPACE-L

- LITA Maker Technology Interest Group
  http://lists.ala.org/sympa/info/lita-makertech

- Make to Learn
  https://list.indiana.edu/sympa/info/maketolearn-1

- Create: Creation and Makerspaces in Libraries
  www.cvl-lists.org/mailman/listinfo/create_cvl-lists.org

NOTES

1. LITA 3D Printing Interest Group, "3D Printing Policies," https://docs.google.com/spreadsheets/d/1tr19eaPzNyKhlxNhIDnwuI5_BCuwFmcJMOYpNU_EVY4/edit#gid=0.
2. Adam Rogers, Emerging Technology Services Librarian at NCSU Raleigh, personal communication, April 2016.
3. TekVenture, "Maker Station," http://tekventure.org/maker-station.
4. Caitlin A. Bagley, *Makerspaces: Top Trailblazing Projects* (Chicago: ALA TechSource, 2014), 32.
5. Brooklyn Public Library, BPL and BRIC, 2016, www.bklynlibrary.org/central/bpl-and-bric.
6. Kristin Fontichiaro, Clinical Assistant Professor at University of Michigan School of Information, personal communication, April 2016.
7. Colleen Graves, Teacher Librarian at Ryan High School in Denton, TX, personal communication, April 2016.
8. Rogers, communication.
9. Graves, communication.

10. Kickstarter, "Kickstarter Basics," 2016, www.kickstarter.com/help/faq/kickstarter+basics.

11. Indiegogo, "How It Works," 2016, www.indiegogo.com/how-it-works.

12. GoFundMe, "Common Questions," 2016, www.gofundme.com/questions.

13. DonorsChoose, "About Us," 2016, www.donorschoose.org/about.

14. The Possible Project, "Makerspace for Teen Entrepreneurs @ The Possible Project," 2014, www.kickstarter.com/projects/1026490730/makerspace-for-teen-entrepreneurs -needs-a-laser-cu/description.

15. Colleen Graves, "Getting Buy-in for Your Makerspace," 2016, http://ideas.demco.com/ blog/getting-buy-in-for-your-makerspace.

16. Bagley, Makerspaces, 6.

17. Rogers, communication.

18. Sue Considine, Executive Director of Fayetteville Free Library, personal conversation, April 2016.

19. Bagley, Makerspaces, 5.

20. Fontichiaro, communication.

21. Ibid.

22. Colleen Graves "Evolution of a Maker Space, From 'Monstie Stuffie' Projects to a Giant Catapult," 2015, www.slj.com/2015/06/programs/evolution-of-a-middle-school-maker -space-from-monster-stuffie-projects-to-a-giant-catapult.

23. Lauren Britton, "A Fabulous Labaratory: The Makerspace at Fayetteville Free Library," 2012, http://publiclibrariesonline.org/2012/10/a-fabulous-labaratory-the-makerspace-at -fayetteville-free-library.

24. Considine, communication.

25. Graves, communication.

26. Ibid.

27. Fontichiaro, communication.

28. Jessica Lachenal, "*Captain Marvel* Author Shannon Hale Highlights the Problems with Gendered Library Programs," 2015, www.themarysue.com/oh-hale-no.

29. Geek Feminism, "Code of Conduct," https://geekfeminism.org/about/code-of-conduct.

30. Patrick Waters (2015). Encouraging Neurodiversity in Your Makerspace or Classroom. www.edutopia.org/blog/encouraging-neurodiversity-in-makerspace-classroom-patrick -waters.

31. Fontichiaro, communication.

32. Judith Schewe, "Out of the Archives: Caution! Artist @ Work! at Rochester Public Library," 2013, www.libraryasincubatorproject.org/?p=11624.

33. Carnegie Library of Pittsburgh, The Labs @ CLP, www.clpgh.org/teens/events/ programs/thelabs.

34. Considine, communication.

35. Mozilla Open Badges, "About," http://openbadges.org/about.

36. Graves, "Evolution."

37. Bagley, *Makerspaces*, 52.

38. Graves, communication.

39. Considine, communication.

40. Rogers, communication.

41. Fontichiaro, communication.

42. Considine, communication.

43. Graves, communication.

44. Colleen Graves, "How Do You Decide What to Buy?" 2016, https://colleengraves.org/2016/04/23/how-do-you-decide-what-to-buy.

45. Ibid.

46. Rogers, communication.

47. Colleen Graves, "Makerspace Resources and Programming Ideas," 2012, http://public librariesonline.org/2012/10/a-fabulous-labaratory-the-makerspace-at-fayetteville-free -library.

REFERENCES

Bagley, Caitlin A. *Makerspaces: Top Trailblazing Projects*. Chicago: ALA TechSource, 2014.

Britton, Lauren. "A Fabulous Laboratory: The Makerspace at Fayetteville Free Library." 2012. http://publiclibrariesonline.org/2012/10/a-fabulous-labaratory-the-makerspace-at -fayetteville-free-library.

Brooklyn Public Library. "BPL and BRIC." 2016. www.bklynlibrary.org/central/bpl-and-bric.

Carnegie Library of Pittsburgh. The Labs @ CLP, www.clpgh.org/teens/events/programs/thelabs.

DonorsChoose. "About Us." www.donorschoose.org/about.

Geek Feminism. "Code of Conduct." https://geekfeminism.org/about/code-of-conduct.

GoFundMe. "Common Questions." www.gofundme.com/questions.

Graves, Colleen. "Evolution of a Maker Space, from 'Monstie Stuffie' Projects to a Giant Catapult." *School Library Journal* (June 2016). www.slj.com/2015/06/programs/evolution-of-a-middle-school-maker-space-from-monster-stuffie-projects-to-a-giant -catapult.

———. "Getting Buy-In for Your Makerspace." http://ideas.demco.com/blog/getting-buy -in-for-your-makerspace.

———. "How Do You Decide What to Buy?" April 26, 2016. https://colleengraves.org/2016/04/23/how-do-you-decide-what-to-buy.

———. Makerspace Resources and Programming Ideas. https://colleengraves.org/maker space-resources-and-programming-ideas.

Indiegogo. "How It Works." www.indiegogo.com/how-it-works.

Kickstarter. "Kickstarter Basics." www.kickstarter.com/help/faq/kickstarter+basics.

Lachenal, Jessica. "Captain Marvel Author Shannon Hale Highlights the Problems with Gendered Library Programs." *The Mary Sue*, 2016. www.themarysue.com/oh-hale-no.

LITA 3D Printing Interest Group. "3D Printing Policies." https://docs.google.com/spread sheets/d/1tr19eaPzNyKhlxNhIDnwuI5_BCuwFmcJMOYpNU_EVY4/edit#gid=0.

Mozilla Open Badges. "About." http://openbadges.org/about.

The Possible Project. Makerspace for Teen Entrepreneurs @ The Possible Project. www.kickstarter.com/projects/1026490730/makerspace-for-teen-entrepreneurs-needs -a-laser-cu/description.

Schewe, Judith. "Out of the Archives: Caution! Artist @ Work! at Rochester Public Library." www.libraryasincubatorproject.org/?p=11624.

TekVenture. Maker Station, http://tekventure.org/maker-station.

Waters, Patrick. "Encouraging Neurodiversity in Your Makerspace or Classroom." www.edutopia.org/blog/encouraging-neurodiversity-in-makerspace-classroom -patrick-waters.

RECOMMENDED READING

Please see the section of this chapter titled "Keeping Up with the Movement" for a list of online resources.

Bagley, Caitlin A. *Makerspaces: Top Trailblazing Projects.* Chicago: ALA TechSource, 2014.

Burke, John J. *Makerspaces: A Practical Guide for Librarians.* Lanham, MD: Rowman and Littlefield, 2014.

Doorley, Scott, and Scott Witthoft. *Make Space: How to Set the Stage for Creative Collaboration.* Hoboken, NJ: John Wiley and Sons, 2012.

Fleming, Laura. *Worlds of Making: Best Practices for Establishing a Makerspace for Your School.* Thousand Oaks, CA: Corwin, 2015.

Hatch, Mark. *The Maker Movement Manifesto: Rules for Innovation in the New World of Crafters, Hackers, and Tinkerers.* New York: McGraw-Hill Education, 2014.

Martinez, Sylvia Libow, and Gary Stager. *Invent to Learn: Making, Tinkering, and Engineering in the Classroom.* Torrance, CA: Constructing Modern Knowledge Press, 2013.

McKnight, John, and Peter Block. *The Abundant Community: Awakening the Power of Families and Neighborhoods.* San Francisco, CA: Berrett-Koehler Publishers, 2010.

Willingham, Theresa, and Jeroen DeBoer. *Makerspaces in Libraries.* Lanham, MD: Rowman & Littlefield, 2015.

The Future of Library Makerspaces

ERIC JOHNSON

“**P**rophecy is a good line of business,” wrote Mark Twain, “but it is full of risks.”[1] This is an important point to bear in mind when committing any kind of forecast to print. Makerspaces are slippery institutions, given the rapidity of their development and the many social, technological, and economic forces that continue to influence their evolution.

This chapter is a reflection on some of the trends, technologies, and service approaches that will affect library makerspaces in the near and long-term future. It starts with an examination of why makerspaces are found in libraries in the first place and moves to consideration of the future of makerspaces in general and of library makerspaces particularly. It then touches on the issue of diversity in makerspaces and explores the idea that library makerspaces can be a response to the call for developing a "twenty-first-century skillset." From there, the discussion focuses on certain practical matters that must be tackled in the future: developments in makerspace programming, emerging technologies, assessment, education, and staffing. Finally, we'll consider some hazards that library makerspaces face before we wrap up by returning to the bigger picture of creating a shared future.

Eric Johnson is Head of Innovative Media at Virginia Commonwealth University Libraries.

The Present Situation

Before diving too deeply into predictions into the future of library makerspaces, it might be helpful to examine some of the reasons that these spaces are to be found in libraries in the first place. Makerspaces and other related creative spaces (such as hackerspaces, FabLabs, and digital scholarship centers) are of course found outside of libraries as well as in schools, university academic departments, museums and science centers, and as freestanding organizations in local communities. Each of these models, like library-based makerspaces, is grounded in the values and needs of the institution and community in which the makerspace is found.

So why should libraries host makerspaces? Throughout their history, libraries have been known as places that offer *preservation of* and *access to* information. This is what Arthur Wayne Hafner referred to when he wrote, "As the public storehouse of knowledge, the public library can be viewed as a free society's insurance that all ideas will be accessible to everyone who may want them."[2] But in addition to those two great purposes, libraries have also always been involved as well in the *creation of* and *sharing of* information and knowledge. Examples of this practice include offering résumé assistance, providing computer labs and coding workshops, circulating recording equipment, making connections through archival metadata, and building digital libraries.

The modern difference is that the creation and sharing of information is now easily done using methods beyond the texts, illustrations, and oral presentations that dominated information output over the past 575-odd years since Gutenberg first laid type to press. The twentieth century was an age of electronic communications: radio, television, movies, and more. In the last decades of the century there developed an unprecedented suite of creation and distributions systems spurred first by personal computers and then by the Internet. The tools of electronic mass communication now no longer rest solely in the hands of professionals with special access to studios, prohibitively expensive cameras, and editing suites; they have now become ubiquitous and commonplace, often literally carried around every day in the form of digital cameras and recorders, laptops, and smartphones. Tools are now available that allow everyone from novices to advanced makers to create and share ideas in *physical* form, too: 3D printers, embroidery machines, laser cutters, CNC machines, programmable microcontrollers, and more.

At their core, library makerspaces are about helping people explore and communicate ideas in ways other than the written word. Because information creation and sharing is headed into the realm of multimedia and physical objects, libraries must embrace this new trend if they are to see themselves as offering comprehensive information services in the modern world. One significant reason for libraries' support of makerspaces is that it helps them fulfill this key purpose.

Another library value reflected in the hosting of makerspaces is that of libraries' commitment to making expensive resources available to all constituents. "After all," wrote Tod Colegrove, "in a very real sense that is what libraries do—and have done, for thousands of years: buy sometimes expensive technology tailored to the needs and interest of the local community and make it available on a shared basis."[3] It is certainly historically true of books and today remains equally true of makerspaces. Books used to be—and laser cutters still are—technologies that few private citizens could easily afford or needed to use frequently. But by pooling the resources of the community to purchase those technologies, they could and can be shared among all its members on an as-needed basis. No one person or group has to carry the fiscal load and all can benefit.

Libraries are also natural places for makerspaces because libraries are institutions that support and encourage cross-disciplinary work—which is a hallmark of makerspaces. Public libraries attract people from all the professional and personal backgrounds represented in their community. Academic libraries serve as hubs for cross-departmental communication and collaboration. Makerspaces can benefit from as well as encourage this multidisciplinary sharing of experience and information, since users very often come in because of personal interests rather than professional requirements. A shared interest on the one hand combined with varied backgrounds and perspectives on the other make for a fertile environment for creative knowledge sharing. A lot of lip service is paid to the idea of this kind of collaborative work; it is hard to find places where it actually happens. Library makerspaces are ideal settings.

Finally, libraries are community hubs. They are places where numbers of people gather together, whether to do research, hold a meeting, take a class or workshop, found a club, or enjoy reading and crafting together. By giving them a chance to create and learn together in a hands-on fashion, a library makerspace is another way for libraries to support, strengthen, and expand opportunities for their communities.

Creativity, common resources, cross-disciplinarity, and community are themes that will come up several times in this chapter. They are the foundation of effective library makerspaces now, and they will remain the bases of effective library makerspaces as those spaces evolve into the future.

The Staying Power of Makerspaces

One crucial question to address when considering the future of library makerspaces is whether makerspaces as a general concept—those inside libraries and those found elsewhere—can be expected to last, and for how long. This is a concern any time there is a rapid adoption of any new technological system: is this just trendy or does it really have legs? Is it a fad or is it a legitimate evolution or revolution? Writing in *Places Journal,* Will Holman relays a cautionary tale of community makerspaces that launched with great fanfare and promise but found themselves foundering on the shores of scalability and sustainability:

> But despite huge attendance at the Maker Faire and a stream of upbeat articles in *Make Magazine,* the makerspace concept is experiencing growing pains. TechShop, a commercial chain, recently announced plans to seed 1,000 locations nationwide, even as it struggles to raise the funding to support such ambitions.... A popular makerspace in Brooklyn, 3rd Ward, closed abruptly in 2013 after an ill-fated expansion into Philadelphia; no matter that some had already paid several thousand dollars for "unlimited lifetime memberships."...With the maker economy projected to hit $8.41 billion by 2020, it is worth asking whether we are witnessing the birth of a durable movement or another trendy notion about civic innovation.[4]

Despite the concern over profitability of private spaces, there is abundant evidence of the growth of makerspaces. True numbers are hard to nail down, but *Popular Science* used self-reported numbers that showed that as of January 2016, 1,393 active or planned makerspaces were to be found around the world ("14 times as many makerspaces as there were a decade ago"), with 483 in the United States alone.[5] A 2015 report by the Royal Society for the Encouragement of Arts, Manufactures and Commerce in the United Kingdom describes three reasons why makerspace development is driven by long-term factors, reasons that pertain to the United States as well:

- *Want to*—More people want to make and view makerspaces as the ideal hubs to do so.
- *Can do*—Making has become easier, cheaper, and more joined up thanks to new tools.
- *Asked to*—There is a growing desire for the products and services of makers.[6]

In addition, article after article in popular journals and newspapers tout the economic potential of the maker movement as a whole with articles sporting titles such as "Why the Maker Movement Is Important to America's Future," "How Makerspaces Help Local Economies," and "Makers Are Radically Changing the World . . . Already."[7] Attendance at Maker Faires, the "all-ages gathering of tech enthusiasts, crafters, educators, tinkerers, hobbyists, engineers, science clubs, authors, artists, students, and commercial exhibitors" sponsored by *Make Magazine* (not to mention the large number of nonaffiliated maker festivals) is burgeoning. Maker Faire reports that "[a] record 215,000 people attended the two flagship Maker Faires in the Bay Area and New York in 2014, with 44 percent of attendees first timers at the Bay Area event, and 61 percent in New York. A family friendly event, 50 percent attend the event with children."[8]

This is not to suggest that all the articles and studies guarantee any kind of long-term future of makerspaces, but in the short term at least there is a strong likelihood that public interest in developing such spaces will remain high both outside and within libraries. Addressing academic libraries, the authors of the New Media Consortium's *NMC Horizon Report: 2015 Library Edition* observe that "university libraries are also integrating makerspaces that invite creative tinkering and experimental learning. Often added as an extension to the digital media labs, the library makerspace is believed by many leaders in the field to support a new form of learning that is key to the future of higher education."[9] Public libraries, too, are seeing growth in makerspaces. A 2013 survey found 16.8 percent of public libraries hosting Science, Technology, Engineering, Math (STEM) makerspaces.[10] The rise of school library makerspaces was celebrated in a dedicated issue of the *School Library Journal* in 2015.[11]

In considering the future of makerspaces in and out of libraries, it is important to draw a distinction between makerspaces and the maker movement. The latter was defined well by *Adweek*:

> The maker movement, as we know, is the umbrella term for independent inventors, designers, and tinkerers ... A convergence of computer hackers and traditional artisans, the niche is established enough to have its own magazine, *Make*, as well as hands-on Maker Faires that are catnip for DIYers who used to toil in solitude. Makers tap into an American admiration for self-reliance and combine that with open-source learning, contemporary design and powerful personal technology like 3-D printers. The creations, born in cluttered local workshops and bedroom offices, stir the imaginations of consumers numbed by generic, mass-produced, made-in–China merchandise.[12]

This movement exists independently of formal makerspaces, as evinced by such examples as the rise of Etsy, an upsurge in cheese-making, canning, and other traditional home crafts, and the growth of the DIY music scene. This same tendency toward creative self-reliance has given rise in recent years to other related trends: Kickstarter and other crowdfunding sites; coworking, co-op spaces, and other flexible, individualized responses to the traditional 9-to-5 workday;

and supplemental income in the form of handcrafted projects (e.g., Etsy, which claims to have 1.6 million active sellers offering more than 35 million items for sale, generated $2.39 billion in gross merchandise sales in 2015).[13]

Despite Will Holman's comments above, a few robust private community makerspaces will likely continue for the foreseeable future because their members often have demands and a willingness to pay for access to higher-end or more specialized maker equipment and resources—such as metal lathes or large CNC machines—than the average library can afford to make available. But it would not be surprising in the least to see smaller private makerspaces getting succeeded in the long run by library-based makerspaces run as community-oriented, common resources.

Library Makerspaces and Their Future

All the above suggests that the near-term future is bright for library makerspaces, not least because they tend not to have the same requirement for self-sustaining profitability that private makerspaces do. The technologies and services in library makerspaces are instead a common good, similar to other library resources.

The longer-term picture is harder to pin down because the environment is changing so rapidly. Technological evolution brings inevitable change to makerspace offerings. Makerspace models continue to evolve. Other related creative spaces are developing in libraries as well, building an ecosystem of creativity in which makerspaces are only a part.

The ongoing evolution—sometimes revolution—of technologies means that the specific technologies that so often seem to define the current makerspaces (e.g., 3D printers) may end up becoming more accessible and will be distributed out into society in new ways as consumer products, which may pull them out of makerspaces entirely. If every home ends up with an inexpensive and accurate 3D printer ready to spit out every nut, bolt, paper clip, and action figure, will there still be a need for library (or other) makerspaces?

For that matter, libraries are hardly the only place for makerspaces: they are found in primary and secondary schools, museums, and throughout communities large and small. They do face a certain kind of competition. In addition, there is a wider ecosystem of related creative spaces found in libraries and other settings, such as media creation labs in school, public, and academic libraries; digital humanities and digital scholarship centers in academic libraries; hackerspaces out in communities; entrepreneurship centers; digital pedagogy centers; and more. Elements of all these are sometimes incorporated into specific library makerspaces and sometimes left as separate entities. It depends on the local creative environment; there is no one-size-fits-all approach.

All of this makes the crucial point that library makerspaces, now and in the future, must take the time to identify their unique missions, grounding those missions in the needs of the library or library makerspace's community or constituency. A makerspace cannot be all things to all people, nor are resources unlimited, so the makerspace staff needs to have a clear understanding of what they are trying to accomplish in their spaces. This understanding in turn flows from knowledge of their community—especially their maker community—and its needs. There may be no more important skillset for library makerspace managers to develop than the abilities to articulate a mission and to understand their community as it changes over time (which necessitates ongoing evaluation). Once the mission and the community are clear, they can make choices on the tools, resources, and services that best fit their circumstances. Mission and audience first; tools later.

Diversity of Makers and Makerspaces

There has been surprisingly little formal, quantitative research done on the demographics of users of makerspaces and of the maker community. The latter is less surprising than the former given the significant challenge of defining members of the maker community. In his seminal book *Makers*, Chris Anderson offers an expansive definition:

> We are all Makers. We are born Makers (just watch a child's fascination with drawing, blocks, Lego, or crafts), and many of us retain that love in our hobbies and passions. It's not just about workshops, garages, and man caves. If you love to cook, you're a kitchen Maker and your stove is your workbench (homemade food is best, right?). If you love to plant, you're a garden Maker. Knitting and sewing, scrap-booking, beading, and cross-stitching—all Making.[14]

In 2014, Intel published an important, survey-based, global study on women's and girls' participation in the maker movement, but the definition of maker they used was, in contrast to Anderson's, very specific:

> For the purposes of the survey, we defined makers as people who make physical objects with electronic tools for their own purposes or with their own designs. To be screened into our online survey, makers needed to have used one of these

tools in the past year: microcontroller, laser cutter, computer development board, open source robotics, 3D manufacturing tools, or a 3D printer.[15]

Such a definition of maker may be so narrow as to limit the conclusions that can be drawn from it.

Which is not to say that there is not still useful—and sobering—information to be gleaned from the existing analyses of the maker movement and its participants. For instance, Maker Media, the publisher of *Make Magazine* and the developer of Maker Faires and one of the public faces of the movement, reports that of the readership of *Make*, 81 percent are male, their median household income is $106,000, 73 percent own their own home, 97 percent attended college, and 83 percent are employed. Of the combined 215,000 attendees of Maker Faire Bay Area 2014 and the World Maker Faire in New York 2014, 70 percent were male, the median household income was $130,000, and 97 percent attended or graduated from college.[16] Such skewed statistics are indeed eye-opening. Although the rhetoric around these spaces is typically one of openness, inclusion, and access ("We are all Makers"), the reality is often one of privilege and exclusivity.

By way of comparison, the Maker Education Initiative (Maker Ed) conducted a survey of fifty-one youth-oriented makerspaces that examined racial diversity in makerspaces. The results revealed that:

> Across all makerspaces surveyed, 42% of program participants were White, 20% were Black/African American, 18% were Hispanic/Latino(a), 14% were Asian, 0.3% were Native American, and 5% did not fall in the given categories. While these represent the mean across all makerspaces responding, the sites vary widely in the populations they serve. . . . This also demonstrates greater diversity than the current U.S. population, based on findings from the U.S. Census data in 2010.[17]

The Maker Ed report expressed a hope that the youth demographics' contrast with those of the adult participants at Maker Faires and subscribers to *Make Magazine* ("i.e., predominantly middle age, white males") points to a more diverse generation of makers on the rise. Diversity of user backgrounds, whether that be race, gender, ability, or other measures, is a strength in a place like a library makerspace that has been designed to serve an entire community and to benefit from varied perspectives.

As a caution, the Maker Ed report points out that the racial diversity they identified is unevenly distributed across the surveyed sites.[18] In the near future, diversity is unlikely to be strengthened or sustained in library makerspaces without a proactive commitment and effort by makerspace staff. This might come in the form of targeted workshops, programs, and other outreach in which minority users are made to feel particularly welcome and valued. In the long run, should the maker movement ignite and remain alight across diverse populations, managers of library makerspaces may not need to do anything special. Until such a time, however, they must exercise vigilance and intentionality to lower the barriers to participation by all groups.

Driving the Future: Twenty-First-Century Skills and Library Makerspaces

Researchers, educators, and policymakers have in recent years identified skills, practices, and habits of mind that are beneficial as society in the United States moves deeper into the twenty-first century. Always prominent on such lists are the development of creativity, technical skills, problem-solving, collaboration, and the creation and understanding of multiple forms of media.

P21, a national nonprofit formed as a partnership among education, business, community, and government leaders that works to ensure "that all learners acquire the knowledge and skills they need to thrive in a world where change is constant and learning never stops," has identified a set of student outcomes that they believe students need to master.[19] Among the top outcomes of their "Framework for 21st Century Learning" are "Learning and Innovation Skills," including creativity and innovation, critical thinking and problem-solving, and communication and collaboration.[20]

Similarly, the major framing guidelines of the International Society for Technology in Education's *ISTE Standards for Students* include "Creativity and innovation," "Communication and collaboration," "Critical thinking, problem solving, and decision making," and "Technology operations and concepts."[21]

Among the "Common Beliefs" guiding the American Association of School Librarians' *Standards for the 21st-Century Learner* are "Inquiry provides a framework for learning" and "Technology skills are crucial for future employment needs." The document lists different skills that students ought to master, including:

- Collaborate with others to exchange ideas, develop new understandings, make decisions, and solve problems.
- Use the writing process, media, and visual literacy, and technology skills to create products that express new understandings.

- Use technology and other information tools to organize and display knowledge and understanding in ways that others can view, use, and assess.
- Use creative and artistic formats to express personal learning.[22]

The Association of College and Research Libraries' *Framework for Information Literacy for Higher Education*, issued recently by the ACRL board as one of several such documents addressing information literacy, includes related language in its description of standards for learners in colleges and universities. In defining information creation as a process, the authors of the framework describe the need for learners to be able to "articulate the . . . emerging processes of information creation and dissemination in a particular discipline" and to "develop, in their own creation processes, an understanding that their choices impact the purposes for which the information product will be used and the message it conveys." The emphasis in this document is on information consumption, but inherent in it is the realization that creative modes of conveying information and the ability to create in these modes are inherent in the twenty-first-century learning environment.[23]

In short, makerspaces, which marry technology, hands-on skills, and collaborative environments, are an excellent way for libraries to respond to the call by prominent educators, activists, and policymakers to equip learners and the workforce with the creative, technical, collaborative, and problem-solving skills needed by people to thrive in our century.

Beyond the Banana Piano: Programming of Library Makerspaces

Much of the current, day-to-day library makerspace programming (workshops, one-on-one instruction, etc.) emphasizes orientation to and skills building on a range of unfamiliar technologies: 3D printing, soldering, Arduino and Makey Makey, laser cutters or engravers, coding, and so on. It is of course crucial that library makerspaces offer such guidance; fundamentally, users cannot imagine a future where they would create with these tools if they do not understand how they operate and what they can achieve. As tools evolve and as new users step up to learn, such an orientation will always be necessary.

However, library makerspaces are doing their communities a deep disservice if that is the totality of their instructional offerings. Knowledge of the tools is necessary, but is not sufficient to increase the creative problem-solving capacity of the community. It is great when someone can use a 3D printer, but it is far more interesting when she learns to see a problem or opportunity, design a solution or response, and then realize how that 3D printer (or other appropriate tool) can help implement her vision.

To offer an analogy, a person who wants soup has several options: 1) he can go to a restaurant and buy some; 2) he can go to the grocery store and buy a can or a mix in a box; 3) he can buy ingredients and strictly follow a recipe; or 4) he can use his knowledge of the science and art of cooking and create a never-before-seen soup from scratch.

Many library makerspace programs are pitched at about levels 2 or 3 as described above. We recognize, for instance, that 3D printing an action figure is "better" than going to the store and buying one. Downloading a file from Thingiverse and printing it is somewhat like the level 2 soup-cooking stage; the design work is already done, there is a hands-on component, and it is helpful to achieving a better understanding of the process, but it is not an entirely creative act. Following the step-by-step instructions in an Arduino kit to get a piezo-electric buzzer to play a song is like the level 3 cooking effort: it offers a more fundamental understanding of the parts and provides some room for tweaking, but at the end of the day it is still about following somebody else's instructions.

Ideal library makerspaces work to move their users into level 4 thinking: rather than obtaining solutions to some physical-world problem by shopping at a store or hiring an expert, the highest-order maker examines the problem, considers solutions, designs the most workable solution, and applies it herself.

For libraries, this means developing an understanding of creative problem-solving approaches such as design thinking. In an article in *Harvard Business Review*, Tim Brown, CEO of the design firm IDEO, defined design thinking as

a methodology that imbues the full spectrum of innovation activities with a human-centered design ethos. By this I mean that innovation is powered by a thorough understanding, through direct observation, of what people want and need in their lives and what they like or dislike about the way particular products are made, packaged, marketed, sold, and supported.[24]

Or as IDEO founder David Kelley put it, "What we, as design thinkers, have, is this creative confidence that, when given a difficult problem, we have a methodology that enables us to come up with a solution that nobody has before."[25]

Effective makerspaces will need to master the methodologies of design thinking and other creative problem-solving approaches. They will need to do it through the development of pedagogies that help equip people to move from level 3 recipe followers to level 4 solution creators. Library makerspace managers should examine (or create!) the studies that will tell makerspace organizers how to maximize their spaces and programs for experiential learning and deep problem-solving.

Much of the current, ubiquitous technology of makerspaces, such as 3D printers and programmable microcontrollers, is still essentially emerging technology. As with the earlier example of makerspaces ceasing to host 3D printers when they become common for home use, library makerspaces should expect their technical offerings to change as technology evolves. A makerspace seven years from now will not offer the same technology as the makerspace of today.

This technical growth and evolution is all the more reason for library makerspaces to broadly emphasize the pedagogy of creativity (while orienting users to the technology of the moment) rather than emphasizing any particular set of technologies as part of the definition of the makerspace itself. Creating a framework that emphasizes creativity and the provision of emerging and hard-to-afford technology means that the library makerspace will be a central place where anybody can learn to create and explore emerging technology no matter what the technology may be.

Emerging Technologies and the Future of Library Makerspaces

Makerspaces will—and must—continue to evolve. More specifically, they must incorporate this expectation of technological and service evolution into their planning. As mentioned, most of the cutting-edge technology available in today's library makerspaces will eventually no longer be found there. The technology will become more affordable to the general user (and therefore more ubiquitous, perhaps even moving into the home), more sophisticated (and therefore will need to be updated to the latest version), or fail to live up to its hype or promise (and will therefore fade away).

Just as importantly, new technology is always in development, and the future-facing makerspace is always preparing itself for what is coming and considering new technology and its relationship to its mission to decide whether to incorporate that tech into the space's offerings or to reject it as a bad fit.

To that end, it is helpful to examine some of those emerging technologies and how they might become part of a library makerspace's offerings in the relatively near future. Makerspaces staff should make a habit of following the development of emerging technologies. Sources for discussion of this tech include Gartner, Inc.'s annual "Hype Cycle for Emerging Technologies"; the New Media Consortium's Horizon Reports for libraries, higher education, museums, and other institutions;

popular journals such as *Wired* and *MIT Technology Review;* technology-oriented blogs and websites such as TechCrunch, Engadget, and The Verge; Kickstarter and other technology crowd-funding sites; reports from the MIT Media Lab, the Consumer Electronics Show, and other tech showcases; and conversations with colleagues, vendors, and others trusted specialists.

This is a good place to insist again that managers of library makerspaces must ground their technology and service choices in a thorough understanding of their space's mission and of the community that the makerspace is designed to serve. New technology emerges constantly, and this understanding serves as the lodestar that helps guide a makerspace to the technology that best serves its mission and benefits its audience. When money and time are limited resources, it is as helpful to understand where *not* to invest—because the tech serves neither mission nor audience—as it is to understand where to spend a unit's resources.

Virtual Reality and Augmented Reality

Virtual reality and augmented reality are two kinds of emerging, primarily visual, technologies that are similar but not quite the same thing.

Augmented reality (AR) is the use of technology—often but not always via headsets—to introduce virtual elements or overlays into the real-world environment, giving users the ability to interact with the virtual while still being able to distinguish between the virtual and the real. Google Glass was one kind of AR technology; iPad apps that show overlays over the surrounding environment are another.

Virtual reality (VR) is more immersive: it entails the computer-based generation of entire, comprehensive interactive environments. Users of VR technology must typically don helmets or goggles so that the system can display the immersive world through which they move. VR technologies that have recently been in the news include the Oculus Rift and HTC Vive headsets, both of which currently (or will soon) offer hand tracking controls that let users interact even further with 3D virtual environments. Another form of virtual reality is offered in large-scale virtual environments consisting of screens surrounding a space in which users stand, such as those offered by the CAVE or CAVE2 systems.

According to the 2015 version of the Gartner Hype Cycle—the annual review of emerging tech that places new technology on a standard curve leading from innovation trigger to plateau of productivity—VR and AR are about to climb onto the "slope of enlightenment" (meaning that while the initial promise may not have delivered immediately, now second- and third-generation products are being delivered based on a better understanding of the actual capabilities of and experience with the technologies).[26]

How does all this fit in a library makerspace? It does not matter whether the user is simply consuming the content made by others or is developing new content with or for these devices themselves; both are appropriate to library makerspaces. The one emphasizes the "makerspace as shared resource for making emerging technology available" aspect of these spaces, while the other emphasizes the idea of "makerspace as place of creative work," especially in the realm of emerging digital tools.

It is important to note that many of these AR and VR systems do not yet run on their own. They often require investments in advanced computers with heavy processing power and sophisticated (read: expensive) graphics cards. Another related technology that is beneficial are gestural sensors. They typically come in the form of handheld devices or as wall-mounted sensors, and some but not all of them come as part of the VR or AR package.

Drones

Drones, or more formally known as unmanned aircraft systems (UAS) or unmanned aerial vehicles (UAV), have been buzzing about and buzzed about for several years. Once the province of the military and intelligence agencies, improvements in electronics and declining costs of components led to an active hobbyist movement for drones in the first decade of the twenty-first century. Starting around 2010, commercially-made drones were made available to average consumers, prompting an enormous upsurge of interest in the platforms for commercial, educational, artistic, and hobbyist applications. Common uses include aerial photography and filming, agriculture, search, and rescue, conservation management, surveying, and simply flying for fun.

In 2012, recognizing the enormous leap in popularity of these devices, Congress instructed the Federal Aviation Administration to develop regulations to integrate drones into the national airspace. Rules clarifications for managing small drones (those under 55 pounds) in commercial and other settings are due in 2016. These may well pave the way to drone delivery of packages, a service that Amazon and other retailers are interested in providing, and prompt an explosion in other forms of commercial drone activity.

All of this has meant a growth in public interest in learning about drones and how to fly them. Library makerspaces will be prime places to provide community access to this emerging and rapidly evolving technology so that people can learn about it and test it out without necessarily investing their own funds. An earlier chapter of this book discusses the current state of drones in the context of library makerspaces; the soon-to-be-announced rule changes seem set to release a pent-up swarm of drone-related developments.

Data Visualization and Visual Literacy

Data visualization, information visualization, infographics—all these are terms that are related to one another and to the larger concept of visual literacy. We now live in the world of "big data," when large sets of data are now available that can be computationally examined and presented for consumption by the public. Computer-based tools are being developed to help people share complex and technical information in understandable ways—often, but not always, in the form of infographics. Creative visualizations can make it possible to grasp patterns in data that textual data sets leave shrouded. We are poised to make the same kind of jump in visualization capabilities as home videos made with the advent of software-based editing suites.

However, the technical tools alone will not create the kind of visual literacy that fuels effective meaning-making through the use of images. Visual literacy "is a set of abilities that enables an individual to effectively find, interpret, evaluate, use, and create images and visual media."[27] Library staff can support the development of these abilities in makerspaces through the provision of 2D visualization systems and 3D modeling tools and through the implementation of an effective and thoughtful visual literacy educational program.

Internet of Things

High-speed Internet is becoming more far-reaching and costing less; chips and sensors are getting smaller, cheaper, and more sophisticated; and wireless connectivity and smartphone use is growing. This crossroads of technological development has set the stage for the "Internet of Things" (IoT), which is "about connecting devices over the Internet, letting them talk to people, applications, and each other."[28] The classic example is the smart refrigerator that communicates with the homeowner to let him know the milk is running low so he can pick some up on the way home from work (or the more sophisticated version in which the refrigerator places an order directly with the grocery store for delivery).

With these sensors, chips, and processors in hand, makers soon will be able to start contributing platforms and solving problems related to the IoT. They will be able to program devices to communicate with each other and execute sophisticated commands in the real world. They will develop apps that take advantage of the interconnected world of things through which they will be traveling. Already under way is the development of a kind of modular library of IoT resources (similar to the approach that littleBits takes in electronics) that will simplify the development of connected systems.

Metrics and Assessment

A world of budgetary and time constraints is often accompanied by a need to prove the "worth" of initiatives such as makerspaces. Not the least means of doing so is by providing metrics on the use of such spaces, with the idea that an increase in numbers over time is a sign of positive impact. The problem is that while such *quantitative* usage metrics—the record of who comes in, why, and in what activities they take part—may be mildly interesting in and of themselves, they do little to provide rigorous *qualitative* feedback about what users are getting from their maker experiences, why they are there, and what that might mean for the space as it continues to develop.

The latter measurements require a more rigorous assessment program, and makerspaces to date have not generally done much of this type of assessment in this way. This must change in the future. As makerspaces become more common, effective qualitative assessment models will no doubt be designed.

One fundamental challenge is that the undirected, playful, experimental uses of makerspaces are much harder to assess than are directed instructional programs, yet the impact may be no less real. How does one say "creativity in our community has increased" or measure a user's problem-solving ability when these might not even show up for years? Are those the right measures or values? Models will arise to help makerspaces assess their effectiveness as creative spaces; the near future will see much discussion at professional conferences on the best means of measurement.

In comparison, it is easier to assess specific programs, such as instructional workshops on the use of 3D printers or sewing machines, or to assess the degree of creativity in an assignment or project. Libraries have many models for assessing instruction sessions formatively and summatively, through direct and indirect measures, and through other approaches.[29] The rise of creativity as an essential twenty-first-century skill has inspired a concomitant rise in tools and rubrics of assessment.[30] The accumulation of these measures is helpful when analyzing the offerings of any makerspace.

That said, measurement of the overall effectiveness of the makerspace requires a clear-eyed articulation of its mission and goals. Only with such a foundation can we get a good read on whether technologies, programs, and personnel are deployed in a manner that most effectively helps goals be achieved. Again, putting technology in a room and calling it a makerspace is an insufficient approach to creating an effective maker program.

The utility of any model or models of assessment will be limited if their results are not applied to the program and technology choices made by makerspace managers. Rapid evolution of technology means rapid evolution of programming, and effective makerspace managers will keep the assessment loop going constantly.

Maker Education of Library Staff

So, where will we learn how to do this "maker stuff" in the future? Will there be a maker track in library schools as there are reference or digital libraries tracks? Do library staff members even need to be experts? Are we more interested in educating ourselves on specific technologies, in learning how (and why) to learn emerging technologies, in developing the pedagogies to teach technologies to others, or a combination of all the above?

Some library schools are starting to explore makerspaces as learning spaces in courses such as "Libraries as Learning Labs in a Digital Age" and "Informal Learning Spaces and Pedagogies."[31] Only a very few schools appear to be teaching the technical skills used in makerspaces.[32] The challenge is that the technology may change too quickly to become part of the curriculum in library schools. In the case of makerspace-related topics, rather than concentrate too deeply on specific technologies, courses on creative spaces like those cited above that take a more broad-based approach to pedagogies of informal learning spaces, are likely to increase across library school curricula.

As for learning the specific skills and hardware, maker culture already champions the twin approaches of self education and community (especially online community) support. Instructional resources abound—manuals, YouTube videos, guides such as this book, websites for hundreds of different tools—to help the aspiring maker librarian to learn the ins and outs of a given technology. In addition, one of the main factors that differentiates today's maker movement from earlier craft-related movements is the opportunity for makers to turn to online communities for learning, support, and assistance. It is incredibly easy for aspiring makers to find like-minded comrades who share interests in particular tools, methods, and outcomes. Both kinds of resources—tools for self-directed learning and communities of support—will only grow in number, sophistication, and interconnectedness.

One role that library makerspace managers and staff should cultivate in the context of makerspaces is that of *facilitator*, rather than that of *expert*. Not all users of library makerspaces will want to be "directed." Many are interested in learning through exploring, so library staff may need to encourage, prod, and question instead of "solving" the problem for the user—even more when there is no explicit "problem" to solve. What is more, it is extremely difficult for library staff to be expert in every emerging technology that might be found in a makerspace, so cultivation of a sense of exploration is not only beneficial for staff who are trying to learn, but also serves as a model for all the users of a space. Some of this exploration may simply mean turning to a more knowledgeable user for help. This attitude does not necessarily come naturally to library staff, some of whom tend to see themselves as the expert resource of last resort.

Staffing Library Makerspaces in the Future

Related to the question of how library makerspace personnel are educated is the issue of staffing. Where will staff come from? The reality is that as makerspaces and maker education become more mainstream, and especially as they permeate primary and secondary educational programs, people who have direct experience with such spaces and the technologies they offer will enter the marketplace.

Few current-day makerspace staff members have been exposed to makerspaces and their technologies from a young age, because the concept of such spaces is still so new. But as time goes on, that will change, as will the baseline understanding of the technologies and their capabilities, how such spaces operate, and how staff in such spaces might function. Indeed, it is not unlikely that children could grow up with an interest in running such spaces as a career goal.

Personal experience and some post-secondary training in these technologies (e.g., in the kinds of library school courses mentioned above, in college courses that rely on makerspace technologies, etc.) will increasingly appear on résumés and CVs. Hiring managers will be able to look for direct experience and not simply rely on demonstrated aptitude and interest alone.

That said, it is likely that new makerspace staff will still need training in pedagogical techniques, the kind of "facilitator mindset" discussed above, and broader approaches to building a successful creative space. It is one thing to know the technologies; it is another to be able to help other people to learn them.

The Dark Side of the Future

Finally, it would be remiss to fail to consider some of the alternative paths that could lead to a future of limited success or outright failure for library makerspaces. Some ideas bear consideration, if not outright resistance:

■ Makerspaces Are Only for STEM Education

It is easy to find news reports trumpeting the makerspace phenomenon as a key solution to the problem of inadequate STEM education in the United States (ignoring for the moment that this crisis may be no real crisis at all).[33] Several tech companies offer grants for STEM-related makerspace creation. Through their grant making and educational initiatives, The National Science Foundation and other federal funding bodies have emphasized the need for informal learning spaces to support STEM education. Many articles in the popular press explicitly describe makerspaces as STEM resources.

Makerspaces truly are good places for addressing STEM-related education—but that is not the only kind of education or creativity that they offer. It makes sense to frame makerspaces in this way: after all, the state of STEM education receives a great deal of attention and funding, and it is entirely reasonable for makerspace managers to tie their spaces to those initiatives so that that they can seek some of funding, especially for expensive technologies.

However, when makerspace rhetoric so closely aligns STEM and making, an enormous array of other kinds of, reasons for, and audiences for making get left behind. How do arts-and-humanities-related makers and traditional crafters fit? Does STEM-related making—given the gender disparities in the STEM fields—sound more welcoming to boys and men than to girls and women? What happens when the "STEM crisis" passes? What are we missing by framing making as a STEM activity?

The opportunities for creativity and creative problem-solving that makerspaces offer extend well beyond STEM fields alone. Creativity writ large is the key twenty-first-century skill, the wellspring from which these other more focused approaches emerge.

2 Makerspaces Are Primarily about Innovation, Product Development, and Entrepreneurship

Similar to the preceding claims about STEM, this argument reflects an unfortunate limitation to the definition of makerspaces. Also, like the STEM assertions, this notion appears to be inspired by the drive for dollars. If a makerspace can help a user develop the next great widget and that user strikes it rich, that will justify the funds allocated to the makerspace. It also reflects a general discomfort with the idea of pursuing creativity for its own sake (or at least without a predetermined end in mind). Further, it touches on a particularly American notion that the best way to measure value is through dollars, so that if people are spending time in such spaces and strengthening their creative skills for reasons *other* than the pursuit of money, then they are wasting their time.

Innovation, product development, and entrepreneurship are forms of what might be termed "applied creativity." As such, they are certainly appropriate and worthy goals for some users of makerspaces. But that is only one portion of a much larger spectrum of creative undertaking that is made possible by makerspaces. Limiting the focus of the space—and the rhetoric of the space—to these areas can blind managers to other opportunities for growth and creative development.

3 Makerspaces Are Defined by Their Tools

This notion has been discussed several times already in this chapter, but it is important to reemphasize the idea that no one tool or set of tools makes a makerspace a makerspace. Tool choices should stem from the mission and goals of the space, not the other way around. On occasion, there have been attempts to define "real" makerspaces as those that have certain tools—3D printers, for instance—while suggesting that those with different emphases and different tools might be "creative spaces" but are not true makerspaces.

This is a silly proposition. Makerspaces are about creation, collaboration, and community. To quote Maker Media, "A collection of tools does not define a Makerspace. Rather, we define it by what it enables: making."[34]

The Future, Together

The future of makerspaces in general and library makerspaces specifically will involve a standoff between those whose goal is to articulate and maintain a broad definition of makerspaces and those who insist on a more limited perspective that suggests that makerspaces are only for specific activities (e.g., STEM or entrepreneurial development) or toolsets. The broader definition absolutely *includes* narrower purposes—but also reaches beyond them toward a wider horizon of possibility.

One way for libraries to pave a path to a more inclusive future is to begin formalizing a cross-institutional discussion about library makerspaces of the future to identify guiding principles that would apply to any library. Such principles should be grounded in the library mission and value. The American Library Association's own core values offer a starting point for a framework for developing these guiding principles. These include:

- an open, inclusive, and collaborative environment
- excellence and innovation
- intellectual freedom
- social responsibility and the public good[35]

Committing to "an open, inclusive, and collaborative environment" would require that library makerspaces work to ensure that a diverse user base is made to feel welcome and explore effective ways to build their user community's capacity to help one another. Pursuing "excellence and innovation" is at the heart of any makerspace—whose entire raison d'etre is creativity. Supporting "intellectual freedom" means that users are welcome in the space for an infinite range of reasons. Emphasizing "social responsibility and the public good" acts as a charge to libraries to be responsible caretakers of common resources.

No doubt other principles will need to be a part of the discussion as well, but any set of principles properly grounded in the mission and values of libraries and the library profession will serve as a guide to which managers of library makerspaces can turn as they develop their service models. A commitment to these principles, along with a grounding in makerspace mission and a deep knowledge of the local community, will ensure library makerspaces' ongoing success into the future—no matter what the next technological revolution or evolution may bring.

NOTES

1. Mark Twain, *Following the Equator: A Journey around the World* (Hartford, CT: American Publishing, 1897).
2. Arthur Wayne Hafner, *Democracy and the Public Library: Essays on Fundamental Issues* (Westport, CT: Greenwood, 1993).
3. Tod Colegrove, "Editorial Board Thoughts: Libraries as Makerspace?" *Information Technology and Libraries* 32, no. 1 (2013): 2–5, doi: http://dx.doi.org/10.6017/ital.v32i1.3793.

4. Will Holman, "Makerspace: Towards a New Civic Infrastructure," *Places Journal*, November 2015, https://placesjournal.org/article/makerspace-towards-a-new-civic -infrastructure/.

5. Nicole Lou and Katie Peek, "By the Numbers: The Rise of the Makerspace," *Popular Science*, February 23, 2016, www.popsci.com/rise-makerspace-by-numbers.

6. Benedict Dellot, *Ours to Master: How Makerspaces Can Help Us Master Technology for a More Human End* (London: The Royal Society for the encouragement of Arts, Man-ufactures and Commerce, 2015), www.thersa.org/discover/publications-and-articles/ reports/ours-to-master/Download.

7. Tim Bajarin, "Why the Maker Movement Is Important to America's Future," *Time*, May 19, 2014, http://time.com/104210/maker-faire-maker-movement/; John Tierney, "How Makerspaces Help Local Economies," *The Atlantic*, April 17, 2015, www.the atlantic.com/technology/archive/2015/04/makerspaces-are-remaking-local-economies/ 390807/; and Mark Hatch, "Makers Are Radically Changing the World . . . Already," *Forbes*, December 23, 2013, www.forbes.com/sites/singularity/2013/12/23/makers-are -radically-changing-the-world-already/#69ae4a4b35ef.

8. "Maker Faire: A Bit of History," http://makerfaire.com/makerfairehistory/.

9. New Media Consortium, *NMC Horizon Report: 2015 Library Edition*, http://cdn.nmc .org/media/2015-nmc-horizon-report-library-EN.pdf.

10. John Carlo Bertot, Paul T. Jaeger, Jean Lee, Kristofer Dubbels, Abigail J. McDermott, and Brian Real, "2013 Digital Inclusion Survey: Survey Findings and Results," *Informa-tion Policy and Access Center*, July 21, 2014, http://digitalinclusion.umd.edu/sites/default/ files/uploads/2013DigitalInclusionNationalReport.pdf.

11. "The Maker Issue," *School Library Journal*, www.slj.com/features/the-maker-issue-slj -2015/.

12. Joan Voight, "Which Big Brands Are Courting the Maker Movement, and Why," *Ad-week*, March 17, 2014, www.adweek.com/news/advertising-branding/which-big-brands -are-courting-maker-movement-and-why-156315.

13. "About Etsy," www.etsy.com/about/.

14. Chris Anderson, *Makers: The New Industrial Revolution* (New York: Crown Business, 2012).

15. Intel Corporation, "MakeHers: Engaging Girls and Women in Technology through Making, Creating, and Inventing," 2014. www.intel.com/content/dam/www/public/us/ en/documents/reports/makers-report-girls-women.pdf.

16. "Fact Sheet," *Maker Media*, http://makermedia.com/press/fact-sheet/.

17. Kylie Peppler, Adam Maltese, Anna Keune, Stephanie Chang, and Lisa Regalla, *The Maker Ed Open Portfolio Project Survey of Makerspaces, Part I*, February 23, 2015, http://makered.org/wp-content/uploads/2015/02/OPP_ResearchBrief6_Surveyof MakerspacesPart1_final.pdf.

18. Ibid., 3.
19. P21, "Our Vision and Mission," www.p21.0rg/about-us/our-mission.
20. ———, "Framework for 21st Century Learning," www.p21.org/about-us/p21-framework.
21. International Society for Technology in Education, *ISTE Standards for Students*, 2007, www.iste.org/standards/iste-standards/standards-for-students.
22. American Association of School Librarians, *Standards for the 21st-Century Learner* (Chicago: American Association of School Librarians, 2007), www.ala.org/aasl/sites/ala.org.aasl/files/content/guidelinesandstandards/learningstandards/AASL_Learning Standards.pdf.
23. Association of College and Research Libraries, *Framework for Information Literacy for Higher Education*, February 2, 2015, www.ala.org/acrl/standards/ilframework.
24. Tim Brown, "Design Thinking," *Harvard Business Review* 86, no. 6 (2008): 84–92.
25. John Brownlee, "Ideo's David Kelley on 'Design Thinking,'" *Fast Company Design*, November 15, 2016, https://www.fastcodesign.com/1139331/ideos-david-kelley-design -thinking.
26. Gartner, Inc., "Hype Cycle," www.gartner.com/technology/research/methodologies/hype-cycle.jsp.
27. Association of College and Research Libraries, *ACRL Visual Literacy Competency Standards for Higher Education*, October 2011, www.ala.org/acrl/standards/visualliteracy.
28. Nicole Kobie, "What is the Internet of Things?" *The Guardian*, May 6, 2015, www .theguardian.com/technology/2015/may/06/what-is-the-internet-of-things-google.
29. Katherine Schilling, and Rachel Applegate, "Best Methods for Evaluating Educational Impact: A Comparison of the Efficacy of Commonly Used Measures of Library Instruction," *Journal of the Medical Library Association* 100, no. 4 (2012): 258–69.
30. Andrew Miller, "Yes, You Can Teach and Assess Creativity!" Edutopia, March 7, 2013, www.edutopia.org/blog/you-can-teach-assess-creativity-andrew-miller.
31. University of Washington, The Information School Library and Information Science [course offerings], www.washington.edu/students/crscat/lis.html; University of Illinois Board of Trustees, School of Library and Information Science, Full Catalog. www.lis .illinois.edu/academics/courses/catalog.
32. See, e.g., Entrepreneurial IT Design in University of Illinois Board of Trustees, School of Library and Information Science, Full Catalog.
33. Michael S. Teitelbaum, "Myth of the Science and Engineering Shortage," *The Atlantic*, March 19, 2014, www.theatlantic.com/education/archive/2014/03/the-myth-of-the -science-and-engineering-shortage/284359/.
34. Maker Media, *Makerspace Playbook: School Edition*, Spring 2013, http://makered.org/wp -content/uploads/2014/09/Makerspace-Playbook-Feb-2013.pdf.
35. American Library Association, "About ALA," www.ala.org/aboutala/.

index